I dedicate this book to my family and my loving partner Yelena.

- Yuri Shkuro

`mapt.io`

Mapt is an online digital library that gives you full access to over 5,000 books and videos, as well as industry leading tools to help you plan your personal development and advance your career. For more information, please visit our website.

Why subscribe?

- Spend less time learning and more time coding with practical eBooks and Videos from over 4,000 industry professionals
- Learn better with Skill Plans built especially for you
- Get a free eBook or video every month
- Mapt is fully searchable
- Copy and paste, print, and bookmark content

Packt.com

Did you know that Packt offers eBook versions of every book published, with PDF and ePub files available? You can upgrade to the eBook version at `www.Packt.com` and as a print book customer, you are entitled to a discount on the eBook copy. Get in touch with us at `customercare@packtpub.com` for more details.

At `www.Packt.com`, you can also read a collection of free technical articles, sign up for a range of free newsletters, and receive exclusive discounts and offers on Packt books and eBooks.

Contributors

About the author

Yuri Shkuro is a software engineer at Uber Technologies, working on distributed tracing, observability, reliability, and performance. He is the technical lead for Uber's tracing team. Before Uber, Yuri spent 15 years on Wall Street, building trading and risk management systems for derivatives at top investment banks, Goldman Sachs, JPMorgan Chase, and Morgan Stanley.

Yuri's open source credentials include being a co-founder of the OpenTracing project, and the creator and the tech lead of Jaeger, a distributed tracing platform developed at Uber. Both projects are incubating at the Cloud Native Computing Foundation. Yuri serves as an invited expert on the W3C Distributed Tracing working group.

Dr. Yuri Shkuro holds a Ph.D. in Computer Science from University of Maryland, College Park, and a Master's degree in Computer Engineering from MEPhI (Moscow Engineering & Physics Institute), one of Russia's top three universities. He is the author of many academic papers in the area of machine learning and neural networks; his papers have been cited in over 130 other publications.

Outside of his academic and professional career, Yuri helped edit and produce several animated shorts directed by Lev Polyakov, including *Only Love* (2008), which screened at over 30 film festivals and won several awards, *Piper the Goat and the Peace Pipe* (2005), a winner at the Ottawa International Animation Festival, and others.

I'd like to say thank you to many people who made this book possible: my producer Andrew, who reached out and convinced me to pursue this book; my editors Tom and Joanne, who reviewed and edited my drafts; my technical reviewer Pavol, who provided many great suggestions on improving the book; Ben Sigelman, who helped me to structure the content and from whom I learned a lot about tracing in general; Lev Polyakov, the author of the Jaeger project's adorable logo, who made brilliant illustrations for this book; and most of all, my family and my partner Yelena, who supported me and put up with me working on the book on weekends over many months.

About the reviewer

Pavol Loffay is a software engineer at Red Hat working on Observability tools for microservice architectures. He is an active maintainer of the Jaeger and OpenTracing projects. He is also a member of the **OpenTracing Specification Council (OTSC)** and a lead for the MicroProfile OpenTracing specification. In his free time, Pavol likes to travel and he is a passionate skier and rock climber.

About the illustrator

Lev Polyakov is an award winning independent animation director and conceptual artist, whose films were featured on WNET 13, Channel Frederator, and ShortsHD.

Lev Polyakov has been active in the animation world since 2004, starting as an intern for Signe Baumane, one of New York's most prominent independent animators, and proceeding to write and direct his own animated films. His first short, *Piper the Goat and the Peace Pipe*, won the first place at the 2005 Ottawa Animation Festival. For his next film, *Morning, Day, Evening, Night… and Morning Again,* Lev was awarded a grant and an honorary membership from the National Board of Review of Motion Pictures. During his junior year at School of Visual Arts, Lev directed and produced *Only Love*, a 15-minute animated short that premiered at the prestigious Woodstock Film Festival, and has been shown at more than 30 film festivals around the world, winning several first place awards.

Lev has done visually appealing, character-driven commercial work such as storyboarding, character design, and animation for an iPad movie-book *Peter and the Wolf in Hollywood,* produced by Giants Are Small in partnership with Universal Music; and for the virtual reality studio, The Glimpse Group.

Lev is currently the Chair of the Art and Technology Committee at the National Arts Club in New York City.

Packt is searching for authors like you

If you're interested in becoming an author for Packt, please visit `authors.packtpub.com` and apply today. We have worked with thousands of developers and tech professionals, just like you, to help them share their insight with the global tech community. You can make a general application, apply for a specific hot topic that we are recruiting an author for, or submit your own idea.

Table of Contents

Preface

Distributed tracing, also known as end-to-end tracing, while not a new idea, has recently began receiving a lot of attention as a must-have observability tool for complex distributed systems. Unlike most other tools that only monitor individual components of the architecture, like a process or a server, tracing plays a rather unique role by being able to observe end-to-end execution of individual requests, or transactions, following them across process and network boundaries. With the rise of such architectural patterns as microservices and functions-as-a-service (or FaaS, or serverless), distributed tracing is becoming the only practical way of managing the complexity of modern architectures.

The book you are about to read is based on my personal experiences of being a technical lead for the tracing team at Uber Technologies. During that time, I have seen the engineering organization grow from a few hundred to several thousand engineers, and the complexity of Uber's microservices-based architecture increasing from a few hundred microservices when we first rolled out Jaeger, our distributed tracing platform, to several thousand microservices we have today. As most practitioners of distributed tracing would tell you, building a tracing system is "the easy part"; getting it widely adopted in a large organization is a completely different challenge altogether, one that unfortunately does not have easy-to-follow recipes. This book is my attempt to provide an end-to-end overview of the problem space, including the history and theoretical underpinning of the technology, the ways to address instrumentation and organizational adoption challenges, the standards emerging in the industry for instrumentation and data formats, and practical suggestions for deploying and operating a tracing infrastructure in real world scenarios.

The book is not intended as a reference material or a tutorial for any particular technology. Instead, I want you to gain an understanding of the underlying principles and trade-offs of distributed tracing and its applications. Equipped with these fundamentals, you should be able to navigate this fairly complex area of technology and find effective ways to apply it to your own use cases and your systems.

Who this book is for

It is my hope that this book may be useful to a wide range of audiences, from beginners who know very little about distributed tracing to active practitioners who are looking to expand their knowledge and find ways to extract more value from their tracing platforms. Different parts of the book may be of interest to these groups of readers:

- *Application developers, SREs, and DevOps,* who are the end users of distributed tracing. This group is generally less interested in how tracing infrastructure and instrumentation work; they are more interested in what the technology can do for their day-to-day work. The book provides many examples of the benefits of distributed tracing, from the simplest use cases of "let's look at one trace and see what performance problems it can help us discover" to advanced data mining scenarios of "how do we process that vast amounts of tracing data we are collecting and gain insights into the behaviors of our distributed system that cannot be inferred from individual transactions."

- *Framework and infrastructure developers,* who are building libraries and tools for other developers and want to make those tools observable through integration with distributed tracing. This group would benefit from the thorough review of the instrumentation techniques and patterns, and the discussion of the emerging standards for tracing.

- *Engineering managers and executives,* who have the "power of the purse" and need to understand and be convinced of the value that tracing provides to an organization.

- Finally, *the tracing teams,* that is, engineers tasked with building, deploying, and operating tracing infrastructure in an organization. This group must deal with many challenges, both technical and organizational, if it wants to scale its technology and its own efforts to amplify the impact of tracing on the organization at large.

What this book covers

Part I, Introduction, provides a general introduction to the area of distributed tracing.

Chapter 1, Why Distributed Tracing, frames the observability problem that distributed tracing aims to solve and explains why other monitoring tools fall short when it comes to troubleshooting pathological behavior in complex distributed systems. The chapter includes a brief history of my personal experience with tracing and an explanation of why I felt that writing this book would be a useful contribution to the industry.

Chapter 2, Take Tracing for a HotROD Ride, dives in with an easy to run, hands-on example used to illustrate the core features, benefits, and capabilities of distributed tracing, using Jaeger, an open source tracing platform, the OpenTracing instrumentation, and a demo application HotROD (Rides on Demand).

Chapter 3, Distributed Tracing Fundamentals, reviews the basic operating principles of end-to-end tracing, such as causality tracking and metadata propagation, and various design decisions historically taken by different implementations that affect the types of problems a given tracing architecture is able to solve. It introduces the reader to two different tracing models, the more expressive event model, and more popular span model.

Part II, Data Gathering Problem, is dedicated to discussions about the different ways of getting tracing data out of the applications, through manual and automatic (agent-based) instrumentation, for both RPC-style and asynchronous (for example, using message queues) applications.

Chapter 4, Instrumentation Basics with OpenTracing, provides a step-by-step guide of manually instrumenting a simple "hello, world" style application for tracing, as it is being evolved from a monolith to a microservices-based system. Three parallel sets of examples are provided in popular programming languages: Go, Java, and Python. The chapter teaches the fundamentals of tracing instrumentation using the OpenTracing API; however, the general patterns are applicable to other instrumentation APIs as well. In the final exercises the chapter introduces automatic (agent-based) instrumentation style that requires little, if any, actual code changes in the application.

Chapter 5, Instrumentation of Asynchronous Applications, continues the lessons from Chapter 4, and applies them to an "online chat" type of application built around asynchronous messaging using Apache Kafka.

Chapter 6, Tracing Standards and Ecosystem, explores the often confusing ecosystem of the tracing industry at large, including the emerging standards such as OpenTracing, W3C Trace Context, and OpenCensus. It provides a useful taxonomy of how to think about the different commercial and open source projects and their positions in relation to each other.

Chapter 7, Tracing with Service Mesh, uses the service mesh Istio, running on Kubernetes, to trace an application and compare the results with tracing an application that is natively instrumented for tracing via the OpenTracing API. It reviews the pros and cons of each approach.

Chapter 8, All About Sampling, explains why tracing platforms are often required to sample transactions and provides an in-depth review of different sampling techniques, from consistent head-based sampling strategies (probabilistic, rate limiting, adaptive, and so on) to the emerging favorite, tail-based sampling.

Part III, Getting Value from Tracing, talks about the different ways engineers and organization can benefit from adopting a distributed tracing solution.

Chapter 9, Turning the Lights On, gives examples of the core value proposition of tracing, covering features that are commonly available in most tracing solutions; such as service graphs; critical path analysis; performance analysis with trace patterns; latency histograms and exemplars; and the long-term profiling techniques.

Chapter 10, Distributed Context Propagation, steps back to discuss context propagation, a technology that underpins most existing tracing infrastructures. It covers Tracing Plane from Brown University, which implements a general-purpose, tool-agnostic framework for context propagation, or "baggage," and covers a number of useful techniques and tools for observability and chaos engineering that have been built on top of context propagation and tracing.

Chapter 11, Integration with Metrics and Logs, shows how all is not lost for traditional monitoring tools, and how combining them with tracing infrastructure gives them new capabilities and makes them more useful in microservices environments.

Chapter 12, Gathering Insights with Data Mining, begins with the basics of data mining and feature extraction from tracing data, followed by a practical example involving the Jaeger backend, Apache Kafka, Elasticsearch, Kibana, an Apache Flink data mining job, and a microservices simulator, `microsim`. It ends with a discussion of further evolution of data mining techniques, such as inferring and observing trends, and historical and ad hoc data analysis.

Part IV, Deploying and Operating Tracing Infrastructure, completes the book with an assortment of practical advice to the tracing teams about implementing and operating tracing platforms in large organizations.

Chapter 13, Implementing Tracing in Large Organizations, discusses how to overcome many technical and organizational challenges that often prevent wide adoption of distributed tracing in enterprises or full realization of its value.

Chapter 14, Under the Hood of a Distributed Tracing System, starts with a brief discussion of build versus buy considerations, then goes deep into many technical details of the architecture and deployment modes of a tracing platform, such as multi-tenancy, security, operation in multiple data centers, monitoring, and resiliency. The Jaeger project is used to illustrate many architectural decisions, yet overall the content is applicable to most tracing infrastructures.

To get the most out of this book

The book is intended for a wide range of audiences interested in solving the observability challenges in complex distributed systems. Some familiarity with the existing monitoring tools, such as metrics, is useful, but not required. Most code examples are written in Java, so a basic level of reading Java code is required.

The included exercises make heavy use of Docker and `docker-compose` to bring up various third-party dependencies, such as MySQL and Elasticsearch databases, Kafka and Zookeeper, and various observability tools like Jaeger, Kibana, Grafana, and Prometheus. A working installation of Docker is required to run most of the examples.

I strongly advise you to not only try running and playing with the provided examples, but also to try adopting them to your own applications and use cases. I have seen time and again how engineers find silly mistakes and inefficiencies simply by looking at a sample trace from their application. If is often surprising how much more visibility into the system behavior is provided by tracing. If this is your first time dealing with this technology, then instrumenting your own application, instead of running the provided abstract examples, is the most effective way to learn and appreciate tracing.

Download the example code files

You can download the example code files for this book from your account at http://www.packt.com. If you purchased this book elsewhere, you can visit http://www.packt.com/support and register to have the files emailed directly to you.

You can download the code files by following these steps:

1. Log in or register at http://www.packt.com.
2. Select the **SUPPORT** tab.
3. Click on **Code Downloads & Errata**.
4. Enter the name of the book in the **Search** box and follow the on-screen instructions.

Once the file is downloaded, please make sure that you unzip or extract the folder using the latest version of:

- WinRAR / 7-Zip for Windows
- Zipeg / iZip / UnRarX for Mac
- 7-Zip / PeaZip for Linux

The code bundle for the book is also hosted on GitHub at `https://github.com/PacktPublishing/Mastering-Distributed-Tracing`. In case there's an update to the code, it will be updated on the existing GitHub repository.

We also have other code bundles from our rich catalog of books and videos available at `https://github.com/PacktPublishing/`. Check them out!

Download the color images

We also provide a PDF file that has color images of the screenshots/diagrams used in this book. You can download it here: `https://www.packtpub.com/sites/default/files/downloads/9781788628464_ColorImages.pdf`.

Conventions used

There are a number of text conventions used throughout this book.

`CodeInText`: Indicates code words in text, database table names, folder names, filenames, file extensions, pathnames, dummy URLs, user input, and Twitter handles. For example; "Mount the downloaded `WebStorm-10*.dmg` disk image file as another disk in your system."

A block of code is set as follows:

```
type SpanContext struct {
        traceID TraceID
        spanID  SpanID
        flags   byte
        baggage map[string]string
        debugID string
}
```

When we wish to draw your attention to a particular part of a code block, the relevant lines or items are set in bold:

```
type SpanContext struct {
        traceID TraceID
        spanID  SpanID
```

```
    flags    byte
    baggage map[string]string
    debugID string
}
```

Any command-line input or output is written as follows:

```
$ go run ./exercise1/hello.go

Listening on http://localhost:8080/
```

Bold: Indicates a new term, an important word, or words that you see on the screen, for example, in menus or dialog boxes, also appear in the text like this. For example: "Select **System info** from the **Administration** panel."

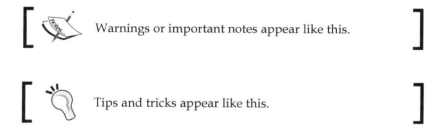

[Warnings or important notes appear like this.]

[Tips and tricks appear like this.]

Get in touch

Feedback from our readers is always welcome.

General feedback: If you have questions about any aspect of this book, mention the book title in the subject of your message and email us at customercare@packtpub.com.

Errata: Although we have taken every care to ensure the accuracy of our content, mistakes do happen. If you have found a mistake in this book we would be grateful if you would report this to us. Please visit, http://www.packt.com/submit-errata, selecting your book, clicking on the Errata Submission Form link, and entering the details.

Piracy: If you come across any illegal copies of our works in any form on the Internet, we would be grateful if you would provide us with the location address or website name. Please contact us at copyright@packt.com with a link to the material.

If you are interested in becoming an author: If there is a topic that you have expertise in and you are interested in either writing or contributing to a book, please visit http://authors.packtpub.com.

Reviews

Please leave a review. Once you have read and used this book, why not leave a review on the site that you purchased it from? Potential readers can then see and use your unbiased opinion to make purchase decisions, we at Packt can understand what you think about our products, and our authors can see your feedback on their book. Thank you!

For more information about Packt, please visit packt.com.

I
INTRODUCTION

1

Why Distributed Tracing?

Modern, internet-scale, **cloud-native applications** are very complex distributed systems. Building them is hard and debugging them is even harder. The growing popularity of **microservices** and **functions-as-a-service** (also known as **FaaS** or serverless) only exacerbates the problem; these architectural styles bring many benefits to the organizations adopting them, while complicating some of the aspects of operating the systems even further.

In this chapter, I will talk about the challenges of monitoring and troubleshooting distributed systems, including those built with microservices, and discuss how and why distributed tracing is in a unique position among the observability tools to address this problem. I will also describe my personal history with distributed tracing and why I decided to write this book.

Microservices and cloud-native applications

In the last decade, we saw a significant shift in how modern, internet-scale applications are being built. Cloud computing (infrastructure as a service) and containerization technologies (popularized by Docker) enabled a new breed of distributed system designs commonly referred to as microservices (and their next incarnation, FaaS). Successful companies like Twitter and Netflix have been able to leverage them to build highly scalable, efficient, and reliable systems, and to deliver more features faster to their customers.

While there is no official definition of microservices, a certain consensus has evolved over time in the industry. Martin Fowler, the author of many books on software design, argues that microservices architectures exhibit the following common characteristics [1]:

- **Componentization via (micro)services**: The componentization of functionality in a complex application is achieved via services, or microservices, that are independent processes communicating over a network. The microservices are designed to provide fine-grained interfaces and to be small in size, autonomously developed, and independently deployable.

- **Smart endpoints and dumb pipes**: The communications between services utilize technology-agnostic protocols such as HTTP and REST, as opposed to smart mechanisms like the **Enterprise Service Bus (ESB)**.

- **Organized around business capabilities**: Products not projects: the services are organized around business functions ("user profile service" or "fulfillment service"), rather than technologies. The development process treats the services as continuously evolving products rather than projects that are considered to be completed once delivered.

- **Decentralized governance**: Allows different microservices to be implemented using different technology stacks.

- **Decentralized data management**: Manifests in the decisions for both the conceptual data models and the data storage technologies being made independently between services.

- **Infrastructure automation**: The services are built, released, and deployed with automated processes, utilizing automated testing, continuous integration, and continuous deployment.

- **Design for failure**: The services are always expected to tolerate failures of their dependencies and either retry the requests or gracefully degrade their own functionality.

- **Evolutionary design**: Individual components of a microservices architecture are expected to evolve independently, without forcing upgrades on the components that depend on them.

Because of the large number of microservices involved in building modern applications, rapid provisioning, rapid deployment via decentralized continuous delivery, strict DevOps practices, and holistic service monitoring are necessary to effectively develop, maintain, and operate such applications. The infrastructure requirements imposed by the microservices architectures spawned a whole new area of development of infrastructure platforms and tools for managing these complex **cloud-native applications**. In 2015, the **Cloud Native Computing Foundation (CNCF)** was created as a vendor-neutral home for many emerging open source projects in this area, such as Kubernetes, Prometheus, Linkerd, and so on, with a mission to "make cloud-native computing ubiquitous."

"Cloud native technologies empower organizations to build and run scalable applications in modern, dynamic environments such as public, private, and hybrid clouds. Containers, service meshes, microservices, immutable infrastructure, and declarative APIs exemplify this approach.

These techniques enable loosely coupled systems that are resilient, manageable, and observable. Combined with robust automation, they allow engineers to make high-impact changes frequently and predictably with minimal toil."

-- Cloud Native Computing Foundation Charter [2]

At the time of writing, the list of graduated and incubating projects at CNCF [3] contained 20 projects (*Figure 1.1*). They all have a single common theme: providing a platform for efficient deployment and operation of cloud-native applications. The observability tools occupy an arguably disproportionate (20 percent) number of slots:

- **Prometheus**: A monitoring and alerting platform

- **Fluentd**: A logging data collection layer

- **OpenTracing**: A vendor-neutral APIs and instrumentation for distributed tracing

- **Jaeger**: A distributed tracing platform

CNCF sandbox projects, the third category not shown in *Figure 1.1*, include two more monitoring-related projects: OpenMetrics and Cortex. Why is observability in such high demand for cloud-native applications?

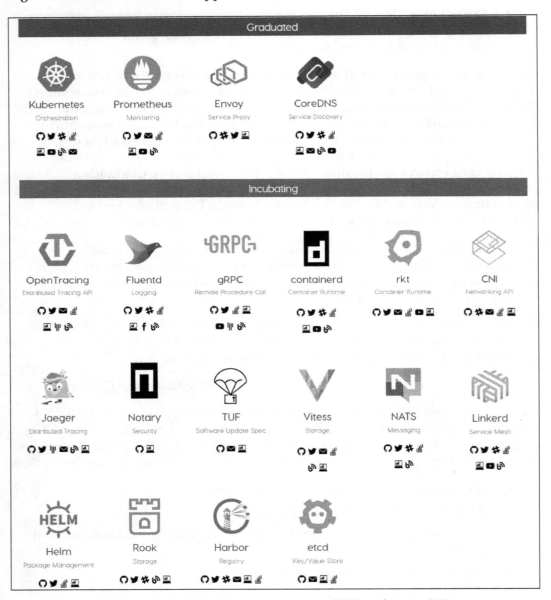

Figure 1.1: Graduated and incubating projects at CNCF as of January 2019.
Project names and logos are registered trademarks of the Linux Foundation.

What is observability?

The term "observability" in control theory states that the system is observable if the internal states of the system and, accordingly, its behavior, can be determined by only looking at its inputs and outputs. At the 2018 Observability Practitioners Summit [4], Bryan Cantrill, the CTO of Joyent and one of the creators of the tool **dtrace**, argued that this definition is not practical to apply to software systems because they are so complex that we can never know their complete internal state, and therefore the control theory's binary measure of observability is always zero (I highly recommend watching his talk on YouTube: https://youtu.be/ U4E0QxzswQc). Instead, a more useful definition of observability for a software system is its "capability to allow a human to ask and answer questions". The more questions we can ask and answer about the system, the more observable it is.

Figure 1.2: The Twitter debate

There are also many debates and Twitter zingers about the difference between monitoring and **observability**. Traditionally, the term monitoring was used to describe metrics collection and alerting. Sometimes it is used more generally to include other tools, such as "using distributed tracing to monitor distributed transactions." The definition by Oxford dictionaries of the verb "monitor" is "to observe and check the progress or quality of (something) over a period of time; keep under systematic review." However, it is better thought of as the process of observing certain a *priori* defined performance indicators of our software system, such as those measuring an impact on the end user experience, like latency or error counts, and using their values to alert us when these signals indicate an abnormal behavior of the system. Metrics, logs, and traces can all be used as a means to extract those signals from the application. We can then reserve the term "observability" for situations when we have a human operator proactively asking questions that were not predefined. As Brian Cantrill put it in his talk, this process is debugging, and we need to "use our brains when debugging." Monitoring does not require a human operator; it can and should be fully automated.

"If you want to talk about (metrics, logs, and traces) as pillars of observability–great.

The human is the foundation of observability!"

-- *Brian Cantrill*

In the end, the so-called "three pillars of observability" (metrics, logs, and traces) are just tools, or more precisely, different ways of extracting sensor data from the applications. Even with metrics, the modern time series solutions like Prometheus, InfluxDB, or Uber's M3 are capable of capturing the time series with many labels, such as which host emitted a particular value of a counter. Not all labels may be useful for monitoring, since a single misbehaving service instance in a cluster of thousands does not warrant an alert that wakes up an engineer. But when we are investigating an outage and trying to narrow down the scope of the problem, the labels can be very useful as observability signals.

The observability challenge of microservices

By adopting microservices architectures, organizations are expecting to reap many benefits, from better scalability of components to higher developer productivity. There are many books, articles, and blog posts written on this topic, so I will not go into that. Despite the benefits and eager adoption by companies large and small, microservices come with their own challenges and complexity. Companies like Twitter and Netflix were successful in adopting microservices because they found efficient ways of managing that complexity. Vijay Gill, Senior VP of Engineering at Databricks, goes as far as saying that the only good reason to adopt microservices is to be able to scale your engineering organization and to "ship the org chart" [2].

Vijay Gill's opinion may not be a popular one yet. A 2018 "Global Microservices Trends" study [6] by Dimensional Research® found that over 91% of interviewed professionals are using or have plans to use microservices in their systems. At the same time, 56% say each additional microservice "increases operational challenges," and 73% find "troubleshooting is harder" in a microservices environment. There is even a famous tweet about adopting microservices:

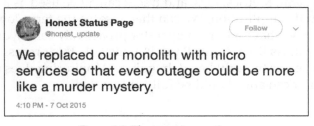

Figure 1.3: The tweet in question

Consider *Figure 1.4*, which gives a visual representation of a subset of microservices in Uber's microservices architecture, rendered by Uber's distributed tracing platform Jaeger. It is often called a service dependencies graph or a topology map. The circles (nodes in the graph) represent different microservices. The edges are drawn between nodes that communicate with each other. The diameter of the nodes is proportional to the number of other microservices connecting to them, and the width of an edge is proportional to the volume of traffic going through that edge.

The picture is already so complex that we don't even have space to include the names of the services (in the real Jaeger UI you can see them by moving the mouse over nodes). Every time a user takes an action on the mobile app, a request is executed by the architecture that may require dozens of different services to participate in order to produce a response. Let's call the path of this request a **distributed transaction**.

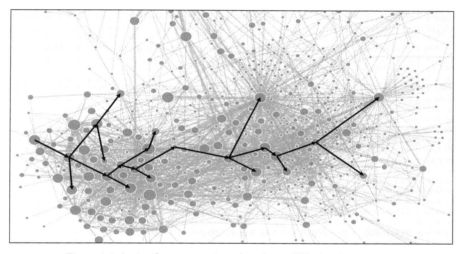

Figure 1.4: A visual representation of a subset of Uber's microservices architecture and a hypothetical transaction

So, what are the challenges of this design? There are quite a few:

- In order to run these microservices in production, we need an advanced orchestration platform that can schedule resources, deploy containers, auto-scale, and so on. Operating an architecture of this scale manually is simply not feasible, which is why projects like Kubernetes became so popular.

- In order to communicate, microservices need to know how to find each other on the network, how to route around problematic areas, how to perform load balancing, how to apply rate limiting, and so on. These functions are delegated to advanced RPC frameworks or external components like network proxies and service meshes.

- Splitting a monolith into many microservices may actually decrease reliability. Suppose we have 20 components in the application and all of them are required to produce a response to a single request. When we run them in a monolith, our failure modes are restricted to bugs and potentially a crush of the whole server running the monolith. But if we run the same components as microservices, on different hosts and separated by a network, we introduce many more potential failure points, from network hiccups, to resource constraints due to noisy neighbors. Even if each microservice succeeds in 99.9% of cases, the whole application that requires all of them to work for a given request can only succeed $0.999^{20} = 98.0\%$ of the time. Distributed, microservices-based applications must become more complicated, for example, implementing retries or opportunistic parallel reads, in order to maintain the same level of availability.

- The latency may also increase. Assume each microservice has 1 ms average latency, but the 99th percentile is $1s$. A transaction touching just one of these services has a 1% chance to take $\geq 1s$. A transaction touching 100 of these services has $1 - (1 - 0.01)^{100} = 63\%$ chance to take $\geq 1s$.

- Finally, the observability of the system is dramatically reduced if we try to use traditional monitoring tools.

When we see that some requests to our system are failing or slow, we want our observability tools to tell us the story about what happens to that request. We want to be able to ask questions like these:

- Which services did a request go through?
- What did every microservice do when processing the request?
- If the request was slow, where were the bottlenecks?
- If the request failed, where did the error happen?
- How different was the execution of the request from the normal behavior of the system?
    - Were the differences structural, that is, some new services were called, or vice versa, some usual services were not called?
    - Were the differences related to performance, that is, some service calls took a longer or shorter time than usual?
- What was the critical path of the request?
- And perhaps most importantly, if selfishly, who should be paged?

Unfortunately, traditional monitoring tools are ill-equipped to answer these questions for microservices architectures.

Traditional monitoring tools

Traditional monitoring tools were designed for monolith systems, observing the health and behavior of a single application instance. They may be able to tell us a story about that single instance, but they know almost nothing about the distributed transaction that passed through it. These tools *lack the context* of the request.

Metrics

It goes like this: "Once upon a time...something bad happened. The end." How do you like this story? This is what the chart in *Figure 1.5* tells us. It's not completely useless; we do see a spike and we could define an alert to fire when this happens. But can we explain or troubleshoot the problem?

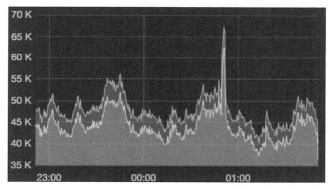

Figure 1.5: A graph of two time series representing (hypothetically) the volume of traffic to a service

Metrics, or stats, are numerical measures recorded by the application, such as counters, gauges, or timers. Metrics are very cheap to collect, since numeric values can be easily aggregated to reduce the overhead of transmitting that data to the monitoring system. They are also fairly accurate, which is why they are very useful for the actual *monitoring* (as the dictionary defines it) and alerting.

Yet the same capacity for aggregation is what makes metrics ill-suited for explaining the pathological behavior of the application. By aggregating data, we are throwing away all the context we had about the individual transactions.

In *Chapter 11, Integration with Metrics and Logs*, we will talk about how integration with tracing and context propagation can make metrics more useful by providing them with the lost context. Out of the box, however, metrics are a poor tool to troubleshoot problems within microservices-based applications.

Logs

Logging is an even more basic observability tool than metrics. Every programmer learns their first programming language by writing a program that prints (that is, logs) "Hello, World!" Similar to metrics, logs struggle with microservices because each log stream only tells us about a single instance of a service. However, the evolving programming paradigm creates other problems for logs as a debugging tool. Ben Sigelman, who built Google's distributed tracing system Dapper [7], explained it in his KubeCon 2016 keynote talk [8] as four types of concurrency (*Figure 1.6*):

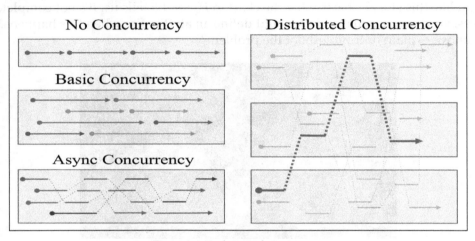

Figure 1.6: Evolution of concurrency

Years ago, applications like early versions of Apache HTTP Server handled concurrency by forking child processes and having each process handle a single request at a time. Logs collected from that single process could do a good job of describing what happened inside the application.

Then came multi-threaded applications and basic concurrency. A single request would typically be executed by a single thread sequentially, so as long as we included the thread name in the logs and filtered by that name, we could still get a reasonably accurate picture of the request execution.

Then came asynchronous concurrency, with asynchronous and actor-based programming, executor pools, futures, promises, and event-loop-based frameworks. The execution of a single request may start on one thread, then continue on another, then finish on the third. In the case of event loop systems like Node.js, all requests are processed on a single thread but when the execution tries to make an I/O, it is put in a wait state and when the I/O is done, the execution resumes after waiting its turn in the queue.

Both of these asynchronous concurrency models result in each thread switching between multiple different requests that are all in flight. Observing the behavior of such a system from the logs is very difficult, unless we annotate all logs with some kind of unique id representing the request rather than the thread, a technique that actually gets us close to how distributed tracing works.

Finally, microservices introduced what we can call "distributed concurrency." Not only can the execution of a single request jump between threads, but it can also jump between processes, when one microservice makes a network call to another. Trying to troubleshoot request execution from such logs is like debugging without a stack trace: we get small pieces, but no big picture.

In order to reconstruct the flight of the request from the many log streams, we need powerful logs aggregation technology and a distributed context propagation capability to tag all those logs in different processes with a unique request id that we can use to stitch those requests together. We might as well be using the real distributed tracing infrastructure at this point! Yet even after tagging the logs with a unique request id, we still cannot assemble them into an accurate sequence, because the timestamps from different servers are generally not comparable due to clock skews. In *Chapter 11, Integration with Metrics and Logs*, we will see how tracing infrastructure can be used to provide the missing context to the logs.

Distributed tracing

As soon as we start building a distributed system, traditional monitoring tools begin struggling with providing observability for the whole system, because they were designed to observe a single component, such as a program, a server, or a network switch. The story of a single component may no doubt be very interesting, but it tells us very little about the story of a request that touches many of those components. We need to know what happens to that request in all of them, end-to-end, if we want to understand why a system is behaving pathologically. In other words, we first want a *macro view*.

At the same time, once we get that macro view and zoom in to a particular component that seems to be at fault for the failure or performance problems with our request, we want a micro view of what exactly happened to that request in that component. Most other tools cannot tell that to us either because they only observe what "generally" happens in the component as a whole, for example, how many requests per second it handles (metrics), what events occurred on a given thread (logs), or which threads are on and off CPU at a given point in time (profilers). They don't have the granularity or context to observe a specific request.

Distributed tracing takes a request-centric view. It captures the detailed execution of causally-related activities performed by the components of a distributed system as it processes a given request. In *Chapter 3, Distributed Tracing Fundamentals*, I will go into more detail on how exactly it works, but in a nutshell:

- Tracing infrastructure attaches **contextual metadata** to each request and ensures that metadata is passed around during the request execution, even when one component communicates with another over a network.

- At various **trace points** in the code, the instrumentation records **events** annotated with relevant information, such as the URL of an HTTP request or an SQL statement of a database query.

- Recorded events are tagged with the contextual metadata and explicit **causality references** to prior events.

That deceptively simple technique allows the tracing infrastructure to reconstruct the whole path of the request, through the components of a distributed system, as a graph of events and causal edges between them, which we call a "trace." A trace allows us to reason about how the system was processing the request. Individual graphs can be aggregated and clustered to infer patterns of behaviors in the system. Traces can be displayed using various forms of visualizations, including Gantt charts (*Figure 1.7*) and graph representations (*Figure 1.8*), to give our visual cortex cues to finding the root cause of performance problems:

Figure 1.7: Jaeger UI view of a single request to the HotROD application, further discussed in chapter 2. In the bottom half, one of the spans (named **GetDriver** from service **redis**, with a warning icon) is expanded to show additional information, such as tags and span logs.

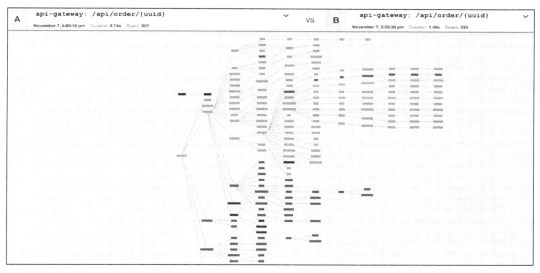

Figure 1.8: Jaeger UI view of two traces A and B being compared structurally in the graph form (best viewed in color). Light/dark green colors indicate services that were encountered more/only in trace B, and light/dark red colors indicate services encountered more/only in trace A.

By taking a request-centric view, tracing helps to illuminate different behaviors of the system. Of course, as Bryan Cantrill said in his KubeCon talk, just because we have tracing, it doesn't mean that we eliminated performance pathologies in our applications. We actually need to know how to use it to ask sophisticated questions that we now can ask with this powerful tool. Fortunately, distributed tracing is able to answer all the questions we posed in *The observability challenge of microservices* section.

My experience with tracing

My first experience with distributed tracing was somewhere around 2010, even though we did not use that term at the time. I was working on a trade capture and trade processing system at Morgan Stanley. It was built as a **service-oriented architecture (SOA)**, and the whole system contained more than a dozen different components deployed as independent Java applications. The system was used for over-the-counter interest rate derivatives products (like swaps and options), which had high complexity but not a huge trading volume, so most of the system components were deployed as a single instance, with the exception of the stateless pricers that were deployed as a cluster.

One of the observability challenges with the system was that each trade had to go through a complicated sequence of additional changes, matching, and confirmation flows, implemented by the different components of the system.

To give us visibility into the various state transitions of the individual trades, we used an APM vendor (now defunct) that was essentially implementing a distributed tracing platform. Unfortunately, our experience with that technology was not particularly stellar, with the main challenge being the difficulty of instrumenting our applications for tracing, which involved creating **aspect-oriented programming (AOP)** - style instructions in the XML files and trying to match on the signature of the internal APIs. The approach was very fragile, as changes to the internal APIs would cause the instrumentation to become ineffective, without good facilities to enforce it via unit testing. Getting instrumentation into existing applications is one of the main difficulties in adopting distributing tracing, as we will discuss in this book.

When I joined Uber in mid-2015, the engineering team in New York had only a handful of engineers, and many of them were working in the metrics system, which later became known as M3. At the time, Uber was just starting its journey towards breaking the existing monolith and replacing it with microservices. The Python monolith, appropriately called "API", was already instrumented with another home-grown tracing-like system called Merckx.

The major shortcoming with Merckx was its design for the days of a monolithic application. It lacked any concept of distributed context propagation. It recorded SQL queries, Redis calls, and even calls to other services, but there was no way to go more than one level deep. It also stored the existing in-process context in a global, thread-local storage, and when many new Python microservices at Uber began adopting an event-loop-based framework Tornado, the propagation mechanism in Merckx was unable to represent the state of many concurrent requests running on the same thread. By the time I joined Uber, Merckx was in maintenance mode, with hardly anyone working on it, even though it had active users. Given the new observability theme of the New York engineering team, I, along with another engineer, Onwukike Ibe, took the mantle of building a fully-fledged distributed tracing platform.

I had no experience with building such systems in the past, but after reading the Dapper paper from Google, it seemed straightforward enough. Plus, there was already an open source clone of Dapper, the Zipkin project, originally built by Twitter. Unfortunately, Zipkin did not work for us out of the box.

In 2014, Uber started building its own RPC framework called TChannel. It did not really become popular in the open source world, but when I was just getting started with tracing, many services at Uber were already using that framework for inter-process communications. The framework came with tracing instrumentation built-in, even natively supported in the binary protocol format. So, we already had traces being generated in production, only nothing was gathering and storing them.

I wrote a simple collector in Go that was receiving traces generated by TChannel in a custom Thrift format and storing them in the Cassandra database in the same format that the Zipkin project used. This allowed us to deploy the collectors alongside the Zipkin UI, and that's how Jaeger was born. You can read more about this in a post on the Uber Engineering blog [9].

Having a working tracing backend, however, was only half of the battle. Although TChannel was actively used by some of the newer services, many more existing services were using plain JSON over HTTP, utilizing many different HTTP frameworks in different programming languages. In some of the languages, for example, Java, TChannel wasn't even available or mature enough. So, we needed to solve the same problem that made our tracing experiment at Morgan Stanley fizzle out: how to get tracing instrumentation into hundreds of existing services, implemented with different technology stacks.

As luck would have it, I was attending one of the Zipkin Practitioners workshops organized by Adrian Cole from Pivotal, the lead maintainer of the Zipkin project, and that same exact problem was on everyone's mind. Ben Sigelman, who founded his own observability company Lightstep earlier that year, was at the workshop too, and he proposed to create a project for a standardized tracing API that could be implemented by different tracing vendors independently, and could be used to create completely vendor-neutral, open source, reusable tracing instrumentation for many existing frameworks and drivers. We brainstormed the initial design of the API, which later became the OpenTracing project [10] (more on that in *Chapter 6, Tracing Standards and Ecosystem*). All examples in this book use the OpenTracing APIs for instrumentation.

The evolution of the OpenTracing APIs, which is still ongoing, is a topic for another story. Yet even the initial versions of OpenTracing gave us the peace of mind that if we started adopting it on a large scale at Uber, we were not going to lock ourselves into a single implementation. Having different vendors and open source projects participating in the development of OpenTracing was very encouraging. We implemented Jaeger-specific, fully OpenTracing-compatible tracing libraries in several languages (Java, Go, Python, and Node.js), and started rolling them out to Uber microservices. Last time I checked, we had close to 2,400 microservices instrumented with Jaeger.

I have been working in the area of distributed tracing even since. The Jaeger project has grown and matured. Eventually, we replaced the Zipkin UI with Jaeger's own, more modern UI built with React, and in April 2017, we open sourced all of Jaeger, from client libraries to the backend components.

By supporting OpenTracing, we were able to rely on the ever-growing ecosystem of open source instrumentation hosted at the opentracing-contrib organization on GitHub [11], instead of writing our own the way some other projects have done. This freed the Jaeger developers to focus on building a best-of-class tracing backend with data analysis and visualization features. Many other tracing solutions have borrowed features first introduced in Jaeger, just like Jaeger borrowed its initial feature set from Zipkin.

In the fall of 2017, Jaeger was accepted as an incubating project to CNCF, following in the footsteps of the OpenTracing project. Both projects are very active, with hundreds of contributors, and are used by many organizations around the world. The Chinese giant Alibaba even offers hosted Jaeger as part of its Alibaba Cloud services [12]. I probably spend 30-50% of my time at work collaborating with contributors to both projects, including code reviews for pull requests and new feature designs.

Why this book?

When I began studying distributed tracing after joining Uber, there was not a lot of information out there. The Dapper paper gave the foundational overview and the technical report by Raja Sambasivan and others [13] provided a very useful historical background. But there was little in the way of a recipe book that would answer more practical questions, such as:

- Where do I start with tracing in a large organization?
- How do I drive adoption of tracing instrumentation across existing systems?
- How does the instrumentation even work? What are the basics? What are the recommended patterns?
- How do I get the most benefit and return on investment from tracing?
- What do I do with all that tracing data?
- How do I operate a tracing backend in real production and not in a toy application?

In the early 2018, I realized that I had pretty good answers to these questions, while most people who were just starting to look into tracing still didn't, and no comprehensive guide has been published anywhere. Even the basic instrumentation steps are often confusing to people if they do not understand the underlying concepts, as evidenced by the many questions posted in the Jaeger and OpenTracing chat rooms.

When I gave the OpenTracing tutorial at the Velocity NYC conference in 2017, I created a GitHub repository that contained step-by-step walkthroughs for instrumentation, from a basic "Hello, World!" program to a small microservices-based application. The tutorials were repeated in several programming languages (I originally created ones for Java, Go, and Python, and later other people created more, for Node.js and C#). I have seen time and again how these most simple tutorials help people to learn the ropes:

Figure 1.9: Feedback about a tutorial

So, I was thinking, maybe I should write a book that would cover not just the instrumentation tutorials, but give a comprehensive overview of the field, from its history and fundamentals to practical advice about where to start and how to get the most benefits from tracing. To my surprise, Andrew Waldron from Packt Publishing reached out to me offering to do exactly that. The rest is history, or rather, this book.

One aspect that made me reluctant to start writing was the fact that the boom of microservices and serverless created a big gap in the observability solutions that can address the challenges posed by these architectural styles, and tracing is receiving a lot of renewed interest, even though the basic idea of distributed tracing systems is not new. Accordingly, there are a lot of changes happening in this area, and there was a risk that anything I wrote would quickly become obsolete. It is possible that in the future, OpenTracing might be replaced by some more advanced API. However, the thought that made me push through was that this book is not about OpenTracing or Jaeger. I use them as examples because they are the projects that are most familiar to me. The ideas and concepts introduced throughout the book are not tied to these projects. If you decide to instrument your applications with Zipkin's Brave library, or with OpenCensus, or even with some vendor's proprietary API, the fundamentals of instrumentation and distributed tracing mechanics are going to be the same, and the advice I give in the later chapters about practical applications and the adoption of tracing will still apply equally.

Summary

In this chapter, we took a high-level look at observability problems created by the new popular architectural styles, microservices and FaaS, and discussed why traditional monitoring tools are failing to fill this gap, whereas distributed tracing provides a unique way of getting both a macro and micro view of the system behavior when it executes individual requests.

I have also talked about my own experience and history with tracing, and why I wrote this book as a comprehensive guide to many engineers coming to the field of tracing.

In the next chapter, we are going to take a hands-on deep dive into tracing, by running a tracing backend and a microservices-based demo application. It will complement the claims made in this introduction with concrete examples of the capabilities of end-to-end tracing.

References

1. Martin Fowler, James Lewis. *Microservices: a definition of this new architectural term*: https://www.martinfowler.com/articles/microservices.html.

2. Cloud Native Computing Foundation (CNCF) Charter: https://github.com/cncf/foundation/blob/master/charter.md.

3. CNCF projects: https://www.cncf.io/projects/.

4. Bryan Cantrill. *Visualizing Distributed Systems with Statemaps*. Observability Practitioners Summit at KubeCon/CloudNativeCon NA 2018, December 10: https://sched.co/HfG2.

5. Vijay Gill. *The Only Good Reason to Adopt Microservices*: https://lightstep.com/blog/the-only-good-reason-to-adopt-microservices/.

6. Global Microservices Trends Report: https://go.lightstep.com/global-microservices-trends-report-2018.

7. Benjamin H. Sigelman, Luiz A. Barroso, Michael Burrows, Pat Stephenson, Manoj Plakal, Donald Beaver, Saul Jaspan, and Chandan Shanbhag. *Dapper, a large-scale distributed system tracing infrastructure*. Technical Report dapper-2010-1, Google, April 2010.

8. Ben Sigelman. Keynote: *OpenTracing and Containers: Depth, Breadth, and the Future of Tracing*. KubeCon/CloudNativeCon North America, 2016, Seattle: https://sched.co/8fRU.

9. Yuri Shkuro. *Evolving Distributed Tracing at Uber Engineering*. Uber Eng Blog, February 2, 2017: https://eng.uber.com/distributed-tracing/.

10. The OpenTracing Project: `http://opentracing.io/`.

11. The OpenTracing Contributions: `https://github.com/opentracing-contrib/`.

12. Alibaba Cloud documentation. OpenTracing implementation of Jaeger: `https://www.alibabacloud.com/help/doc-detail/68035.htm`.

13. Raja R. Sambasivan, Rodrigo Fonseca, Ilari Shafer, Gregory R. Ganger. *So, You Want to Trace Your Distributed System? Key Design Insights from Years of Practical Experience*. Carnegie Mellon University Parallel Data Lab Technical Report CMU-PDL-14-102. April 2014.

2
Take Tracing for a HotROD Ride

A picture is worth a thousand words. So far, we have only talked about distributed tracing in the abstract terms. In this chapter, we are going to look at concrete examples of the diagnostic and troubleshooting tools provided by a tracing system. We are going to use Jaeger (pronounced \yā-gər\), an open source distributed tracing system, originally created by Uber Technologies [1] and now hosted with the Cloud Native Computing Foundation [2].

The chapter will:

- Introduce HotROD, an example application provided by the Jaeger project, which is built with microservices and instrumented with the OpenTracing API (we will discuss OpenTracing in detail in *Chapter 4, Instrumentation Basics with OpenTracing*)

- Use Jaeger's user interface to understand the architecture and the data flow of the HotROD application

- Compare standard logging output of the application with contextual logging capabilities of distributed tracing

- Investigate and attempt to fix the root causes of latency in the application

- Demonstrate the distributed context propagation features of OpenTracing

Prerequisites

All relevant screenshots and code snippets are included in this chapter, but you are strongly encouraged to try running the example and explore the features of the web UIs, in order to better understand the capabilities of distributed tracing solutions like Jaeger.

Both the Jaeger backend and the demo application can be run as downloadable binaries for macOS, Linux, and Windows, as Docker containers, or directly from the source code. Since Jaeger is an actively developed project, by the time you read this book, some of the code organization or distributions may have changed. To ensure you are following the same steps as described in this chapter, we are going to use **Jaeger version 1.6.0**, released in July 2018.

Running from prepackaged binaries

Downloading pre packaged binaries is likely the easiest way to get started, since it requires no additional setup or installations. All Jaeger backend components, as well as the HotROD demo application, are available as executable binaries for macOS, Linux, and Windows from GitHub: `https://github.com/jaegertracing/jaeger/releases/tag/v1.6.0/`. For example, to run the binaries on macOS, download the archive `jaeger-1.6.0-darwin-amd64.tar.gz` and extract its content into a directory:

```
$ tar xvfz jaeger-1.6.0-darwin-amd64.tar.gz
x jaeger-1.6.0-darwin-amd64/
x jaeger-1.6.0-darwin-amd64/example-hotrod
x jaeger-1.6.0-darwin-amd64/jaeger-query
```

```
x jaeger-1.6.0-darwin-amd64/jaeger-standalone
x jaeger-1.6.0-darwin-amd64/jaeger-agent
x jaeger-1.6.0-darwin-amd64/jaeger-collector
```

This archive includes the production-grade binaries for the Jaeger backend, namely `jaeger-query`, `jaeger-agent`, and `jaeger-collector`, which we will not use in this chapter. We only need the all-in-one packaging of the Jaeger backend `jaeger-standalone`, which combines all the backend components into one executable, with no additional dependencies.

The Jaeger backend listens on half a dozen different ports, so if you run into port conflicts, you may need to find out which other software listens on the same ports and shut it down temporarily. The risk of port conflicts is greatly reduced if you run Jaeger all-in-one as a Docker container.

The executable `example-hotrod` is the HotROD demo application we will be using in this chapter to demonstrate the features of distributed tracing.

Running from Docker images

Like most software designed for the cloud-native era, Jaeger components are distributed in the form of Docker container images, so we recommend installing a working Docker environment. Please refer to the Docker documentation (https://docs.docker.com/install/) for installation instructions. To quickly verify your Docker setup, run the following command:

```
$ docker run --rm jaegertracing/all-in-one:1.6 version
```

You may first see some Docker output as it downloads the container images, followed by the program's output:

```
{"gitCommit":"77a057313273700b8a1c768173a4c663ca351907","GitVersion":"v1.6.0","BuildDate":"2018-07-10T16:23:52Z"}
```

Running from the source code

The HotROD demo application contains some standard tracing instrumentation, as well as a number of custom instrumentation techniques that give more insight into the application's behavior and performance. We will discuss these techniques in this chapter and show some code examples. If you want to dive deeper into the code and maybe tweak it, we recommend downloading the full source code.

Go language development environment

The HotROD application, just like Jaeger itself, is implemented in the Go language, thus a working Go v1.10 or later development environment is required to run it from source. Please refer to the documentation (`https://golang.org/doc/install`) for installation instructions.

Jaeger source code

The HotROD application is located in the `examples` directory of the main Jaeger backend repository, `https://github.com/jaegertracing/jaeger/`. If you have Git installed, you can check out the source code as follows:

```
$ mkdir -p $GOPATH/src/github.com/jaegertracing
$ cd $GOPATH/src/github.com/jaegertracing
$ git clone https://github.com/jaegertracing/jaeger.git jaeger
$ cd jaeger
$ git checkout v1.6.0
```

Alternatively, you can download the source code bundle from the Jaeger release page (`https://github.com/jaegertracing/jaeger/releases/tag/v1.6.0/`), and make sure that the code is extracted into the `$GOPATH/src/github.com/jaegertracing/jaeger/` directory.

Jaeger 1.6 uses the `github.com/Masterminds/glide` utility as the dependencies manager, so you would need to install it:

```
$ go get -u github.com/Masterminds/glide
```

After installing `glide`, run it to download the libraries that Jaeger depends on:

```
$ cd $GOPATH/src/github.com/jaegertracing/jaeger/
$ glide install
```

Now you should be able to build and run the HotROD binary:

```
$ go run ./examples/hotrod/main.go help
HotR.O.D. - A tracing demo application.

Usage:
  jaeger-demo [command]

Available Commands:
  all         Starts all services
```

```
customer      Starts Customer service
driver        Starts Driver service
frontend      Starts Frontend service
help          about any command
route         Starts Route service
[... skipped ...]
```

It is also possible to run the Jaeger backend from the source code. However, it requires an additional setup of Node.js in order to compile the static assets for the UI, which may not even work on an OS like Windows, so I do not recommend it for this chapter's examples.

Start Jaeger

Before we run the demo application, let's make sure we can run the Jaeger backend to collect the traces, as otherwise we might get a lot of error logs. A production installation of the Jaeger backend would consist of many different components, including some highly scalable databases like Cassandra or Elasticsearch. For our experiments, we do not need that complexity or even the persistence layer. Fortunately, the Jaeger distribution includes a special component called **all-in-one** just for this purpose. It runs a single process that embeds all other components of a normal Jaeger installation, including the web user interface. Instead of a persistent storage, it keeps all traces in memory.

If you are using Docker, you can run Jaeger all-in-one with the following command:

```
$ docker run -d --name jaeger \
    -p 6831:6831/udp \
    -p 16686:16686 \
    -p 14268:14268 \
    jaegertracing/all-in-one:1.6
```

The -d flag makes the process run in the background, detached from the terminal. The --name flag sets a name by which this process can be located by other Docker containers. We also use the -p flag to expose three ports on the host network that the Jaeger backend is listening to.

The first port, 6831/udp, is used to receive tracing data from applications instrumented with Jaeger tracers, and the second port, 16686, is where we can find the web UI. We also map the third port, 14268, in case we have issues with UDP packet limits and need to use HTTP transport for sending traces (discussed as follows).

The process listens to other ports as well, for example, to accept traces in other formats, but they are not relevant for our exercise. Once the container starts, open `http://127.0.0.1:16686/` in the browser to access the UI.

If you chose to download the binaries instead of Docker images, you can run the executable named `jaeger-standalone`, without any arguments, which will listen on the same ports. `jaeger-standalone` is the binary used to build the `jaegertracing/all-in-one` Docker image (in the later versions of `Jaeger`, it has been renamed `jaeger-all-in-one`).

```
$ cd jaeger-1.6.0-darwin-amd64/
$ ./jaeger-standalone
[... skipped ...]
{"msg":"Starting agent"}
{"msg":"Starting jaeger-collector TChannel server","port":14267}
{"msg":"Starting jaeger-collector HTTP server","http-port":14268}
[... skipped ...]
{"msg":"Starting jaeger-query HTTP server","port":16686}
{"msg":"Health Check state change","status":"ready"}
[... skipped ...]
```

We removed some fields of the log statements (`level`, `timestamp`, and `caller`) to improve readability.

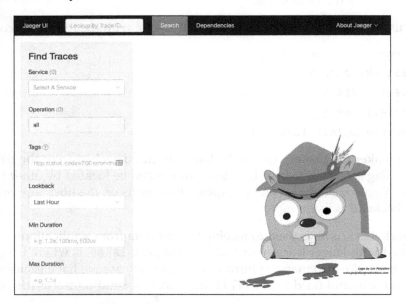

Figure 2.1: Jaeger UI front page: the search screen

Since the all-in-one binary runs the Jaeger backend with an in-memory database, which is initially empty, there is not much to see in the UI right away. However, the Jaeger backend has self-tracing enabled, so if we reload the home page a few times, we will see the **Services** dropdown in the top-left corner display **jaeger-query**, which is the name of the microservice running the UI component. We can now hit the **Search** button to find some traces, but let's first run the demo application to get more interesting traces.

Meet the HotROD

HotROD is a mock-up "ride-sharing" application (**ROD** stands for **Rides on Demand**) that is maintained by the Jaeger project. We will discuss its architecture later, but first let's try to run it. If you are using Docker, you can run it with this command:

```
$ docker run --rm -it \
    --link jaeger \
    -p8080-8083:8080-8083 \
    jaegertracing/example-hotrod:1.6 \
    all \
    --jaeger-agent.host-port=jaeger:6831
```

Let's quickly review what is going on with this command:

- The `rm` flag instructs Docker to automatically remove the container once the program exits.

- The `it` flags attach the container's standard in and out streams to the terminal.

- The `link` flag tells Docker to make the hostname `jaeger` available inside the container's networking namespace and resolve it to the Jaeger backend we started earlier.

- The string `all`, after the image name, is the command to the HotROD application, instructing it to run all microservices from the same process. It is possible to run each microservice as a separate process, even on different machines, to simulate a truly distributed application, but we leave this as an exercise for you.

- The final flag tells the HotROD application to configure the tracer to send data to UDP port `6831` on hostname `jaeger`.

To run HotROD from downloaded binaries, run the following command:

```
$ example-hotrod all
```

If we are running both the Jaeger all-in-one and the HotROD application from the binaries, they bind their ports directly to the host network and are able to find each other without any additional configuration, due to the default values of the flags.

Sometimes users experience issues with getting traces from the HotROD application due to the default UDP settings in the OS. Jaeger client libraries batch up to 65,000 bytes per UDP packet, which is still a safe number to send via the loopback interface (that is, localhost) without packet fragmentation. However, macOS, for example, has a much lower default for the maximum datagram size. Rather than adjusting the OS settings, another alternative is to use the HTTP protocol between Jaeger clients and the Jaeger backend. This can be done by passing the following flag to the HotROD application:

```
--jaeger-agent.host-port=http://localhost:14268/api/traces
```

Or, if using the Docker networking namespace:

```
--jaeger-agent.host-port=http://jaeger:14268/api/traces
```

Once the HotROD process starts, the logs written to the standard output will show the microservices starting several servers on different ports (for better readability, we removed the timestamps and references to the source files):

```
INFO Starting all services
INFO Starting {"service": "route", "address":
"http://127.0.0.1:8083"}
INFO Starting {"service": "frontend", "address":
"http://127.0.0.1:8080"}
INFO Starting {"service": "customer", "address":
"http://127.0.0.1:8081"}
INFO TChannel listening {"service": "driver", "hostPort":
"127.0.0.1:8082"}
```

Let's navigate to the application's web frontend at http://127.0.0.1:8080/:

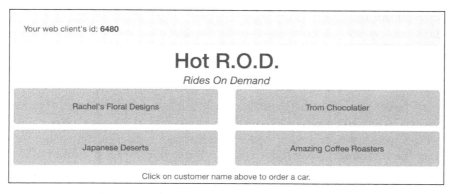

Figure 2.2: The HotROD single-page web application

We have four customers, and by clicking one of the four buttons, we summon a car to arrive to the customer's location, perhaps to pick up a product and deliver it elsewhere. Once a request for a car is sent to the backend, it responds with the car's license plate number, **T757183C**, and the expected time of arrival of two minutes:

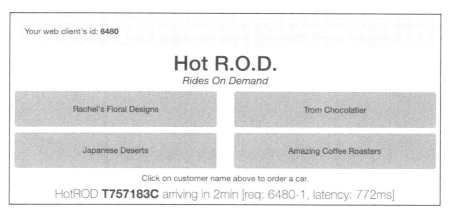

Figure 2.3: We ordered a car that will arrive in two minutes

There are a few bits of debugging information we see on the screen:

1. In the top-left corner, there is a web client id: **6480**. This is a random session ID assigned by the JavaScript UI. If we reload the page, we get a different session ID.

2. In the brackets after the car information, we see a request ID, **req: 6480-1**. This is a unique ID assigned by the JavaScript UI to each request it makes to the backend, composed of the session ID and a sequence number.

3. The last bit of debugging data, **latency: 772ms**, is measured by the JavaScript UI and shows how long the backend took to respond.

This additional information has no impact on the behavior of the application but will be useful when we investigate performance problems.

The architecture

Now that we have seen what the HotROD application does, we may want to know how it is architected. After all, maybe all those servers we saw in the logs are just for show, and the whole application is simply a JavaScript frontend. Rather than asking someone for a design document, wouldn't it be great if our monitoring tools could build the architecture diagram automatically, by observing the interactions between the services? That's exactly what distributed tracing systems like Jaeger can do. That request for a car we executed earlier has provided Jaeger with enough data to connect the dots.

Let's go to the **Dependencies** page in the Jaeger UI. At first, we will see a tiny diagram titled **Force Directed Graph**, but we can ignore it, as that particular view is really designed for showing architectures that contain hundreds or even thousands of microservices. Instead, click on the **DAG** tab (**Directed Acyclic Graph**), which shows an easier-to-read graph. The graph layout is non-deterministic, so your view may have the second-level nodes in a different order than in the following screenshot:

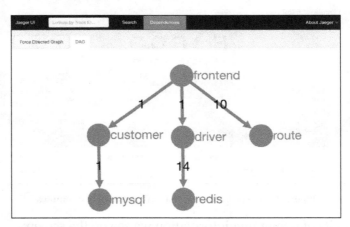

Figure 2.4: Empirically constructed diagram of a services call graph

As it turns out, the single HotROD binary is actually running four microservices and, apparently, two storage backends: Redis and MySQL. The storage nodes are not actually real: they are simulated by the application as internal components, but the top four microservices are indeed real. We saw each of them logging a network address of the servers they run. The `frontend` microservice serves the JavaScript UI and makes RPC calls to the other three microservices.

The graph also shows the number of calls that were made to handle the single request for a car, for example, the `route` service was called 10 times, and there were 14 calls to Redis.

The data flow

We have learned that the application consists of several microservices. What exactly does the request flow look like? It is time to look at the actual trace. Let's go to the **Search** page in the Jaeger UI. Under the **Find Traces** caption, the **Services** dropdown contains the names of the services we saw in the dependency diagram. Since we know that **frontend** is the root service, let's choose it and click the **Find Traces** button.

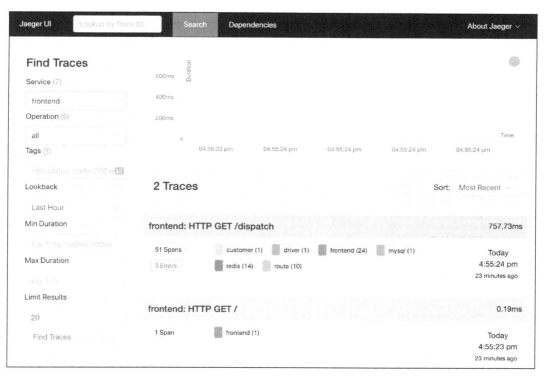

Figure 2.5: Results of searching for all traces in the last hour from the service **frontend**

The system found two traces and displayed some metadata about them, such as the names of different services that participated in the traces, and the number of spans each service emitted to Jaeger. We will ignore the second trace that represents the request to load the JavaScript UI and focus on the first trace, named **frontend: HTTP GET /dispatch**. This name is a concatenation of the service name **frontend** and the operation name of the top-level span, in this case **HTTP GET /dispatch**.

On the right side, we see that the total duration of the trace was **757.73ms**. This is shorter than the **772ms** we saw in the HotROD UI, which is not surprising because the latter was measured from the HTTP client side by JavaScript, while the former was reported by the Go backend. The 14.27ms difference between these numbers can be attributed to the network latency. Let's click on the trace title bar.

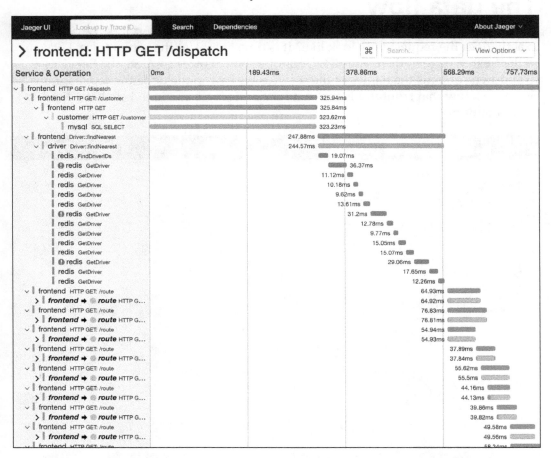

Figure 2.6: Trace timeline view. At the top is the name of the trace, which is combined from the service name and the operation name of the root span. On the left is the hierarchy of calls between microservices, as well as within microservices (internal operations can also be represented as spans). The calls from the **frontend** service to the **route** service are collapsed to save space. Some of the calls from the **driver** service to Redis have red circles with white exclamation points in them, indicating an error in the operation. On the right side is the Gantt chart showing spans on the horizontal timeline. The Gantt chart is interactive and clicking on a span can reveal additional information.

The timeline view shows a typical view of a trace as a time sequence of nested spans, where a span represents a unit of work within a single service. The top-level span, also called the **root span**, represents the handling of the main HTTP request from the JavaScript UI by the `frontend` service (server span), which in turn called the `customer` service, which in turn called a MySQL database. The width of the spans is proportional to the time a given operation took. This may represent a service doing some work or waiting on a downstream call.

From this view, we can see how the application handles a request:

1. The `frontend` service receives the external HTTP GET request at its `/dispatch` endpoint.
2. The `frontend` service makes an HTTP GET request to the `/customer` endpoint of the `customer` service.
3. The `customer` service executes `SELECT` SQL statement in MySQL. The results are returned back to the `frontend` service.
4. Then the `frontend` service makes an RPC request, `Driver::findNearest`, to the `driver` service. Without drilling more into the trace details, we cannot tell which RPC framework is used to make this request, but we can guess it is not HTTP (it is actually made over TChannel [1]).
5. The `driver` service makes a series of calls to Redis. Some of those calls show a red circle with an exclamation point, indicating failures.
6. After that, the `frontend` service executes a series of HTTP GET requests to the `/route` endpoint of the `route` service.
7. Finally, the `frontend` service returns the result to the external caller (for example, the UI).

We can tell all of this pretty much just by looking at the high-level Gantt chart presented by the end-to-end tracing tool.

Contextualized logs

We now have a pretty good idea about what the HotROD application does, if not exactly how it does it. For example, why does the `frontend` service call the `/customer` endpoint of the `customer` service? Of course, we can look at the source code, but we are trying to approach this from the point of view of application monitoring. One direction we could take is to look at the logs the application writes to its standard output (*Figure 2.7*).

Figure 2.7: Typical logging output

It is quite difficult to follow the application logic from these logs and we are only looking at the logs when a single request was executed by the application.

We are also lucky that the logs from four different microservices are combined in a more-or-less consistent stream. Imagine many concurrent requests going through the system and through microservices running in different processes! The logs would become nearly useless in that case. So, let's take a different approach. Let's view the logs collected by the tracing system. For example, click on the root span to expand it and then click on the **Logs (18)** section to expand and see the logs (18 refers to the number of log statements captured in this span). These logs give us more insight into what the /dispatch endpoint was doing (*Figure 2.8*):

1. It called the `customer` service to retrieve some information about the customer given `customer_id=123`.

2. It then retrieved *N* available drivers closest to the customer location (115,277). From the Gantt chart, we know this was done by calling the `driver` service.

3. Finally, it called the `route` service to find the shortest route between driver location (indicated as "pickup") and customer location (indicated as "drop-off").

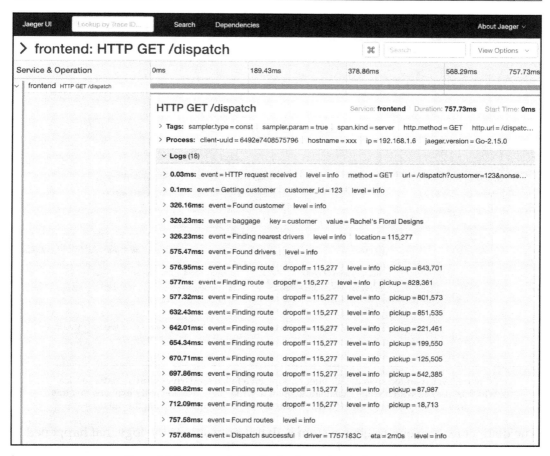

Figure 2.8: Logs recorded by the tracing system in the root span.
The hostname is masked in all screenshots for privacy.

Let's close the root span and open another one; specifically, one of the failed calls to Redis (*Figure 2.9*). The span has a tag `error=true`, which is why the UI highlighted it as failed. The log statement explains the nature of the error as "Redis timeout." The log also includes the `driver_id` that the `driver` service was attempting to retrieve from Redis. All these details may provide very useful information during debugging.

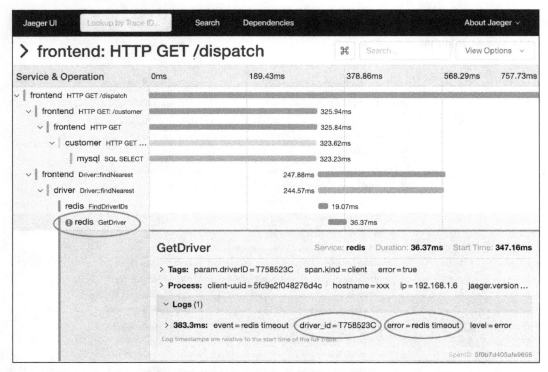

Figure 2.9: Expanded span details after clicking on a failed **GetDriver** span, in **redis** service
which is marked with a white exclamation point in a red circle. The log entry explains that this
was a **redis timeout** and indicates which driver ID was queried from the database.

The distinct feature of a tracing system is that it only shows the logs that happened
during the execution of a given request. We call these logs **contextualized** because
they are captured not only in the context of a specific request, but also in the context
of a specific span within the trace for that request.

In the traditional log output, these log statement would have been mixed with a lot
of other statements from parallel requests, but in the tracing system, they are neatly
isolated to the service and span where they are relevant. Contextualized logs allow
us to focus on the behavior of the application, without worrying about logs from
other parts of the program or from other concurrent requests.

As we can see, using a combination of a Gantt chart, span tags, and span logs, the
end-to-end tracing tool lets us easily understand the architecture and data flow of
the application, and enables us to zoom in on the details of individual operations.

Span tags versus logs

Let's expand a couple more spans.

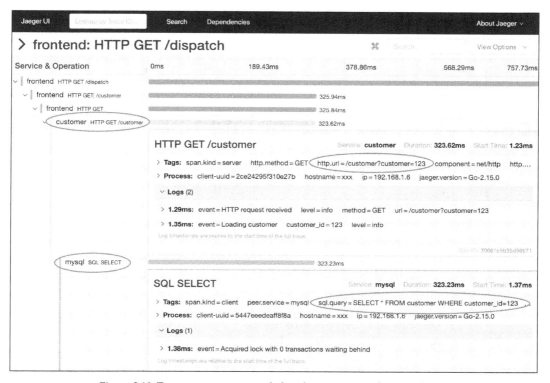

Figure 2.10: Two more spans expanded to show a variety of tags and logs.
Each span also contains a section called "Process" that also looks like a collection of tags.
The process tags describe the application that was producing the tracing record, rather than an individual span.

In the `customer` span, we can see a tag `http.url` that shows that the request at the `/customer` endpoint had a parameter `customer=123`, as well as two logs narrating the execution during that span. In the `mysql` span, we see an `sql.query` tag showing the exact SQL query that was executed: `SELECT * FROM customer WHERE customer_id=123`, and a log about acquiring some lock.

What is the difference between a span *tag* and a span *log*? They are both annotating the span with some contextual information. Tags typically apply to the whole span, while logs represent some events that happened during the span execution. A log always has a timestamp that falls within the span's start-end time interval. The tracing system does not explicitly track causality between logged events the way it keeps track of causality relationships between spans, because it can be inferred from the timestamps.

An acute reader will notice that the /customer span records the URL of the request twice, in the http.url tag and in the first log. The latter is actually redundant but was captured in the span because the code logged this information using the normal logging facility, which we will discuss later in this chapter.

The OpenTracing Specification [3] defines semantic data conventions that prescribe certain well-known tag names and log fields for common scenarios. Instrumentation is encouraged to use those names to ensure that the data reported to the tracing system is well defined and portable across different tracing backends.

Identifying sources of latency

So far, we have not discussed the performance characteristics of the HotROD application. If we refer to *Figure 2.6*, we can easily make the following conclusions:

1. The call to the customer service is on the critical path because no other work can be done until we get back the customer data that includes the location to which we need to dispatch the car.
2. The driver service retrieves N nearest drivers given the customer's location and then queries Redis for each driver's data in a sequence, which can be seen in the staircase pattern of Redis GetDriver spans. If these operations can be done in parallel, the overall latency can be reduced by almost 200ms.
3. The calls to the route service are not sequential, but not fully parallel either. We can see that, at most, three requests can be in progress, and as soon as one of them ends, another request starts. This behavior is typical when we use a fixed-size executor pool.

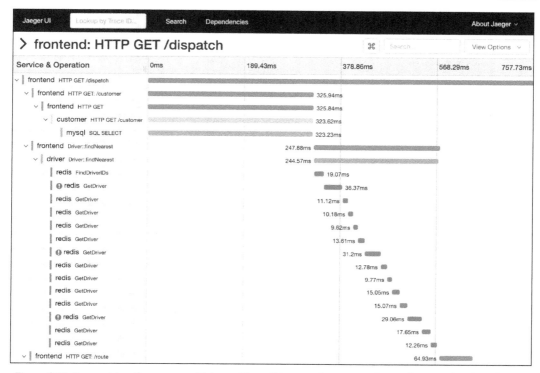

Figure 2.11: Recognizing the sources of latency. The call to **mysql** appears to be on the critical path and takes almost 40% of the trace time, so clearly it is a good target for some optimization. The calls from the **driver** service to Redis look like a staircase, hinting at a strictly sequential execution that perhaps can be done in parallel to expedite the middle part of the trace.

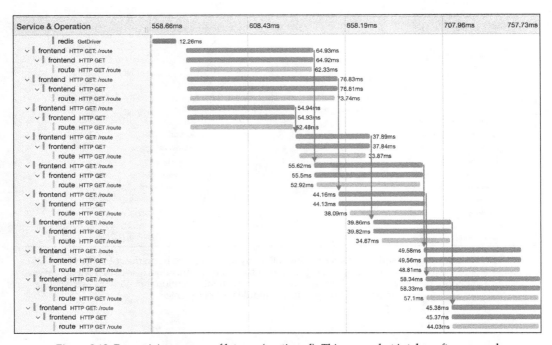

Figure 2.12: Recognizing sources of latency (continued). This screenshot is taken after we used a zoom-in feature in the mini-map to only look at the last 200ms of the trace (by dragging the mouse horizontally across the area of interest). It is easy to see that the requests from the **frontend** service to the route service are done in parallel, but no more than three requests at a time. Red arrows point out how as soon as one request ends, another one starts. This pattern indicates some sort of contention, most likely a worker pool that only has three workers.

What happens if we make many requests to the backend simultaneously?
Let's go to the HotROD UI and click on one of the buttons repeatedly (and quickly).

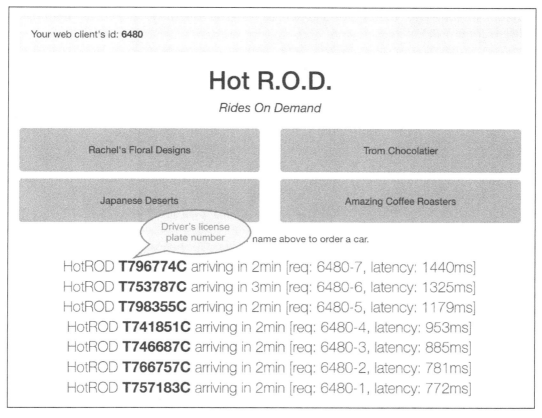

Figure 2.13: Executing many requests simultaneously shows increasing latency of the responses

As we can see, the more requests that are being processed concurrently, the longer it takes for the backend to respond. Let's take a look at the trace of the longest request. We could do it in two ways. We can simply search for all traces and pick the one with the highest latency, represented by the longest cyan-colored title bar (*Figure 2.14*):

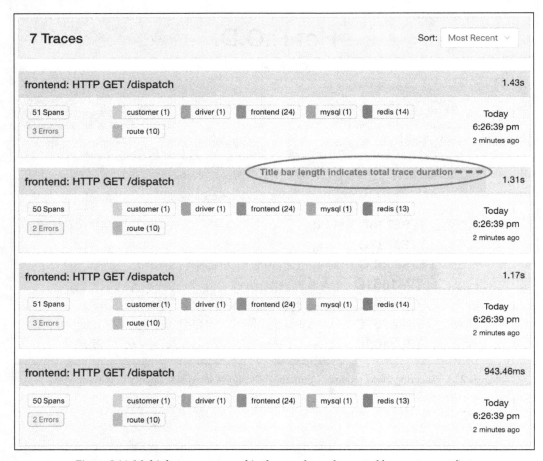

Figure 2.14: Multiple traces returned in the search results, sorted by most recent first

Another way is to search by tags or logs on the span. The root span emits a final log, where it records the license plate number of the closest car as one of the log fields:

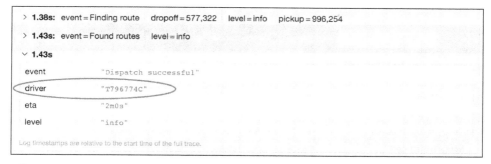

Figure 2.15: License plate number **T796774C** recorded in one of the log events as the field **driver**. Each log entry can be individually expanded to show fields in a table, as opposed to a single row.

The Jaeger backend indexes all spans by both tags and log fields, and we can find that trace by specifying `driver=T796774C` in the **Tags** search box:

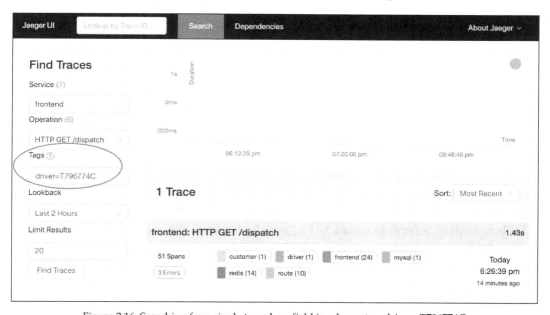

Figure 2.16: Searching for a single trace by a field in a log entry: driver=T796774C

This trace took 1.43 seconds, about 90% longer than our first trace, which took only 757ms (measured from the server side). Let's open it and investigate what is different:

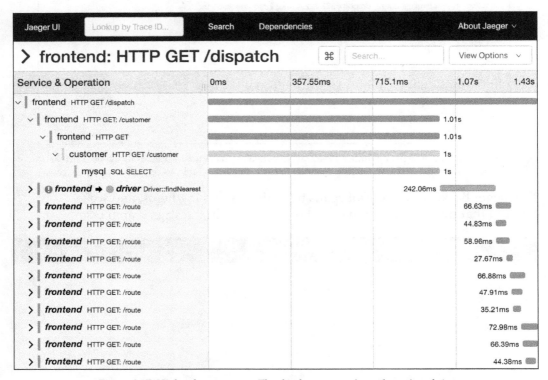

Figure 2.17: Higher-latency trace. The database query (mysql span) took 1s, significantly longer than the 300ms or so that it took when only a single request was processed by the application.

The most apparent difference is that the database query (the `mysql` span) takes a lot longer than before: 1s instead of 323ms. Let's expand that span and try to find out why:

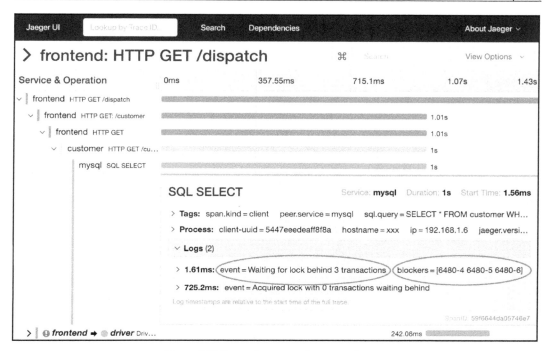

Figure 2.18: Inspecting a very long mysql span

In the log entries of the span, we see that execution was blocked waiting for a lock for more than 700ms. This is clearly a bottleneck in the application, but before we dive into that, let's look at the first log record, evidently emitted before getting blocked on the lock: `Waiting for lock behind 3 transactions. Blockers=[6480-4 6480-5 6480-6]`. It tells us how many other requests were already queued for this lock, and even gives us the identity of those requests. It is not too hard to imagine a lock implementation that keeps track of how many goroutines are blocked, but where would it get the *identity* of the requests?

If we expand the previous span for the customer service, we can see that the only data passed to it via an HTTP request was the customer ID `392`. In fact, if we inspect every span in the trace, we will not find any remote call where the request ID, like `6480-5`, was passed as a parameter.

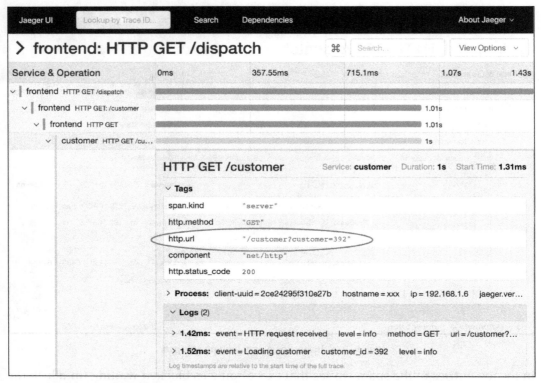

Figure 2.19: The parent span of the database call expanded. It represents an HTTP call from the **frontend** service to the **customer** service. The Tags section of the span is expanded to show tags in a tabular format. The **http.url** tag shows that **customer=392** was the only parameter passed by the caller to the HTTP endpoint.

This *magic* appearance of blocking request IDs in the logs is due to a custom instrumentation in HotROD that makes use of a distributed context propagation mechanism, which is called **baggage** in the OpenTracing API.

As we will see in *Chapter 3, Distributed Tracing Fundamentals*, end-to-end tracing works because tracing instrumentation is designed to propagate certain metadata across thread, component, and process boundaries, throughout the whole distributed call graph. Trace and span IDs are examples of such metadata. Another example is baggage, which is a general-purpose key-value store embedded in every inter-process request. HotROD's JavaScript UI stores session ID and request ID in the baggage before making the request to the backend, and that baggage is transparently made available via OpenTracing instrumentation to every service involved in handling the request, without the need to pass that information explicitly as request parameters.

It is an extremely powerful technique that can be used to propagate various useful pieces of information (such as tenancy) in the context of a single request throughout the architecture, without needing to change every service to understand what they are propagating. We will discuss more examples of using metadata propagation for monitoring, profiling, and other use cases in *Chapter 10, Distributed Context Propagation*.

In our example, knowing the identities of the requests stuck in the queue ahead of our slow request allows us to find traces for those requests, and analyze them as well. In real production systems, this could lead to unexpected discoveries, such as a long-running request spoiling a lot of other requests that are normally very fast. Later in this chapter, we will see another example of using baggage.

Now that we know that the `mysql` call gets stuck on a lock, we can easily fix it. As we mentioned earlier, the application does not actually use the MySQL database, just a simulation of it, and the lock is meant to represent a single database connection shared between multiple goroutines. We can find the code in the file `examples/hotrod/services/customer/database.go`:

```
if !config.MySQLMutexDisabled {
    // simulate misconfigured connection pool that only gives
    // one connection at a time
    d.lock.Lock(ctx)
    defer d.lock.Unlock()
}

// simulate db query delay
delay.Sleep(config.MySQLGetDelay, config.MySQLGetDelayStdDev)
```

If the locking behavior is not disabled via configuration, we acquire the lock before simulating the SQL query delay. The statement `defer d.lock.Unlock()` is used to release the lock before we exit the surrounding function.

Notice how we pass the `ctx` parameter to the lock object. `context.Context` is a standard way in Go to pass request-scoped data throughout an application. The OpenTracing span is stored in the Context, which allows the lock to inspect it and retrieve the JavaScript's request ID from the baggage. The code for this custom implementation of a mutex can be found in the source file `examples/hotrod/pkg/tracing/mutex.go`.

We can see that the mutex behavior is protected by a configuration parameter

```
if !config.MySQLMutexDisabled {
    // . . .
}
```

Fortunately, the HotROD applications expose command line flags to change these configuration parameters. We can find the flags by running the HotROD binary with `help` command:

```
$ ./example-hotrod help
HotR.O.D. - A tracing demo application.
[... skipped ...]
Flags:
  -D, --fix-db-query-delay, duration      Average lagency of MySQL DB
                                          query (default 300ms)
  -M, --fix-disable-db-conn-mutex         Disables the mutex guarding
                                          db connection
  -W, --fix-route-worker-pool-size, int   Default worker pool size
                                          (default 3)
[... skipped ...]
```

The flags that control parameters for latency-affecting logic all start with the `--fix` prefix. In this case, we want the flag `--fix-disable-db-conn-mutex`, or `-M` as a short form, to disable the blocking behavior. We also want to reduce the default `300ms` latency of simulated database queries, controlled by flag `-D`, to make it easier to see the results of this optimization.

Let's restart the HotROD application using these flags, to pretend that we fixed the code to use a connection pool with enough capacity that our concurrent requests do not have to compete for connections (the logs are again trimmed for better readability):

```
$ ./example-hotrod -M -D 100ms all
INFO Using expvar as metrics backend
INFO fix: overriding MySQL query delay {"old": "300ms", "new":
"100ms"}
INFO fix: disabling db connection mutex
INFO Starting all services
```

We can see in the logs that the changes are taking effect. To see how it works out, reload the HotROD web page and repeat the experiment of issuing many simultaneous requests by clicking one of the buttons many times in quick succession.

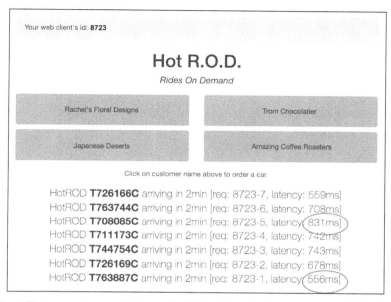

Figure 2.20: Partially improved request latency after "fixing" the database query bottleneck. No requests run longer than a second, but some are still pretty slow; for example, request #5 is still 50% slower than request #1.

The latency still increases as we add more requests to the system, but it no longer grows as dramatically as with the single database bottleneck from before. Let's look at one of the longer traces again.

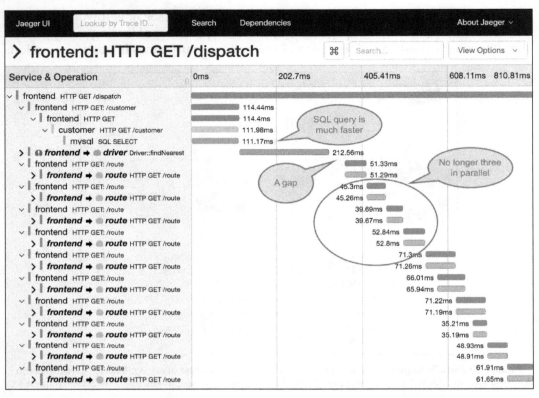

Figure 2.21: Trace of another pretty slow request, after removing the database query bottleneck

As expected, the `mysql` span stays at around `100ms`, regardless of the load. The `driver` span is not expanded, but it takes the same time as before. The interesting change is in the `route` calls, which now take more than 50% of the total request time. Previously, we saw these requests executing in parallel three at a time, but now we often see only one at a time, and even a gap right after the `frontend` to `driver` call when no requests to `route` service are running. Clearly, we have a contention with other goroutines on some limited resource and we can also see that the gaps happen between the spans of the `frontend` service, which means the bottleneck is not in the `route` service, but in how the `frontend` service calls it.

Let's look at function `getRoutes()` in the source file `services/frontend/best_eta.go`:

```
// getRoutes calls Route service for each (customer, driver) pair
func (eta *bestETA) getRoutes(
    ctx context.Context,
    customer *customer.Customer,
    drivers []driver.Driver,
) []routeResult {
```

```
results := make([]routeResult, 0, len(drivers))
wg := sync.WaitGroup{}
routesLock := sync.Mutex{}
for _, dd := range drivers {
    wg.Add(1)
    driver := dd // capture loop var
    // Use worker pool to (potentially) execute
    // requests in parallel
    eta.pool.Execute(func() {
        route, err := eta.route.FindRoute(
            ctx, driver.Location, customer.Location
        )
        routesLock.Lock()
        results = append(results, routeResult{
            driver: driver.DriverID,
            route:  route,
            err:    err,
        })
        routesLock.Unlock()
        wg.Done()
    })
}
wg.Wait()
return results
}
```

This function receives a customer record (with address) and a list of drivers (with their current locations), then calculates the **expected time of arrival (ETA)** for each driver. It calls the route service for each driver inside an anonymous function executed via a pool of goroutines, by passing the function to eta.pool.Execute().

Since all functions are executed asynchronously, we track their completion with the wait group, wg, which implements a countdown latch: for every new function, we increment its count with we.Add(1), and then we block on wg.Wait() until each of the spawned functions calls wg.Done().

As long as we have enough executors (goroutines) in the pool, we should be able to run all calculations in parallel. The size of the executor pool is defined in services/config/config.go:

```
RouteWorkerPoolSize = 3
```

The default value of three explains why we saw, at most, three parallel executions in the very first trace we inspected. Let's change it to 100 (goroutines in Go are cheap) using the -W command line flag, and restart HotROD:

```
$ ./example-hotrod -M -D 100ms -W 100 all
INFO   Using expvar as metrics backend
```

```
INFO   fix: overriding MySQL query delay {"old": "300ms", "new":
"100ms"}
INFO   fix: disabling db connection mutex
INFO   fix: overriding route worker pool size {"old": 3, "new": 100}
INFO   Starting all services
```

One more time, reload the HotROD web UI and repeat the experiment. We have to click on the buttons really quickly now because the requests return back in less than half a second.

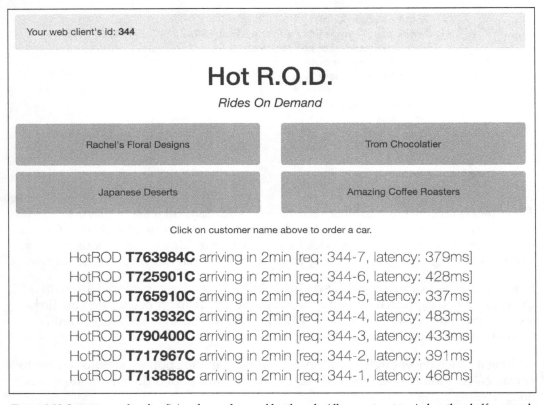

Figure 2.22: Latency results after fixing the worker pool bottleneck. All requests return in less than half a second.

If we look at one of these new traces, we will see that, as expected, the calls from `frontend` to the `route` service are all done in parallel now, thus minimizing the overall request latency. We leave the final optimization of the driver service as an exercise for you.

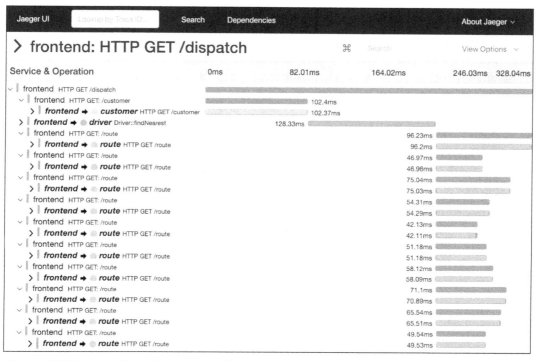

Figure 2.23: Trace after fixing the worker pool bottleneck. The **frontend** is able to fire 10 requests to the **route** service almost simultaneously.

Resource usage attribution

In this last example, we will discuss a technique that is not, strictly speaking, a functionality commonly provided by distributed tracing systems, but rather a side effect of the distributed context propagation mechanism that underlies all tracing instrumentation and can be relied upon in applications instrumented for tracing. We saw an example of this earlier when we discussed an implicit propagation of the frontend request ID used to tag transactions that were blocking in a mutex queue. In this section, we will discuss the use of metadata propagation for resource usage attribution.

Resource usage attribution is an important function in large organizations, especially for capacity planning and efficiency improvements. We can define it as a process of measuring the usage of some resource, such as CPU cores, or disk space, and attributing it to some higher-level business parameter, such as a product or a business line. For example, consider a company that has two lines of business that together require 1,000 CPU cores to operate, as maybe measured by some cloud provider.

Let's assume the company projects that one line of business will grow 10% next year, while the other will grow 100%. Let's also assume, for simplicity, that the hardware needs are proportional to the size of each business. We are still not able to predict how much extra capacity the company will need because we do not know how those current 1,000 CPU cores are attributed to each business line.

If the first business line is actually responsible for consuming 90% of hardware, then its hardware needs will increase from 900 to 990 cores, and the second business line's needs will increase from 100 to 200 CPU cores, to the total of an extra 190 cores across both business lines. On the other hand, if the current needs of the business lines are split 50/50, then the total capacity requirement for next year will be 500 * 1.1 + 500 * 2.0=1550 cores.

The main difficulty in resource usage attribution stems from the fact that most technology companies use shared resources for running their business. Consider such products as Gmail and Google Docs. Somewhere, at the top level of the architecture, they may have dedicated pools of resources, for example, load balancers and web servers, but the lower we go down the architecture, the more shared resources we usually find.

At some point, the dedicated resource pools, like web servers, start accessing shared resources like Bigtable, Chubby, Google File System, and so on. It is often inefficient to partition those lower layers of architecture into distinct subsets in order to support multi-tenancy. If we require all requests to explicitly carry the tenant information as a parameter, for example, `tenant="gmail"` or `tenant="docs"`, then we can accurately report resource usage by the business line. However, such a model is very rigid and hard to extend if we want to break down the attribution by a different dimension, as we need to change the APIs of every single infrastructure layer to pass that extra dimension. We will now discuss an alternative solution that relies on metadata propagation.

We have seen in the HotROD demo that the calculation of the shortest route performed by the `route` service is a relatively expensive operation (probably CPU intensive). It would be nice if we could calculate how much CPU time we spend per customer. However, the `route` service is an example of a shared infrastructure resource that is further down the architectural layers from the point where we know about the customer. It does not need to know about the customer in order to calculate the shortest route between two points.

Passing the customer ID to the `route` service just to measure the CPU usage would be poor API design. Instead, we can use the distributed metadata propagation built into the tracing instrumentation. In the context of a trace, we know for which customer the system is executing the request, and we can use metadata (baggage) to transparently pass that information throughout the architecture layers, without changing all the services to accept it explicitly.

If we want to perform CPU usage aggregation by some other dimension, say, the session ID from the JavaScript UI, we can do so without changing all the components as well.

To demonstrate this approach, the `route` service contains the code to attribute the CPU time of calculations to the customer and session IDs, which it reads from the baggage. In the `services/route/server.go` file, we can see this code:

```
func computeRoute(
    ctx context.Context,
    pickup, dropoff string,
) *Route {
    start := time.Now()
    defer func() {
        updateCalcStats(ctx, time.Since(start))
    }()
    // actual calculation ...
}
```

As with the instrumented mutex we saw earlier, we don't pass any customer/session IDs because they can be retrieved from baggage via the context. The code actually uses some static configuration to know which baggage items to extract and how to report the metrics.

```
var routeCalcByCustomer = expvar.NewMap(
    "route.calc.by.customer.sec",
)
var routeCalcBySession = expvar.NewMap(
    "route.calc.by.session.sec",
)
var stats = []struct {
    expvar  *expvar.Map
    baggage string
}{
    {routeCalcByCustomer, "customer"},
    {routeCalcBySession, "session"},
}
```

This code uses the `expvar` package ("exposed variables") from Go's standard library. It provides a standard interface to global variables that can be used to accumulate statistics about the application, such as operation counters, and it exposes these variables in JSON format via an HTTP endpoint, `/debug/vars`.

The `expvar` variables can be standalone primitives, like `float` and `string`, or they can be grouped into named maps for more dynamic statistics. In the preceding code, we define two maps: one keyed by customer ID and another by session ID, and combine them in the `stats` structure (an array of anonymous structs) with the names of metadata attributes that contain the corresponding ID.

The `updateCalcStats()` function first converts the elapsed time of an operation into seconds as a `float` value, then iterates through the `stats` array and checks if the `span` metadata contains the desired key (`"customer"` or `"session"`). If the baggage item with that key is not empty, it increments the counter for that key by calling `AddFloat()` on the respective `expvar.Map` to aggregate the time spent on computing the route.

```go
func updateCalcStats(ctx context.Context, delay time.Duration) {
    span := opentracing.SpanFromContext(ctx)
    if span == nil {
        return
    }
    delaySec := float64(delay/time.Millisecond) / 1000.0
    for _, s := range stats {
        key := span.BaggageItem(s.baggage)
        if key != "" {
            s.expvar.AddFloat(key, delaySec)
        }
    }
}
```

If we navigate to `http://127.0.0.1:8083/debug/vars`, which is one of the endpoints exposed by the HotROD application, we can see `route.calc.by.*` entries that give us the breakdown of time (in seconds) spent in calculation on behalf of each customer, and some UI sessions.

```
route.calc.by.customer.sec: {
    Amazing Coffee Roasters: 1.479,
    Japanese Deserts: 2.019,
    Rachel's Floral Designs: 5.938,
    Trom Chocolatier: 2.542
},
route.calc.by.session.sec: {
    0861: 9.448,
    6108: 2.530
},
```

This approach is very flexible. If necessary, this static definition of the stats array can be easily moved to a configuration file to make the reporting mechanism even more flexible. For example, if we wanted to aggregate data by another dimension, say the type of web browser (not that it would make a lot of sense), we would need to add one more entry to the configuration and make sure that the frontend service captures the browser type as a baggage item.

The key point is that we do not need to change anything in the rest of the services. In the HotROD demo, the frontend and route services are very close to each other, so if we had to change the API it would not be a major undertaking. However, in real-life situations, the service where we may want to calculate resource usage can be many layers down the stack, and changing the APIs of all the intermediate services, just to pass an extra resource usage aggregation dimension, is simply not feasible. By using distributed context propagation, we vastly minimize the number of changes needed. In *Chapter 10, Distributed Context Propagation*, we will discuss other uses of metadata propagation.

In a production environment, using the expvar module is not the best approach, since the data is stored individually in each service instance. However, our example has no hard dependency on the expvar mechanism. We could have easily used a real metrics API and had our resource usage statistics aggregated in a central metrics system like Prometheus.

Summary

This chapter introduced a demo application, HotROD, that is instrumented for distributed tracing, and by tracing that application with Jaeger, an open source distributed tracing system, demonstrated the following features common to most end-to-end tracing systems:

- **Distributed transaction monitoring**: Jaeger records the execution of individual requests across the whole stack of microservices, and presents them as traces.

- **Performance and latency optimization**: Traces provide very simple visual guides to performance issues in the application. The practitioners of distributed tracing often say that fixing the performance issue is the easy part, but finding it is the hard part.

- **Root cause analysis**: The highly contextualized nature of the information presented in the traces allows for quickly narrowing down to the parts of the execution that are responsible for issues with the execution (for example, the timeouts when calling Redis, or the mutex queue blocking).

- **Service dependency analysis**: Jaeger aggregates multiple traces and constructs a service graph that represents the architecture of the application.

- **Distributed context propagation**: The underlying mechanism of metadata propagation for a given request enables not only tracing, but various other features, such as resource usage attribution.

In the next chapter, we will review more of the theoretical underpinnings of distributed tracing, the anatomy of a tracing solution, different implementation techniques that have been proposed in the industry and academia, and various trade-offs that implementors of tracing infrastructure need to keep in mind when making certain architectural decisions.

References

1. Yuri Shkuro, *Evolving Distributed Tracing at Uber Engineering*, Uber Engineering blog, February 2017: `https://eng.uber.com/distributed-tracing/`.

2. Natasha Woods, *CNCF Hosts Jaeger*, Cloud Native Computing Foundation blog, September 2017: `https://www.cncf.io/blog/2017/09/13/cncf-hosts-jaeger/`.

3. The OpenTracing Authors. *Semantic Conventions*, The OpenTracing Specification: `https://github.com/opentracing/specification/blob/master/semantic_conventions.md`.

3

Distributed Tracing Fundamentals

Distributed tracing, also known as end-to-end or workflow-centric tracing, is a family of techniques that aim to capture the detailed execution of causally-related activities, performed by the components of a distributed system. Unlike the traditional code profilers or host-level tracing tools, such as **dtrace** [1], end-to-end tracing is primarily focused on profiling the individual executions cooperatively performed by many different processes, usually running on many different hosts, which is typical of modern, cloud-native, microservices-based applications.

In the previous chapter, we saw a tracing system in action from the end user perspective. In this chapter, we will discuss the basic underlying ideas of distributed tracing, various approaches that have been presented in the industry, academic works for implementing end-to-end tracing; the impact and trade-offs of the architectural decisions taken by different tracing systems on their capabilities, and the types of problems they can address.

The idea

Consider the following, vastly simplified architectural diagram of a hypothetical e-commerce website. Each node in the diagram represents numerous instances of the respective microservices, handling many concurrent requests. To help with understanding the behavior of this distributed system and its performance or user-visible latency, end-to-end tracing records information about all the work performed by the system on behalf of a given client or request initiator. We will refer to this work as **execution** or **request** throughout this book.

The data is collected by means of instrumentation **trace points**. For example, when the client is making a request to the web server, the client's code can be instrumented with two trace points: one for sending the request and another for receiving the response. The collected data for a given execution is collectively referred to as **trace**. One simple way to visualize a trace is via a Gantt chart, as shown on the right in in *Figure 3.1*:

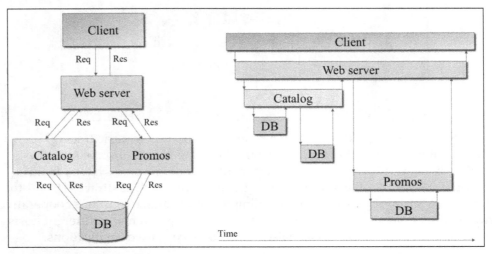

Figure 3.1: Left: a simplified architecture of a hypothetical e-commerce website and inter-process communications involved in executing a single request from a client. Right: a visualization of a single request execution as a Gantt chart.

Request correlation

The basic concept of distributed tracing appears to be very straightforward:

- Instrumentation is inserted into chosen points of the program's code (trace points) and produces profiling data when executed

- The profiling data is collected in a central location, correlated to the specific execution (request), arranged in the causality order, and combined into a trace that can be visualized or further analyzed

Of course, things are rarely as simple as they appear. There are multiple design decisions taken by the existing tracing systems, affecting how these systems perform, how difficult they are to integrate into existing distributed applications, and even what kinds of problems they can or cannot help to solve.

The ability to collect and correlate profiling data for a given execution or request initiator, and identify causally-related activities, is arguably the most distinctive feature of distributed tracing, setting it apart from all other profiling and observability tools. Different classes of solutions have been proposed in the industry and academia to address the correlation problem. Here, we will discuss the three most common approaches: black-box inference, domain-specific schemas, and metadata propagation.

Black-box inference

Techniques that do not require modifying the monitored system are known as black-box monitoring. Several tracing infrastructures have been proposed that use statistical analysis or machine learning (for example, the Mystery Machine [2]) to infer causality and request correlation by consuming only the records of the events occurring in the programs, most often by reading their logs. These techniques are attractive because they do not require modifications to the traced applications, but they have difficulties attributing causality in the general case of highly concurrent and asynchronous executions, such as those observed in event-driven systems. Their reliance on "big data" processing also makes them more expensive and higher latency compared to the other methods.

Schema-based

Magpie [3] proposed a technique that relied on manually-written, application-specific event schemas that allowed it to extract causality relationships from the event logs of production systems. Similar to the black-box approach, this technique does not require the applications to be instrumented explicitly; however, it is less general, as each application requires its own schemas.

This approach is not particularly suitable for modern distributed systems that consist of hundreds of microservices because it would be difficult to scale the manual creation of event schemas. The schema-based technique requires all events to be collected before the causality inference can be applied, so it is less scalable than other methods that allow sampling.

Metadata propagation

What if the instrumentation trace points could annotate the data they produce with a global identifier – let's call it an **execution identifier** – that is unique for each traced request? Then the tracing infrastructure receiving the annotated profiling data could easily reconstruct the full execution of the request, by grouping the records by the execution identifier. So, how do the trace points know which request is being executed when they are invoked, especially trace points in different components of a distributed application? The global execution identifier needs to be passed along the execution flow. This is achieved via a process known as **metadata propagation** or **distributed context propagation**.

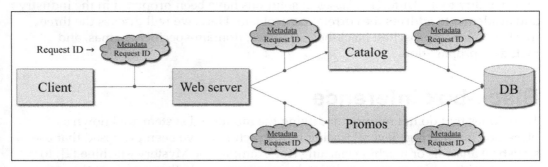

Figure 3.2: Propagating the execution identifier as request metadata. The first service in the architecture (client) creates a unique execution identifier (Request ID) and passes it to the next service via metadata/context. The remaining services keep passing it along in the same way.

Metadata propagation in a distributed system consists of two parts: **in-process** and **inter-process** propagation. In-process propagation is responsible for making the metadata available to trace points inside a given program. It needs to be able to carry the context between the inbound and outbound network calls, dealing with possible thread switches or asynchronous behavior, which are common in modern applications. Inter-process propagation is responsible for transferring metadata over network calls when components of a distributed system communicate to each other during the execution of a given request.

Inter-process propagation is typically done by decorating communication frameworks with special tracing middleware that encodes metadata in the network messages, for example, in HTTP headers, Kafka records headers, and so on.

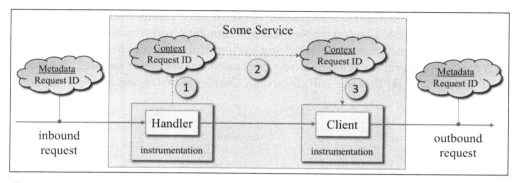

Figure 3.3: Metadata propagation in a single service. (1) The Handler that processes the inbound request is wrapped into instrumentation that extracts metadata from the request and stores it in a Context object in memory. (2) Some in-process propagation mechanism, for example, based on thread-local variables. (3) Instrumentation wraps an RPC client and injects metadata into outbound (downstream) requests.

The key disadvantage of metadata propagation-based tracing is the expectation of a white-box system whose components can be modified accordingly. However, it is more scalable and provides much higher accuracy of the data compared to black-box techniques, since all trace points are explicitly annotating the data with execution identifiers. In many programming languages, it is even possible to inject trace points automatically, without changes to the application itself, through a technique known as **agent-based instrumentation** (we will discuss this in more detail in *Chapter 6, Tracing Standards and Ecosystem*). Distributed tracing based on metadata propagation is by far the most popular approach and used by virtually all industrial-grade tracing systems today, both commercial and open source. Throughout the rest of this book, we will focus exclusively on this type of tracing systems. In *Chapter 6, Tracing Standards and Ecosystem*, we will see how new industry initiatives, such as the OpenTracing project [11], aim to reduce the cost of white-box instrumentation and make distributed tracing a standard practice in the development of modern cloud-native applications.

An acute reader may have noticed that the notion of propagating metadata alongside request execution is not limited to only passing the execution identifier for tracing purposes. Metadata propagation can be thought of as a prerequisite for distributed tracing, or distributed tracing can be thought of as an application built on top of distributed context propagation. In *Chapter 10, Distributed Context Propagation* we will discuss a variety of other possible applications.

Anatomy of distributed tracing

The following diagram shows a typical organization of distributed tracing systems, built around metadata propagation. The microservices or components of a distributed application are instrumented with trace points that observe the execution of a request. The trace points record causality and profiling information about the request and pass it to the tracing system through calls to a Tracing API, which may depend on the specific tracing backend or be vendor neutral, like the OpenTracing API [11] that we will discuss in *Chapter 4, Instrumentation Basics with OpenTracing*.

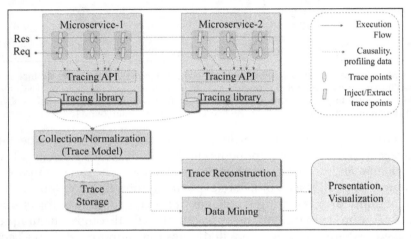

Figure 3.4: Anatomy of distributed tracing

Special trace points at the edges of the microservice, which we can call **inject** and **extract** trace points, are also responsible for encoding and decoding metadata for passing it across process boundaries. In certain cases, the inject/extract trace points are used even between libraries and components, for example, when a Python code is making a call to an extension written in C, which may not have direct access to the metadata represented in a Python data structure.

The Tracing API is implemented by a concrete tracing library that reports the collected data to the tracing backend, usually with some in-memory batching to reduce the communications overhead. Reporting is always done asynchronously in the background, off the critical path of the business requests. The tracing backend receives the tracing data, normalizes it to a common trace model representation, and puts it in a persistent trace storage. Because tracing data for a single request usually arrives from many different hosts, the trace storage is often organized to store individual pieces incrementally, indexed by the execution identifier. This allows for later reconstruction of the whole trace for the purpose of visualization, or additional processing through aggregations and data mining.

Sampling

Sampling affects which records produced by the trace points are captured by the tracing infrastructure. It is used to control the volume of data the tracing backend needs to store, as well as the performance overhead and impact on the applications from executing tracing instrumentation. We discuss sampling in detail in *Chapter 8, All About Sampling.*

Preserving causality

If we only pass the execution identifier as request metadata and tag tracing records with it, it is sufficient to reassemble that data into a single collection, but it is not sufficient to reconstruct the execution graph of causally-related activities. Tracing systems need to capture causality that allows assembling the data captured by the trace points in the correct sequence. Unfortunately, knowing which activities are truly causally-related is very difficult, even with very invasive instrumentation. Most tracing systems elect to preserve Lamport's **happens-before** relation [4], denoted as $\rightarrow$ and formally defined as the least strict partial order on events, such that:

- If events a and b occur in the same process, then $a \rightarrow b$ if the occurrence of event a preceded the occurrence of event b

- If event a is the sending of a message and event b is the reception of the message sent in event a, then $a \rightarrow b$

The happens-before relation can be too indiscriminate if applied liberally: *may have influenced* is not the same as *has influenced*. The tracing infrastructures rely on the additional domain knowledge about the systems being traced, and the execution environment, to avoid capturing irrelevant causality. By threading the metadata along the individual executions, they establish the relationships between items with the same or related metadata (that is, metadata containing different trace point IDs by the same execution ID). The metadata can be static or dynamic throughout the execution.

Tracing infrastructures that use **static metadata**, such as a single unique execution identifier, throughout the life cycle of a request, must capture additional clues via trace points, in order to establish the happens-before relationships between the events. For example, if part of an execution is performed on a single thread, then using the local timestamps allows correct ordering of the events. Alternatively, in a client-server communication, the tracing system may infer that the sending of a network message by the client happens before the server receiving that message. Similar to black-box inference systems, this approach cannot always identify causality between events when additional clues are lost or not available from the instrumentation. It can, however, guarantee that all events for a given execution will be correctly identified.

Most of today's industrial-grade tracing infrastructures use **dynamic metadata**, which can be fixed-width or variable-width. For example, X-Trace [5], Dapper [6], and many similar tracing systems use **fixed-width dynamic metadata**, where, in addition to the execution identifier, they record a unique ID (for example, a random 64-bit value) of the event captured by the trace point. When the next trace point is executed, it stores the inbound event ID as part of its tracing data, and replaces it with its own ID.

In the following diagram, we see five trace points causally linked to a single execution. The metadata propagated after each trace point is a three-part tuple (execution ID, event ID, and parent ID). Each trace point stores the parent event ID from inbound metadata as part of its captured trace record. The fork at trace point *b* and join at trace point *e* illustrate how causal relationships forming a directed acyclic graph can be captured using this scheme.

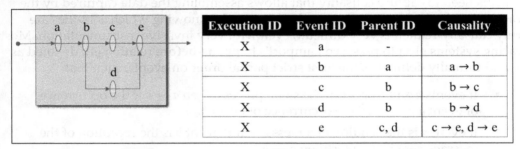

Execution ID	Event ID	Parent ID	Causality
X	a	-	
X	b	a	a → b
X	c	b	b → c
X	d	b	b → d
X	e	c, d	c → e, d → e

Figure 3.5: Establishing causal relationships using dynamic, fixed-width metadata

Using fixed-width dynamic metadata, the tracing infrastructure can explicitly record happens-before relationships between trace events, which gives it an edge over the static metadata approach. However, it is also somewhat brittle if some of the trace records are lost because it will no longer be able to order the events in the order of causality.

Some tracing systems use a variation of the fixed-width approach by introducing the notion of a **trace segment**, which is represented by another unique ID that is constant within a single process, and only changes when metadata is sent over the network to another process. It reduces the brittleness slightly, by making the system more tolerant to the loss of trace records within a single process, in particular when the tracing infrastructure is proactively trying to reduce the volume of trace data to control the overhead, by keeping the trace points only at the edges of a process and discarding all the internal trace points.

When using end-to-end tracing on distributed systems, where profiling data loss is a constant factor, some tracing infrastructures, for example, Azure Application Insights, use **variable-width dynamic metadata**, which grows as the execution travels further down the call graph from the request origin.

The following diagram illustrates this approach, where each next event ID is generated by appending a sequence number to the previous event ID. When a fork happens at event 1, two distinct sequence numbers are used to represent parallel events **1.1** and **1.2**. The benefit of this scheme is higher tolerance to data loss; for example, if the record for event **1.2** is lost, it is still possible to infer the happens-before relationship *1 → 1.2.1*.

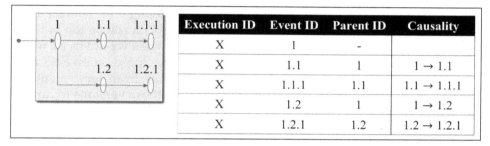

Execution ID	Event ID	Parent ID	Causality
X	1	-	
X	1.1	1	1 → 1.1
X	1.1.1	1.1	1.1 → 1.1.1
X	1.2	1	1 → 1.2
X	1.2.1	1.2	1.2 → 1.2.1

Figure 3.6: Establishing causal relationships using dynamic, variable-width metadata

Inter-request causality

Sambasivan and others [10] argue that another critical architectural decision that significantly affects the types of problems an end-to-end tracing infrastructure is able to address is the question of how it attributes *latent work*. For example, a request may write data to a memory buffer that is flushed to the disk at a later time, after the originating request has been completed. Such buffers are commonly implemented for performance reasons and, at the time of writing, the buffer may contain data produced by many different requests. The question is: who is responsible for the use of resources and the time spent by the system on writing the buffer out?

The work can be attributed to the last request that made the buffer full and caused the write (trigger-preserving attribution), or it can be attributed proportionally to all requests that produced the data into the buffer before the flush (submitter-preserving attribution). Trigger-preserving attribution is easier to implement because it does not require access to the instrumentation data about the earlier executions that affected the latent work.

However, it disproportionally penalizes the last request, especially if the tracing infrastructure is used for monitoring and attributing resource consumption. The submitter-preserving attribution is fair in that regard but requires that the profiling data for all previous executions is available when latent work happens. This can be quite expensive and does not work well with some forms of sampling usually applied by the tracing infrastructure (we will discuss sampling in chapter 8).

Trace models

In *Figure 3.4*, we saw a component called "Collection/Normalization." The purpose of this component is to receive tracing data from the trace points in the applications and convert it to some normalized **trace model**, before saving it in the trace storage. Aside from the usual architectural advantages of having a façade on top of the trace storage, the normalization is especially important when we are faced with the diversity of instrumentations. It is quite common for many production environments to be using numerous versions of instrumentation libraries, from very recent ones to some that are several years old. It is also common for those versions to capture trace data in very different formats and models, both physical and conceptual. The normalization layer acts as an equalizer and translates all those varieties into a single logical trace model, which can later be uniformly processed by the trace visualization and analysis tools. In this section, we will focus on two of the most popular conceptual trace models: event model and span model.

Event model

So far, we have discussed tracing instrumentation taking the form of **trace points** that record **events** when the request execution passes through them. An event represents a single point in time in the end-to-end execution. Assuming that we also record the happens-before relationships between these events, we intuitively arrive to the model of a trace as a directed acyclic graph, with nodes representing the events and edges representing the causality.

Some tracing systems (for example, X-Trace [5]) use such an **event model** as the final form of the traces they surface to the user. The diagram in *Figure 3.7* illustrates an event graph observed from the execution of an RPC request/response by a client-server application. It includes events collected at different layers of the stack, from application-level events (for example, "client send" and "server receive") to events in the TCP/IP stack.

The graph contains multiple forks used to model request execution at different layers, and multiple joins where these logical parallel executions converge to higher-level layers. Many developers find the event model difficult to work with because it is too low level and obscures useful higher-level primitives. For example, it is natural for the developer of the client application to think of the RPC request as a single operation that has start (*client sent*) and end (*client receive*) events. However, in the event graph these two nodes are far apart.

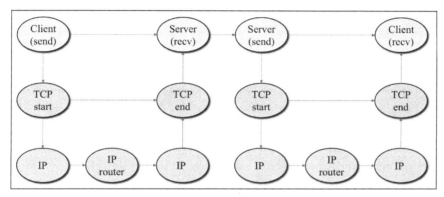

Figure 3.7: Trace representation of an RPC request between client and server in the event model, with trace events recorded at application and TCP/IP layers

The next diagram (*Figure 3.8*) shows an even more extreme example, where a fairly simple workflow becomes hard to decipher when represented as an event graph. A frontend Spring application running on Tomcat is calling another application called remotesrv, which is running on JBoss. The remotesrv application is making two calls to a PostgreSQL database.

It is easy to notice that aside from the "info" events shown in boxes with rounded corners, all other records come in pairs of entry and exit events. The info events are interesting in that they look almost like a noise: they most likely contain useful information if we had to troubleshoot this particular workflow, but they do not add much to our understanding of the shape of the workflow itself. We can think of them as info logs, only captured via trace points. We also see an example of fork and join because the info event from tomcat-jbossclient happens in parallel with the execution happening in the remotesrv application.

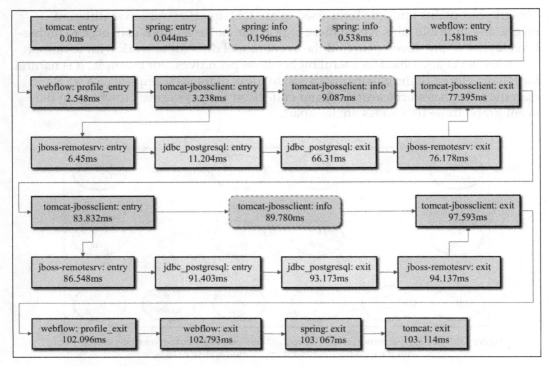

Figure 3.8: Event model-based graph of an RPC request between a Spring application running on Tomcat and a remotesrv application running on JBoss, and talking to a PostgreSQL database. The boxes with rounded corners represent simple point-in-time "info" events.

Span model

Having observed that, as in the preceding example, most execution graphs include well-defined pairs of entry/exit events representing certain operations performed by the application, Sigelman and others [6], proposed a simplified trace model, which made the trace graphs much easier to understand. In Dapper [6], which was designed for Google's RPC-heavy architecture, the traces are represented as trees, where tree nodes are basic units of work referred to as **spans**. The edges in the tree, as usual, indicate causal relationships between a span and its **parent span**. Each span is a simple log of timestamped records, including its start and end time, a human-readable operation name, and zero or more intermediary application-specific annotations in the form of (timestamp, description) pairs, which are equivalent to the info events in the previous example.

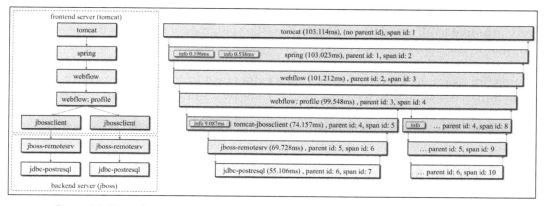

Figure 3.9: Using the span model to represent the same RPC execution as in as in Figure 3.8.
Left: the resulting trace as a tree of spans. Right: the same trace shown as a Gantt chart. The info events
are no longer included as separate nodes in the graph; instead they are modeled as timestamped annotations
in the spans, shown as pills in the Gantt chart.

Each span is assigned a unique ID (for example, a random 64-bit value), which is
propagated via metadata along with the execution ID. When a new span is started,
it records the ID of the previous span as its **parent ID**, thus capturing the causality.
In the preceding example, the remote server represents its main operation in the
span with ID=6. When it makes a call to the database, it starts another span with
ID=7 and parent ID=6.

Dapper originally advocated for the model of **multi-server spans**, where a client
application that makes an RPC call creates a new span ID, and passes it as part of
the call, and the server that receives the RPC logs its events using the same span ID.
Unlike the preceding figure, the multi-server span model resulted in fewer spans
in the tree because each RPC call is represented by only one span, even though two
services are involved in doing the work as part of that RPC. This multi-server span
model was used by other tracing systems, such as Zipkin [7] (where spans were
often called **shared spans**). It was later discovered that this model unnecessarily
complicates the post-collection trace processing and analysis, so newer tracing
systems like Jaeger [8] opted for a **single-host** span model, in which an RPC call
is represented by two separate spans: one on the client and another on the server,
with the client span being the parent.

The tree-like span model is easy to understand for the programmers, whether they
are instrumenting their applications or retrieving the traces from the tracing system
for analysis. Because each span has only one parent, the causality is represented with
a simple call-stack type view of the computation that it is easy to implement and to
reason about.

Effectively, traces in this model look like **distributed stack traces**, a concept very intuitive to all developers. This makes the span model for traces the most popular in the industry, supported by the majority of tracing infrastructures. Even tracing systems that collect instrumentations in the form of single point-in-time events (for example, Canopy [9]) go to the extra effort to convert trace events into something very similar to the span model. Canopy authors claim that "events are an inappropriate abstraction to expose to engineers adding instrumentation to systems," and propose another representation they call **modeled trace**, which describes the requests in terms of execution units, blocks, points, and edges.

The original span model introduced in Dapper was only able to represent executions as trees. It struggled to represent other execution models, such as queues, asynchronous executions, and multi-parent causality (forks and joins). Canopy works around that by allowing instrumentation to record edges for non-obvious causal relationships between points. The OpenTracing API, on the other hand, sticks with the classic, simpler span model but allows spans to contain multiple "references" to other spans, in order to support joins and asynchronous execution.

Clock skew adjustment

Anyone working with distributed systems programming knows that there is no such thing as accurate time. Each computer has a hardware clock built in, but those clocks tend to drift, and even using synchronization protocols like NTP can only get the servers maybe within a millisecond of each other. Yet we have seen that end-to-end tracing instrumentation captures the timestamp with most tracing events. How can we trust those timestamps?

Clearly, we cannot trust the timestamps to be actually correct, but this is not what we often look for when we analyze distributed traces. It is more important that timestamps in the trace are correctly aligned relative to each other. When the timestamps are from the same process, such as the start of the `server` span and the extra info annotations in the following diagram, we can assume that their relative positions are correct. The timestamps from different processes on the same host are generally incomparable because even though they are not subject to the hardware clock skew, the accuracy of the timestamps depends on many other factors, such as what programming language is used for a given process and what time libraries it is using and how. The timestamps from different servers are definitely incomparable due to hardware clock drifts, but we can do something about that.

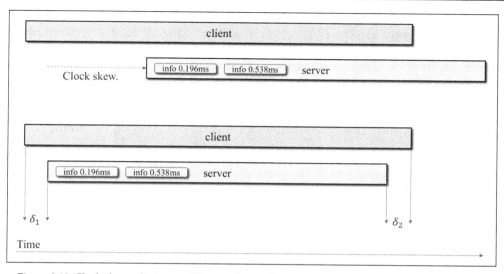

Figure 3.10: Clock skew adjustment. When we know the causality relationships between the events, such as "client-send must happen before server-receive", we can consistently adjust the timestamps for one of the two services, to make sure that the causality constraints are satisfied. The annotations within the span do not need to be adjusted, since we can assume their timestamps to be accurate relative to the beginning and end timestamps of the span.

Consider the `client` and `server` spans at the top diagram in *Figure 3.10*. Let's assume that we know from instrumentation that this was a blocking RPC request, that is, the server could not have received the request before the client sent it, and the client could not have received the response before the server finished the execution (this reasoning only works if the `client` span is longer than the `server` span, which is not always the case). These basic causality rules allow us to detect if the `server` span is misaligned on the timeline based on its reported timestamps, as we can see in the example. However, we don't know *how much* it is misaligned.

We can adjust the timestamps for all events originating from the `server` process by shifting it to the left until its start and end events fall within the time range of the larger `client` span, as shown at the bottom of the diagram. After this adjustment, we end up with two variables, δ_1 and δ_2, that are still unknown to us. If there are no more occurrences of client and server interaction in the given trace, and no additional causality information, we can make an arbitrary decision on how to set the variables, for example, by positioning the `server` span exactly in the middle of the `client` span:

$$\delta_1 = \delta_2 = \frac{len(client) - len(server)}{2}$$

The values of δ_1 and δ_2 calculated this way provide us with an estimate of the time spent by RPC in network communication. We are making an arbitrary assumption that both request and response took roughly the same time to be transmitted over the network. In other cases, we may have additional causality information from the trace, for example the server may have called a database and then another node in the trace graph called the same database server. That gives us two sets of constraints on the possible clock skew adjustment of the database spans. For example, from the first parent we want to adjust the database span by -2.5 ms and from the second parent by -5.5 ms. Since it's the same database server, we only need one adjustment to its clock skew, and we can try to find the one that works for both calling nodes (maybe it's -3.5 ms), even though the child spans may not be exactly in the middle of the parent spans, as we have arbitrarily done in the preceding formula.

In general, we can walk the trace and aggregate a large number of constraints using this approach. Then we can solve them as a set of linear equations for a full set of clock skew adjustments and we can apply to the trace to align the spans.

In the end, the clock skew adjustment process is always heuristic, since we typically don't have other reliable signals to calculate it precisely. There are scenarios when this heuristic technique goes wrong and the resulting trace views make little sense to the users. Therefore, the tracing systems are advised to provide both adjusted and unadjusted views of the traces, as well as to clearly indicate when the adjustments are applied.

Trace analysis

Once the trace records are collected and normalized by the tracing infrastructure, they can be used for analysis, using visualizations or data mining algorithms. We will cover some of the data mining techniques in *Chapter 12, Gathering Insights with Data Mining*.

Tracing system implementers are always looking for new creative visualizations of the data, and end users often build their own views based on specific features they are looking for. Some of the most popular and easy-to-implement views include Gantt charts, service graphs, and request flow graphs.

We have seen examples of Gantt charts in this chapter. Gantt charts are mostly used to visualize individual traces. The x axis shows relative time, usually from the beginning of the request, and the y axis represents different layers and components of the architecture participating in the execution of the request. Gantt charts are good for analyzing the latency of the requests, as they easily show which spans in the trace take the longest time, and combined with critical path analysis can zoom in on problematic areas. The overall shape of the chart can reveal other performance problems at a glance, like the lack of parallelism among sub-requests or unexpected synchronization/blocking.

Service graphs are constructed from a large corpus of traces. Fan-outs from a node indicate calls to other components. This visualization can be used for analysis of service dependencies in large microservices-based applications. The edges can be decorated with additional information, such as the frequency of calls between two given components in the corpus of traces.

Request flow graphs represent the execution of individual requests, as we have seen in the examples in the section on the event model. When using the event model, the fan-outs in the flow graph represent parallel execution and fan-ins are joins in the execution. With the span model, the flow graphs can be shown differently; for example, fan-outs can simply represent the calls to other components similar to the service graph, rather than implying concurrency.

Summary

This chapter introduced the fundamental principles underlying most open source, commercial, and academic distributed tracing systems, and the anatomy of a typical implementation. Metadata propagation is the most-popular and frequently-implemented approach to correlating tracing records with a particular execution, and capturing causal relationships. Event model and span model are the two completing trace representations, trading expressiveness for ease of use.

We briefly mentioned a few visualization techniques, and more examples of visualization, and data mining use cases, will be discussed in subsequent chapters.

In the next chapter, we will go through an exercise to instrument a simple "Hello, World!" application for distributed tracing, using the OpenTracing API.

References

1. Bryan M. Cantrill, Michael W. Shapiro, and Adam H. Leventhal. *Dynamic Instrumentation of Production Systems*. Proceedings of the 2004 USENIX Annual Technical Conference, June 27-July 2, 2004.

2. Michael Chow, David Meisner, Jason Flinn, Daniel Peek, Thomas F. Wenisch. *The Mystery Machine: End-to-end Performance Analysis of Large-scale Internet Services*. Proceedings of the 11th USENIX Symposium on Operating Systems Design and Implementation. October 6–8, 2014.

3. Paul Barham, Austin Donnelly, Rebecca Isaacs, and Richard Mortier. *Using Magpie for request extraction and workload modelling*. OSDI '04: Proceedings of the 6th USENIX Symposium on Operating Systems Design and Implementation, 2004.

4. Leslie Lamport. *Time, clocks, and the ordering of events in a distributed system.* Communications of the ACM, 21 (7), July1978.

5. Rodrigo Fonseca, George Porter, Randy H. Katz, Scott Shenker, and Ion Stoica. *X-Trace: a pervasive network tracing framework.* In NSDI '07: Proceedings of the 4th USENIX Symposium on Networked Systems Design and Implementation, 2007.

6. Benjamin H. Sigelman, Luiz A. Barroso, Michael Burrows, Pat Stephenson, Manoj Plakal, Donald Beaver, Saul Jaspan, and Chandan Shanbhag. *Dapper, a large-scale distributed system tracing infrastructure.* Technical Report dapper-2010-1, Google, April 2010.

7. Chris Aniszczyk. *Distributed Systems Tracing with Zipkin.* Twitter Engineering blog, June 2012: `https://blog.twitter.com/engineering/en_us/a/2012/distributed-systems-tracing-with-zipkin.html`.

8. Yuri Shkuro. *Evolving Distributed Tracing at Uber Engineering.* Uber Engineering blog, February 2017: `https://eng.uber.com/distributed-tracing/`.

9. Jonathan Kaldor, Jonathan Mace, Michał Bejda, Edison Gao, Wiktor Kuropatwa, Joe O'Neill, Kian Win Ong, Bill Schaller, Pingjia Shan, Brendan Viscomi, Vinod Venkataraman, Kaushik Veeraraghavan, and Yee Jiun Song. *Canopy: An End-to-End Performance Tracing and Analysis System.* Symposium on Operating Systems Principles, October 2017.

10. Raja R. Sambasivan, Rodrigo Fonseca, Ilari Shafer, and Gregory R. Ganger. *So, You Want To Trace Your Distributed System? Key Design Insights from Years of Practical Experience.* Carnegie Mellon University Parallel Data Lab Technical Report CMU-PDL-14-102, April 2014.

11. The OpenTracing Project: `http://opentracing.io/`.

II
DATA GATHERING PROBLEM

4
Instrumentation Basics with OpenTracing

In the previous chapter, we looked into the theory behind end-to-end tracing, and various architectural decisions one must make when building a distributed tracing infrastructure, including which data formats can be used for propagating metadata between processes and for exporting tracing data to a tracing backend. Fortunately, as we will see in this chapter, an end user of a tracing infrastructure, someone who wants to instrument their business application, or their open source framework, or library, typically does not need to worry about those decisions.

We only briefly touched upon the notion of instrumentation and trace points before, so in this chapter, we will dive deep into the question of instrumentation, using three canonical "Hello, World!" applications in Go, Java, and Python. You may be having Jules Winnfield's reflex right now: "Say Hello, World! again," but I promise to make it interesting.

The application will be built with microservices, using a database, and occasionally will spit out "politically incorrect" responses. We will use the OpenTracing APIs from the OpenTracing project [1] to make our instrumentation portable across many tracing vendors, and we will cover such topics as creating entry/exit trace points; annotating spans with tags and timestamped events; encoding and decoding metadata for transferring it over the wire; and the mechanisms for in-process context propagation provided by the OpenTracing APIs.

Using three programming languages allows us to demonstrate how the same general concepts of the OpenTracing APIs are manifested in each language, and how they are sometimes different due to language restrictions.

The chapter is organized as a series of exercises, each covering a particular topic:

- Exercise 1: The Hello application:
  - Run the application
  - Review its structure

- Exercise 2: The first trace:
  - Instantiate a tracer
  - Create a simple trace
  - Annotate the trace

- Exercise 3: Tracing functions and passing context:
  - Trace individual functions and database calls
  - Combine multiple spans into a single trace
  - Propagate request context in-process

- Exercise 4: Tracing RPC requests:
  - Break up the monolith
  - Trace a transaction across more than one microservice
  - Pass the context between processes using inject and extract trace points
  - Apply OpenTracing-recommended tags

- Exercise 5: Using baggage:
  - Understand distributed context propagation
  - Use baggage to pass data through the call graph

- Exercise 6: Auto-instrumentation:
  - ° Use existing open source instrumentation
  - ° Use zero-touch instrumentation
- Exercise 7: Extra credit

After completing this chapter, you will have the knowledge and understanding of how to apply instrumentation to your own applications or frameworks to hit the ground running with distributed tracing.

Prerequisites

In order to run the examples in this chapter, we need to prepare the development environment for each of the three programming languages and run the tracing backend. This section provides instructions on setting up the required dependencies.

Project source code

One third of the examples are written in Go, which expects the source code [2] to be placed in the specific directories relative to the GOPATH (this was written before Go 1.11 and modules support). The examples have been tested with Go version 1.10. Follow these steps to download the source code:

```
$ mkdir -p $GOPATH/src/github.com/PacktPublishing
```

```
$ cd $GOPATH/src/github.com/PacktPublishing
```

```
$ git clone https://github.com/PacktPublishing/Mastering-Distributed-
Tracing.git Mastering-Distributed-Tracing
```

The last argument to the `git clone` command is to ensure that the directory is not created with the `.git` suffix, otherwise it will confuse the Go compiler. If you are not planning on running Go examples, then you can clone the source code in any directory of your choosing, as Python and Java won't care.

To make it easier to refer to the main directory throughout this chapter, let's define an environment variable for convenience:

```
$ cd Mastering-Distributed-Tracing/Chapter04
```

```
$ export CH04='pwd'
```

```
$ echo $CH04
```

```
/Users/yurishkuro/gopath/src/github.com/PacktPublishing/Mastering-
Distributed-Tracing/Chapter04
```

The source code for examples is organized in the following structure:

```
Mastering-Distributed-Tracing/
   Chapter04/
      go/
         exercise1/
         exercise2/
         lib/
         ...
      java/
         src/main/java/
            exercise1/
            exercise2/
            ...
         pom.xml
      python/
         exercise1/
         exercise2/
         lib/
         ...
         requirements.txt
```

All examples are grouped by language first. The main directory for the language contains project files, such as pom.xml or requirements.txt, and a list of exercise# directories with the final code for each exercise. You may also find lib directories, which are used for code that is shared across exercises.

All code examples, except for exercise1 and exercise4a, are built upon the previous exercises. You can take the code in {lang}/exercise1 modules as the starting point and keep improving it in the first half of the chapter, and then move onto {lang}/exercise4a to do the same.

Go development environment

Please refer to the documentation (https://golang.org/doc/install) for Go development environment installation instructions. The examples have been tested with Go version 1.10.x. In addition to the standard toolchain, you will need to have dep, a dependency management tool. Please see https://github.com/golang/dep for installation instructions. Once installed, run dep ensure to download all the necessary dependencies:

```
$ cd $CH04/go
$ dep ensure
```

The dependencies are declared in the `Gopkg.toml` file, for example:

```
[[constraint]]
  name = "github.com/uber/jaeger-client-go"
  version = "^2.14.0"
```

In order to guarantee repeatable builds, `dep` uses a `Gopkg.lock` file, where the dependencies are resolved to specific versions or Git commits. When we run `dep ensure`, it downloads all the dependencies and stores them in the `vendor` folder.

Java development environment

The Java examples have been tested with Java 8, but most likely will work with newer JDK versions. You may download the OpenJDK from `http://jdk.java.net/java-se-ri/8`. I used Maven to build and run the examples, and included Maven wrapper scripts `mvnw` and `mvnw.cmd`, so that you do not have to install Maven globally. Run it once to let it download all the necessary dependencies:

```
$ cd $CH04/java
$ ./mvnw install
```

Python development environment

To follow the Python examples, please install Python version 2.7.x or 3.7.x (see instructions at `https://www.python.org/downloads/`). We will also need the dependency manager tool `pip` (see `https://pypi.org/project/pip/`) and virtual environment manager `virtualenv` (see `https://pypi.org/project/virtualenv/`). Initialize your workspace and install the dependencies as follows:

```
$ cd $CH04/python
$ virtualenv env
$ source env/bin/activate
$ pip install -r requirements.txt
```

This will create a subdirectory `env` containing the virtual environment, which we then activate, and we run `pip` to install the dependencies. If you are more comfortable with other Python environment tools, like `pipenv` or `pyenv`, feel free to use those.

MySQL database

The application we are going to use will be making calls to MySQL database. We do not have exotic requirements, so any version of MySQL should work, but I specifically tested with the Community Server edition version 5.6. You can download and install it locally from `https://dev.mysql.com/downloads/mysql/`, but I recommend running it as a Docker container:

```
$ docker run -d --name mysql56 -p 3306:3306 \
        -e MYSQL_ROOT_PASSWORD=mysqlpwd mysql:5.6
cae5461f5354c9efd4a3a997a2786494a405c7b7e5b8159912f691a5b3071cf6
$ docker logs mysql56 | tail -2
2018-xx-xx 20:01:17 1 [Note] mysqld: ready for connections.
Version: '5.6.42'  socket: '/var/run/mysqld/mysqld.sock'  port: 3306
MySQL Community Server (GPL)
```

You may need to define a user and permissions to create the database, which is outside of the scope of this book. For simplicity, we used the default user `root` to access the database (which you should never do in production) with password `mysqlpwd`.

The source code contains a file called `database.sql` with SQL instructions to create the database `chapter04` and the table `people`, and populate it with some data:

```
$ docker exec -i mysql56 mysql -uroot -pmysqlpwd < $CH04/database.sql
Warning: Using a password on the command line interface can be insecure.
```

If you are using a local installation, you can run `mysql` directly:

```
$ mysql -u root -p < $CH04/database.sql
Enter password:
```

Query tools (curl or wget)

The sample application is going to expose a REST API, so we will need a way to interact with it. One option is to type the URLs in the browser. An easier way is to use the command-line utilities like `curl` (`https://curl.haxx.se/`):

```
$ curl http://some-domain.com/some/url
```

Or `wget` (`https://www.gnu.org/software/wget/`), which requires a couple of extra arguments to print the response back to the screen:

```
$ wget -q -o- http://some-domain.com/some/url
```

Tracing backend (Jaeger)

Finally, we will be using Jaeger [3] as the tracing backend, so I recommend you start it and keep it running. Please refer to the instructions in *Chapter 2, Take Tracing for a HotROD Ride*, on how to run its all-in-one binary or Docker container. Once the backend is started, verify that you can open the web frontend at `http://localhost:16686/`.

OpenTracing

Before we jump into the exercises, let's talk about the OpenTracing project. In October 2015, Adrian Cole, the lead maintainer of Zipkin, organized and hosted a "Distributed Tracing and Zipkin Workshop" at the Pivotal office in San Francisco. The attendees were a mix of commercial tracing vendors, open source developers, and engineers from a number of companies who were in charge of building or deploying tracing infrastructure in their organizations.

A common theme in the hallway conversations was that the single largest obstacle to the wide adoption of tracing in large organizations was the lack of reusable instrumentation for a vast number of open source frameworks and libraries, due to the absence of standard APIs. It was forcing all vendors; open source tracing systems, like Zipkin; and the end users to implement instrumentation over and over for the same popular software and frameworks.

The group collaborated on the first version of a common instrumentation API, which eventually became the OpenTracing project, incubating at the **Cloud Native Computing Foundation** (**CNCF**) (`https://cncf.io`). It now includes standard tracing APIs in a number of major programming languages and maintains over 100 modules that provide instrumentation for various popular open source frameworks. We will use the examples of that off-the-shelf instrumentation in the last exercise, but first let's talk about the general principles of OpenTracing.

One common mistake people make about the OpenTracing project is thinking that it provides the actual end-to-end tracing infrastructure. We will see in *Chapter 6, Tracing Standards and Ecosystem*, that there are five different problems that someone deploying a tracing system in an organization needs to address. The OpenTracing project solves one and only one of those problems: providing vendor-neutral APIs for the instrumentation, as well as the reusable instrumentation libraries for popular frameworks. This is very likely the problem that has the largest audience because if we have an organization of several thousand software engineers, only a few of them will be actually dealing with deploying the tracing infrastructure. The rest of the engineers are going to develop their own applications and will expect either to have the tracing instrumentation included with their infrastructure libraries, or to have a narrow, well-defined API that they can use to instrument their own code.

The OpenTracing APIs allow developers to focus on what they know best: describing the semantic behavior of the distributed transactions executed by their software. All other concerns of tracing, such as the exact wire format of metadata and the format of span data, are delegated to the implementations of the OpenTracing APIs that the end users can swap without changing their code.

The OpenTracing APIs define two primary entities: a **tracer** and a **span**. A tracer is a singleton that is responsible for creating spans and exposing methods for transferring the context across process and component boundaries. For example, in Go, the `Tracer` interface has just three methods:

```
type Tracer interface {
    StartSpan(operationName string, opts
...StartSpanOption) Span
    Inject(sc SpanContext, format interface{}, carrier
interface{}) error
    Extract(format interface{}, carrier interface{})
(SpanContext, error)
}
```

A **span** is an interface for implementing a given trace point in the application. As we discussed in the previous chapter, in the context of the span model, a span represents a unit of work done by the application on behalf of a particular distributed execution. This unit of work is given a name, called the "operation name" in OpenTracing (sometimes also referred to as the "span name"). Each span has a start and end time, and in most cases includes a causal link to its predecessors in the execution, provided in the form of "span references" to the `StartSpan()` method.

All spans started by the tracer must be finished by calling their `Finish()` method, at which point the tracer implementation can send the accumulated data immediately to the tracing backend, or buffer it and send it later as part of a larger batch with the other finished spans, for efficiency reasons. The `Span` interface also has methods for annotating the span with tags (key-value pairs) and logs (timestamped events with their own tags). The `Span` interface in Go looks like this (I excluded some overloaded methods):

```
type Span interface {
    SetOperationName(operationName string) Span
    SetTag(key string, value interface{}) Span
    LogFields(fields ...log.Field)

    SetBaggageItem(restrictedKey, value string) Span
    BaggageItem(restrictedKey string) string

    Finish()

    Context() SpanContext
    Tracer() Tracer
}
```

As we can see, span is mostly a write-only API. With the exception of the baggage API, which we will discuss later, all other methods are used to write data to the span, without being able to read it back. This is intentional, since requiring implementations to provide a read API for the recorded data would impose additional restrictions in how the implementation can process that data internally.

Span context is another important concept in the OpenTracing APIs. In the previous chapter, we discussed that tracing systems are able to track distributed executions by propagating metadata along the execution path of the request. Span context is the in-memory representation of that metadata. It is an interface that does not actually have any methods, except for the baggage iterator, because the actual representation of the metadata is implementation-specific. Instead, the `Tracer` interface provides `Inject()` and `Extract()` methods that allow the instrumentation to encode metadata represented by the span context to and from some wire representation.

The causal relationship between two spans is represented with the **span reference**, which is a combination of two values; a reference type, which describes the nature of the relationship; and a span context, which identifies the referenced spans. Span references can only be recorded in the span when it is started, which prevents loops in the causality graph. We will come back to span references later in this chapter.

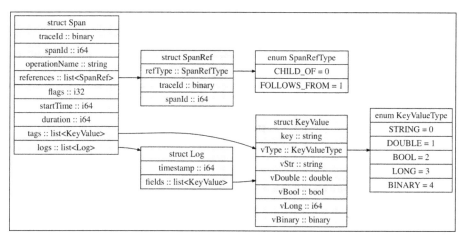

Figure 4.1: A representation of the OpenTracing conceptual model in the physical Thrift data model in Jaeger

To finish this brief introduction to the OpenTracing conceptual model, it may be useful to look at its concrete representation in Jaeger in *Figure 4.1*. On the left, we see the `Span` structure, which contains the expected fields, like `operationName`, `startTime`, `duration`, and `tags`, and `logs`. We also see the `traceId` and `spanId` fields, which are specific to Jaeger, in the sense that another implementation of the OpenTracing API might have a different representation of these fields or even completely different fields.

The `references` list contains the links to ancestor spans in the causality DAG. The tags are represented with the `KeyValue` struct, which contains a key and a value of one of the five types.

The `Log` struct is a combination of a timestamp and a nested list of key-value pairs (called "log fields" in the OpenTracing API). There is no data type for span context because this is Jaeger's backend data model, and span context is only needed when the execution is in progress, in order to pass the metadata, and establish causality references between spans. If we look at the actual Jaeger implementation of the OpenTracing API for Go, we will find this implementation of `SpanContext` interface:

```
type SpanContext struct {
        traceID  TraceID
        spanID   SpanID
        flags    byte
        baggage  map[string]string
        debugID  string
}
```

Now that we have reviewed the basics of the OpenTracing API, let's see it in action.

Exercise 1 – the Hello application

In the first exercise, we are going to run a simple, single-process "Hello" application, and review its source code, so that we can later instrument it for distributed tracing. The application is implemented as a web service, which we can access by sending it HTTP requests like this:

```
$ curl http://localhost:8080/sayHello/John
Hello, John!
```

```
$ curl http://localhost:8080/sayHello/Margo
Hello, Margo!
```

The application has some creepy big brother tendencies, however, by occasionally volunteering additional knowledge about the person:

```
$ curl http://localhost:8080/sayHello/Vector
Hello, Vector! Committing crimes with both direction and magnitude!
```

```
$ curl http://localhost:8080/sayHello/Nefario
Hello, Dr. Nefario! Why ... why are you so old?
```

It looks up the information in the MySQL database that we created and seeded earlier. In the later exercises, we will extend this application to run several microservices.

Hello application in Go

The working directory for all Go exercises is `$CH04/go`.

Let's run the application (I removed the date and timestamps from the log messages for brevity):

```
$ go run ./exercise1/hello.go
Listening on http://localhost:8080/
```

Now we have the HTTP server running, let's query it from another Terminal window:

```
$ curl http://localhost:8080/sayHello/Gru
Hello, Felonius Gru! Where are the minions?%
```

Let's review how the application's code is structured:

```
$ ls exercise1/*
exercise1/hello.go

exercise1/people:
repository.go
```

We can see that the application consists of the main file, `hello.go`, and a data repository module called `people`. The data repository uses a self-explanatory `Person` type defined in a shared location, `lib/model/person.go`:

```
package model

// Person represents a person.
type Person struct {
        Name        string
        Title       string
        Description string
}
```

The data repository, `people/repository.go`, is also fairly straightforward. It starts with the imports:

```
package people

import (
    "database/sql"
    "log"

    "github.com/go-sql-driver/mysql"

    "github.com/PacktPublishing/Mastering-Distributed-Tracing/
Chapter04/go/lib/model"
)
```

We can see that it imports a driver for MySQL and the `model` package that defines the `Person` struct. Then we have a couple of declarations: the connection URL for the MySQL database (where `root:mysqlpwd` refers to the username and password) and the `Repository` type:

```
const dburl = "root:mysqlpwd@tcp(127.0.0.1:3306)/chapter04"

// Repository retrieves information about people.
type Repository struct {
    db *sql.DB
}
```

The constructor function creates a database connection and stores it in the `Repository` object:

```
// NewRepository creates a new Repository backed by MySQL database.
func NewRepository() *Repository {
    db, err := sql.Open("mysql", dburl)
    if err != nil {
        log.Fatal(err)
    }
    err = db.Ping()
    if err != nil {
        log.Fatalf("Cannot ping the db: %v", err)
    }
    return &Repository{
        db: db,
    }
}
```

It uses `log.Fatal` to cause a panic in the program immediately, since it will not function without a database connection. The main method, `GetPerson()`, retrieves the person's information from the database given the person's name:

```
// GetPerson tries to find the person in the database by name.
// If not found, it still returns a Person object with only name
// field populated.
func (r *Repository) GetPerson(name string) (model.Person, error)
{
    query := "select title, description from people where name =
?"
    rows, err := r.db.Query(query, name)
    if err != nil {
       return model.Person{}, err
    }
    defer rows.Close()

    for rows.Next() {
       var title, descr string
        err := rows.Scan(&title, &descr)
        if err != nil {
           return model.Person{}, err
        }
        return model.Person{
            Name:        name,
            Title:       title,
            Description: descr,
        }, nil
    }
    return model.Person{
        Name: name,
    }, nil
}
```

The `Close()` method closes the database connection:

```
// Close calls close on the underlying db connection.
func (r *Repository) Close() {
    r.db.Close()
}
```

This is all a pretty standard use of Go's `database/sql` module. With this out of the way, let's take a look at the main application code in `hello.go`. We need to import the `people` package to get access to the repository:

```
package main

import (
    "log"
    "net/http"
    "strings"

    "github.com/PacktPublishing/Mastering-Distributed-Tracing/chapter-
04/go/exercise1/people"
)
```

The main function creates the repository and starts an HTTP server listening on port `8080`, and serving a single endpoint, `sayHello`:

```
var repo *people.Repository

func main() {
    repo = people.NewRepository()
    defer repo.Close()

    http.HandleFunc("/sayHello/", handleSayHello)

    log.Print("Listening on http://localhost:8080/")
    log.Fatal(http.ListenAndServe(":8080", nil))
}
```

The endpoint is implemented by the `handleSayHello()` function. It reads the name of the person from the URL path and calls another function, `SayHello(name)`:

```
func handleSayHello(w http.ResponseWriter, r *http.Request) {
    name := strings.TrimPrefix(r.URL.Path, "/sayHello/")
    greeting, err := SayHello(name)
    if err != nil {
        http.Error(w, err.Error(), http.StatusInternalServerError)
        return
    }
    w.Write([]byte(greeting))
}
```

The function `SayHello()` uses the repository to load the `Person` object by name, and formats the greeting using the information it may have found:

```go
// SayHello creates a greeting for the named person.
func SayHello(name string) (string, error) {
    person, err := repo.GetPerson(name)
    if err != nil {
        return "", err
    }
    return FormatGreeting(
        person.Name,
        person.Title,
        person.Description,
    ), nil
}

// FormatGreeting combines information about a person into a
greeting.
func FormatGreeting(name, title, description string) string {
    response := "Hello, "
    if title != "" {
        response += title + " "
    }
    response += name + "!"
    if description != "" {
        response += " " + description
    }
    return response
}
```

Hello application in Java

The working directory for all Java exercises is `$CH04/java`. The application is using the Spring Boot framework (`http://spring.io/projects/spring-boot`). We use the Maven wrapper to build and run the app. The dependencies are defined in the file `pom.xml`, and include artifacts for Spring Boot, a JPA adapter for accessing the database, a MySQL connection, and finally, the Jaeger client library:

```xml
<dependency>
    <groupId>io.jaegertracing</groupId>
    <artifactId>jaeger-client</artifactId>
    <version>0.31.0</version>
</dependency>
```

The file also includes a commented-out dependency, `opentracing-spring-cloud-starter`:

```
<!--
<dependency>
    <groupId>io.opentracing.contrib</groupId>
    <artifactId>opentracing-spring-cloud-starter</artifactId>
    <version>0.1.13</version>
</dependency>
-->
```

Please do not uncomment it until *Exercise 6*. Since all exercises are defined in the same module, we have multiple classes that define the `main()` function, and therefore we must tell Spring which main class we want to run, like this:

```
$ ./mvnw spring-boot:run -Dmain.class=exercise1.HelloApp
[... a lot of logs ...]
INFO 57474 --- [main] exercise1.HelloApp: Started HelloApp in 3.844
seconds
```

Compared to Go and Python apps, both Maven and Spring generate *a lot of logs*. The last log should be stating that the application has started. We can test it the same way as the others:

```
$ curl http://localhost:8080/sayHello/Gru
Hello, Felonius Gru! Where are the minions?%
```

The source code of the application consists of two packages. One of them (`lib.people`) is shared across all exercises and defines the `Person` class as the data model, and the data access `PeopleRepository` interface:

```
@Entity
@Table(name = "people")
public class Person {
    @Id
    private String name;

    @Column(nullable = false)
    private String title;

    @Column(nullable = false)
    private String description;

    public Person() {}

    public Person(String name) { this.name = name; }
}

public interface PersonRepository
    extends CrudRepository<Person, String> {
}
```

The `Person` class also includes getters for its members, which is omitted here. Together, these two classes allow us to use Spring's Data to access the database. The database connection details are defined in `src/main/resources/application.properties`:

```
spring.jpa.hibernate.ddl-auto=none
spring.datasource.url=jdbc:mysql://localhost:3306/Chapter04
spring.datasource.username=root
spring.datasource.password=mysqlpwd
```

The main application code can be found in the `exercise1` package. It contains a very simple main class, `HelloApp`, where we point Spring to the `lib.people` package to auto-discover the data model and the repository interface:

```
@EnableJpaRepositories("lib.people")
@EntityScan("lib.people")
@SpringBootApplication
public class HelloApp {
    public static void main(String[] args) {
        SpringApplication.run(HelloApp.class, args);
    }
}
```

The main logic is in the `HelloController` class:

```
@RestController
public class HelloController {

    @Autowired
    private PersonRepository personRepository;

    @GetMapping("/sayHello/{name}")
    public String sayHello(@PathVariable String name) {
        Person person = getPerson(name);
        String response = formatGreeting(person);
        return response;
    }

    private Person getPerson(String name) { ... }

    private String formatGreeting(Person person) { ... }
}
```

It defines a single endpoint sayHello and calls two functions to get the person by name and to format the greeting for that person:

```java
private Person getPerson(String name) {
    Optional<Person> personOpt = personRepository.findById(name);
    if (personOpt.isPresent()) {
        return personOpt.get();
    }
    return new Person(name);
}

private String formatGreeting(Person person) {
    String response = "Hello, ";
    if (!person.getTitle().isEmpty()) {
        response += person.getTitle() + " ";
    }
    response += person.getName() + "!";
    if (!person.getDescription().isEmpty()) {
        response += " " + person.getDescription();
    }
    return response;
}
```

Hello application in Python

The working directory for all Python exercises is $CH04/python. We can find the basic Hello application in the execrise1 module. It is using the Flask framework to implement an HTTP server (http://flask.pocoo.org/). Let's run it:

```
$ python -m exercise1.hello
 * Serving Flask app "py-1-hello" (lazy loading)
 * Environment: production
   WARNING: Do not use the development server in a production
environment.
   Use a production WSGI server instead.
 * Debug mode: off
 * Running on http://127.0.0.1:8080/ (Press CTRL+C to quit)
```

Now we can query it with curl:

```
$ curl http://localhost:8080/sayHello/Gru
Hello, Felonius Gru! Where are the minions?
```

The application consists of two files at this point. The `database.py` module contains the basic code to read from the database using the ORM framework SQL Alchemy:

```python
from sqlalchemy import create_engine
from sqlalchemy.ext.declarative import declarative_base
from sqlalchemy.orm import sessionmaker
from sqlalchemy.schema import Column
from sqlalchemy.types import String


db_url = 'mysql+pymysql://root:mysqlpwd@localhost:3306/chapter04'
engine = create_engine(db_url, echo=False)
Session = sessionmaker(bind=engine)
session = Session()
Base = declarative_base()


class Person(Base):
    __tablename__ = 'people'
    name = Column(String, primary_key=True)
    title = Column(String)
    description = Column(String)

    @staticmethod
    def get(name):
        return session.query(Person).get(name)
```

It allows us to do queries like `Person.get("name")`. The main application defines an HTTP handler function and two helper functions to read the person's data from the database, and to format the greeting:

```python
from flask import Flask
from .database import Person

app = Flask('py-1-hello')

@app.route("/sayHello/<name>")
def say_hello(name):
    person = get_person(name)
    resp = format_greeting(
        name=person.name,
        title=person.title,
        description=person.description,
    )
    return resp

def get_person(name):
```

```
        person = Person.get(name)
        if person is None:
            person = Person()
            person.name = name
        return person

    def format_greeting(name, title, description):
        greeting = 'Hello, '
        if title:
            greeting += title + ' '
        greeting += name + '!'
        if description:
            greeting += ' ' + description
        return greeting

    if __name__ == "__main__":
        app.run(port=8080)
```

Exercise summary

In this first exercise, we familiarized ourselves with the source code of the "Hello" application and learned how to run it. In the following exercises, we will instrument this program with the OpenTracing API, and also refactor it into multiple microservices.

Exercise 2 – the first trace

Now that we are familiar with the sample application, let's add some very basic instrumentation to it to create a trace for each HTTP request that it handles. We will do it in three steps:

1. Create a tracer instance
2. Start a span in the HTTP handler function
3. Annotate the span with additional details in a few places in the code

Step 1 – create a tracer instance

As mentioned, OpenTracing is just an API, so we need to instantiate a concrete implementation of the tracer. We will be using the Jaeger tracer as an example, but the function that creates the tracer will be the only place in the whole program that is Jaeger-specific. It can be easily replaced with any other OpenTracing-compatible tracer, such as Zipkin or tracers from commercial vendors.

Tracers are expected to be used as singletons: one tracer per application. There are rare scenarios when an application needs more than one tracer. For example, as we will see in *Chapter 7, Tracing with Service Mesh*, service meshes can create spans on behalf of different applications, which may require multiple instances of the tracer. The exact mechanism for ensuring a singleton instance of a tracer is language-and framework-specific. The OpenTracing API libraries usually provide a mechanism for defining a global tracer using a global variable, however, the applications are not required to use that and can instead rely on dependency injection.

Jaeger libraries in different languages have a convention that they provide a `Configuration` class that can act as a builder for the `Tracer`. By default, the builder creates a *production-ready* tracer, including a sampling strategy that only samples approximately one in 1,000 traces. For our purposes, we would rather have all traces sampled, so we override the sampling strategy by instructing the `Configuration` class to use a `"const"` strategy, meaning that it always makes the same decision, with a parameter `param=1`, which translates to that decision always being "yes" (this sampler treats the parameter as a Boolean value). Another small tweak we make to the defaults is to instruct the reporter to write a log entry for all finished spans. The reporter is an internal component of the Jaeger tracer that is responsible for exporting finished spans out of the process to the tracing backend.

`Configuration` classes expect us to provide a **service name**, which is used by the tracing backend to identify the service instance in the distributed call graph. In this exercise, we only have a single service, but in the later exercises, we will split it into multiple microservices, and by giving them different names, we will be able to more clearly see the shape of the distributed execution call graph. We will be using a simple notation to name the services:

```
{language}-{exercise number}-{microservice name}
```

For example, the Go service in this exercise will be called "go-2-hello." This naming scheme will allow us to clearly separate services in the tracing UI.

Create a tracer in Go

Creating a tracer will be something we will need to do across all exercises, so rather than repeating that code under each exercise, I placed it into a shared module under `$CH04/go/lib/tracing`, in the file called `init.go`. Let's look at the imports:

```
package tracing

import (
    "io"
    "log"

    opentracing "github.com/opentracing/opentracing-go"
    jaeger "github.com/uber/jaeger-client-go"
    config "github.com/uber/jaeger-client-go/config"
)
```

Here we're importing the `opentracing-go` module that defines the official OpenTracing API for Go. We're renaming it to `opentracing`, which is, strictly speaking, not necessary, since that is the package name it has anyway, but we just want to be more explicit, since its import path ends with a different name.

We also import two modules from the Jaeger client library that implement the OpenTracing API. The `config` module is used to create the tracer parameterized with some settings. The `jaeger` module is only needed because we use the `jaeger.StdLogger` type to bind the Jaeger tracer to the standard library logger, which we used in the rest of the program. The main function looks like this:

```go
// Init returns an instance of Jaeger Tracer that samples 100%
// of traces and logs all spans to stdout.
func Init(service string) (opentracing.Tracer, io.Closer) {
    cfg := &config.Configuration{
        Sampler: &config.SamplerConfig{
            Type:  "const",
            Param: 1,
        },
        Reporter: &config.ReporterConfig{
            LogSpans: true,
        },
    }
    tracer, closer, err := cfg.New(
        service,
        config.Logger(jaeger.StdLogger),
    )
    if err != nil {
        log.Fatalf("ERROR: cannot init Jaeger: %v", err)
    }
    return tracer, closer
}
```

The function returns an instance of the tracer implementing the `opentracing.Tracer` interface, and a `Closer` instance that can be used to close the tracer before the program ends, to ensure that it will flush any spans that may still be stored in the internal memory buffer. The `Init()` function accepts the service name as the argument because we will be varying it from exercise to exercise.

Now we can add a call to this function to our main application in the `hello.go` file. First, we add the imports:

```go
import (
    "log"
    "net/http"
    "strings"
```

```
opentracing "github.com/opentracing/opentracing-go"

    "github.com/PacktPublishing/Mastering-Distributed-Tracing/
Chapter04/go/exercise2/people"
    "github.com/PacktPublishing/Mastering-Distributed-Tracing/
Chapter04/go/lib/tracing"
)
```

Then we declare a global variable called `tracer` (so that we don't have to pass it to functions), and initialize it by calling `tracing.Init()` in `main()`:

```go
var repo *people.Repository
var tracer opentracing.Tracer

func main() {
    repo = people.NewRepository()
    defer repo.Close()

    tr, closer := tracing.Init("go-2-hello")
    defer closer.Close()
    tracer = tr
```

As previously discussed, we are passing the string `"go-2-hello"` as the service name. To make sure that the tracer can flush any spans it accumulates in the buffer when we stop the program, we defer a call to `closer.Close()`.

Create a tracer in Java

Unlike Go and Python, creating a tracer is Java is the least verbose, so we include it directly in the main `HelloApp`. We declare it as a bean, so that it can be provided in other places via dependency injection:

```java
@Bean
public io.opentracing.Tracer initTracer() {
    SamplerConfiguration samplerConfig =
        new SamplerConfiguration()
        .withType("const").withParam(1);
    ReporterConfiguration reporterConfig =
        new ReporterConfiguration().withLogSpans(true);
    return new Configuration("java-2-hello")
        .withSampler(samplerConfig)
        .withReporter(reporterConfig)
        .getTracer();
}
```

Create a tracer in Python

Similar to the Go program, creating a tracer will be something we will need to do across all exercises, so rather than repeating that code each time, I placed it into a shared module called `tracing.py` under `$CH04/python/lib`:

```python
import logging
from jaeger_client import Config

def init_tracer(service):
    logging.getLogger('').handlers = []
    logging.basicConfig(format='%(message)s', level=logging.DEBUG)

    config = Config(
        config={
            'sampler': {
                'type': 'const',
                'param': 1,
            },
            'logging': True,
            'reporter_batch_size': 1,
        },
        service_name=service,
    )

    # this call sets global variable opentracing.tracer
    config.initialize_tracer()
```

The first thing we do here is to configure Python's logging. It's probably not the best place, but the tracer is the only component using it, so we do it here for convenience. Then we see the already-familiar configuration overrides. The additional parameter `reporter_batch_size=1` is used to instruct the tracer to flush the spans immediately without buffering them.

As we can see in the comment, the last function, `config.initialize_tracer()`, not only creates and returns an instance of the Jaeger tracer (we actually ignore the return value), but also sets it in the global variable `opentracing.tracer` provided by the Python OpenTracing library that is implicitly imported by the Jaeger client. We will be using this instance later and having it in a global variable is convenient, allowing us to avoid implementing dependency injection.

With this utility function in place, we just need to call it from the main `hello.py`:

```python
from flask import Flask
from .database import Person
from lib.tracing import init_tracer

app = Flask('py-2-hello')
init_tracer('py-2-hello')
```

Note that we're passing the service name `py-2-hello` to the tracer.

Step 2 – start a span

In order to start tracing the program, we need to create at least one span. When we create a very first span in the trace, the tracer does some one-time internal work. For example, the Jaeger tracer will generate a unique trace ID and will execute a sampling strategy to decide if the given execution should be sampled. The decision taken by the sampling strategy is "sticky": once made, it applies to all spans in the same trace, which would be the descendants of the first span, often called the "root span".

When the sampling decision is "no", some of the API calls to the span may be short-circuited, for example, trying to annotate the span with tags will be a no-op. However, the trace ID, span ID, and other metadata will still be propagated alongside the distributed execution, even for unsampled traces. We will go into more detail about sampling in *Chapter 8, All About Sampling*, where we will see that the so-called "upfront" or "head-based sampling" implemented by Jaeger is not the only possible sampling technique, although it is the prevailing one in the industry.

Since we want to have a new trace for each HTTP request handled by our application, we will add the instrumentation code to the HTTP handler functions. Every time we start a span, we need to give it a name, called the "operation name" in OpenTracing. The operation names help with later analysis of the traces, and can be used for the grouping of traces, building latency histograms, tracking endpoint **service level objectives (SLOs)**, and so on. Now, because of this frequent use in aggregations, operation names should never have high cardinality. For example, in the Hello application the name of the person is encoded as the HTTP path parameter, for example, `/sayHello/Margo`. Using this exact string as the operation name would be a bad idea because the service may be queried with thousands of different names, and each will result in a unique span name, which will make any aggregate analysis of the spans, such as investigation of the endpoint latency profile, very difficult.

If the application is using a web framework, as we did in the Java and Python examples, then they typically define a pattern for the URLs, often referred to as a route, for example, the `"/sayHello/{name}"` pattern in the Java example:

```
@GetMapping("/sayHello/{name}")
public String hello(@PathVariable String name) { ... }
```

The route pattern is fixed and does not depend on the actual value of the `{name}` parameter, so it would be a good option to use as the span operation name. In this exercise, however, we will be using the string `"say-hello"` as the operation name, for consistency across languages.

As we discussed earlier, a span is a unit of work with a start and end timestamps. In order to capture the end timestamp of the span, the instrumentation code must call the `Finish()` method on it. If the `Finish()` method is not called, the span may not be reported to the tracing backend at all because quite often, the only reference to the span object is in the function that created it. Some tracer implementations may provide additional tracking capabilities and still report unfinished spans, but it is not a guaranteed behavior. Therefore, the OpenTracing specification requires an explicit call to the `Finish()` method.

Start a span in Go

In Go, the HTTP handler function is `handleSayHello`. We can start a span right at the beginning:

```go
func handleSayHello(w http.ResponseWriter, r *http.Request) {
    span := tracer.StartSpan("say-hello")
    defer span.Finish()

    name := strings.TrimPrefix(r.URL.Path, "/sayHello/")
    ...
}
```

To ensure that the span is finished when the handler returns (either successfully or with an error), we invoke `Finish()` with the `defer` keyword right after starting it.

Start a span in Java

In Java, starting the span looks a bit different than in Go and Python. Rather than having a `startSpan()` function with variadic arguments for options, the Java OpenTracing API uses a Builder pattern, which allows the options to be added via fluid syntax, which we will see later in this chapter. At this point, we do not need any options, so we start the span in the `sayHello()` function like this:

```java
@GetMapping("/sayHello/{name}")
public String sayHello(@PathVariable String name) {
    Span span = tracer.buildSpan("say-hello").start();
    try {
        ...
        return response;
    } finally {
        span.finish();
    }
}
```

To ensure that the span is always finished, even in the case of an exception, we are using a `try-finally` statement. In order to get access to the tracer singleton, we need to declare it as auto-injected by the Spring framework:

```
@Autowired
private Tracer tracer;
```

Start a span in Python

The `Span` class in OpenTracing for Python implements the context manager and can be used in a `with` statement. It's useful because it allows the span to be finished automatically, even if the code inside raises an exception. We can start a span in the handler function like this:

```
import opentracing

@app.route("/sayHello/<name>")
def say_hello(name):
    with opentracing.tracer.start_span('say-hello'):
        person = get_person(name)
        resp = format_greeting(
            name=person.name,
            title=person.title,
            description=person.description,
        )
        return resp
```

Step 3 – annotate the span

If we run the code with the instrumentation that starts and finishes the span, we will be able to see the traces in the Jaeger UI. However, the traces are pretty bare bones. We do see the service name, the operation name, and the latency. We also see some tags automatically added by Jaeger, including the details of the sampling strategy and the process information, such as the IP address. Otherwise, there is no custom information about our application, and the traces look pretty different from what we saw in the HotROD demo:

Figure 4.2: A single span without any custom annotations

The primary objective of a span is to tell a story about the operation it represents. Sometimes a name and a couple of timestamps are enough. In other cases, we may need more information if we want to analyze the behavior of our system.

As developers, we know best what might be useful in the context: the remote address of the server we called; the identity of a database replica we accessed; the details and the stack trace of an exception that was encountered; the account number we tried to access; the number of records we retrieved from storage, and so on. The rules here are similar to logging: record what you think may be useful and control the overhead with sampling. If you find some crucial piece of data is missing, add it! This is what instrumentation is all about.

The OpenTracing APIs provide two facilities for recording custom information in the spans: "tags" and "logs". Tags are key-value pairs that apply to the span as a whole, and are often used to query and filter trace data. For example, if a span represents an HTTP call, then recording the HTTP method, such as GET or POST, is best done with a tag.

Logs, on the other hand, represent point-in-time events. In that sense, they are very closely related to traditional log statements that we often use throughout the program, only contextualized to a single span. OpenTracing logs are also structured, that is, represented as a timestamp and a nested collection of key-value pairs. Span logs can be used to record additional events that occur during the span lifetime, if we do not want to model them as their own nested spans. For example, if we have a single span for an HTTP request, we might want to log the following lower-level events:

- Starting DNS lookup
- DNS lookup finished
- Attempting TCP connection
- TCP connection established
- HTTP headers written
- Finished writing HTTP request body

Recording these events as span logs establishes a basic causality relationship between them, based on the recording order and the timestamps. In some cases, it may be a sufficient level of detail for analyzing performance problems. In other cases, we may want to have a more structured representation and, for example, represent DNS lookup and TCP handshake as their own spans, since they also have well-defined start and end points.

The fact that span logs are called "logs" is often confusing and leads to questions like "when should I use regular logs and when should I use span logs?" There is no one-size-fits-all answer to that. Some logs simply do not make sense as part of the span; we have seen the examples in the HotROD demo, where the custom logging API reserved the term "background logs" for those events that occur as part of the application lifecycle, rather than as part of a specific request execution.

For logs that are related to a single request, there are other aspects to consider. Most tracing systems are not designed as log aggregation services, so they may not provide the same capabilities as, say, the **Elasticsearch–Logstash–Kibana (ELK)** stack. The sampling generally works differently for logs and traces: logs are sometimes sampled (or throttled) per-process, while traces are always sampled per-request (distributed execution). In retrospect, it would be better if the OpenTracing specification used the term "events" instead of logs, until the industry decides how to deal with both. In fact, OpenTracing recommends that one of the key-value pairs in every span log is a pair with `key = "event"` that describes the overall event being logged, with other attributes of the event provided as additional fields.

What kind of information might we need to record in the span in case we are troubleshooting some issue in our Hello application? It might be useful to know what response string (formatted greeting) the service returns, and maybe the details loaded from the database. There's no clear-cut answer whether these should be recorded as tags or logs (we will see more relevant examples later). We chose to record the response string as a tag, since it corresponds to the span overall, and used a log for the contents of the `Person` object loaded from the database because it is structured data and a span log allows multiple fields.

We also have another special case where we may want to add custom annotations to the span: the error handling. In all three languages, the query to the database may fail for one reason or another, and we will receive an error of some sort. When we are troubleshooting an application in production, it is very useful if it can record these errors in the correct span.

The tag and log APIs do not enforce any specific semantics or meaning on the values recorded as key-value pairs. This allows the instrumentation to easily add completely custom data. For example, in our case we can store the response string as a tag named `"response"`. However, there are data elements that are frequently recorded in the spans with the same meaning, such as HTTP URLs, HTTP status codes, database statements, errors/exception, and so on. To ensure that all disparate instrumentations still record these common concepts in a consistent way, the OpenTracing project provides a set of "standard tags" and "fields", and a guideline on the exact way of using them, in a document called "Semantic Conventions" [4].

The tag and field names prescribed in this document are usually available as constants exposed by the respective OpenTracing APIs, and we will be using those in this exercise to record the error information in a standardized way. In the later exercise, we will use those constants to record other data, such as HTTP attributes and a SQL query.

Annotate the span in Go

First, let's add the code to annotate the span in the `handleSayHello()` function:

```go
func handleSayHello(w http.ResponseWriter, r *http.Request) {
    span := tracer.StartSpan("say-hello")
    defer span.Finish()

    name := strings.TrimPrefix(r.URL.Path, "/sayHello/")
    greeting, err := SayHello(name, span)
    if err != nil {
        span.SetTag("error", true)
        span.LogFields(otlog.Error(err))
        http.Error(w, err.Error(), http.StatusInternalServerError)
        return
    }

    span.SetTag("response", greeting)
    w.Write([]byte(greeting))
}
```

Here, we made three changes. In the error handling branch, we set an `error = true` tag on the span, to indicate that the operation failed, and we log the error using the `span.LogFields()` method. It is a structured way to pass the log fields to the span that minimizes memory allocations. We need to import an additional package that we labeled `otlog`:

```go
otlog "github.com/opentracing/opentracing-go/log"
```

In the case of a successful request, just before we write the response, we store the `greeting` string in the span tag called `response`. We also change the signature of the `SayHello()` function and pass the span to it so that it can do its own annotation, like this:

```go
func SayHello(name string, span opentracing.Span) (string, error) {
    person, err := repo.GetPerson(name)
    if err != nil {
        return "", err
    }
```

```
span.LogKV(
    "name", person.Name,
    "title", person.Title,
    "description", person.Description,
)

...
}
```

Here, we are using a different span log function, LogKV, which is conceptually still the same, but takes the arguments as an even-length list of values, that is, alternating (key, value, key, value, ...) pairs.

Annotate the span in Java

Let's log to the span the person's details after we load them from the database, and capture the response as a tag on the span:

```
@GetMapping("/sayHello/{name}")
public String sayHello(@PathVariable String name) {
    Span span = tracer.buildSpan("say-hello").start();
    try {
        Person person = getPerson(name);
        Map<String, String> fields = new LinkedHashMap<>();
        fields.put("name", person.getName());
        fields.put("title", person.getTitle());
        fields.put("description", person.getDescription());
        span.log(fields);

        String response = formatGreeting(person);
        span.setTag("response", response);

        return response;
    } finally {
        span.finish();
    }
}
```

The Java OpenTracing API for span logs is rather inefficient at this time, requiring us to create a new instance of a map. Perhaps in the future a new API will be added with alternating key/value pairs.

Annotate the span in Python

To record the `response` tag in the `say_hello()` function, we first need to capture the span created in the `with` statement as a named variable:

```python
@app.route("/sayHello/<name>")
def say_hello(name):
    with opentracing.tracer.start_span('say-hello') as span:
        person = get_person(name, span)
        resp = format_greeting(
            name=person.name,
            title=person.title,
            description=person.description,
        )
        span.set_tag('response', resp)
        return resp
```

We also want to pass that span to the `get_person()` function, where we can log the person's information to that span:

```python
def get_person(name, span):
    person = Person.get(name)
    if person is None:
        person = Person()
        person.name = name
    span.log_kv({
        'name': person.name,
        'title': person.title,
        'description': person.description,
    })
    return person
```

Exercise summary

If we now run the program (for example, `go run ./exercise2/hello.go`) and query it with `curl`, we will see a span that looks slightly more interesting (*Figure 4.3*). The relative timing of the log entry is 451.85 ms, which is only slightly earlier than the end of the span at 451.87 ms, which is not surprising, since the majority of the time is spent in the database query.

Figure 4.3: A single-span trace with custom annotations

In this second exercise, we have learned that in order to use the OpenTracing API, we need to instantiate a concrete tracer, just like you would need to use a concrete logging implementation if you wanted to use SLF4J logging API in Java. We wrote instrumentation that starts and finishes a span representing the work done by the HTTP handler of the Hello application. Next, we added custom annotations to the span in the form of tags and logs.

Exercise 3 – tracing functions and passing context

When looking at the trace generated by the version of the Hello application from the second exercise, we noticed that the log entry we added to the span happens very close to the end of the span. We hypothesized that this is because most of the time is spent querying the database, but this is why we are doing distributed tracing in the first place: not to guess, but to measure! We already have the main chunks of the logic, the database access and formatting of the greeting, separated into functions, so let's give each of them a span and get a more meaningful trace.

In this exercise we will:

- Trace individual functions
- Combine multiple spans into a single trace
- Learn to propagate the context in-process

Step 1 – trace individual functions

Let's start with adding spans in our two "worker" functions: reading from the database and formatting the greeting.

Trace individual functions in Go

Our `FormatGreeting()` function is located in the `main` package, so it has access to the global `tracer` variable that we will need to start a span. The database access code, however, is in another package, and we don't want to have a circular dependency between them. Since this is a rather common problem, the OpenTracing API provides a dedicated global variable that can be used to access the tracer. Generally, relying on global variables is not a great idea, but for simplicity, we will use it in the Hello application.

Let's change the `main()` to not have its own global variable `tracer`, and instead initialize the one in the OpenTracing library:

```go
// var tracer opentracing.Tracer - commented out

func main() {
    repo = people.NewRepository()
    defer repo.Close()

    tracer, closer := tracing.Init("go-3-hello")
    defer closer.Close()
    opentracing.SetGlobalTracer(tracer)

    ...
}
```

We then replace all references to the `tracer` variable with `opentracing.GlobalTracer()`. That way, we can add new spans to the worker functions, starting with the `Repository` (in file `people/repository.go`):

```go
func (r *Repository) GetPerson(name string) (model.Person, error) {
    query := "select title, description from people where name = ?"

    span := opentracing.GlobalTracer().StartSpan(
        "get-person",
        opentracing.Tag{Key: "db.statement", Value: query},
    )
    defer span.Finish()

    rows, err := r.db.Query(query, name)
    ...
}
```

Notice that we record the SQL query we are about to execute as a span tag.
Let's make a similar change in the `FormatGreeting()` function:

```
func FormatGreeting(name, title, description string) string {
    span := opentracing.GlobalTracer().StartSpan("format-
greeting")
    defer span.Finish()

    response := "Hello, "
    ...
}
```

Trace individual functions in Java

Adding new spans to the `getPerson()` and `formatGreeting()` functions in `hello.go` is very similar to how we did it in the `sayHello()` function:

```
private Person getPerson(String name) {
    Span span = tracer.buildSpan("get-person").start();
    try {
        ...
        return new Person(name);
    } finally {
        span.finish();
    }
}

private String formatGreeting(Person person) {
    Span span = tracer.buildSpan("format-greeting").start();
    try {
        ...
        return response;
    } finally {
        span.finish();
    }
}
```

Even though the `get-person` span represents a call to the database, we do not
have access to a lot of information about that call, since it is handled by the ORM
framework for us. Later in this chapter, we will see how we can get instrumentation
to that level as well, for example, to save the SQL statement in the span.

Trace individual functions in Python

Let's start new spans in the `get_person()` and `format_greeting()` functions:

```python
def get_person(name, span):
    with opentracing.tracer.start_span('get-person') as span:
        person = Person.get(name)
        ...
        return person

def format_greeting(name, title, description):
    with opentracing.tracer.start_span('format-greeting'):
        greeting = 'Hello, '
        ...
        return greeting
```

We could also add a span to the `Person.get()` method, however it would be more useful if we could have access to the SQL query, which we don't have because it's hidden by the ORM framework. In Exercise 6, we will see how we can get that.

Step 2 – combine multiple spans into a single trace

Now that we have additional instrumentation, we are ready to run the example. Unfortunately, we will soon find that the result is not what we expected. We don't even need to look in the Jaeger UI; we can look at the logs printed, for example, by the Go application:

```
Initializing logging reporter
Listening on http://localhost:8080/
Reporting span 419747aa37e1a31c:419747aa37e1a31c:0:1
Reporting span 1ffddd91dd63e202:1ffddd91dd63e202:0:1
Reporting span 796caf0b9ddb47f3:796caf0b9ddb47f3:0:1
```

The instrumentation did create three spans, as expected. The long hexadecimal strings are the representation of the span context for each span, in the format `trace-id:span-id:parent-id:flags`. The important part is the first segment, representing the trace ID – they are all different! Instead of creating a single trace with three spans, we created three independent traces. Well, rookie mistake. What we neglected to do was to establish causal relationships between the spans, so that the tracer would know that they belong to the same trace. As we discussed earlier in this chapter, these relationships are represented by **span references** in OpenTracing.

There are two types of span references currently defined by the OpenTracing specification: "child-of" and "follows-from". For example, we can say that span B is a "child-of" span A, or it "follows-from" span A. In both cases, it means that span A is the ancestor of span B, that is, A *happens-before* B. The difference between the two relationships, as defined by the OpenTracing specification, is that if B is child-of A, then A *depends on the outcome* of B. For example, in the Hello application, the span "say-hello" depends on the outcome of spans "get-person" and "format-greeting", so the latter should be created with child-of references to the former.

There are cases, however, when the span that happens-before does not depend on the outcome of the descendent span. One classic example is when the second span is a fire-and-forget type of operation, such as an opportunistic write to a cache. Another classic example is a producer-consumer pattern in the messaging systems, where the producer generally has no idea when and how the consumer will process the message, yet the producer's span (the act of writing to the queue) has the causal link to the consumer span (the act of reading from the queue). These kinds of relationships are modeled with follows-from span references.

In order to add a reference to happens-before span A when creating a new span B, we need to have access to span A, or more precisely to its span context.

Combine multiple spans into a single trace in Go

Let's pass the parent span to the worker functions and use its span context to create a child-of reference:

```go
func FormatGreeting(
    name, title, description string,
    span opentracing.Span,
) string {
    span = opentracing.GlobalTracer().StartSpan(
        "format-greeting",
        opentracing.ChildOf(span.Context()),
    )
    defer span.Finish()
    ...
}

func (r *Repository) GetPerson(
    name string,
    span opentracing.Span,
) (model.Person, error) {
    query := "select title, description from people where name = ?"
```

```
        span = opentracing.GlobalTracer().StartSpan(
            "get-person",
            opentracing.ChildOf(span.Context()),
            opentracing.Tag{Key: "db.statement", Value: query},
        )
        defer span.Finish()
        ...
    }

    func SayHello(name string, span opentracing.Span) (string, error) {
        person, err := repo.GetPerson(name, span)
        if err != nil {
            return "", err
        }

        span.LogKV(...)

        return FormatGreeting(
            person.Name,
            person.Title,
            person.Description,
            span,
        ), nil
    }
```

The resulting code can be found in the exercise3a package.

Combine multiple spans into a single trace in Java

Let's change the code to pass the top span to the getPerson() and
formatGreeting() functions, and use it to create a child-of reference:

```
        private Person getPerson(String name, Span parent) {
            Span span = tracer
                .buildSpan("get-person")
                .asChildOf(parent)
                .start();
            ...
        }

        private String formatGreeting(Person person, Span parent) {
            Span span = tracer
                .buildSpan("format-greeting")
                .asChildOf(parent)
                .start();
            ...
        }
```

Here we see the use of the fluid syntax of the span builder. The method `asChildOf()` needs a span context, but it has an overload that accepts a full span and extracts the context from it. The changes to the `sayHello()` function are trivial, so we will omit them here. The resulting code can be found in the `exercise3a` package.

Combine multiple spans into a single trace in Python

Let's link the two spans in the lower functions to the top span created in the HTTP handler. We already pass that span to the `get_person()` function as an argument, so we need to do the same for the `format_greeting()` function:

```python
@app.route("/sayHello/<name>")
def say_hello(name):
    with opentracing.tracer.start_span('say-hello') as span:
        person = get_person(name, span)
        resp = format_greeting(
            name=person.name,
            title=person.title,
            description=person.description,
            span=span,
        )
        span.set_tag('response', resp)
        return resp
```

Now let's change the calls to `start_span()` and pass a child-of reference:

```python
def get_person(name, span):
    with opentracing.tracer.start_span(
        'get-person', child_of=span,
    ) as span:
        person = Person.get(name)
        ...
        return person


def format_greeting(name, title, description, span):
    with opentracing.tracer.start_span(
        'format-greeting', child_of=span,
    ):
        greeting = 'Hello, '
        ...
        return greeting
```

Note that the `child_of` argument generally expects a span context, but the Python library has a convenient fallback that allows us to pass the full span, and the library will automatically retrieve span context from it. The resulting code can be found in the `exerice3a` directory.

Step 3 – propagate the in-process context

If we run the application after the last changes, we will see that it correctly produces a single trace for each request.

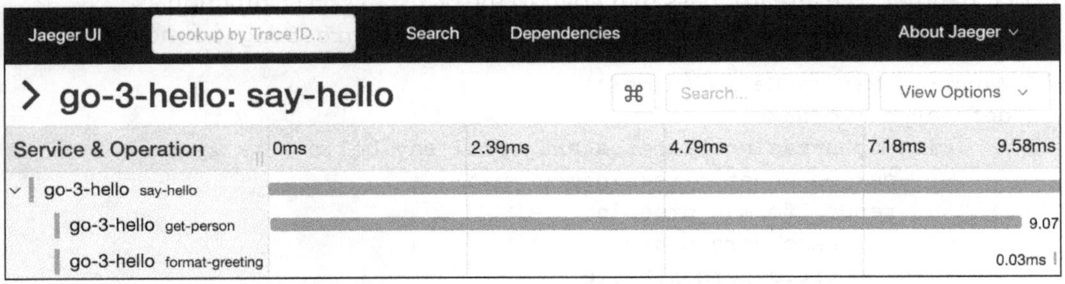

| Jaeger UI | Lookup by Trace ID... | Search | Dependencies | | | About Jaeger ∨ |

| > go-3-hello: say-hello | | ⌘ | Search... | | View Options ∨ |

Service & Operation	0ms	2.39ms	4.79ms	7.18ms	9.58ms
∨ go-3-hello say-hello					
go-3-hello get-person					9.07
go-3-hello format-greeting					0.03ms

Figure 4.4: A three-span trace that includes spans for the worker functions

Each trace contains three spans, as expected, and we can confirm our earlier suspicion that the database lookup is indeed responsible for the majority of the time spent by the system on the request. We can drilldown into the database span and see the SQL query as a tag (but only in the Go version where we did not use the ORM framework).

One major downside of our approach, however, is that we had to explicitly change the signatures of many methods in our application to accept a span, so that we could use its span context when creating a child-of reference. This approach is clearly not scalable to large applications. In general, this problem is known as **in-process context propagation**, and it's one of the hardest to solve in a world with increasingly frequent use of asynchronous frameworks and programming styles.

To complicate things further, the solutions differ across programming languages and frameworks. For example, in Node.js one could use **continuation local storage** (**CLS**) to pass the context, which itself is not standard in the language and has multiple implementations. In Java and Python, we can use thread-local variables, unless the application is using an asynchronous programming style, for example, `asyncio` in Python. The Go language has neither CLS nor thread-local mechanisms and requires a completely different approach. The OpenTracing project has recently defined a high-level approach called **Scope Managers** that allows the instrumentation to be (mostly) abstracted from the details of the in-process context propagation mechanism.

In this step, we will amend our function instrumentation to avoid passing spans explicitly as parameters and use the in-process propagation mechanism from OpenTracing instead. Since Go language is a special case, we will start with Python and Java. In both Python and Java, the OpenTracing APIs have introduced the notion of an "active span," "a scope," and a "scope manager." The easiest way to think about them is to imagine an application where each request executes in its own thread (a very common model). When the server receives a new request, it starts a span for it, and makes that span "active," meaning that any other instrumentation that, for example, wants to add annotations to it can access the active span directly from the tracer (just for that thread). If the server executes some long operation, or maybe a remote call, it would create another span as a `child-of` the currently active span and make the new span "active." Effectively, the old active span is pushed onto the stack while the child span is executing. Once the child span is finished, its parent is popped from the stack and made active again. The scope manager is the component responsible for managing and storing these active spans.

The idea of a stack is just an analogy, as in practice it is not always implemented as a stack, especially when we are not dealing with thread-per-request programming, but some event-loop-based frameworks. However, the scope manager abstracts that away and gives a logical equivalent of a stack. There are different implementations of scope managers suitable for specific programming styles and frameworks. The one limitation is that we cannot mix and match different scope managers in the same application, as each one is a singleton for a given tracer instance.

The management of the active spans is done through scopes. When we ask the scope manager to activate a span, we get back a scope object that contains the span. Each scope can be closed once, which removes it from the top of the stack and makes the previous scope (and its span) active. Scopes can be configured to auto-finish the span when the scope is closed, or to leave the span open–which one of these modes is used depends on the threading model of the code. For example, if we are using futures-based asynchronous programming, and we make a remote call, then the result handler for that call will most likely be handled in another thread. So, the scope that was created on the thread that started the request should not finish the span. We will discuss this in *Chapter 5, Instrumentation of Asynchronous Applications*.

One very convenient feature of using active spans is that we no longer need to explicitly tell the tracer that the new span should be the child-of the currently active span. If we do not explicitly pass another span reference, the tracer will automatically establish that relationship, assuming there is an active span at the time. This makes the code for starting spans simpler.

Writing instrumentation code that is fully relying on scope managers has one danger. If the application flow is not correctly instrumented, it is possible to arrive at a certain place in the program where the stack of scopes stored in the scope manager is empty, and statements that unconditionally expect an active span to be present, such as `tracer.activeSpan().setTag(k, v)`, might raise a null pointer exception or a similar error. Defensive coding and checking for null would address this issue, but in a well-structured application with clear flow, it may not be a problem. The examples I use in this chapter do not include these null checks because they are structured so that it is not possible to find oneself in a situation where an expected active span is null. Another recommendation is to keep code that accesses the scope close to the code that starts it, thus also avoiding the null situation altogether.

In-process context propagation in Python

To use scope managers and active spans, we need to call the `start_active_span()` method of the tracer, which returns a scope object instead of a span. First, let's change the HTTP handler:

```python
@app.route("/sayHello/<name>")
def say_hello(name):
    with opentracing.tracer.start_active_span('say-hello') as scope:
        person = get_person(name)
        resp = format_greeting(
            name=person.name,
            title=person.title,
            description=person.description,
        )
        scope.span.set_tag('response', resp)
        return resp
```

Since the active span is directly accessible from the tracer, we no longer need to pass it to the other two functions. However, when we want to set the `response` tag, we need to retrieve the span from its scope.

The other two functions are changed in a similar way. The main difference is that we get a scope back, and we do not have to specify the parent span anymore:

```python
def get_person(name):
    with opentracing.tracer.start_active_span(
        'get-person',
    ) as scope:
        person = Person.get(name)
        if person is None:
            person = Person()
            person.name = name
```

```
        scope.span.log_kv({
            'name': person.name,
            'title': person.title,
            'description': person.description,
        })
        return person

    def format_greeting(name, title, description):
        with opentracing.tracer.start_active_span(
            'format-greeting',
        ):
            greeting = 'Hello, '
            ...
            return greeting
```

This code is available in the directory `exercise3b`.

In-process context propagation in Java

To use scope managers and active spans, we need to pass the span to the `activate()` method of the scope manager, which returns a scope object. First, let's change the HTTP handler:

```
    @GetMapping("/sayHello/{name}")
    public String sayHello(@PathVariable String name) {
        Span span = tracer.buildSpan("say-hello").start();
        try (Scope s = tracer.scopeManager().activate(span, false)) {
            ...
        } finally {
            span.finish();
        }
    }
```

We are using a try-with-resource statement that automatically calls the `close()` method on the scope, which restores the previously active span in the scope manager. We are passing `false` as the second argument to the `activate()` method, which tells the scope manager to not finish the span when the scope is closed. This is different from what we did in Python. The OpenTracing API for Java v0.31 supported scopes with auto-finish behavior, but they were being deprecated in the later versions because they could lead to inadvertent mistakes in the instrumentation. Also, according to the variable scoping rules of the try-with-resource statement, the closeable variable declared in the `try()` part is only visible inside its body, but not visible in the `catch()` and `finally` blocks.

This means that logging an exception or the error status to the span is not possible, that is, the following code is invalid, even though it would be a lot simpler:

```
try (Scope scope = tracer.buildSpan("get-person").startActive(true)) {
    ...
} catch (Exception e) {
    // will not compile since the scope variable is not visible
    scope.span().setTag("error", true);
    scope.span().log(...);
}
```

The changes to the `getPerson()` and `formatGreeting()` functions are similar. We no longer need to explicitly pass the parent span as a function argument and use it to create a `child-of` reference because the tracer does that automatically, as long as there is a current active span:

```
private Person getPerson(String name) {
    Span span = tracer.buildSpan("get-person").start();
    try (Scope s = tracer.scopeManager().activate(span, false)) {
        ...
    } finally {
        span.finish();
    }
}

private String formatGreeting(Person person) {
    Span span = tracer.buildSpan("format-greeting").start();
    try (Scope s = tracer.scopeManager().activate(span, false)) {
        ...
    } finally {
        span.finish();
    }
}
```

The new code does not look significantly simpler than before; however, in a real program there may be many nested levels of functions, and not having to pass the span object through all of them ends up saving a lot of typing and API churn.

The final version of the code is available in the `exercise3b` package.

In-process context propagation in Go

The availability of thread-local variables in Python and Java makes the in-process propagation relatively easy. Go does not have such a mechanism and does not even provide any means of obtaining a unique identity of a goroutine, which could have allowed us to build some internal mapping to keep track of the context. One of the reasons for that is due to one of Go's design principles, "no magic", which encourages a programming style where the behavior of the program is always obvious and easy to follow through. Even reflection-based dependency injection frameworks, hugely popular in Java, are frowned upon in Go because they do look like you are getting parameters to your functions from somewhere, as if by magic.

On the other hand, Go is one of the most popular languages for developing cloud-native software. In-process context propagation is not only useful for distributed tracing, but for other techniques, such as implementing RPC deadlines, timeouts, and cancellations, which are important for high-performing applications. To address this issue, the Go standard library provides a standard module, context, which defines an interface called context.Context, used as a container to hold and pass the in-process request context. If you are not familiar with this, you may want to read the blog post that first introduced the Context type (https://blog.golang.org/context). Here's an interesting quote from this blog:

> *"At Google, we require that Go programmers pass a Context parameter as the first argument to every function on the call path between incoming and outgoing requests. This allows Go code developed by many different teams to interoperate well. It provides simple control over timeouts and cancelation and ensures that critical values like security credentials transit Go programs properly."*

So, Go's solution is to ensure that the applications explicitly pass the Context object between all function calls. This is very much in the spirit of the "no magic" principle because the program itself is fully in charge of propagating the context. It completely solves the problem of in-process propagation for the purpose of distributed tracing. It is certainly more invasive than in Java or Python, and might seem like we just traded passing one thing (span) for another (context). However, since it is the language standard, and Go's Context has much wider applications than just distributed tracing, it is not a tough sell in an organization where many Go applications are already written in the style recommended by the standard library.

The OpenTracing API for Go recognized this early on and provided helper functions that simplify passing the current span as part of the `Context` object and starting new spans from it. Let's use that to clean up our Hello application. The first span is created in the HTTP handler function and we need to store that span in the context to be passed down, by calling `ContextWithSpan()`. The context itself is already provided by the `http.Request` object. Then we pass the new `ctx` object to the `SayHello()` function as the first argument, instead of passing the span:

```
func handleSayHello(w http.ResponseWriter, r *http.Request) {
    span := opentracing.GlobalTracer().StartSpan("say-hello")
    defer span.Finish()
    ctx := opentracing.ContextWithSpan(r.Context(), span)

    name := strings.TrimPrefix(r.URL.Path, "/sayHello/")
    greeting, err := SayHello(ctx, name)
    ...
}
```

We change the function `SayHello()` similarly, by passing the context to both the `GetPerson()` and the `FormatGreeting()` functions. By convention, we always put `ctx` as the first argument. Since we no longer have a reference span to call the `LogKV()` method, we call another OpenTracing helper, `SpanFromContext()`, to retrieve the current span:

```
func SayHello(ctx context.Context, name string) (string, error) {
    person, err := repo.GetPerson(ctx, name)
    if err != nil {
        return "", err
    }

    opentracing.SpanFromContext(ctx).LogKV(
        "name", person.Name,
        "title", person.Title,
        "description", person.Description,
    )

    return FormatGreeting(
        ctx,
        person.Name,
        person.Title,
        person.Description,
    ), nil
}
```

Now let's change the `GetPerson()` function to work with the context:

```
func (r *Repository) GetPerson(
    ctx context.Context,
    name string,
) (model.Person, error) {
    query := "select title, description from people where name = ?"

    span, ctx := opentracing.StartSpanFromContext(
        ctx,
        "get-person",
        opentracing.Tag{Key: "db.statement", Value: query},
    )
    defer span.Finish()

    rows, err := r.db.QueryContext(ctx, query, name)
    ...
}
```

We are using the `opentracing.StartSpanFromContext()` helper function to start a new span as a `child-of` the span currently stored in the context. The function returns a new span and a new instance of the `Context` that contains the new span. We do not need to pass the `child-of` reference explicitly: it is done by the helper. Since our code is now context-aware, we try to be good citizens and pass it further to the database API, `db.QueryContext()`. We do not need it for tracing purposes right now, but it could be used for request cancellations, and so on.

Finally, we make similar changes to the `FormatGreeting()` function:

```
func FormatGreeting(
    ctx context.Context,
    name, title, description string,
) string {
    span, ctx := opentracing.StartSpanFromContext(
        ctx,
        "format-greeting",
    )
    defer span.Finish()
    ...
}
```

The final version of the code is available in the exercise3b package. We can verify that the spans are connected correctly by running the program and checking that all trace IDs are the same:

```
$ go run ./exercise3b/hello.go
Initializing logging reporter
Listening on http://localhost:8080/
Reporting span 158aa3f9bfa0f1e1:1c11913f74ab9019:158aa3f9bfa0f1e1:1
Reporting span 158aa3f9bfa0f1e1:1d752c6d320b912c:158aa3f9bfa0f1e1:1
Reporting span 158aa3f9bfa0f1e1:158aa3f9bfa0f1e1:0:1
```

Exercise summary

In this exercise, we have increased our instrumentation coverage to three spans representing three functions in the application. We have discussed how OpenTracing allows us to describe the causal relationships between spans by using span references. Also, we used the OpenTracing scope managers and Go's context. Context mechanisms to propagate the context in-process between function calls. In the next exercise, we will replace the two inner functions with RPC calls to other microservices and will see what additional instrumentation that requires in order to support **inter-process context propagation**.

Exercise 4 – tracing RPC requests

I promised at the beginning of this chapter to make this application interesting. So far, it was just a single process and not particularly exciting as a testbed for distributed tracing. In this exercise, we will turn the Hello application from a monolith into a microservices-based application. While doing that, we will learn how to:

- Trace a transaction across more than one microservice
- Pass the context between processes using inject and extract trace points
- Apply OpenTracing-recommended tags

Step 1 – break up the monolith

Our main application internally performs two primary functions: retrieving a person's information from the database and formatting it into a greeting. We can extract these two functions into their own microservices. We will call the first one "Big Brother" and the second "Formatter." The Big Brother service will listen on HTTP port 8081 and serve a single endpoint getPerson, reading the name of the person as the path parameter, similar to the Hello application itself.

It will return the information about the person as a JSON string. We could test that service like this:

```
$ curl http://localhost:8081/getPerson/Gru
{"Name":"Gru","Title":"Felonius","Description":"Where are the minions?"}
```

The Formatter service will listen on HTTP port 8082 and serve a single endpoint formatGreeting. It will take three parameters: name, title, and description encoded as URL query parameters, and respond with a plain text string. Here's an example of calling it:

```
$ curl 'http://localhost:8082/formatGreeting?name=Smith&title=Agent'
Hello, Agent Smith!
```

Since we are now using three microservices, we will need to start each of them in a separate Terminal window.

Microservices in Go

The refactored code for the Hello application broken down into three microservices is available in package exercise4a. I will not reproduce all of it here, since most of it is the same as before, just moved around. The main hello.go application is refactored to have two local functions, getPerson() and formatGreeting(), which make HTTP calls to the Big Brother and Formatter services respectively. They are using a helper function, xhttp.Get(), from a shared module, lib/http/, to execute HTTP requests and handle errors.

We added two submodules, bigbrother and formatter, each containing a single main.go file, which is similar to the former hello.go in that it instantiates a new tracer with a unique service name and starts an HTTP server. For example, here's how the main() function for the Formatter service looks:

```
func main() {
    tracer, closer := tracing.Init("go-4-formatter")
    defer closer.Close()
    opentracing.SetGlobalTracer(tracer)

    http.HandleFunc("/formatGreeting", handleFormatGreeting)

    log.Print("Listening on http://localhost:8082/")
    log.Fatal(http.ListenAndServe(":8082", nil))
}
```

The initialization of the data repository is moved from hello.go to bigbrother/main.go, since it's the only service that needs access to the database.

Microservices in Java

Package `exercise4a` contains the refactored code from *Exercise 3 - tracing functions and passing context*, that reimplements the Hello application as three microservices. The class `HelloController` still has the same `getPerson()` and `formatGreeting()` functions, but they now execute HTTP requests against two new services, implemented in packages `exercise4a.bigbrother` and `exercise4a.formatter`, using Spring's `RestTemplate` that we ask to be auto-injected:

```
@Autowired
private RestTemplate restTemplate;
```

Each sub-package has an `App` class (`BBApp` and `FApp`) and a controller class. All `App` classes instantiate their own tracer with a unique name, so that we can separate the services in the traces. The JPA annotations are moved from `HelloApp` to `BBApp`, as it is the only one accessing the database. Since we need the two new services to run on different ports, they each override the `server.port` environment variable in the `main()` function:

```
@EnableJpaRepositories("lib.people")
@EntityScan("lib.people")
@SpringBootApplication
public class BBApp {

    @Bean
    public io.opentracing.Tracer initTracer() {
        ...
        return new Configuration("java-4-bigbrother")
            .withSampler(samplerConfig)
            .withReporter(reporterConfig)
            .getTracer();
    }

    public static void main(String[] args) {
        System.setProperty("server.port", "8081");
        SpringApplication.run(BBApp.class, args);
    }
}
```

The two new controllers are similar to the `HelloController` and contain the code that it previously had in the `getPerson()` and `formatGreeting()` functions. We also added new spans at the top of the HTTP handler functions.

The new services can be run in separate Terminal windows similar to the main one:

```
$ ./mvnw spring-boot:run -Dmain.class=exercise4a.bigbrother.BBApp
$ ./mvnw spring-boot:run -Dmain.class=exercise4a.formatter.FApp
```

Microservices in Python

The refactored code for the Hello application broken down into three microservices is available in package exercise4a. I will not reproduce all of it here, since most of it is the same as before, just moved around. The functions get_person() and format_greeting() in hello.py are changed to execute HTTP requests against two new microservices, which are implemented by the bigbrother.py and formatter.py modules. They both create their own tracers; for example, the Big Brother code looks like this:

```python
from flask import Flask
import json
from .database import Person
from lib.tracing import init_tracer
import opentracing

app = Flask('py-4-bigbrother')
init_tracer('py-4-bigbrother')


@app.route("/getPerson/<name>")
def get_person_http(name):
    with opentracing.tracer.start_active_span('/getPerson') as scope:
        person = Person.get(name)
        if person is None:
            person = Person()
            person.name = name
        scope.span.log_kv({
            'name': person.name,
            'title': person.title,
            'description': person.description,
        })
        return json.dumps({
            'name': person.name,
            'title': person.title,
            'description': person.description,
        })


if __name__ == "__main__":
    app.run(port=8081)
```

The new services can be run in separate Terminal windows similar to the main one:

```
$ python -m exercise4a.bigbrother
$ python -m exercise4a.formatter
```

Step 2 – pass the context between processes

Let's run a test against our refactored application in your preferred language. Here is how it looks for the Go app:

```
$ go run exercise4a/hello.go
Initializing logging reporter
Listening on http://localhost:8080/
Reporting span 2de55ae657a7ddd7:2de55ae657a7ddd7:0:1


$ go run exercise4a/bigbrother/main.go
Initializing logging reporter
Listening on http://localhost:8081/
Reporting span e62f4ea4bfb1e34:21a7ef50eb869546:e62f4ea4bfb1e34:1
Reporting span e62f4ea4bfb1e34:e62f4ea4bfb1e34:0:1


$ go run exercise4a/formatter/main.go
Initializing logging reporter
Listening on http://localhost:8082/
Reporting span 38a840df04d76643:441462665fe089bf:38a840df04d76643:1
Reporting span 38a840df04d76643:38a840df04d76643:0:1


$ curl http://localhost:8080/sayHello/Gru
Hello, Felonius Gru! Where are the minions?
```

As far as its greeting output, the application is working as expected. Unfortunately, we see that the refactoring reintroduced the old problem of a broken trace, that is, a single request to the Hello application results in three independent traces, indicated by different trace IDs in the logs. Of course, we should have expected that. In the monolith application, we were using in-process context propagation to make sure all spans are linked to each other and into the same trace. Making RPC requests broke our context propagation, so we need another mechanism. The OpenTracing APIs require all traces to implement a pair of methods, Inject() and Extract(), that are used to transfer the context between processes.

The design of this API had an interesting history because it had to work with several assumptions:

- It could not assume any knowledge about the contents of the metadata used by the tracing implementation, since virtually all existing tracing systems use different representations.

- It could not assume any knowledge of the serialized format of the metadata because again, even systems with conceptually very similar metadata (for example, Zipkin, Jaeger, and Stackdriver) use very different formats for transmitting it over the wire.

- It could not assume any knowledge about the transmission protocol and where in that protocol the metadata is encoded. For example, it is common to pass metadata as plain text headers when using HTTP, but when transmitting it via Kafka, or via custom transport protocols used by many storage systems (for example, Cassandra), the plain text HTTP format might not be suitable.

- It could not require tracers to be aware of all the different transmission protocols either, so that the teams that maintain the tracers could focus on a narrow and well-defined scope without worrying about all possible custom protocols that may exist.

OpenTracing was able to solve this by abstracting most of these concerns and delegating them to the tracer implementation. First, the inject/extract methods operate on the span context interface, which is already an abstraction. To address the difference in the transports, a notion of a "format" was introduced. It does not refer to the actual serialization format, but to the type of metadata support that exists in different transports. There are three formats defined in OpenTracing: "text-map," "binary," and "http-headers." The latter was a special nod to HTTP being the prevailing protocol with certain not-so-friendly idiosyncrasies, such as having case-insensitive header names, and other quirks. Conceptually, the http-headers format is similar to text-map in that it expects the transport to support a notion of metadata as a collection of string key-value pairs. The binary format is for use with protocols where the metadata can only be represented as an opaque sequence of bytes (for example, in the Cassandra wire protocol).

The second abstraction introduced in the OpenTracing APIs is the notion of a carrier. The carrier is actually tightly coupled with the format (there are discussions in the OpenTracing of merging them into a single type) in that it provides a physical container that the tracer can use to store the metadata according to the chosen format. For example, for the text-map format, the carrier can be a `Map<String, String>` in Java or `map[string]string` in Go; while the carrier for the binary format in Go is the standard `io.Writer` or `io.Reader` (depending on whether we are injecting or extracting the span context). The instrumentation that invokes these OpenTracing APIs to inject/extract metadata always knows which transport it is dealing with, so it can construct the appropriate carrier, typically tied to the underlying RPC request object, and let the tracer populate it (inject) or read from it (extract) through a well-defined carrier interface. This allows for the decoupling of tracer inject/extract implementation from the actual transport used by the application.

To use this mechanism in the Hello application, we need to add calls to `Inject()` in the main Hello service, and calls to `Extract()` in the Big Brother and Formatter services. We will also be starting new spans to represent each outbound HTTP call. This is customary in distributed tracing, since we do not want to attribute the time spent in the downstream service to the top-level `say-hello` span. As a general rule, every time an application makes a remote call to another service, for example, to a database, we want to create a new span wrapping just that call.

Passing context between processes in Go

Let's first change `hello.go` to inject the metadata into the HTTP request before calling the other services. The two internal functions, `getPerson()` and `formatGreeting()`, are using the helper function `xhttp.Get()` to execute HTTP requests. Let's replace them with calls to a new local function, `get()`, that looks like this:

```go
func get(ctx context.Context, operationName, url string) ([]byte,
error) {
    req, err := http.NewRequest("GET", url, nil)
    if err != nil {
        return nil, err
    }

    span, ctx := opentracing.StartSpanFromContext(ctx,
operationName)
    defer span.Finish()

    opentracing.GlobalTracer().Inject(
        span.Context(),
        opentracing.HTTPHeaders,
        opentracing.HTTPHeadersCarrier(req.Header),
    )

    return xhttp.Do(req)
}
```

A couple of new things are happening here. First, we start a new span that wraps the HTTP request, as discussed. Then, we call the `Inject()` function on the tracer and pass it the span context, the desired representation format `opentracing.HTTPHeaders`, and the carrier created as a wrapper (adapter) around the HTTP request headers. What's left is to replace the call sites:

```go
func getPerson(ctx context.Context, name string) (*model.Person,
error) {
    url := "http://localhost:8081/getPerson/"+name
    res, err := get(ctx, "getPerson", url)
    . . .
```

```
    }

func formatGreeting(
    ctx context.Context,
    person *model.Person,
) (string, error) {
    ...
    url := "http://localhost:8082/formatGreeting?" + v.Encode()
    res, err := get(ctx, "formatGreeting", url)
    ...
}
```

Now we need to change the other two services to extract the encoded metadata from the request and use it when creating a new span. For example, in the Big Brother service, it looks like this:

```
func handleGetPerson(w http.ResponseWriter, r *http.Request) {
    spanCtx, _ := opentracing.GlobalTracer().Extract(
        opentracing.HTTPHeaders,
        opentracing.HTTPHeadersCarrier(r.Header),
    )
    span := opentracing.GlobalTracer().StartSpan(
        "/getPerson",
        opentracing.ChildOf(spanCtx),
    )
    defer span.Finish()

    ctx := opentracing.ContextWithSpan(r.Context(), span)
    ...
}
```

Similar to the calling side, we are using tracer's `Extract()` method with `HTTPHeaders` format and carrier to decode span context from the request headers. We then start a new span, using the extracted span context to establish a child-of reference to the caller span. We can apply a similar change to the handler in the Formatter service. Also, since our top-level Hello service is also an HTTP server, it is conceivable that it might be called by a client that has already started a trace. So, let's replace the code that starts the `say-hello` span with a similar extract-and-start span code.

We are ignoring the error returned from the `Extract()` function because it does not affect the rest of our code, for example, if the tracer is not able to extract the context from the request, maybe because it is malformed or missing, it returns `nil` and an error. We can pass `nil` into the `ChildOf()` function without ill effect: it would simply be ignored and the tracer would start a new trace.

Passing context between processes in Java

In Java, invoking the tracer's `inject()` and `extract()` methods requires a bit more work, since we do not have the same standard conventions for representing HTTP headers as we do in Go and Python, that is, the representation is dependent on the HTTP framework. To save us some typing, we can use a helper base class, `TracedController`, that the other three controllers extend. This new class provides two helper methods, `get()` and `startServerSpan()`:

```
protected <T> T get(
        String operationName,
        URI uri,
        Class<T> entityClass,
        RestTemplate restTemplate) {
    Span span = tracer.buildSpan(operationName).start();
    try (Scope s = tracer.scopeManager().activate(span,
false)) {
        HttpHeaders headers = new HttpHeaders();
        HttpHeaderInjectAdapter carrier =
            new HttpHeaderInjectAdapter(headers);
        tracer.inject(scope.span().context(),
            Format.Builtin.HTTP_HEADERS, carrier);
        HttpEntity<String> entity = new HttpEntity<>(headers);
        return restTemplate.exchange(
            uri, HttpMethod.GET, entity,
            entityClass).getBody();
    } finally {
        span.finish();
    }
}
```

The method `get()` is used for executing outbound HTTP requests. We need to inject the trace context into request headers, so we use Spring's `HttpHeaders` object and wrap it in an adapter class `HttpHeaderInjectAdapter`, which makes it look like an implementation of OpenTracing's `TextMap` interface. The `TextMap` is an interface that has method `iterator()` used by `tracer.extract()` and method `put()` used by `tracer.inject()`. Since we are only doing the `inject()` call here, we do not implement the iterator:

```
private static class HttpHeaderInjectAdapter implements
TextMap {
    private final HttpHeaders headers;

    HttpHeaderInjectAdapter(HttpHeaders headers) {
        this.headers = headers;
```

```
        }

        @Override
        public Iterator<Entry<String, String>> iterator() {
            throw new UnsupportedOperationException();
        }

        @Override
        public void put(String key, String value) {
            headers.set(key, value);
        }
    }
```

Once the `HttpHeaders` object is populated by the tracer, via our adapter, with the headers carrying the trace context, we create `HttpEntity`, which is used by Spring's `restTemplate` to execute the request.

For the inbound HTTP requests implemented by HTTP handlers in the controllers, we implement a `startServerSpan()` method that performs the reverse of `get()`: it extracts the span context from the headers and passes it as the parent when starting a new server-side span:

```
    protected Span startServerSpan(
        String operationName, HttpServletRequest request)
    {
        HttpServletRequestExtractAdapter carrier =
            new HttpServletRequestExtractAdapter(request);
        SpanContext parent = tracer.extract(
            Format.Builtin.HTTP_HEADERS, carrier);
        Span span = tracer.buildSpan(operationName)
            .asChildOf(parent).start();
        return span;
    }
```

This time we are dealing with HTTP headers from `HttpServletRequest`, which does not expose an API to get them all at once, but only one at a time. Since we again need a `TextMap` interface for the tracer, we use another adapter class:

```
    private static class HttpServletRequestExtractAdapter
        implements TextMap
    {
        private final Map<String, String> headers;

        HttpServletRequestExtractAdapter(HttpServletRequest
request) {
            this.headers = new LinkedHashMap<>();
```

```
        Enumeration<String> keys = request.getHeaderNames();
        while (keys.hasMoreElements()) {
            String key = keys.nextElement();
            String value = request.getHeader(key);
            headers.put(key, value);
        }
    }

    @Override
    public Iterator<Entry<String, String>> iterator() {
        return headers.entrySet().iterator();
    }

    @Override
    public void put(String key, String value) {
        throw new UnsupportedOperationException();
    }
}
```

This time we are only interested in the `iterator()` method, so the other one always throws an exception. The constructor takes the servlet request and copies all HTTP headers into a plain map, which is later used to get the iterator. There are more efficient implementations, for example, `HttpServletRequestExtractAdapter` from the `https://github.com/opentracing-contrib/java-web-servlet-filter` library, but they are more complicated, so we provided our own version that is simpler but less efficient, since it always copies the headers.

With the base controller class in place, we make small changes to the main controllers, for example:

```
@RestController
public class HelloController extends TracedController {

    @Autowired
    private RestTemplate restTemplate;

    @GetMapping("/sayHello/{name}")
    public String sayHello(@PathVariable String name,
                           HttpServletRequest request) {
        Span span = startServerSpan("/sayHello", request);
        try (Scope s = tracer.scopeManager().activate(span, false)) {
            ...
            return response;
        } finally {
            span.finish();
```

```
        }
    }

    private Person getPerson(String name) {
        String url = "http://localhost:8081/getPerson/" + name;
        URI uri = UriComponentsBuilder
            .fromHttpUrl(url).build(Collections.emptyMap());
        return get("get-person", uri, Person.class, restTemplate);
    }
```

Similar changes are made to the HTTP handlers in BBController and FController.

Passing context between processes in Python

Let's first change how hello.py makes HTTP requests. Previously, we used the requests module directly, so instead let's wrap it into the following function _get():

```
def _get(url, params=None):
    span = opentracing.tracer.active_span
    headers = {}
    opentracing.tracer.inject(
        span.context,
        opentracing.Format.HTTP_HEADERS,
        headers,
    )
    r = requests.get(url, params=params, headers=headers)
    assert r.status_code == 200
    return r.text
```

In order to inject the span context, we need to get access to the current span, which we can do via the tracer.active_span property. Then we create a carrier headers as an empty dictionary and use tracer's inject() method to populate it, asking for the http-headers format. Then we simply pass the resulting dictionary as HTTP headers to the requests module.

On the receiving side, we need to read from those same headers to extract the context and use it to create a child-of reference. Flask exposes an object request that we can use to access inbound HTTP headers. Here's how we do it in bigbrother.py:

```
from flask import request

@app.route("/getPerson/<name>")
def get_person_http(name):
    span_ctx = opentracing.tracer.extract(
        opentracing.Format.HTTP_HEADERS,
```

```
        request.headers,
    )
with opentracing.tracer.start_active_span(
        '/getPerson',
        child_of=span_ctx,
    ) as scope:
        person = Person.get(name)
        ...
```

We need to make the same changes in the HTTP handlers in `hello.py` and `formatter.py`. After that, all spans emitted by the three microservices should have the same trace ID.

Step 3 – apply OpenTracing-recommended tags

If we repeat the test of the application, we will see that all three services are now attributing spans to the same trace ID. The trace is starting to look a lot more interesting. In particular, we see that the database call is no longer taking most of the time of the top-level request because we introduced two more network calls into the call graph. We can even see the latency introduced by those network calls, especially at the beginning of the requests. This just illustrates how introducing microservices into the application complicates its distributed behavior:

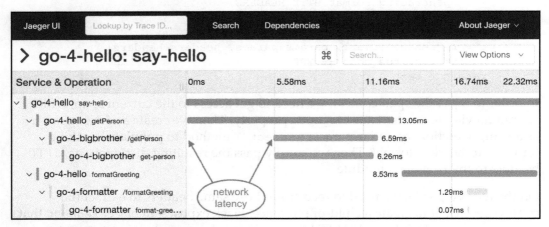

Figure 4.5: A trace that spans three microservices. Network latency can be clearly observed when descending from the inner spans in the go-4-hello service to the spans representing HTTP server endpoints in the downstream microservices.

There is just one thing left to do. Earlier we talked about the OpenTracing semantic conventions. HTTP requests are such a common pattern that OpenTracing defines a number of recommended tags that should be used to annotate the spans representing HTTP requests.

Having those tags allows tracing backends to perform standard aggregations and analysis, as well as understand the semantics of the trace better. In this last step, we want to apply the following standard tags:

- `span.kind`: This tag is used to identify the role of the service in an RPC request. Most frequently used values are `client` and `server`, which we want to use in our example. Another pair used in messaging systems is `producer` and `consumer`.

- `http.url`: This tag records the URL requested by the client or served by the server. The client-side URL is usually more interesting, since the URL known to the server may have been rewritten by upstream proxies.

- `http.method`: GET or POST, and so on.

Standard tags in Go

Since we already encapsulated tracing instrumentation for outbound HTTP calls, it's easy to add the standard tags in one place: the `get()` function. We just need one extra import for the extensions package `ext` (which we rename to `ottag`) that defines the tags as objects with strongly typed `Set()` methods, such as `Set(Span, string)`, in contrast to the more generic `span.SetTag(key, value)` method, where the second parameter can be of any type:

```
import ottag "github.com/opentracing/opentracing-go/ext"

func get(ctx context.Context, operationName, url string) ([]byte,
error) {
    ...
    span, ctx := opentracing.StartSpanFromContext(ctx,
operationName)
    defer span.Finish()

    ottag.SpanKindRPCClient.Set(span)
    ottag.HTTPUrl.Set(span, url)
    ottag.HTTPMethod.Set(span, "GET")
    opentracing.GlobalTracer().Inject(
        span.Context(),
        opentracing.HTTPHeaders,
        opentracing.HTTPHeadersCarrier(req.Header),
    )

    return xhttp.Do(req)
}
```

On the server side, we will only add the `span.kind` tag. The OpenTracing API provides an option `RPCServerOption` for the `StartSpan()` method that combines setting the `span.kind = server` tag and adding a child-of reference:

```
func handleFormatGreeting(w http.ResponseWriter, r *http.Request)
{
    spanCtx, _ := opentracing.GlobalTracer().Extract(
        opentracing.HTTPHeaders,
        opentracing.HTTPHeadersCarrier(r.Header),
    )
    span := opentracing.GlobalTracer().StartSpan(
        "/formatGreeting",
        ottag.RPCServerOption(spanCtx),
    )
    defer span.Finish()
    ...
}
```

The complete code for the exercise can be found in the package `exercise4b`.

Standard tags in Java

We can add the three tags for the outbound call to the `get()` method in the `TracedController`. Similar to Go, the standard tags are defined by the OpenTracing library as objects that expose a strongly typed `set(span, value)` method. For example, the constant `Tags.HTTP_URL` expects value to be a string, while `Tags.HTTP_STATUS` (which we are not using here) expects the value to be an integer:

```
import io.opentracing.tag.Tags;


protected <T> T get(String operationName, URI uri,
                    Class<T> entityClass,
                    RestTemplate restTemplate) {
    Span span = tracer.buildSpan(operationName).start();
    try (Scope s = tracer.scopeManager().activate(span,
false)) {
        Tags.SPAN_KIND.set(scope.span(), Tags.SPAN_KIND_CLIENT);
        Tags.HTTP_URL.set(scope.span(), uri.toString());
        Tags.HTTP_METHOD.set(scope.span(), "GET");
        ...
    } finally {
        span.finish();
    }
}
```

The span.kind=server tag can be added to the startServerSpan() method:

```
protected Span startServerSpan(
        String operationName, HttpServletRequest request)
{
    ...
    Span span = tracer.buildSpan(operationName)
        .asChildOf(parent).start();
    Tags.SPAN_KIND.set(span, Tags.SPAN_KIND_SERVER);
    return span;
}
```

The final code, with all modifications, is available in package exercise4b.

Standard tags in Python

We can first add the tags for outbound HTTP requests to the _get() function. Unlike Go and Java, the OpenTracing library for Python defines tag constants as simple strings, so we need to use the set_tag() method on the span:

```
from opentracing.ext import tags

def _get(url, params=None):
    span = opentracing.tracer.active_span
    span.set_tag(tags.HTTP_URL, url)
    span.set_tag(tags.HTTP_METHOD, 'GET')
    span.set_tag(tags.SPAN_KIND, tags.SPAN_KIND_RPC_CLIENT)
    headers = {}
    ...
```

On the server side, we will only add the span.kind = server tag, right when we create the new span (we'll only show the snippet from formatter.py):

```
from opentracing.ext import tags

@app.route("/formatGreeting")
def handle_format_greeting():
    span_ctx = opentracing.tracer.extract(
        opentracing.Format.HTTP_HEADERS,
        request.headers,
    )
    with opentracing.tracer.start_active_span(
        '/formatGreeting',
        child_of=span_ctx,
        tags={tags.SPAN_KIND: tags.SPAN_KIND_RPC_SERVER},
    ) as scope:
        ...
```

The final code, with all modifications, is available in package exercise4b.

Exercise summary

In this exercise, we have divided the formerly monolithic Hello application into three microservices. We discussed the inject/extract mechanisms provided by the OpenTracing APIs for propagating tracing metadata between processes in a variety of network protocols. We used OpenTracing-recommended standard tags to enhance the client and server spans with additional semantic annotations.

Exercise 5 – using baggage

In the previous exercise, we implemented a distributed context propagation mechanism in our microservices. It is easy to see that neither in-process nor inter-process context propagation mechanisms are very specific to distributed tracing metadata: they are generic enough to pass other types of metadata throughout the call graph of a distributed execution. The OpenTracing authors recognized that fact and defined another general-purpose container for arbitrary metadata called "baggage." The term was originally coined by Prof. Rodrigo Fonseca, one of the authors of the X-Trace system. The OpenTracing baggage is an arbitrary collection of key/value pairs that are defined and used by the application itself. In *Chapter 10, Distributed Context Propagation*, we will discuss various uses of this mechanism. In this exercise, we want to try it out in the Hello application.

One of the biggest advantages of baggage is that it can be used to pass data through the call graph without changing the APIs of the microservices. Needless to say, this should only be used for legitimate use cases, not as an excuse to cheat your way out of designing proper service APIs. In the case of the Hello application, it could be considered as an example of such cheating, but we will be doing it for demonstration only.

Specifically, our Formatter service always returns a string that starts with the word "Hello." We are going to build an Easter egg that will allow us to change the greeting word by specifying it as baggage to the request. The Jaeger instrumentation libraries recognize a special HTTP header that can look like this: `jaeger-baggage: k1=v1, k2=v2, ....` It is useful for manually providing some baggage items for testing purposes, which we can exploit. Alternatively, the baggage can always be explicitly set on the span inside the application by using the `Span.SetBaggageItem()` API.

In this exercise, we will make a simple change to the `FormatGreeting()` function in the Formatter service to read the greeting word from the baggage item named `greeting`. If that baggage item is not set, then we will continue to default to the word "Hello." With no other changes elsewhere in the application, we will be able to run queries like this:

```
$ curl -H 'jaeger-baggage: greeting=Bonjour' \
        http://localhost:8080/sayHello/Kevin
Bonjour, Kevin!
```

Using baggage in Go

```go
func FormatGreeting(
    ctx context.Context,
    name, title, description string,
) string {
    span, ctx := opentracing.StartSpanFromContext(
        ctx,
        "format-greeting",
    )
    defer span.Finish()

    greeting := span.BaggageItem("greeting")
    if greeting == "" {
        greeting = "Hello"
    }
    response := greeting + ", "
    ...
}
```

Using baggage in Java

```java
@GetMapping("/formatGreeting")
public String formatGreeting(
        @RequestParam String name,
        @RequestParam String title,
        @RequestParam String description,
        HttpServletRequest request)
{
    Scope scope = startServerSpan("/formatGreeting", request);
    try {
        String greeting = tracer
            .activeSpan().getBaggageItem("greeting");
        if (greeting == null) {
            greeting = "Hello";
        }
        String response = greeting + ", ";
        ...
        return response;
    finally {
        scope.close();
    }
}
```

Using baggage in Python

```python
def format_greeting(name, title, description):
    with opentracing.tracer.start_active_span(
        'format-greeting',
    ) as scope:
        greeting = scope.span.get_baggage_item('greeting') or 'Hello'
        greeting += ', '
        if title:
            greeting += title + ' '
        greeting += name + '!'
        if description:
            greeting += ' ' + description
        return greeting
```

Exercise summary

This exercise demonstrates the use of OpenTracing baggage to transparently pass values throughout the whole distributed call graph, without any changes to the application APIs. It is a toy example only, and we will discuss serious usage of baggage in *Chapter 10, Distributed Context Propagation*.

Exercise 6 – auto-instrumentation

In the previous exercises, we added a lot of manual instrumentation to our application. One may get the impression that it always takes so much work to instrument code for distributed tracing. In reality, things are a lot better thanks to a large amount of already-created, open source, vendor-neutral instrumentation for popular frameworks that exists in the OpenTracing project under its community contributions organization: https://github.com/opentracing-contrib/meta. In this exercise, we will explore some of those modules to minimize the amount of manual, boiler-plate instrumentation in the Hello application.

Open source instrumentation in Go

Due to its "no magic" design principle, with Go it is a bit tougher to get away from explicit code instrumentation, compared to other languages. In this exercise, we will focus our attention on the HTTP server and client instrumentation. We will be using one of the contributed libraries, github.com/opentracing-contrib/go-stdlib, that contains a module nethttp, with functions that allow wrapping the HTTP server and client with OpenTracing middleware. For the server side, we define a function ListenAndServe() in a new internal package othttp:

```
package othttp

import (
    "log"
    "net/http"

    "github.com/opentracing-contrib/go-stdlib/nethttp"
    "github.com/opentracing/opentracing-go"
)


// ListenAndServe starts an instrumented server with a single
endpoint.
func ListenAndServe(hostPort string, endpoint string) {
    mw := nethttp.Middleware(
        opentracing.GlobalTracer(),
        http.DefaultServeMux,
        nethttp.OperationNameFunc(func(r *http.Request) string {
            return "HTTP " + r.Method + ":" + endpoint
        }),
    )

    log.Print("Listening on http://" + hostPort)
    log.Fatal(http.ListenAndServe(hostPort, mw))
}
```

`nethttp.Middleware()` takes care of extracting metadata from an incoming request and starting a new span. This allows us to simplify our main and handler functions, for example, in `hello.go`:

```
func main() {
    tracer, closer := tracing.Init("go-6-hello")
    defer closer.Close()
    opentracing.SetGlobalTracer(tracer)

    http.HandleFunc("/sayHello/", handleSayHello)
    othttp.ListenAndServe(":8080", "/sayHello")
}

func handleSayHello(w http.ResponseWriter, r *http.Request) {
    span := opentracing.SpanFromContext(r.Context())

    name := strings.TrimPrefix(r.URL.Path, "/sayHello/")
    greeting, err := SayHello(r.Context(), name)
    if err != nil {
        span.SetTag("error", true)
```

```
            span.LogFields(otlog.Error(err))
            http.Error(w, err.Error(), http.StatusInternalServerError)
            return
    }

    span.SetTag("response", greeting)
    w.Write([]byte(greeting))
}
```

We no longer create any spans, but we still have some OpenTracing code. Some of it is unavoidable, since it's completely custom logic, like setting the `response` tag on the span. The error handling code is a bit unfortunate, as it's completely boilerplate and we would rather avoid writing it (of course, it should be encapsulated in a helper function in a larger code base). However, it's not completely avoidable, due to the way Go defines the HTTP API, which does not include any error handling facilities. If we used some more advanced RPC framework than the standard library, that is, something that actually allows our handlers to return an error (for example, gRPC), then this code could also be encapsulated in a standard instrumentation.

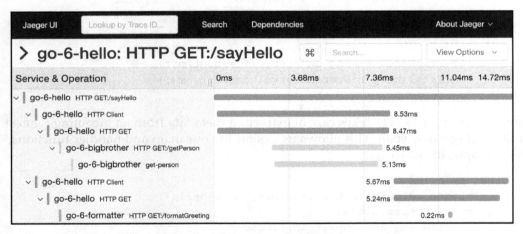

Figure 4.6: An example trace from Go after replacing custom
instrumentation with github.com/opentracing-contrib/go-stdlib

We use the `nethttp` module to instrument the outbound HTTP calls as well, which also reduces some boilerplate code. You will find the complete code in the `exercise6` package.

Auto-instrumentation in Java

The auto-instrumentation exercise for Java is especially interesting because we can remove *all instrumentation*, and still get a very detailed trace showing all HTTP and database calls.

This is in part due to how the Spring framework is designed, since it allows us to provide it with instrumentation classes simply by adding a jar file to the class path. All we need to do is to uncomment the dependency in the pom.xml file:

```
<dependency>
    <groupId>io.opentracing.contrib</groupId>
    <artifactId>opentracing-spring-cloud-starter</artifactId>
    <version>0.1.13</version>
</dependency>
```

After that, try running the code from package exercise6 (in separate Terminal windows):

```
$ ./mvnw spring-boot:run -Dmain.class=exercise6.bigbrother.BBApp
$ ./mvnw spring-boot:run -Dmain.class=exercise6.formatter.FApp
$ ./mvnw spring-boot:run -Dmain.class=exercise6.HelloApp
$ curl http://localhost:8080/sayHello/Gru
Hello, Felonius Gru! Where are the minions?%
```

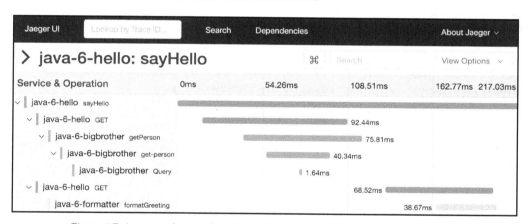

Figure 4.7: An example trace from Java after removing all custom instrumentation
and adding opentracing-spring-cloud-starter jar

The trace still looks very detailed, including our only remaining manual instrumentation for the get-person span in the Big Brother service. The server-side spans that represent the HTTP handlers get the name derived from name of the handler method, that is, the route /sayHello/{name} is handled by the method sayHello() and results in the span name sayHello.

The outbound HTTP requests, on the other hand, have a very generic span name, GET (that is, just the HTTP method), which is not surprising since the client does not really know how the server calls its endpoints, and the automatic instrumentation only has the target URL, which, as we discussed previously, cannot be used as an operation name due to potentially high cardinality.

The database query is represented by the span named Query. If we expand that span, we will find a number of useful span tags added by the automatic instrumentation, including the database query.

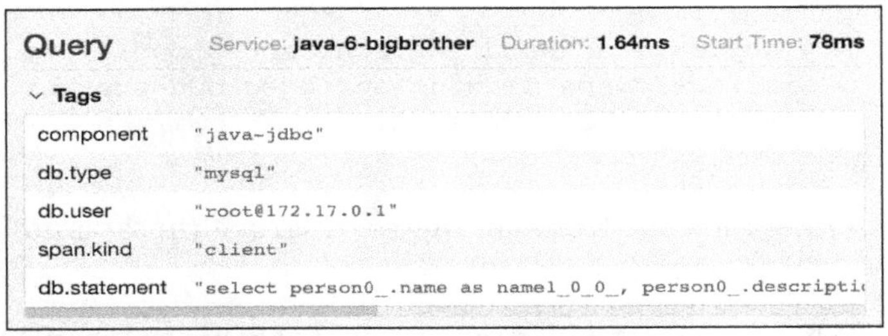

Figure 4.8: A number of useful tags added to the database query span by the automatic instrumentation

Not too bad for a completely automatic, near zero-touch instrumentation! However, you may have noticed something peculiar about that trace: the spans representing HTTP endpoints in the downstream microservices end later than their parent spans. I have rerun the tests several times and always got the same results, while the traces from *Exercise 5 - using baggage* that used manual instrumentation always looked "normal." One possible explanation for this is that the automatic instrumentation may be done at a lower level in the Spring framework, where the spans are finished after the server has already sent the response to the client, that is, during some request pipeline clean-up performed by the framework.

This style of instrumentation is somewhat similar to the so-called "agent-based instrumentation" often provided by the commercial APM vendors. Agent-based instrumentation often works by augmenting the code of the application or libraries using various techniques, like monkey patching and bytecode rewriting, thus requiring no changes to the application.

Our version is similarly nearly zero-touch, but we still had code in the App classes to instantiate the Jaeger tracer. It could be made completely zero-touch (not counting adding the jar to the class path) by using a traceresolver module (https://github.com/opentracing-contrib/java-tracerresolver) that allows tracers to implement an API that automatically registers the tracer as a global tracer. Then, the global tracer can be automatically registered as a Spring bean by using another module from OpenTracing: https://github.com/opentracing-contrib/java-spring-tracer-configuration.

Some people in the Java community may consider the traceresolver approach to be an anti-pattern, since it creates a dependency on a global variable. An alternative, specifically for the Spring framework, is to use another module, https://github.com/opentracing-contrib/java-spring-jaeger, which exports Jaeger configuration to Spring and provides a tracer bean to the application. I leave this as an exercise to you to try out these modules.

Auto-instrumentation in Python

In this exercise, we will be using two open source libraries that provide almost automatic instrumentation of many parts of our application. The first one is the instrumentation for Flask from `https://github.com/opentracing-contrib/python-flask`. While it is not fully automatic, it allows us to install a middleware for the Flask application with one line (two if you count the `import` statement):

```
from flask_opentracing import FlaskTracer

app = Flask('py-6-hello')
init_tracer('py-6-hello')
flask_tracer = FlaskTracer(opentracing.tracer, True, app)
```

Unfortunately, at the time of writing the library has not been upgraded to support the scope manager API that was only recently released for Python. As a result, even though the framework does create a span for every inbound request, it does not set it as the active span. To address that, I have included a simple adapter function in `lib/tracing.py`:

```
def flask_to_scope(flask_tracer, request):
    return opentracing.tracer.scope_manager.activate(
        flask_tracer.get_span(request),
        False,
    )
```

Using the Flask `request` object, we ask `FlaskTracer` to give us the span it created for the current request. We then activate that span through the OpenTracing scope manager but pass `False` as the last argument, indicating that we do not want the span to be finished once the scope is closed because `FlaskTracer` will take care of finishing the span it started. With this helper function in place, we can replace rather verbose instrumentation in our HTTP handlers with a single line:

```
@app.route("/getPerson/<name>")
def get_person_http(name):
    with flask_to_scope(flask_tracer, request) as scope:
        person = Person.get(name)
        ...
```

Let's go ahead and make the same change in the other two microservices. Once the `flask_opentracing` library is upgraded to work with scope manager and active span, even this call to `flask_to_scope()` will not be necessary: the span will be available automatically. If we want to get access to it, without having the `scope` variable, we can always get it from the tracer via the `active_span` property:

```
opentracing.tracer.active_span.set_tag('response', resp)
```

The second library we want to use is `opentracing_instrumentation` by Uber: `https://github.com/uber-common/opentracing-python-instrumentation`.

This library has a submodule called `client_hooks` that uses the monkey-patching technique (that is, dynamically rewriting well-known library functions) to add tracing to a number of modules, such as `urllib2`, `requests`, `SQLAlchemy`, `redis` (client), and so on. Other than activating this library in the main module, it requires no changes to the source code of our application:

```
from opentracing_instrumentation.client_hooks import install_all_
patches

app = Flask('py-6-hello')
init_tracer('py-6-hello')
install_all_patches()
```

That means we can remove our manual instrumentation of HTTP requests in the `_get()` function to be as simple as:

```
def _get(url, params=None):
    r = requests.get(url, params=params)
    assert r.status_code == 200
    return r.text
```

It also means we can get a deeper instrumentation of SQL queries that were hidden from us by the ORM in SQL Alchemy. At the same time, if we still want to keep some of our custom instrumentation, like the extra span in the `get_person()` function, we can easily do it and both included libraries are compatible with that.

Figure 4.9: An example trace from Python after replacing custom instrumentation with Flask-OpenTracing and Uber's opentracing-python-instrumentation

After applying these changes (which can be found in module `exercise6`), we can still get detailed traces similar to the one in the preceding screenshot. We can see that the auto-instrumentation added a span called "SQL SELECT". If we inspect that span, we will see that one of its tags includes the complete SQL query executed by the ORM framework:

```
SELECT people.name AS people_name, people.title AS people_title,
people.description AS people_description
FROM people
WHERE people.name = %(param_1)s
```

Exercise 7 – extra credit

This exercise does not have any specific code examples or even recommendations. Instead, it's an invitation to go and explore the large amount of community-contributed instrumentation libraries listed in the OpenTracing Registry [5]. Check whether a framework you are using in your application is already supported there and give it a try. If it's not supported, maybe use the skills you acquired by reading this chapter to contribute a new module. Alternatively, if you know the developers of the framework, ask them to add OpenTracing instrumentation and enable tracing in their framework.

Another option to explore for "extra credit" is trying to use the same Hello application with a different implementation of OpenTracing. You can find OpenTracing-compatible libraries for Zipkin, and for other tracing systems [5], both free and commercial. The only places that need changing in the exercises are the `InitTracer` functions.

Summary

In this chapter, we talked about tracing instrumentation. We discussed common tasks that need to be addressed by the instrumentation, from simple annotations to in-process context propagation, to using inject/extract trace points to transfer distributed context across processes.

We took a brief detour and looked at using the baggage API for passing additional metadata alongside the distributed call graph.

We finished with a review of using off-the-shelf open source instrumentation for popular libraries, which can be applied with minimal changes to your application, from a few lines of code to literally zero changes. Best of all, all the instrumentation we reviewed was completely vendor-agnostic. We used it with Jaeger tracers, but they can be easily swapped for any other OpenTracing-compatible tracers.

In the next chapter, we will look at a more advanced case of instrumentation involving applications with asynchronous behavior: either internal-using futures or external-using messaging between microservices.

References

1. The OpenTracing Project: `http://opentracing.io/`.

2. Code examples: `https://github.com/PacktPublishing/Mastering-Distributed-Tracing/`.

3. The Jaeger Project: `https://jaegertracing.io/`.

4. The OpenTracing Semantic Conventions: `https://github.com/opentracing/specification#semantic-conventions`.

5. Inventory of OpenTracing-compatible tracers and instrumentation libraries: `https://opentracing.io/registry/`.

5
Instrumentation of Asynchronous Applications

In *Chapter 4, Instrumentation Basics with OpenTracing*, we reviewed the basics of instrumenting a microservices-based application for distributed tracing using the OpenTracing APIs. If you went through all the exercises, you deserve a medal! The Hello application was intentionally very simple and involved only blocking synchronous calls between microservices.

In this chapter, we will attempt to instrument an online chat application, Tracing Talk, which uses asynchronous messaging-based interactions between microservices built on top of Apache Kafka. We will see how metadata context can be passed through messaging systems using the same OpenTracing primitives we already discussed, and how causal relationships between spans can be modeled differently than in the plain RPC scenarios.

We will continue using the OpenTracing API, even though the same instrumentation principles would apply to other tracing APIs, such as Zipkin's Brave and OpenCensus. Since the chat application is slightly more complex, we will only look at implementing it in Java, with the Spring framework.

After completing this chapter, you will have the knowledge and understanding to apply instrumentation to your own asynchronous applications.

Prerequisites

In order to run the Tracing Talk chat application, we need to deploy a number of infrastructure dependencies:

- Apache Kafka, as the messaging platform
- Redis, as the backend store for the chat messages
- Apache Zookeeper, used by Kafka
- Jaeger tracing backend to collect and analyze the traces

This section provides instructions on setting up the environment to run the chat application.

Project source code

The examples can be found in the Chapter05 directory of the book's source code repository on GitHub. Please refer to *Chapter 4, Instrumentation Basics with OpenTracing*, for instructions on how to download it, then switch to the Chapter05 directory to run the examples.

The source code of the application is organized in the following structure:

```
Mastering-Distributed-Tracing/
  Chapter05/
    exercise1/
      chat-api/
      giphy-service/
      storage-service/
    lib/
    webapp/
    pom.xml
```

The application is composed of three microservices, defined in the submodule `exercise1`. We will review their roles in the following section. The microservices are using some shared components and classes defined in the module `lib`. The `webapp` directory contains the source code for the JavaScript frontend of the chat application; however, the static HTML assets it generates are already precompiled and checked in under `webapp/public`, so we will not need to build them.

Java development environment

Similar to the examples in *Chapter 4, Instrumentation Basics with OpenTracing*, we will need a JDK 8 or higher. The Maven wrappers are checked in and will download Maven as needed. The Maven project in `pom.xml` is set up as a multi-module project, so make sure to run `install` to install the dependencies in Maven's local repository:

```
$ ./mvnw install
[... skip a lot of Maven logs ...]
[INFO] Reactor Summary:
[INFO]
[INFO] Tracing Talk 0.0.1-SNAPSHOT ........... SUCCESS [  0.420 s]
[INFO] lib ................................... SUCCESS [  1.575 s]
[INFO] exercise1 ............................ SUCCESS [  0.018 s]
[INFO] chat-api-1 ........................... SUCCESS [  0.701 s]
[INFO] giphy-service-1 ...................... SUCCESS [  0.124 s]
[INFO] storage-service-1 0.0.1-SNAPSHOT ...... SUCCESS [  0.110 s]
[INFO] ------------------------------------------------------------
[INFO] BUILD SUCCESS
[INFO] ------------------------------------------------------------
```

Kafka, Zookeeper, Redis, and Jaeger

Downloading and installing each of these systems is quite a bit of work. Rather than running them all independently, I provided provided a Docker Compose configuration that spins up all the required dependencies as Docker containers.

Please refer to the Docker documentation (`https://docs.docker.com/install/`) on how to install Docker on your machine. The `docker-compose` tool might be installed along with it, or you can install it manually (`https://docs.docker.com/compose/install/`). We can start all the dependencies with `docker-compose`:

```
$ docker-compose up
Starting chapter-06_kafka_1                ... done
Starting chapter-06_jaeger-all-in-one_1 ... done
Starting chapter-06_redis_1                ... done
Starting chapter-06_zookeeper_1            ... done
[... lots and lots of logs ...]
```

You should leave this running in a separate Terminal, although, if you want to run everything in the background, you can pass the `--detach` flag: `docker-compose up --detach`. To check that all dependencies have started successfully, run the `docker ps` or `docker-compose ps` command. You should see four processes in the Up state, for example:

```
$ docker ps | cut -c1-55,100-120
CONTAINER ID        IMAGE                          STATUS
b6723ee0b9e7        jaegertracing/all-in-one:1.6   Up 6 minutes
278eee5c1e13        confluentinc/cp-zookeeper:5.0.0-2   Up 6 minutes
84bd8d0e1456        confluentinc/cp-kafka:5.0.0-2   Up 6 minutes
60d721a94418        redis:alpine                   Up 6 minutes
```

If you prefer to install and run each dependency without Docker, the Tracing Talk application should still work without any additional changes, but the installation instructions are outside of the scope of this book.

Once you are finished with this chapter, you may want to stop all the dependencies by killing the `docker-compose` command, or, if you detached it from the Terminal, by executing:

```
$ docker-compose down
```

The Tracing Talk chat application

Before we talk about instrumentation, let's review the chat application. It was adopted from a demo (`https://github.com/saada/tracing-kafka`) presented at the inaugural Distributed Tracing NYC meetup [1] by Mahmoud (Moody) Saada, a site reliability engineer at machine learning company Agolo.

Once the application is running, we will be able to access its web frontend at `http://localhost:8080/`. Each visitor is given a random screen name, such as **Guest-1324**, which can be changed using the **Edit** button. The chat functionality is exceedingly basic: the new messages appear at the bottom, with the name of the sender and a relative timestamp. One can enter a message in the form of **/giphy <topic>**, which causes the application to make a call to the `giphy.com` REST API and display a random image on the specified topic.

Figure 5.1: The frontend view of the Tracing Talk chat application

The application consists of several frontend and backend components, depicted in the architecture diagram in *Figure 5.2*:

- The JavaScript frontend is implemented with React (`https://reactjs.org/`). The static assets are served by the `chat-api` microservice running on port `8080`. The frontend polls for all messages every couple of seconds, which is not the most efficient way of implementing the chat application, but keeps it simple to allow us to focus on the backend messaging.

- The `chat-api` microservice receives API calls from the frontend to record new messages or to retrieve all already-accumulated messages. It publishes new messages to a Kafka topic, as a way of asynchronous communication with the other microservices. It reads the accumulated messages from Redis, where they are stored by the `storage-service` microservice.

- The `storage-service` microservice reads messages from Kafka and stores them in Redis in a set.

- The `giphy-service` microservice also reads messages from Kafka and checks whether they start with a **/giphy <topic>** string. The internal message structure has an `image` field and if that field is empty, the service makes a remote HTTP call to the `giphy.com` REST API, querying for 10 images related to the **<topic>**. Then the service picks one of them randomly, stores its URL in the `image` field of the message, and publishes the message to the same Kafka topic, where it will be again picked up by the `storage-service` microservice and updated in Redis.

- The Apache Zookeeper is used internally by Kafka to keep the state of the topics and subscriptions.

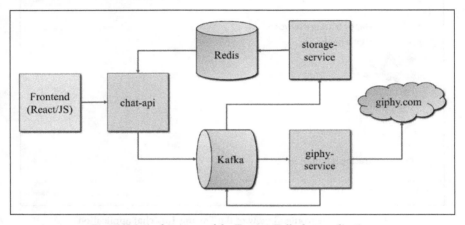

Figure 5.2: Architecture of the Tracing Talk chat application

Implementation

We will review the implementation and source code of the main components of the application now.

The lib module

The `lib` module contains several classes that are used by all three microservices. Some of them are simple value objects (`AppId` and `Message`), while others are Spring configuration beans that register other beans (`KafkaConfig` and `RedisConfig`), and the rest (`GiphyService`, `KafkaService`, and `RedisService`) are in-process services encapsulating the functionality for communicating with `giphy.com`, Kafka, and Redis respectively.

AppId

The `AppId` class defines a bean that exposes the name of the current service. It is created in the main `App` classes in all three services, for example:

```
@Bean
public AppId appId() {
    return new AppId("chat-api");
}
```

The service name is used by `KafkaConfig` to compose a client ID string used by the Kafka driver.

Message

The `Message` class is a value object that defines the structure of chat messages used by the overall application application:

```
public class Message {
    public String event;
    public String id;
    public String author;
    public String message;
    public String room;
    public String date;
    public String image;
}
```

It has an `init()` method that is called by the `chat-api` service when receiving a new message from the frontend. It is used to populate some of the metadata in the message, such as the unique ID and the timestamp.

KafkaConfig and KafkaService

The `KafkaConfig` class is a Spring configuration that exposes two beans: a Kafka template, used to send messages, and a listener container factory, used to receive Kafka messages and execute application-specific handlers. The `KafkaService` class is a helper used by the other microservices to send messages to Kafka, and to start the OpenTracing spans in the message handlers. We will discuss the details of the instrumentation a bit later.

RedisConfig and RedisService

Similar to the Kafka classes, the `RedisConfig` class defines the beans for communicating with Redis, and the `RedisService` class is a business helper to store and retrieve messages using the `Message` class.

GiphyService

The `GiphyService` class is a helper that encapsulates the logic of calling the `giphy.com` REST API and retrieving the URL of one of the returned 10 images at random. It uses Spring's `RestTemplate`, which is auto-instrumented with OpenTracing, to make HTTP calls.

The chat-api service

The `chat-api` service is composed of two classes: `App`, which contains the main function and populates the `AppId` bean, and `ChatController`, which implements the REST API. Spring automatically serves the static HTML assets for the frontend because we include them in the artefact in the module's `pom.xml` file:

```
<build>
    <resources>
        <resource>
            <directory>../../webapp</directory>
            <includes>
                <include>public/**</include>
            </includes>
        </resource>
    </resources>
</build>
```

The controller defines two main methods: `getMessages()` and `postMessage()`. The `getMessages()` method implements the request handler for HTTP GET requests to /message endpoint. It uses `RedisService` to retrieve all currently stored messages for the chat room and return them as JSON to the frontend. Note that the current implementation of the frontend does not allow the creation of different chat rooms, so it is always defaulted to `"lobby"`:

```
@RequestMapping(value = "/message", method = RequestMethod.GET)
public @ResponseBody List<Message> index(
    @RequestParam(value = "room", defaultValue = "lobby")
    String room
        )throws Exception {
    List<Message> messages = redis.getMessages(room);
    System.out.println("Retrieved " + messages.size()
        + " messages.");
    return messages;
}
```

The second method, `postMessages()`, handles HTTP POST requests to the same endpoint. It reads the message JSON from the request body, calls `msg.init()` to initialize some metadata, and sends the message to Kafka using the `KafkaService` helper.

```
@RequestMapping(value = "/message",
    consumes = { "application/json" },
    produces = { MediaType.APPLICATION_JSON_VALUE },
    method = RequestMethod.POST)
public ResponseEntity<Message> postMessage(
        @RequestBody Message msg
) throws Exception {
    msg.init();
    System.out.println("Received message: " + msg);

    kafka.sendMessage(msg);
    System.out.println("Message sent sync to Kafka");
    return new ResponseEntity<Message>(msg, HttpStatus.OK);
}
```

The actual code of this method, in the source code repository, looks slightly more complex because it allows choosing between the `kafka.sendMessage()` and `kafka.sendMessageAsync()` methods of the helper, based on the environment variable. We will come back to that later in this chapter. If we run the service with default parameters, it will use the synchronous method that we showed in the preceding listing.

The storage-service microservice

The `storage-service` microservice has a single class, `App`, which implements both the main function and the Kafka message handler, which, in its simplest form, looks like this:

```
@KafkaListener(topics = "message")
public void process(@Payload Message message,
        @Headers MessageHeaders headers) throws Exception
{
    System.out.println("Received message: " + message.message);
    redis.addMessage(message);
    System.out.println("Added message to room.");
}
```

Once again, the code in the repository looks slightly different because it contains extra statements to create OpenTracing span and scope, which we will discuss later.

The giphy-service microservice

Similar to the `storage-service`, the `giphy-service` microservice is implemented in a single `App` class that contains the main function and the Kafka message handler. The handler checks whether the message has no image attached to it and whether the text in the message starts with the string `/giphy`, and if so, it reads the remainder of the string as a topic used to query the `giphy.com` REST API, via the `query()` method of `GiphyService`. The service then stores the URL of the image in the `message.image` field and sends it back to Kafka, where it will be picked up by the `storage-service` microservice again and updated in Redis. Notice that the `giphy-service` microservice will also receive that updated message again but will not do anything with it, since the message will already have its `image` field populated:

```
@KafkaListener(topics = "message")
public void process(
        @Payload Message message,
        @Headers MessageHeaders headers
) throws Exception {
    System.out.println("Received message: " + message.message);
    if (message.image == null &&
            message.message.trim().startsWith("/giphy")) {
        String query = message.message.split("/giphy")[1].trim();
        System.out.println("Giphy requested: " + query);
        message.image = giphy.query(query);
        if (message.image != null) {
            kafka.sendMessage(message);
            System.out.println("Updated message, url=" +
                message.image);
        }
    }
}
```

Once again, we omitted the tracing code from the preceding listing.

Running the application

Assuming you followed the *Prerequisites* section, you should already have Kafka, Redis, and Jaeger running as Docker containers. To start the rest of the components of the Tracing Talk application, we need to run them manually using the provided `Makefile` (make sure you have run `./mvnw install` first). In separate Terminal windows, run these three commands:

```
$ make storage
$ make giphy
$ make chatapi
```

They will all produce a lot of logs. The `chat-api` service will log a message **Started App in x.xx seconds** once it is ready. The `storage-service` and `giphy-service microservices` also log this message, but you may not notice it because it is followed by the logs from the Kafka consumer. We have observed that those services are ready when they log a line like this:

```
2018-xx-xx 16:43:53.023  INFO 6144 --- [ntainer#0-0-C-1]
o.s.k.l.KafkaMessageListenerContainer   : partitions assigned:
[message-0]
```

Here `[message-0]` refers to partition 0 of the `message` topic used by the application.

When all three microservices are ready, access the frontend at `http://localhost:8080/`. Try sending a message with a `/giphy` command, for example, `/giphy hello`. You may observe peculiar behavior, where the message will appear in the chat, then disappear, then appear again, and then the image will show up, all with delays of about one second. This is due to the polling nature of the frontend, that is, what might be happening in that instance is the following:

- The frontend sends a message to the `chat-api` service. The service writes it to Kafka and returns it back to the frontend, which displays it in the chat panel.

- In a second or so, the frontend polls the `chat-api` service for all current messages and may not get the latest message back, since it hasn't been processed yet by the `storage-service` microservice. The frontend removes it from the screen.

- The `storage-service` microservice receives the message from Kafka and stores it in Redis. The next poll from the frontend picks it up and displays it again.

- Finally, the `giphy-service` microservice updates the image in the message, and on the next poll the frontend displays the message with the image.

This flip-flopping behavior is not something we expect to see in a production application, so there is room for improvement, namely by using a persistent WebSocket connection between the frontend and the `chat-api` service. However, it does provide a useful illustration of the asynchronous nature of the application. You may not always notice this behavior; I have observed it most often after a cold start of the microservices, due to class loading, establishing connections to other servers, and so on.

Observing traces

Once the application is running and you have sent at least one message with the `/giphy` command, we can check how it looks in the Jaeger UI. The **Services** dropdown in Jaeger should be showing the names of our three microservices:

chat-api-1, **storage-service-1**, and **giphy-service-1**. We want to search for traces that include **chat-api-1**. However, that service produces many different spans, so we also want to filter on the operation name **postMessage** in the **Operation** dropdown.

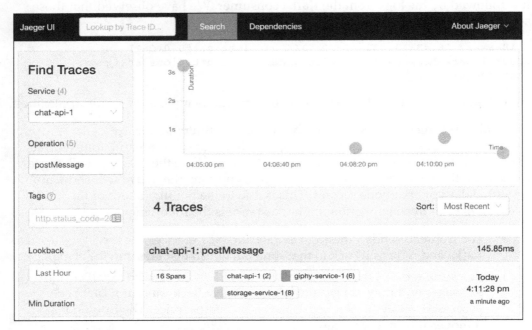

Figure 5.3: Searching for a trace for the postMessage endpoint in the chat-api service

If the trace was for a message that contained a /giphy command, we should see all three services in it. We do not see, however, any spans from Kafka or Redis, which is expected. We have encountered this behavior already in *Chapter 4, Instrumentation Basics with OpenTracing*, where we also saw no spans from the MySQL database. The reason is because all these third-party technologies are not yet instrumented with OpenTracing, and the only spans we are able to observe are the client-side spans from the application when it communicates to these backends. We hope the situation will change in the future.

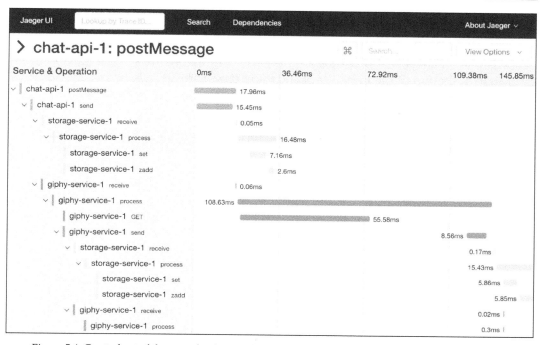

Figure 5.4: Gantt chart of the trace for the request to the postMessage endpoint in the chat-api service

If we go to the Gantt chart trace view for our request, we will see more details about all the interactions that occurred in the application, and how much time they took. The chat-api service handled the POST request by sending the message to Kafka (the send span).

Once the message was published, both storage-service and giphy-service received it at almost simultaneously, indicated by the receive spans. The storage-service microservice relatively quickly stored it in Redis, while the giphy-service microservice took a while to make a query to the giphy.com REST API, and then resend the updated message to Kafka.

The update was again received by both `storage-service` and `giphy-service`, and processed much quicker this time. These final spans are rather short when compared to the rest of the trace that it's difficult to understand their timeline. Fortunately, the Jaeger UI provides a time selector functionality via the trace mini-map at the top of the screen (not shown in the pictures), which can use to zoom in on the last portion of the trace by dragging the mouse horizontally around the area of interest.

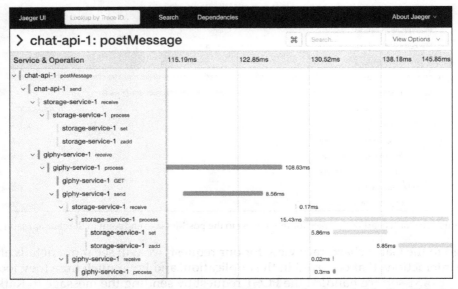

Figure 5.5: The Gantt chart of the same trace as in Figure 5.4 but zoomed to the end of the first Giphy interaction.

In this zoomed-in view, we see that the `storage-service` microservice again received the message and stored it in Redis. The `giphy-service` microservice also received the message, but did not make the REST API call, since the message already contained the image URL.

Sometimes the `send` span in the `giphy-service` looks a bit peculiar because it extends beyond the end time of its parent span `process`, and even beyond the time when the `storage-service` received that sent message from Kafka. We have seen this behavior already with Spring instrumentation in *Chapter 4, Instrumentation Basics with OpenTracing*. Without going deeper, with more instrumentation, the best guess is that this is caused by the asynchronous behavior of the `send()` method in the Kafka template, which may be closing the span in another thread after the message has already been produced to Kafka and even consumed by the other services. This is not an unusual occurrence for asynchronous applications and only emphasizes how difficult it is to analyze their behavior without a tool like distributed tracing.

Instrumenting with OpenTracing

Now that we have run the application and got a pretty-looking trace, it is time to get to the main point of this chapter and discuss how it was instrumented to achieve this. As we discussed earlier, the primary goal of the OpenTracing project is to provide an API that allows for the creation of open source instrumentation for other open source projects and frameworks. In the Tracing Talk application, we rely heavily on such open source instrumentation for Kafka, Redis, and the Spring framework, to the point that there is very little manual instrumentation in the code, and that small amount is only due to the relative immaturity of the respective instrumentation libraries, rather than a fundamental limitation. We also made this example completely agnostic to which tracing library we are using. Unlike *Chapter 4, Instrumentation Basics with OpenTracing*, where we had explicit code instantiating the Jaeger tracer, this time we are using the "tracer resolver" mechanism, which automatically instantiates whichever tracer can be found on the class path.

Spring instrumentation

Similar to *Chapter 4, Instrumentation Basics with OpenTracing*, we can use the `opentracing-spring-cloud-starter` library to automatically enable tracing instrumentation in many Spring components, including the `RestTemplate` class, as long as the Spring container has a bean of type `io.opentracing.Tracer`:

```
<dependency>
    <groupId>io.opentracing.contrib</groupId>
    <artifactId>opentracing-spring-cloud-starter</artifactId>
    <version>0.1.13</version>
</dependency>
```

Tracer resolver

Tracer resolver (`https://github.com/opentracing-contrib/java-tracerresolver`) is a library that supports instantiating the tracer from the class path using Java's Service Loader mechanism. In order to make such a tracer available in the Spring container, we used another artefact, `opentracing-spring-tracer-configuration-starter` (it transitively pulls the `tracerresolver` dependency):

```
<dependency>
    <groupId>io.opentracing.contrib</groupId>
    <artifactId>
        opentracing-spring-tracer-configuration-starter
    </artifactId>
    <version>0.1.0</version>
</dependency>
```

```
<dependency>
    <groupId>io.jaegertracing</groupId>
    <artifactId>jaeger-client</artifactId>
    <version>0.31.0</version>
</dependency>
```

By including the `jaeger-client` dependency, we make the Jaeger tracer factory available on the class path to the `tracerresolver` module. The `opentracing-spring-tracer-configuration-starter` module then binds the instantiated tracer from `tracerresolver` to the Spring context. There are other ways of achieving the same result. For example, the `https://github.com/opentracing-contrib/java-spring-jaeger` library avoids the singleton-based `tracerresolver` approach and integrates Jaeger configuration directly with Spring. However, `tracerresolver` is a more general mechanism that works with other frameworks, not just Spring, without requiring the authors of the tracer implementation to write integration with multiple frameworks.

Since we no longer write any code to configure the Jaeger tracer, we are using environment variables to pass some parameters, which is done in the `Makefile`. For example, we start the `storage-service` microservice with the following parameters passed to Maven via the `-D` switch:

```
JAEGER_SAMPLER_TYPE=const
JAEGER_SAMPLER_PARAM=1
JAEGER_SERVICE_NAME=storage-service-1
```

Once this is all done, we can get access to the tracer, if we need to, by declaring an auto-wired dependency, for example, in the `KafkaConfig` class:

```
import io.opentracing.Tracer;

@Configuration
public class KafkaConfig {

    @Autowired
    Tracer tracer;

    . . .
}
```

Redis instrumentation

For the purposes of the Tracing Talk application, Redis is just another service we call, similar to calling the `giphy.com` API with Spring's `RestTemplate`. Unfortunately, the OpenTracing instrumentation for Spring does not yet support `RedisTemplate` instrumentation.

Therefore, we are using one of the Redis clients directly, namely
`io.lattuce:lettuce-core`. Fortunately, there is already an OpenTracing
library, `java-redis-client`, that provides instrumentation for this Redis client:

```
<dependency>
    <groupId>io.opentracing.contrib</groupId>
    <artifactId>opentracing-redis-lettuce</artifactId>
    <version>0.0.5</version>
</dependency>
```

With this dependency, we are able to create a `RedisCommands` bean that
includes tracing instrumentation, by wrapping the Redis connection with
the `TracingStatefulRedisConnection` decorator:

```
import io.lettuce.core.RedisClient;
import io.lettuce.core.api.StatefulRedisConnection;
import io.lettuce.core.api.sync.RedisCommands;
import io.opentracing.Tracer;
import io.opentracing.contrib.redis.lettuce.
TracingStatefulRedisConnection;

@Configuration
public class RedisConfig {
    @Autowired Tracer tracer;

    @Bean
    public StatefulRedisConnection<String, String> redisConn() {
        RedisClient client = RedisClient.create("redis://localhost");
        return new TracingStatefulRedisConnection<>(
                client.connect(), tracer, false);
    }

    @Autowired StatefulRedisConnection<String, String> redisConn;

    @Bean
    public RedisCommands<String, String> redisClientSync() {
        return redisConn.sync();
    }
}
```

One remaining downside of this approach is that the connection created by
calling `client.connect()` is explicitly of type `StatefulRedisConnection<String, String>`; that is, it only supports keys and values as strings. If we were using
Spring Data, we would have been able to use our `Message` class as the value,
serialized to JSON.

Instead, we are forced to do it manually, using `ObjectMapper` from FasterXML/Jackson, as we can see in the `RedisService` class:

```
@Service
public class RedisService {
    @Autowired
    RedisCommands<String, String> syncCommands;

    public void addMessage(Message message) throws Exception {
        ObjectMapper objectMapper = new ObjectMapper();
        String jsonString = objectMapper.writeValueAsString(message);

        syncCommands.set("message:" + message.id, jsonString);

        Long epoch = Instant.parse(message.date).getEpochSecond();
        syncCommands.zadd(message.room,
            epoch.doubleValue(), message.id);
    }
}
```

Kafka instrumentation

The situation is slightly better for Kafka, which already has OpenTracing support for Spring. We are using the following dependencies:

```
<dependency>
    <groupId>org.springframework.kafka</groupId>
    <artifactId>spring-kafka</artifactId>
    <version>2.1.8.RELEASE</version>
</dependency>
<dependency>
    <groupId>org.apache.kafka</groupId>
    <artifactId>kafka-clients</artifactId>
    <version>2.0.0</version>
</dependency>
<dependency>
    <groupId>io.opentracing.contrib</groupId>
    <artifactId>opentracing-kafka-spring</artifactId>
    <version>0.0.14</version>
</dependency>
```

The low 0.0.14 version of the last module hints at it being an early experimental version. It provides the decorators for producers and consumers, but does not have the ability to auto-enable them as part of Spring initialization.

Producing messages

Our `KafkaConfig` class registers the `KafkaTemplate` bean used to send messages to Kafka:

```
@Bean
public KafkaTemplate<String, Message> kafkaTemplate() throws Exception
{
    return new KafkaTemplate<>(producerFactory());
}
```

The producer factory is the one that is decorated with `TracingProducerFactory`:

```
private ProducerFactory<String, Message> producerFactory()
    throws Exception
{
    Map<String, Object> props = new HashMap<>();
    props.put(ProducerConfig.BOOTSTRAP_SERVERS_CONFIG,
                "localhost:9092");
    props.put(ProducerConfig.CLIENT_ID_CONFIG, clientId());
    ProducerFactory<String, Message> producer =
        new DefaultKafkaProducerFactory<String, Message>(
            props,
            new StringSerializer(),
            new JsonSerializer<Message>());
    return new TracingProducerFactory<String, Message>(producer,
tracer);
}
```

This is simple enough and because we are using the Spring template, we can take advantage of Spring's serialization mechanisms by registering a JSON serializer for the `Message` class. Given this template, we can send a message to Kafka like this:

```
@Service
public class KafkaService {
    private static final String TOPIC = "message";

    @Autowired
    KafkaTemplate<String, Message> kafkaTemplate;

    public void sendMessage(Message message) throws Exception {
        ProducerRecord<String, Message> record =
            new ProducerRecord<>(TOPIC, message);
        kafkaTemplate.send(record).get();
    }
}
```

Figure 5.6: Tags in the Kafka producer span captured by instrumentation
from the opentracing-kafka-spring library

If we go back to the trace we collected in the Jaeger UI and expand one of the
send spans, we will see that it is indeed created by the java-kafka component,
with a span.kind=producer tag, and the topic name message is captured in the
message_bus.destination tag.

Recording of a span, by itself, is not difficult; we have done it previously with
the calls to the database. What is special in the preceding instrumentation is
that the span context is not lost, as often happens with the database calls that
typically end up as leaf nodes in the trace. Instead, the span context is recorded
into the Kafka message headers. Readers can follow the chain of execution from
TracingProducerFactory, but we can jump right to the interesting place: the
inject() method in io.opentracing.contrib.kafka.TracingKafkaUtils:

```
static void inject(SpanContext spanContext, Headers headers,
    Tracer tracer) {
  tracer.inject(spanContext, Format.Builtin.TEXT_MAP,
    new HeadersMapInjectAdapter(headers, false));
}
```

This should look familiar. The span context is serialized and stored in the
Kafka message headers using the tracer.inject() call. The only new part is
the HeadersMapInjectAdapter, whose job it is to adapt the Kafka record headers
to OpenTracing's TextMap carrier API.

Elsewhere, this method is called by passing it the span context from the currently active span, accessed via `scope.span()`, and the record headers:

```
try {
    TracingKafkaUtils.inject(scope.span().context(),
        record.headers(), tracer);
} catch (Exception e) {
    logger.error("failed to inject span context", e);
}
```

Consuming messages

Now let's review how the tracing instrumentation works on the consumer side. We have already seen from the trace that our current instrumentation results in two spans: one called `receive`, which is typically very short, and another called `process`, which wraps the actual execution of the message handler.

Unfortunately, the Jaeger UI currently does not display what span reference type is used by these spans (tracing through messaging is a relatively new field). We can still find that out by using the **View Options** dropdown menu in the top-right corner and selecting **Trace JSON**. This will open a new browser window with JSON representation of the trace.

If we search for span names `receive` and `process`, we will see that both of these types of spans are defined with a follows-from span reference type. As we discussed briefly in *Chapter 4, Instrumentation Basics with OpenTracing*, the follows-from reference is used to link the current span to its predecessor, and indicate that the predecessor did not have a dependency on the outcome of the current span. This makes sense in the case of asynchronous messaging applications: a producer writes a message to the queue and does not wait for a response. Most often, it does not even know who the consumer is, or if there are many of them, or if they are all down at the moment. According to the semantic definition in OpenTracing, the producer does not depend on the outcome of some process consuming the message later. Therefore, the `receive` span using a follows-from reference makes perfect sense.

The relationship between the `receive` and `process` spans is actually similar to that of a producer/consumer relationship. The `receive` span is executed somewhere deep inside the Kafka driver, when a whole batch of messages is read from the queue. The `process` span is started in the application code, asynchronously. The `receive` span does not directly depend on the outcome of the `process` span, so they are linked via a follows-from reference.

People who are new to tracing sometimes ask why we cannot have a span that starts from the moment of the producer writing the message and ends when the consumer receives it.

It would certainly make the Gantt chart of the trace look better because they can get really sparse when used for messaging workflows. There are a few reasons why this is not the best approach:

- It goes against the model recommended by OpenTracing that each span is associated with only a single process. This is not enforced, but many tracing systems are not designed to represent multi-host spans.

- Modeling the time spent waiting in the queue as a multi-host span does not provide a lot of benefits. The wait time can still be easily inferred from the trace by using single-host spans at the producer and consumer separately, as we have seen earlier in our trace.

- There may be multiple consumers! They can each read messages at different times, so associating the end of the multi-host span to a single receive event is not practical.

The problem of the sparse Gantt charts is better solved with improvements to the UIs.

Let's look at how all span creation is achieved in the code on the consumer side. The `receive` span is created by `TracingConsumerFactory`, which decorates the default consumer factory:

```
private ConsumerFactory<String, Message> consumerFactory()
        throws Exception
{
    . . .
    return new TracingConsumerFactory<>(
            new DefaultKafkaConsumerFactory<String, Message>(
                props,
                new StringDeserializer(),
                new JsonDeserializer<>(Message.class)));
}
```

This factory is then used to create a listener container factory:

```
@Bean
public Object kafkaListenerContainerFactory() throws Exception {
    ConcurrentKafkaListenerContainerFactory<String, Message> factory =
            new ConcurrentKafkaListenerContainerFactory<>();
    factory.setConsumerFactory(consumerFactory());
    return factory;
}
```

Unfortunately, this is where the immature status of the library comes though: with this code, we are only getting the receive span, but not the process span. We can only speculate as to why; maybe the maintainers did not have time to write proper Spring wiring for the message handlers. Another reason could be that the Kafka driver does not provide a place to store the span context of the receive span so that the process span can refer to it later. Sometimes, we have to work with the limitations of frameworks that do not expose enough hooks for middleware. We can look into the io.opentracing.contrib.kafka.TracingKafkaConsumer code, where we find the following method:

```
@Override
public ConsumerRecords<K, V> poll(long timeout) {
    ConsumerRecords<K, V> records = consumer.poll(timeout);
    for (ConsumerRecord<K, V> record : records) {
        TracingKafkaUtils.buildAndFinishChildSpan(
            record, tracer, consumerSpanNameProvider);
    }
    return records;
}
```

As we can see, the consumer reads multiple Kafka records at once and then creates a span for each of them, finishing them immediately. There is no other state, so the instrumentation uses a trick to preserve the span context of the receive span: it serializes it back into the message headers under a different set of keys, by prefixing them with the string second_span_. The code can be found in the buildAndFinishChildSpan() method in the class TracingKafkaUtils:

```
static <K,V> void buildAndFinishChildSpan(ConsumerRecord<K, V> record,
    Tracer tracer)
{
    SpanContext parentContext = extract(record.headers(), tracer);
    if (parentContext != null) {
        Tracer.SpanBuilder spanBuilder = tracer.buildSpan("receive")
            .withTag(
                Tags.SPAN_KIND.getKey(), Tags.SPAN_KIND_CONSUMER);

        spanBuilder.addReference(References.FOLLOWS_FROM,
            parentContext);

        Span span = spanBuilder.start();
        SpanDecorator.onResponse(record, span);
        span.finish();

        // Inject created span context into record headers
        // for extraction by client to continue span chain
        injectSecond(span.context(), record.headers(), tracer);
    }
}
```

The `injectSecond()` function uses the familiar `tracer.inject()` call:

```
static void injectSecond(SpanContext spanContext, Headers headers,
                Tracer tracer)
{
    tracer.inject(spanContext, Format.Builtin.TEXT_MAP,
        new HeadersMapInjectAdapter(headers, true));
}
```

The custom `HeadersMapInjectAdapter` class is responsible for prefixing the keys with the string `second_span_`:

```
public class HeadersMapInjectAdapter implements TextMap {

    private final Headers headers;
    private final boolean second;

    HeadersMapInjectAdapter(Headers headers, boolean second) {
        this.headers = headers;
        this.second = second;
    }

    @Override
    public void put(String key, String value) {
        if (second) {
            headers.add("second_span_" + key,
                        value.getBytes(StandardCharsets.UTF_8));
        } else {
            headers.add(key, value.getBytes(StandardCharsets.UTF_8));
        }
    }
}
```

If the instrumentation does not create the `process` span automatically, how did we get it into the trace? When we showed earlier the examples of the message handlers in the Tracing Talk application, we mentioned that they were slightly simplified. Now let's look at their full form, for example, in the `storage-service` microservice:

```
@KafkaListener(topics = "message")
public void process(@Payload Message message,
        @Headers MessageHeaders headers) throws Exception
{
    Span span = kafka.startConsumerSpan("process", headers);
    try (Scope scope = tracer.scopeManager().activate(span, true)) {
        System.out.println("Received message: " + message.message);
        redis.addMessage(message);
        System.out.println("Added message to room.");
    }
}
```

We are using a helper method, `startConsumerSpan`, from `KafkaService` to start the `process` span manually and make it active in the current scope. This allows the rest of the instrumentation, such as that in the Redis connection, to pick up the current span and continue the trace.

The helper method uses another adapter for the headers to extract the keys with the `second_span_` prefix (unfortunately, the identical class in the instrumentation library is private):

```
public Span startConsumerSpan(String name, MessageHeaders headers) {
    TextMap carrier = new MessageHeadersExtractAdapter(headers);
    SpanContext parent = tracer.extract(
            Format.Builtin.TEXT_MAP, carrier);
    return tracer.buildSpan(name)
            .addReference(References.FOLLOWS_FROM, parent)
            .start();
}
```

If we did not start this span manually, as shown, our top-level trace would have stopped with the `receive` span as a leaf, and calls to Redis or to the `giphy.com` API would have started new traces. We leave it as an exercise to you to verify this by commenting out the span creation statements in the message handlers.

Instrumenting asynchronous code

Using messaging between services is not the only way to implement asynchronous applications. Sometimes, the code within a single service is asynchronous. In environments like Node.js, it is the standard way of writing code and requires a different style of in-process context propagation.

In Java, the asynchronous code is often written with the use of futures and executors. In our Tracing Talk application, we have already used those APIs, only in the synchronous manner. For example, the `KafkaService.sendMessage()` method calls the `send()` function, which returns `ListenableFuture`, a sign of the asynchronous API. We turn it back to synchronous by calling `get()` and blocking until it is completed:

```
public void sendMessage(Message message) throws Exception {
    ProducerRecord<String, Message> record =
        new ProducerRecord<>(TOPIC, message);
    kafkaTemplate.send(record).get();
}
```

The tracing implementation we used takes care of transferring the tracing context correctly through the asynchronous API boundaries. However, what if we wanted to try it ourselves? The KafkaService class contains another method for sending messages: sendMessageAsync(). It pretends that kafkaTemplate.send() is a blocking call and uses a CompletableFuture and an executor to execute that call on a thread that is different from the caller thread:

```
public void sendMessageAsync(Message message, Executor executor)
        throws Exception
{
    CompletableFuture.supplyAsync(() -> {
        ProducerRecord<String, Message> record =
                new ProducerRecord<>(TOPIC, message);
        kafkaTemplate.send(record);
        return message.id;
    }, executor).get();
}
```

The chat-api service uses the environment variable KSEND to toggle between using the sendMessage() and sendMessageAsync() methods. Since the second function requires an executor, the chat-api service constructs one as follows:

```
@Bean
public Executor asyncExecutor() {
    ThreadPoolTaskExecutor executor = new
ThreadPoolTaskExecutor();
    executor.setCorePoolSize(2);
    executor.setMaxPoolSize(2);
    executor.setQueueCapacity(10);
    executor.setThreadNamePrefix("send-to-kafka-");
    executor.initialize();
    return executor;
}

Executor executor1 = asyncExecutor();
```

To use this executor, we can start the chat-api with the KSEND=async1 parameter:

```
$ make chatapi KSEND=async1
```

For convenience, we added a separate make target for this command:

```
$ make chatapi-async1
```

If we post a message to the chat and look for a trace, we will find that instead of one trace, as we would expect, we created two traces: one for the top-level endpoint that contains a single span **postMessage**, and one that starts with the send span as the root, and contains the rest of the usual trace. Remember that in order to find the second trace, you may need to select **send** in the **Operation** dropdown box.

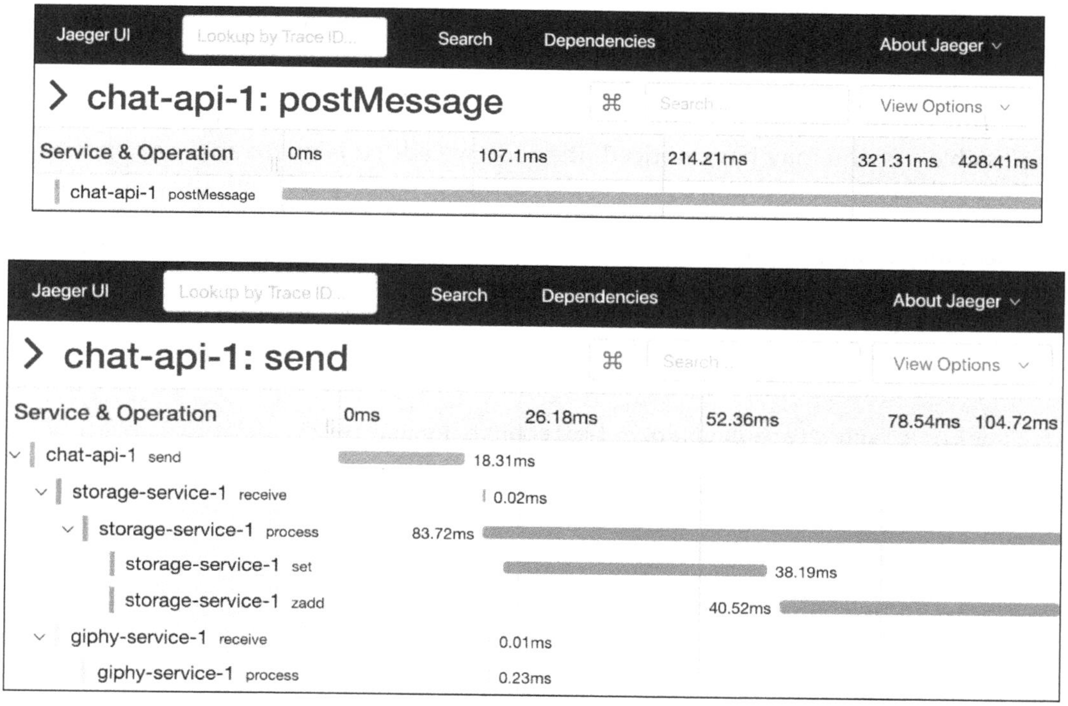

Figure 5.7: Two traces instead of one when running the chat-api service with KSEND=async1 parameter

Clearly, breaking a trace like that is not what we intended. We used an asynchronous `CompletableFuture` to execute the request, which is not that much different from the future used by the Kafka template. The problem is that we did not take care of passing the in-process context between the threads correctly. The lambda function passed to the future executes on a different thread, which has no access to the active span from the caller thread. In order to bridge the gap, we can get the current active span and re activate it inside the lambda code that runs in the other thread:

```java
public void sendMessageAsync(Message message, Executor executor)
        throws Exception
{
    final Span span = tracer.activeSpan();
    CompletableFuture.supplyAsync(() -> {
      try (Scope scope = tracer.scopeManager().activate(span, false))
      {
          ProducerRecord<String, Message> record =
                  new ProducerRecord<>(TOPIC, message);
          kafkaTemplate.send(record);
          return message.id;
      }
    }, executor).get();
}
```

If we apply this change and rerun the test with a chat message (don't forget to run `mvn install` first), we will see that the trace is back to normal, with `postMessage` and `send` spans properly connected. Unfortunately, it requires adding tracing code directly into the application code, which we were trying to avoid as much as possible. As you may have noticed, the code we added is not in any way specific to the lambda function that we pass to the future. If we step through the call to the `supplyAsync()` code, we will eventually reach a point where a runnable is passed to an executor. Until that point, all execution happens on the same caller thread that has access to the current active span. Thus, the generic solution would be to instrument the executor (by decorating it) to perform the active span transfer between threads. This is exactly what the `TracedRunnable` class in the `opentracing-contrib/java-concurrent` library does:

```
public class TracedRunnable implements Runnable {

    private final Runnable delegate;
    private final Span span;
    private final Tracer tracer;

    public TracedRunnable(Runnable delegate, Tracer tracer) {
        this.delegate = delegate;
        this.tracer = tracer;
        this.span = tracer.activeSpan();
    }

    @Override
    public void run() {
        Scope = span == null ? null :
            tracer.scopeManager().activate(span, false);
        try {
            delegate.run();
        } finally {
            if (scope != null) {
                scope.close();
            }
        }
    }
}
```

The `TracedRunnable` class captures the current span when the decorator is created and activates it in the new thread, before calling `run()` on the delegate. We could wrap our executor into `TracedExecutor` from this library, which internally uses `TracedRunnable`. However, that would still require changes to our code to apply the decorator. Instead, we can let the Spring instrumentation do it automatically!

The method `asyncExecutor()` is already annotated with `@Bean`, meaning it is injected into the Spring context, where the auto-instrumentation can detect it and auto-decorate for tracing. We just need to get that bean back from the Spring context, instead of calling the function to create a new one:

```
Executor executor1 = asyncExecutor();

@Autowired
Executor executor2;
```

As you probably have already guessed (or looked into the source code), we can tell the `chat-api` service to use the second executor with the `KSEND=async2` parameter:

$ make chatapi KSEND=async2

Alternatively, we can use the `make` target: `make chatapi-async2`.

If we run the chat message test again, we will see that the trace is back to normal, with up to 16 spans if the message contains the `/giphy` command.

To close this section, here is one final comment about using follows-from versus child-of span references with asynchronous programming. Sometimes, the code at the lower levels of the stack does not know its true relationship with the current active span in the thread. For example, consider sending a message to Kafka, which is done using an asynchronous `send()` method on the Kafka template.

We have seen that the producer decorator always creates the `send` span using a child-of reference to the span active in the caller thread. In the case of the `chat-api` service, it turns out to be the correct choice because we always call `get()` on the future returned from `send()`, that is, our HTTP response is not produced until the `send` span is finished. However, that is not a strict dependency and it is easy to imagine a situation where an asynchronous API is called without expecting its completion to affect the higher-level span. A follows-from reference is more appropriate in that scenario, yet the lower-level instrumentation cannot infer the intent.

The best advice here is to make the caller responsible for attributing correct causality to spans. If the caller knows that it is making a fire-and-forget type of asynchronous call, it can pre-emptively start a follows-from span, so that the child-of span created at the lower level has the correct causality reference. Fortunately, it is quite rare that this needs to be done explicitly because even when we use asynchronous programming, there is often the expectation that the parent span depends on the outcome of the child.

Summary

In this chapter, we covered the more advanced topic of tracing instrumentation for asynchronous applications. Using Apache Kafka as an example of asynchronous communication between services, we discussed how tracing context can be propagated through messaging infrastructure, and how producer and consumer spans are created at both ends of the message bus. We finished off with a discussion about instrumenting applications that use asynchronous programming in-process, such as futures and executors in Java. While the instrumentation itself was OpenTracing-specific, the principles of instrumenting asynchronous applications were general and applicable to any tracing API built around the span model.

Most of the instrumentation we used in this chapter came from various off-the-shelf open source modules from the `opentracing-contrib` organization on GitHub. We even avoided the code to instantiate the Jaeger tracer and used runtime configuration options instead. Since all the instrumentation was vendor-agnostic, any other OpenTracing-compatible tracer could be used.

OpenTracing solves the instrumentation problem, which is arguably the largest one standing in the way of wider adoption of distributed tracing in the industry, but it is not the only problem.

In the next chapter, we will take a look at a larger ecosystem of tracing beyond OpenTracing, to see what other emerging standards are being developed. Some projects are competing and some overlap in non-trivial ways, so we will introduce a classification by the types of problems the projects are solving, and by their primary audience.

References

1. Distributed Tracing NYC meetup: `https://www.meetup.com/Distributed-Tracing-NYC/`.

6
Tracing Standards and Ecosystem

In the microservices-ruled world, end-to-end tracing is no longer a "nice-to-have" feature, but "table stakes" for understanding modern cloud-native applications. In *Chapter 4, Instrumentation Basics with OpenTracing*, we saw an example of what it takes to manually instrument a simple "Hello, world!" application for distributed tracing. If, after reading it, you were left with the impression, "oh, that is a lot of work," then it achieved one of its goals. Developing and deploying instrumentation in order to get high-quality tracing data is absolutely the largest, but not the only, challenge of rolling out a distributed tracing solution in an organization. In *Chapter 13, Implementing Tracing in Large Organizations*, we will review some practical techniques for making the process easier from an organizational point of view.

In this chapter, we will discuss:

- Open source projects aiming to ease or eliminate the instrumentation challenge
- Standards initiatives trying to address the problem of interoperability and siloed data, which is exacerbated when companies are adopting managed cloud services, such as AWS Kinesis or Cloud Spanner

Styles of instrumentation

The completely manual instrumentation we did in *Chapter 4, Instrumentation Basics with OpenTracing*, was useful to demonstrate the core principles, but in practice, that instrumentation style is very rare, as it is very expensive and simply not scalable for large, cloud-native applications. It is also quite unnecessary because in a microservices-based application, most instrumentation trace points occur next to process boundaries, where the communications are performed by the means of a small number of frameworks, such as RPC libraries.

If we instrument the frameworks, we need to do it only once and then reuse that instrumentation across the application. This does not mean that manual instrumentation in the application has no place at all, but usually it is reserved for special cases where some unique application logic warrants it, for example, to monitor access to some custom shared resource.

There is another style of instrumentation commonly referred to as **agent-based**, which promises automatic, zero-touch instrumentation of the applications. In dynamic languages, like Python and JavaScript, it is often done through a technique known as **monkey-patching**, which involves dynamic modification of classes or modules at runtime, transparently to the application. As an example, a popular Python module, `requests`, has a static function, `requests.get()`, used to execute HTTP requests. The tracing instrumentation agent might replace that function with a wrapper that would create a client-side tracing span, invoke the original function, and then finish the span, annotated with the results of the request, such as the HTTP status code.

In Java applications, where dynamic code modifications like that are not allowed, a similar effect is achieved though byte code manipulation. For example, the Java runtime executable has a command line switch, `-javaagent`, that loads a library that interacts with the `java.lang.instrument` API to automatically apply instrumentation as classes are being loaded.

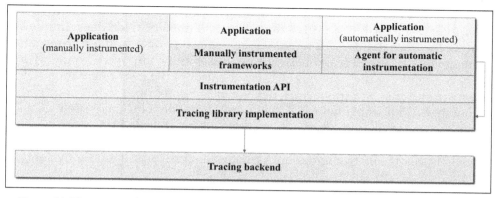

Figure 6.1: Three types of tracing instrumentation and their interactions with the Instrumentation API. The API abstracts the exact metadata propagation and trace reporting formats from the application and framework developers, delegating it to the tracing library implementation, which communicates with the tracing backend. Agent-based instrumentations often bypass the API and go to the implementation directly, making them non-portable across tracing vendors.

Agent-based instrumentation is often much more complicated to maintain than instrumentation directly integrated with frameworks. When frameworks are designed with extensibility in mind, adding the tracing code in the form of middleware, interceptors, filters, and so on is generally very straightforward. Unfortunately, some frameworks do not provide the extensibility path. In those cases, monkey-patching and agent-based instrumentation are often the only recourse. Historically, only large commercial APM vendors like New Relic or AppDynamics provided agents for multiple languages, sinking a lot of engineering resources into maintaining them, as the underlying frameworks kept evolving and multiplying. Today, agent-based instrumentation can be found from newer vendors like DataDog and Elastic, and some open source projects, such as Apache SkyWalking. Unfortunately, those libraries are typically coupled with the specific tracing backend of the vendor.

In my early days of trying to implement tracing instrumentation in Python, I wrote a module `opentracing_instrumentation` [1] that used the monkey-patching style to alter a few popular Python modules like `urllib2`, `requests`, `MySQLdb`, `SQLAlchemy`, and a few others. That module applied vendor-neutral instrumentation via the OpenTracing API [2], so that it could be used with any compliant tracer implementation. In late 2018, another group of OpenTracing developers started a new project for Java called "Special Agent" [3], which automatically instruments Java applications to produce trace events via the OpenTracing API.

Both manual and frameworks instrumentation require a certain **instrumentation API** for describing the distributed transactions. The API must provide the primitives for annotating the trace points with semantics and causality data, and for propagating the context metadata within and between processes and component boundaries. As we have seen from the previous chapter, the user of the instrumentation API, that is, an application or a framework developer, does not need to be concerned with how that API is implemented, for example, what data format it used to represent the metadata in the network requests, or the collected traces as they are reported to the backend. The part that is most important to the application developers is that the instrumentation API is used *consistently by all the frameworks*.

A typical microservice (*Figure 6.2*) contains some proprietary business logic, while using a number of standard frameworks, usually open source, for its infrastructure needs, such as a server framework for serving the inbound requests; potentially a separate RPC framework for making calls to other microservices; database and queue drivers for talking to infrastructure components, and so on. All of these frameworks should be instrumented for tracing, but without a common API, they won't even know how to pass the context metadata to each other.

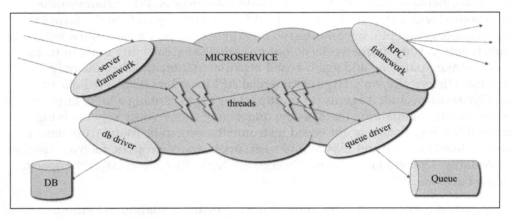

Figure 6.2 A typical microservice composed of proprietary business logic and open source frameworks

We can summarize the requirements for the instrumentation API as follows:

- It must be expressive, to capture sufficient semantic meaning and causality of operations involved in a distributed transaction.

- It should provide similar tracing primitives across different programming languages. It is quite common for cloud-native applications to be polyglot and having to deal with conceptually different APIs creates an additional cognitive overhead for developers.

- At the same time, the API should feel natural to the specific programming language, using established idioms and naming conventions.

- The primitives must abstract away how the context metadata is formatted on the wire, and how collected traces are reported to the tracing backend. Those considerations are important for the operators of a tracing system and for successful deployment, but they are irrelevant at the time of the instrumentation and must be decoupled.

- It must be vendor-neutral. Writing instrumentation for a framework or an application is an expensive proposition; it does not need to be coupled with the simultaneous decision of which tracing system will be used with that instrumentation. I will use the term "vendor" in this chapter to refer to any of the commercial APM vendors, managed tracing systems from cloud providers, and open source tracing projects.

- It must be lightweight, ideally packaged as a standalone library without extra dependencies.

The additional soft requirement for the instrumentation API is that it needs to be widely adopted. As with any standardization efforts, competing standards fracture the community. Competition is good for implementations, but not for standards because it saddles the other open source developers with a difficult choice: which competing API should they use to instrument their framework? If they choose wrongly, their tracing code becomes incompatible with the other frameworks that someone else might use to compose their application.

In the previous chapters, we used the OpenTracing API, an instrumentation API that satisfies all the preceding criteria. It has been developed through collaboration between many tracing practitioners, including APM vendors like LightStep, Instana, DataDog, New Relic, and SolarWinds; open source projects like OpenZipkin, Jaeger, Stagemonitor, Hawkular, and SkyWalking; and end users like Uber Technologies, one of the earliest adopters.

Anatomy of tracing deployment and interoperability

As I alluded to earlier, standardization on the instrumentation API is not the only aspect of a successful rollout of a tracing solution in an organization. Consider the following imaginary application in Company X (*Figure 6.3*), where all microservices are instrumented with the OpenTracing API and use Jaeger libraries to collect traces in a single installation of the Jaeger backend.

Assuming that this is the complete architecture and the microservices do not communicate with any external systems (which is actually not realistic, at least for the **Billing** component, which usually needs to make calls to the external payment processor), there are no interoperability issues in this deployment that would prevent the collection of complete traces covering all the components of the application.

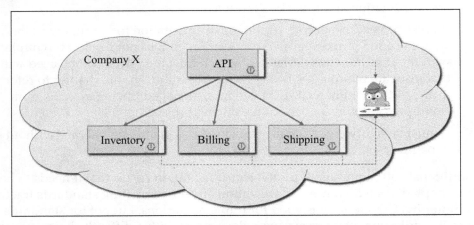

Figure 6.3: Imaginary application deployed in the cloud or on premises,
instrumented with OpenTracing and collecting all traces in a single installation of Jaeger.
Solid arrows represent business requests and dashed arrows represent trace data collection.

In reality, things are usually more complicated. Imagine that our company needs to meet data protection and privacy regulations, and after some analysis, we realize that the fastest way to get there is to move the **Billing** component, which handles credit cards, to Amazon's cloud service, AWS, because it has sufficient controls in place. AWS provides its own tracing solution, X-Ray, which is also integrated with other services it provides, so we may decide to use X-Ray instead of Jaeger to trace the Billing service.

Also imagine that the database used by the **Inventory** module is no longer scaling and we decide to replace it with a managed database service, for example, Google's Cloud Spanner. Spanner, as with most managed Google services, is internally traced with Google's StackDriver.

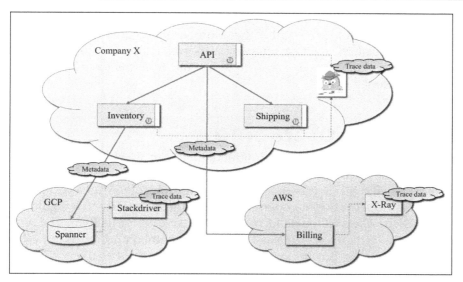

Figure 6.4: More complicated deployment of the imaginary application introduces integration points between different tracing backends in order to be able to observe a full view of the system in the traces. All three tracing systems, Jaeger, Stackdriver, and X-Ray, use different data formats for encoding the metadata in the requests, and for storing and exposing collected trace data.

Figure 6.4 shows the extended architecture, which includes the components running both on premises and in the cloud. The complexity of the system has only increased, so even more than before, we want to see the complete, end-to-end traces of the transactions. Unfortunately, we have two new problems to solve before we can do that. The first problem is that we won't even get a single complete trace for a given transaction.

You may remember from *Chapter 3, Distributed Tracing Fundamentals,* that tracing systems propagate context metadata when services make network calls, usually by encoding it in a certain way as request headers. In our case, the metadata is being exchanged between components instrumented with different tracing systems: Jaeger, Stackdriver, and X-Ray. They need to agree on the wire format for metadata in order to preserve causality relationships between tracing data. We will discuss one such proposed format later in this chapter.

The second problem is that different parts of the trace are now collected by different tracing backends. In order to assemble them into a single view, we need to export them into a single system, *and* in a single data format. At the time of writing, no such standard format for trace data exists, although some attempts have been made in the industry to create one.

Five shades of tracing

The tracing ecosystem today is fairly fragmented and probably confusing. Traditional APM vendors made a lot of investment in the agent-based instrumentation, all with their own APIs and data protocols. After Twitter released Zipkin, the first industrial-grade open source tracing system, it started gaining traction among the users as the de facto standard, at least for its B3 metadata propagation format (many systems at Twitter were named after birds, and Zipkin was originally called Big Brother Bird, or B3, which was used as the prefix for HTTP headers, for example, `X-B3-TraceId`).

In 2016, both Google and Amazon announced the availability of their own managed tracing systems, Stackdriver and X-Ray, both with their own metadata and trace data formats. These systems can be used to trace the applications running in the respective clouds, as well as receive tracing data from the internal applications running, by their customers on premises. A number of other tracing systems were created and open sourced in 2016-2018.

All this activity increased the interest in distributed tracing in the industry but did not help with interoperability or moving tracing instrumentation into the mainstream as a required component of application frameworks, the way logging and metrics instrumentations have been for some time now. This led to the creation of several open source projects aiming for the standardization of various aspects of tracing solutions. However, some of the projects have overlaps, confusing newcomers even further.

At a recent KubeCon EU 2018 conference, Ben Sigelman, one of the creators of Google's Dapper and a co-founder of the OpenTracing project, hypothesized that the confusion and sometimes even hurt feelings between the projects stem from the fact that they are not defining clearly which part of the tracing puzzle they are solving, and they use the same word *tracing* when referring to four different tasks: analyzing, recording, federating, and describing transactions. I think this mental exercise can be extended even further, at least to five categories, all under the name of *tracing* (*Figure 6.5*).

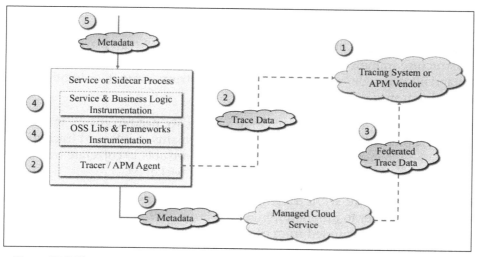

Figure 6.5: Different meanings of tracing: analyzing transactions (1), recording transactions (2), federating transactions (3), describing transactions (4), and correlating transactions (5)

The very first notion that comes to mind when you hear *tracing* is the actual tracing system that collects the data and provides users with the means to **analyze transactions** using the tracing tool. When we took the HotROD for a test drive in *Chapter 2, Take Tracing for a HotROD Ride*, we said we **traced** it, even though all we did was use the Jaeger UI to look at the traces.

There will be people (and projects) to whom *tracing* means something else. They will say tracing is about **recording transactions** in a process and sending them to the tracing backend. For example, a service mesh sidecar, or an APM agent, might be in the position to both capture the traces for a service and record them.

As we discussed in the previous section, the introduction of managed cloud services creates additional challenges for getting a complete picture of distributed transactions. As an example, an application might use a messaging service like AWS Kinesis, which is different from using a managed database because a message bus is typically not the leaf node in the trace, since the business logic acts as both producer and consumer.

Understanding the behavior of such a system is much easier if we can trace the transactions end to end through the message bus, but because it is a managed service, it is much more likely to send its part of the traces to the tracing system run by the cloud provider. By uniting or **federating transactions**, we can get them to a single place where they can be analyzed end to end.

If we are developing a business service, we are usually running and deploying a lot of code, some of which we wrote, and some of which we brought as dependencies from shared repositories like Maven Central, GitHub, NPM, and so on, either as infrastructure frameworks or some extensions of business functionality. To understand all that code, we need to **trace** it by instrumenting it, or in other words, by **describing transactions**.

Finally, coming back to the managed cloud service, we need to ensure that the traces are not interrupted when transactions cross the domains of different tracing vendors. By agreeing on the metadata encoding format, we are able to **correlate transactions**, even when they are recorded into different tracing backends.

All these meanings of the word **tracing** are valid and have people who care about them, but they all refer to different things. It is important to make sure that these different aspects are decoupled from each other, and the projects working on them are clear about their scope.

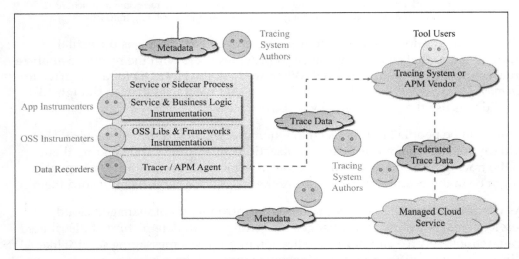

Figure 6.6: Different audiences for different meanings of tracing

Know your audience

Just like many projects care about different aspects of tracing, different groups of people are their target audience:

- Tracing system authors care about recording, federating, and correlating transactions, and about the projects attempting to standardize data formats for trace data and for metadata.

- Tool users, for example, DevOps, SREs, and application developers, generally only care that the tool works and helps them to analyze transactions. They are not involved in most projects around the standardization efforts.

- Data recorders, which often, but not always, include tracing system authors, care about recording transactions and work on tools that may include tracing libraries. For example, the OpenCensus project is focused on data recording, but it is explicitly agnostic to the actual tracing backend that receives the data. It is not maintained by the same people who maintain the tracing backends.

- Application developers care about instrumentation APIs that help them to describe transactions in their systems and gain visibility.

- **OSS** (**open source software**) framework developers, similar to application developers, care about describing transactions by means of the instrumentation API, which allows them to provide their users with best-in-class visibility into the operation of their libraries and frameworks.

The ecosystem

In this section, we will attempt to classify some of the projects in the distributed tracing space by the dimensions described earlier. The following table provides a quick summary of the areas where each project has some exposure, such as a dependency or an influence on a specific data format.

Project	Analyzing transactions Tracing tool	Recording transactions Tracer/agent	Federating transactions Trace data	Describing transactions App/OSS instrumentation	Correlating transactions Metadata
Zipkin	✔	✔	✔	✔	✔
Jaeger	✔	✔	✔		✔
SkyWalking	✔	✔	✔	✔	✔
Stackdriver, X-Ray, and so on	✔	✔	✔	✔	✔
W3C Trace Context					✔
W3C "Data Interchange Format"			✔		

OpenCensus		✔	✔	✔	✔
OpenTracing				✔	

Tracing systems

First, let us consider a few complete tracing systems and see which areas of the problem space they occupy.

Zipkin and OpenZipkin

Zipkin was the first highly scalable distributed tracing system made available as an open source project. Released in 2012 by Twitter, it accumulated a lot of followers and a healthy community. Being the first, Zipkin had to cover all aspects of tracing we discussed in this chapter, so it is no surprise that it ticks a box in every column, including the instrumentation columns. This is because the Zipkin project actively supports its own tracer called Brave, which brings with it a lot of standard instrumentation for many popular frameworks, such as Spring, Spark, Kafka, gRPC, and so on. The instrumentation itself is tightly coupled to the Brave API, and therefore can only interoperate with the other tracing systems at the data-format level.

Jaeger

Jaeger was created at Uber in 2015 and released as an open source project in 2017. It is a relatively new project but gaining in popularity due to its focus on OpenTracing compatibility and a neutral home at the Cloud Native Computing Foundation. Jaeger provides a feature set similar to that of Zipkin. The Jaeger project does not provide any instrumentation by itself. Instead, it maintains a set of OpenTracing-compatible tracers in multiple languages that can be used with the wealth of existing OpenTracing-based instrumentation (discussed later in this chapter). Therefore, Jaeger has no exposure in the instrumentation column in the table. Some of Jaeger's tracing libraries are able to send data in Zipkin format, as well as use Zipkin's B3 metadata format.

SkyWalking

SkyWalking is another relatively new project, which originated in China, and was accepted at incubation stage to Apache Foundation in 2017. Started as a tracing system, it has been gradually transforming into a full-blown APM solution, providing metrics and alerting functionality, and even logs. As far as its tracing capability is concerned, it is partially OpenTracing-compatible (only in Java), but the authors invested heavily into agent-based instrumentation for a number of frameworks popular in China, thus earning the checkmarks in the instrumentation columns.

X-Ray, Stackdriver, and more

Many of the managed services run by large cloud providers are traced with their respective cloud-hosted tracing systems, such as AWS X-Ray or Google Stackdriver. This creates problems for their customers who are running their own in-house tracing backends, including the open source ones like Zipkin or Jaeger, because the tracing data about transactions becomes siloed in different tracing backends. This makes the cloud vendors very interested in the data standardization efforts, which we will describe next. At the same time, as of writing, every one of these cloud-hosted tracing backends ships its own set of SDKs for instrumenting customer applications, which makes those instrumentations non-portable.

Standards projects

As we can see, all of the tracing systems we discussed earlier have unique solutions for each area of the problem space, including data formats for traces and metadata, trace recording libraries, and, with the exception of Jaeger, their individual instrumentation APIs. This makes them mostly incompatible with each other without some special adapters. A number of standardization efforts have appeared in the past two years trying to bridge the gaps and bring vendor neutrality in areas that do not require strong differentiation, such as, "how do we instrument an HTTP endpoint?"

W3C Trace Context

In 2017, a group of vendors, cloud providers, and open source projects formed a committee called the "Distributed Tracing Working Group" [4] under the umbrella of the **World Wide Web Consortium (W3C)** with the goal of defining standards for interoperability between tracing tools. The main active project of that working group is called Trace Context [5]. As can be seen from the preceding table, this project's purpose is very narrowly focused on a single dimension: the format of the tracing metadata passed between the processes over standard protocols, such as HTTP or AMQP.

The Trace Context project reached one major milestone in early 2018 when all participating vendors agreed on the conceptual model for trace identifiers. Previously, there was a lot of disagreement on whether such a standard would be workable for all participating tracing systems. As an example, the OpenTracing API had for two years refrained from requiring the span context API to expose anything resembling trace and span ID, in fear that some tracing systems would not be able to support that. Since the decision in the W3C Trace Context, that hurdle has been removed.

The Trace Context working draft suggests two protocol headers to propagate the tracing metadata. The first header, `traceparent`, holds a canonical representation of the trace and span IDs as 16-bytes and 8-bytes arrays, respectively, encoded as hexadecimal strings, and a `flags` field, which carries the indicator of a sampling decision made upstream from the current service. As an example, it might look like this:

```
Traceparent: 00-4bf92f3577b34da6a3ce929d0e0e4736-00f067aa0ba902b7-01
```

The leading `00` is the version of the specification, and the `01` at the end is an 8-bit mask with the least significant bit indicating that the trace was sampled upstream. The second header, `tracestate`, is designed to provide tracing vendors with a place to store and pass additional metadata that may be specific to the vendor and not supported in the canonical format of the `traceparent` header. As an example, SkyWalking propagates additional fields that cannot be represented in the `traceparent` header, such as parent span id or parent service instance id [6].

Compliant tracers are required to pass `tracestate` values to the next node in the call graph, which is useful when the transaction execution leaves the domain of one tracing vendor and then comes back to it. Each vendor uses a unique key to mark its own state, for example:

```
Tracestate: vendorname1=opaqueValue1,vendorname2=opaqueValue2
```

Despite the narrow focus, and relative simplicity of the format proposal, the project has been running for over a year. This shows why the narrow focus is very important for the open source projects, as even such a simple format takes many months to get agreement from many stakeholders and to work out all the edge cases. As of the time of writing, the following questions remain unresolved:

- If a new version of the Trace Context format specification is released, and a tracer encounters a version, v, in the incoming request that is different from the version v' it is using, how should it behave? As an example, if the incoming version is lower, $v < v'$, is it allowed to upgrade and send the newer version in the following requests? What if the incoming version is higher, $v > v'$? Should it ignore it and start a new trace?

- What happens if a cloud provider does not want to respect the incoming trace IDs? A managed service, such as Cloud Spanner, is most likely to be traced by the internal tracing system of the cloud provider. A malicious actor may send requests to this service that all contain the same trace ID, which will result in bad data or "infinite" traces for the managed service. At the same time, completely discarding the customer's inbound trace ID is not a solution either, since most customers will be playing by the rules and would want to get visibility into their transactions.

In the case of a leaf service like Spanner (leaf from the customer point of view), there is a simple solution: the incoming trace ID is not respected, but recorded in the trace as a tag, for example "correlation ID", which still allows the traces from the customer tracing system to be correlated with traces in the cloud provider tracing systems. But what if the managed service is not a leaf, for example, a messaging system like AWS Kinesis?

- If a commercial APM vendor encodes the name or ID of the customer in the custom vendor state, and two of its customers, A and B, are exchanging requests, how should it represent its vendor state in the `tracestate` header once the request with a state for A arrives to customer B? Since there is a chance that later requests may come back to the first customer, A, the vendor might want to preserve both, but how should that be encoded in a single field in the header?

I hope these edge cases will be resolved soon and the specification ratified with an official recommendation version. The header standard will open up an opportunity for distributed transactions crossing systems with different tracing libraries to maintain a single view of distributed traces.

W3C "Data Interchange Format"

It would be much easier to join traces from different tracing backends, a process that we earlier called *federating transactions*, if all tracing backends exposed the traces in the same common format. The same Distributed Tracing Working Group has started discussions on what that format might look like, but there is no official project as of the time of writing. This is another example of a problem in the distributed tracing space that greatly benefits from narrow scope, and yet is still difficult to solve due to a wide variety of ways that different tracing systems represent their tracing data. Today, in the absence of a common format, this problem can only be solved via a so-called "N-squared" solution: each vendor needs to implement an adapter for the data format of each other vendor.

OpenCensus

The OpenCensus project [7] originates from an internal set of libraries at Google that were called Census. It defines its mission as a "vendor-agnostic single distribution of libraries to provide metrics collection and tracing for your services." Its roadmap also mentions logs collection, so in the future, it may increase in scope even more.

The OpenCensus project occupies a wider problem area space than the other standardization efforts, as it combines the instrumentation API with the underlying implementation of trace recording and the logical data model, especially of the metadata.

OpenCensus is very opinionated about the metadata and follows the original Google Dapper format of trace ID, span ID, and a bitmask for flags. For example, its Go library defines the `SpanContext` as follows:

```
type TraceID      [16]byte
type SpanID       [8]byte
type TraceOptions uint32

// SpanContext contains the state that must propagate
// across process boundaries.
type SpanContext struct {
    TraceID      TraceID
    SpanID       SpanID
    TraceOptions TraceOptions
}
```

This representation is the exact match for the metadata used by Google Stackdriver, as well as the Zipkin and Jaeger projects, all of which can trace their roots to Dapper. It is fully compatible with the W3C Trace Context format, without the need to pass any additional data in the `tracestate` header. However, many other existing tracing systems define their metadata quite differently. For example, an APM vendor Dynatrace [8] has a much more complex metadata propagation format that contains seven fields:

```
<clusterId>;<serverId>;<agentId>;<tagId>;<linkId>;<tenantId>;<pathInf
o>
```

For the purpose of this discussion, it is not important what those fields mean, but it is clear that they do not fit cleanly into the OpenCensus view of the metadata. In contrast, the OpenTracing API that we will discuss next imposes no restrictions on what data goes into the span context.

One obvious strength of the OpenCensus project is combining tracing and metrics functionality. On the surface, it sounds like those two are completely different problem domains and should be kept separately. However, as we have seen in the HotROD example in *Chapter 2, Take Tracing for a HotROD Ride*, some metrics might benefit from the additional labels, such as partitioning a single metric into many time series depending on the top-level customer or the product line.

This is only possible through the use of distributed context propagation, which is usually available in the tracing libraries. Thus, unless the access to the propagated context is completely de-coupled from the tracing functionality (more on that in the Tracing Plane discussion in *Chapter 10, Distributed Context Propagation*), the metrics API inevitably becomes coupled with tracing. This coupling, however, is one way: the metrics functionality depends on the context propagation feature of tracing functionality, but not vice versa. The same considerations will apply to the logging APIs once OpenCensus implements them.

The OpenCensus project does not get a checkmark in the trace data column in our table because, fortunately, it is not opinionated about that external format. Instead, it uses special modules called **exporters** whose job it is to convert the internal span data model into some external representation and send it to a particular tracing backend. As of the time of writing, OpenCensus by default ships with exporters for Zipkin, Jaeger, and Stackdriver tracing systems.

There is an inevitable question about the relationship between OpenCensus and OpenTracing. We can put aside the metrics capability because I already said that it is mostly built *on top of* the context propagation provided by the tracing functionality, and for all practical purposes can be a completely separate module. As for the domain of tracing instrumentation, both OpenCensus and OpenTracing have nearly identical semantic models of the spans and context propagation facilities, yet slightly different APIs, which unfortunately makes the instrumentations programmed to these APIs mutually incompatible. An ideal state would be for these two projects to converge to a single tracing API that would then allow a reuse of the existing open source instrumentation with either of them. In late 2018, the two projects started discussions toward that goal.

OpenTracing

Finally, we come back to the OpenTracing project [2]. We already know from the previous chapters that it is a collection of instrumentation APIs in different programming languages. The goals of the OpenTracing project are:

- To provide a single API that application and framework developers can use to instrument their code

- To enable truly reusable, portable, and composable instrumentation, especially for the other open source frameworks, libraries, and systems

- To empower other developers, not just those working on the tracing systems, to write instrumentation for their software and be comfortable that it will be compatible with other modules in the same application that are instrumented with OpenTracing, while not being bound to a specific tracing vendor

We can see from our comparison table that there are no other problems that OpenTracing is trying to solve. OpenTracing has no opinion on the format of metadata encoding, or the format of trace data, or the method of recording and collecting the traces, because those are not the concerns of the instrumentation domain.

This was a conscientious choice on the part of the project founders, who believe that decoupling unrelated problems is a good engineering practice, and that a pure API leaves a lot more freedom for innovation to the implementers than devising a single implementation.

As an example, Jaeger tracing libraries implement a number of features that, for a long time, were not available in any other implementations, including OpenCensus. It is also much harder to get an agreement on the implementation from all different vendors and parties involved, and by de-scoping that problem, the OpenTracing project was able to move much quicker in an already difficult domain of multi-lingual API design.

At the time of writing, the OpenTracing project defines official instrumentation APIs in nine programming languages: Go, JavaScript, Java, Python, Ruby, PHP, Objective-C, C++, and C#. These APIs have been used by the community to create tracing instrumentations for dozens of popular open source projects and frameworks, from RPC libraries to database and queueing drivers, and even standalone products like Envoy and NGINX. Being an abstract way of describing the semantics and causality of distributed transactions, the OpenTracing API can even be used for purposes unrelated to tracing, as we will see in later chapters.

The OpenTracing project is an incubation-stage project at the Cloud Native Computing Foundation. It has a strong governance model [9] that gives ultimate decision-making authority to the **OpenTracing Specification Council (OTSC)**, which consists of representatives from several tracing system authors and vendors who are actively involved in the project.

Another group of mostly end users of tracing, called the **OpenTracing Industrial Advisory Board (OTIAB)**, is tasked with advising the OTSC based on their experiences, successes, and challenges. Proposals to make changes to the specification and language APIs go through a formal and rigorous **request for comment (RFC)** process. Sometimes, breaking changes have to be made, a decision that is not taken lightly by the project members. As an example, the change of the Java API from version 0.30 to 0.31 was accompanied by the development of a large test suite illustrating how the new features were to be used in a variety of instrumentation scenarios. It even included a separate adapter module to ease the transition from version 0.30.

The OpenTracing project includes another GitHub organization, `opentracing-contrib` [10], which is a home to the actual open source instrumentation for popular frameworks. As of the time of writing, it has about 80 repositories instrumenting over 100 libraries, modules, and frameworks. The OpenTracing Registry [11] lists them, as well as externally hosted libraries. It supports search by keywords for finding tracers or instrumentation libraries for various technologies and frameworks (*Figure 6.7*).

Figure 6.7 Search for Python-related libraries in the OpenTracing registry

Summary

Deploying a tracing system is not just a matter of instrumenting your code or running a tracing backend. In this chapter, we discussed five problem areas that must be addressed in order to "have a good time" when collecting traces, and being able to analyze your system behavior and performance. The areas are analyzing, recording, federating, describing, and correlating transactions.

Most existing tracing systems cover all those areas, but in their own ways, which are incompatible with other tracing systems. This limits interoperability, which is especially problematic when using managed cloud services. There are four standardization projects that exist in the industry and they are trying to address different problem areas. We reviewed the scope of each project and discussed why having a narrow scope is important for them to be successful.

In the next chapter, we will discuss how other technologies, specifically service mesh proxies, can be used to standardize methods of extracting tracing data from applications.

References

1. A collection of Python instrumentation tools for the OpenTracing API: `https://github.com/uber-common/opentracing-python-instrumentation/`.

2. The OpenTracing Project: `http://opentracing.io/`.

3. Automatic OpenTracing instrumentation for 3rd-party libraries in Java applications: `https://github.com/opentracing-contrib/java-specialagent/`.

4. Distributed Tracing Working Group. **World Wide Web Consortium (W3C)**: `https://www.w3.org/2018/distributed-tracing/`.

5. Trace Context: Specification for distributed tracing context propagation format: `https://www.w3.org/TR/trace-context/`.

6. Apache SkyWalking Cross-Process Propagation Headers Protocol: `https://github.com/apache/incubator-skywalking/blob/master/docs/en/protocols/Skywalking-Cross-Process-Propagation-Headers-Protocol-v2.md`.

7. The OpenCensus Project: `https://opencensus.io/`.

8. Dynatrace: Software intelligence for the enterprise cloud: `https://www.dynatrace.com/`.

9. The OpenTracing Specification and Project Governance: `https://github.com/opentracing/specification`.

10. The OpenTracing Contributions: `https://github.com/opentracing-contrib/`.

11. The OpenTracing Registry: `https://opentracing.io/registry/`.

7

Tracing with Service Meshes

In previous chapters, we discussed multiple methods of extracting tracing data from applications, either by adding instrumentation directly to the application code, or enabling the instrumentation dynamically at runtime through configuration. I also mentioned agent-based instrumentation, often provided by commercial APM vendors, which works by injecting trace points externally into the customer's program, using techniques such as monkey-patching and bytecode manipulation. All these methods can be classified as white-box instrumentation, since they all require modification of the application's code, either explicitly or implicitly at runtime. In *Chapter 3, Distributed Tracing Fundamentals,* we also discussed black-box techniques that work purely by correlating externally observed telemetry, such as logs used by the Mystery Machine [1].

In this chapter, we will discuss and try in practice how **service meshes**, a relatively new phenomenon in the cloud-native landscape, can be used to deploy distributed tracing using an approach that is somewhat in between the white-box and black-box techniques. We will use Istio [2], a service mesh platform developed by Google, IBM, and Lyft, which comes with built-in Jaeger integration. We will use Kubernetes [3] to deploy both Istio and our sample application.

Service meshes

Service meshes have become increasingly popular in the past two-to-three years, as more and more organizations have embarked on the path of replacing the old monolithic applications with distributed architectures based on microservices. In *Chapter 1, Why Distributed Tracing*, we discussed the benefits and challenges of these transitions. As microservices-based applications grow in size and complexity, the communications between the services require more and more support from the infrastructure, to address problems like discovery, load balancing, rate limiting, failure recovery and retries, end-to-end authentication, access control, A/B testing, canary releases, and so on. Given a common trend in the industry, where different parts of distributed applications are often written in different programming languages, implementing all this infrastructure functionality as libraries, included in the individual services in every language, becomes intractable. We would much rather implement it once and find a way to reuse the functionality across different services.

The pattern of consolidating inter-service communication functionality into a reusable component is not new. In the early 2000s, it became fairly popular under the name of **Enterprise Service Bus (ESB)**. Wikipedia [4] defines the duties of an ESB as follows:

- Route messages between services
- Monitor and control routing of message exchange between services
- Resolve contention between communicating service components
- Control deployment and versioning of services
- Marshal use of redundant services
- Provide commodity services like event handling, data transformation and mapping, message and event queuing and sequencing, security or exception handling, protocol conversion, and enforcing proper quality of communication services

It sounds very similar to what we need for the microservices-based applications, doesn't it? However, even though ESB was an abstract architecture pattern, it was often implemented as a central layer or hub through which all the inter-service communications were proxied.

From a performance point of view, that means every time two services, A and B, need to talk to each other, there must be two network hops: A → ESB and ESB → B. For modern cloud-native applications, where a single user request may involve dozens, or even hundreds of microservices, these extra network hops quickly add up and contribute to the application latency. Also, a problem or a bug in the single central layer could bring the whole application down.

With the advent of containers, popularized by Docker, a new architectural pattern known as a **sidecar** has emerged. In this pattern, a set of tasks complementary to the main application functionality, and common across many services within the distributed application, are collocated with each service but placed inside their own lightweight process or container, providing a homogeneous interface for platform services across languages. Instead of all inter-service communications going through a central ESB, a sidecar container is deployed next to each microservice that takes care of the infrastructure needs required for the communication, such as service discovery, routing, and so on. The advantages of using a sidecar pattern include:

- A sidecar can be implemented in its own language, independent of the main application.

- A sidecar is collocated with the main application, so there is no significant latency between them (but a small latency does exist).

- Each sidecar handles just a single instance of a single service, so a misbehaving sidecar process may affect the health of that instance but will not affect the rest of the application (although a bad global configuration change may theoretically affect all sidecars at once).

- A sidecar acts as an extension mechanism for the main application, even if the application itself provides no extension capabilities. For example, a third-party application may not expose any monitoring signals, but a sidecar can compensate for that.

- A sidecar's life cycle and identity are tied to the main application's life cycle and identity, which allows the sidecar to take on such duties as authentication and transport-level security.

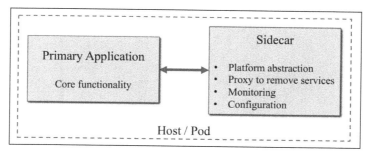

Figure 7.1: The sidecar pattern

The term *service mesh* often refers to the use of the sidecar pattern to provide the infrastructure for microservices communications. The term itself is a bit misleading, since the dictionary definition of a "mesh" would more accurately apply to *the network of microservices* that make up a distributed application and *the interactions between them*. However, the industry seems to be converging on using *service mesh* to refer to the actual communications routing and management infrastructure, and so will we in this book.

Service mesh platforms typically provide two separate components, the **data plane** and the **control plane**. The data plane is a set of network proxies deployed as sidecars that are responsible for the runtime tasks, such as routing, load balancing, rate limiting, circuit breaking, authentication and security, and monitoring. In other words, the data plane's job is to translate, forward, and observe every network packet that goes in and out of the service instance. There is a separate design pattern used to describe this category of sidecars, known as the *Ambassador pattern* and named this way because the sidecar handles all the external communications on behalf of the application. Examples of network proxies that can be used as a service mesh data plane include Envoy, Linkerd, NGINX, HAProxy, and Traefik.

The control plane decides how the data plane should perform its tasks. For example, how does the proxy know where to find service X on the network? Where does it get the configuration parameters for load balancing, timeouts, and circuit breaking? Who configures the authentication and authorization settings? The control plane is in charge of these decisions. It provides policy and configuration for all the network proxies (data plane) that run in a service mesh. The control plane does not touch any packets/requests in the system, as it is never on the critical path. Istio, which we will use in this chapter, is an example of a service mesh control plane. It uses Envoy as the default data plane.

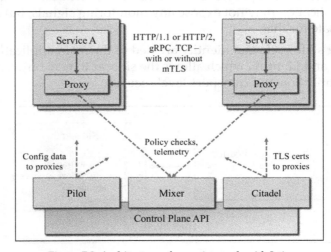

Figure 7.2: Architecture of a service mesh with Istio

The diagram in *Figure 7.2* shows an architecture of the Istio service mesh platform. It is not in the scope of this book to complete a thorough review of Istio, so I will only provide a brief overview. The data plane is represented by the network proxies collocated with the service instances. The control plane at the bottom consists of an API layer and three components:

- Pilot provides service discovery for the proxy sidecars, traffic management capabilities for intelligent routing (for example, A/B tests, canary deployments, and so on), and resiliency (timeouts, retries, circuit breakers, and so on).

- Mixer enforces access control and usage policies across the service mesh, and collects telemetry data from the proxy sidecars and other services.

- Citadel provides strong service-to-service and end-user authentication, with built-in identity and credential management.

Istio supports distributed tracing with Jaeger, Zipkin, and other tracing systems. With the emergence of the standards for tracing data formats that we discussed in *Chapter 6, Tracing Standards and Ecosystem*, the tracing capabilities provided by the service meshes should become completely portable across different tracing backends.

Observability via a service mesh

If we place a service mesh in the path of every network request between the services in an application, it makes it an ideal place to collect consistent, standardized telemetry about the application. This standardized observability alone may be enough to compensate for a small performance loss introduced by going through a proxy for every request because it dramatically enhances the operational properties of the system, making it easier to monitor and troubleshoot:

- The sidecar can emit uniformly named metrics about the traffic going in and out of a service instance, such as throughput, latency, and error rates (also known as the **RED** method (**Rate, Error, Duration**). These metrics can be used to monitor the health of the services and for creating standardized dashboards.

- The sidecar can produce rich access logs. Sometimes these logs need to be produced and stored securely for compliance reasons. Having a single logical component responsible for all those logs is very convenient, especially for applications that are implemented with multiple languages and frameworks, which makes standardizing log format and processing rather difficult.

- The sidecar can generate traces as well. Network proxies like Envoy can handle not only the standard RPC traffic through common protocols like HTTP or gRPC, but other types of network calls as well, such as calls to MySQL databases or Redis cache. By understanding the call protocols, the sidecars can generate rich tracing spans with many useful attributes and annotations.

The ability of the service mesh to generate traces is obviously the most interesting in the context of this book. By generating traces outside of the application, in the routing sidecar, the method looks almost like the holy grail of the black-box approach, which works without any changes to the application. Unfortunately, if something seems too good to be true, it probably is. As we will see, the service mesh tracing does not quite rise up to the level of treating the application as a complete black box. Without the application doing some minimal work to propagate the context, even a service mesh cannot guarantee complete traces.

Prerequisites

In the rest of this chapter, we will focus on collecting tracing data via Istio. We will use a modified version of the Hello application we developed in *Chapter 4, Instrumentation Basics with OpenTracing*, and deploy it along with Istio onto a Kubernetes cluster. First, we will describe some dependencies and installations you will need to do in order to run the examples.

I should note that setting up Kubernetes and Istio is not a particularly easy endeavor. If you are able to follow the following directions and get everything running, then great, you will have a platform where you can experiment more with the ideas introduced in this chapter. However, if you run into a wall and cannot get everything running, do not despair; just read on and simply understand the concepts, and the integration between tracing and a service mesh.

Project source code

The examples can be found in the Chapter07 directory of the book's source code repository on GitHub. Please refer to *Chapter 4, Instrumentation Basics with OpenTracing*, for instructions on how to download it, then switch to the Chapter07 directory, from where all examples can be run.

The source code of the application is organized in the following structure:

```
Mastering-Distributed-Tracing/
  Chapter07/
    exercise1/
```

```
    formatter/
    hello/
 Dockerfile
 Makefile
 app.yml
 gateway.yml
 routing.yml
 pom.xml
```

This version of the application contains only two microservices defined in the submodule `exercise1`. Included is a `Dockerfile` used to build container images that we deploy to Kubernetes, and a `Makefile` with some convenience targets for building and deploying the application. The three YAML (`*.yml`) files contain Kubernetes and Istio configurations.

Java development environment

Similar to the examples in *Chapter 4*, *Instrumentation Basics with OpenTracing*, we will need a JDK 8 or higher installed. The Maven project in `pom.xml` is set up as a multi-module project, so make sure to run the `install` target to install the dependencies in Maven's local repository:

```
$ ./mvnw install
[... skip a lot of Maven logs ...]
[INFO] Reactor Summary:
[INFO]
[INFO] Tracing with Service Mesh ............... SUCCESS [  0.316 s]
[INFO] exercise1 ............................... SUCCESS [  0.006 s]
[INFO] hello-1 ................................. SUCCESS [  2.447 s]
[INFO] formatter-1 ............................. SUCCESS [  0.330 s]
[INFO] ------------------------------------------------------------
[INFO] BUILD SUCCESS
[INFO] ------------------------------------------------------------
```

Kubernetes

In order to run Istio, we need a working Kubernetes installation. The examples in this chapter were tested with **minikube** (version 0.28.2), which runs a single-node Kubernetes cluster inside a virtual machine. Instructions on how to install it are beyond the scope of this book, so please refer to the documentation at `https://kubernetes.io/docs/setup/minikube/`.

Istio

I used Istio version 1.0.2 to run the examples in the chapter. Full installation instructions can be found at `https://istio.io/docs/setup/kubernetes/quick-start/`. Here, I will summarize the steps I took to get it working on minikube.

First, download the release from `https://github.com/istio/istio/releases/tag/1.0.2/`. Unpack the archive and switch to the root directory of the installation, for example, `~/Downloads/istio-1.0.2/`. Add the `/bin` directory to the path to allow you to run the `istioctl` command later:

```
$ cd ~/Downloads/istio-1.0.2/
$ export PATH=$PWD/bin:$PATH
```

Install the custom resource definitions:

```
$ kubectl apply -f install/kubernetes/helm/istio/templates/crds.yaml
```

Install Istio without mutual TLS authentication between components:

```
$ kubectl apply -f install/kubernetes/istio-demo.yaml
```

Ensure that the pods are deployed and running:

```
$ kubectl get pods -n istio-system
```

NAME	READY	STATUS	RESTARTS	AGE
grafana-6cbdcfb45-49vl8	1/1	Running	0	6d
istio-citadel-6b6fdfdd6f-fshfk	1/1	Running	0	6d
istio-cleanup-secrets-84vdg	0/1	Completed	0	6d
istio-egressgateway-56bdd5fcfb-9wfms	1/1	Running	0	6d
istio-galley-96464ff6-p2vhv	1/1	Running	0	6d
istio-grafana-post-install-kcrq6	0/1	Completed	0	6d
istio-ingressgateway-7f4dd7d699-9v2fl	1/1	Running	0	6d
istio-pilot-6f8d49d4c4-m5rjz	2/2	Running	0	6d
istio-policy-67f4d49564-2jxk9	2/2	Running	0	6d
istio-sidecar-injector-69c4bc7974-w6fr	1/1	Running	0	6d
istio-statsd-prom-bridge-7f44bb5ddb-c7t	1/1	Running	0	6d
istio-telemetry-76869cd64f-jk8dc	2/2	Running	0	6d
istio-tracing-ff94688bb-rn7zk	1/1	Running	0	6d
prometheus-84bd4b9796-166qg	1/1	Running	0	6d
servicegraph-c6456d6f5-v7f47	1/1	Running	0	6d

Note: This installation includes Jaeger as part of `istio-tracing`, and a `servicegraph` component. Therefore, we will not be running the Jaeger backend separately as we did in the previous chapters. If you still have it running from earlier exercises, for example, as a Docker container, please make sure to shut it down to avoid port conflicts.

The Hello application

The Hello application implemented as an exercise for this chapter is very similar to the one we used in *Chapter 4, Instrumentation Basics with OpenTracing*. However, since we already have a lot of moving components with Kubernetes, I decided to simplify the setup and dropped the `bigbrother` service, so that we would not need to run a MySQL database. The `bigbrother` service was a bit creepy anyway: it knew too much personal information. Instead, I added some logic to the `formatter` service that gives a bit of conversation to the greeting when given the person's name:

```
@RestController
public class FController {

    private final String template;

    public FController() {
        if (Boolean.getBoolean("professor")) {
            template = "Good news, %s! If anyone needs me " +
                "I'll be in the Angry Dome!";
        } else {
            template = "Hello, puny human %s! Morbo asks: " +
                "how do you like running on Kubernetes?";
        }
        System.out.println("Using template: " + template);
    }


    @GetMapping("/formatGreeting")
    public String formatGreeting(@RequestParam String name,
                                 @RequestHeader HttpHeaders headers) {
        System.out.println("Headers: " + headers);

        return String.format(template, name);
    }
}
```

The Formatter's controller checks for the Java system property
`professor=true|false` and defines a template string it uses for the response.
This property is set in the `Dockerfile` from the same-named environment variable:

```
CMD java \
    ...
    -Dformatter.host=${formatter_host:-formatter} \
    -Dformatter.port=${formatter_port:-8080} \
    -Dprofessor=${professor:-false} \
    -jar ${app_name:?'app_name must be set'}.jar
```

The environment variable `professor` is defined in the Kubernetes' resource `app.yml` file. We use it to simulate two different versions of the service: `v1` without the environment variable, and `v2` with the environment variable set to `true` to make the Formatter produce a different response:

```
apiVersion: extensions/v1beta1
kind: Deployment
metadata:
  name: formatter-svc-v2
spec:
  replicas: 1
  template:
    metadata:
      labels:
        app: formatter-svc
        version: v2
    spec:
      containers:
      - name: formatter-svc
        image: hello-app:latest
        imagePullPolicy: Never
        ports:
        - name: http
          containerPort: 8080
        env:
        - name: app_name
          value: "formatter"
        - name: professor
          value: "true"
```

The entry point to the application is the `hello` service. Since we don't have the `bigbrother` service to call anymore, the `hello` service acts as a simple proxy, by calling the endpoint `/formatGreeting` of the `formatter` service.

It is easy to notice that there is no tracing instrumentation in the code. `HelloController` has one statement that reads the `User-Agent` header from the incoming HTTP request and stores it in the span baggage. I will return to that later in the chapter, as obviously that statement does not generate traces for the execution. Instead, we are using Spring Boot integration with OpenTracing to automatically enable tracing in the application, just like we did in *Chapter 4, Instrumentation Basics with OpenTracing*, by using the following dependencies in `exercise1/hello/pom.xml`:

```
<dependency>
    <groupId>io.opentracing.contrib</groupId>
    <artifactId>opentracing-spring-cloud-starter</artifactId>
</dependency>
<dependency>
    <groupId>io.opentracing.contrib</groupId>
    <artifactId>opentracing-spring-tracer-configuration-starter</artifactId>
</dependency>
<dependency>
    <groupId>io.jaegertracing</groupId>
    <artifactId>jaeger-client</artifactId>
</dependency>
<dependency>
    <groupId>io.jaegertracing</groupId>
    <artifactId>jaeger-zipkin</artifactId>
</dependency>
```

In order to configure the Jaeger tracer automatically, we pass some parameters to it via environment variables that can be found in the `Dockerfile`, which is shared by all microservices:

```
CMD java \
    -DJAEGER_SERVICE_NAME=${app_name} \
    -DJAEGER_PROPAGATION=b3 \
    -DJAEGER_ENDPOINT=http://jaeger-collector.istio-system:14268/api/traces \
    ...
    -jar ${app_name:?'app_name must be set'}.jar
```

> **Note**: We are setting the JAEGER_PROPAGATION=b3 parameter and including the jaeger-zipkin artifact. This is necessary because the Envoy proxy does not recognize Jaeger's default on-the-wire representation of the trace context, but it does recognize Zipkin's B3 headers. This configuration instructs the Jaeger tracer to use B3 headers instead of its default ones.

Distributed tracing with Istio

We are now ready to run the Hello application. First, we need to build a Docker image, so that we can deploy it to Kubernetes. The build process will store the image in the local Docker registry, but that's not good since minikube is run entirely in a virtual machine and we need to push the image to the image registry in that installation. Therefore, we need to define some environment variables to instruct Docker where to push the build. This can be done with the following command:

```
$ eval $(minikube docker-env)
```

After that, we can build the application:

```
$ make build-app
mvn install
[INFO] Scanning for projects...
[... skipping lots of logs ...]
[INFO] BUILD SUCCESS
[INFO] ------------------------------------------------------------------
docker build -t hello-app:latest .
Sending build context to Docker daemon  44.06MB
Step 1/7 : FROM openjdk:alpine
[... skipping lots of logs ...]
Successfully built 67659c954c30
Successfully tagged hello-app:latest
*** make sure the right docker repository is used
*** on minikube run this first: eval $(minikube docker-env)
```

We added a few help messages at the end to remind you to build against the right Docker registry. After the build is done, we can deploy the application:

```
$ make deploy-app
```

The make target executes these commands:

```
deploy-app:
    istioctl kube-inject -f app.yml | kubectl apply -f -
    kubectl apply -f gateway.yml
    istioctl create -f routing.yml
```

The first one instructs Istio to decorate our deployment instructions in app.yml with the sidecar integration, and applies the result. The second command configures the ingress path, so that we can access the hello service from outside of the networking namespace created for the application. The last command adds some extra routing based on the request headers, which we will discuss later in this chapter.

To verify that the services have been deployed successfully, we can list the running pods:

```
$ kubectl get pods
```

NAME	READY	STATUS	RESTARTS	AGE
formatter-svc-v1-59bcd59547-81br5	2/2	Running	0	1m
formatter-svc-v2-7f5c6dfbb6-dx79b	2/2	Running	0	1m
hello-svc-6d789bd689-624jh	2/2	Running	0	1m

As expected, we see the hello service and two versions of the formatter service. In case you run into issues deploying the application, the Makefile includes useful targets to get the logs from the pods:

```
$ make logs-hello
```

```
$ make logs-formatter-v1
```

```
$ make logs-formatter-v2
```

We are almost ready to access the application via curl, but first we need to get the address of the Istio ingress endpoint. I have defined a helper target in the Makefile for that:

```
$ make hostport
export GATEWAY_URL=192.168.99.103:31380
```

Either execute the export command manually or run eval $(make hostport). Then use the GATEWAY_URL variable to send a request to the application using curl:

```
$ curl http://$GATEWAY_URL/sayHello/Brian
Hello, puny human Brian! Morbo asks: how do you like running on
Kubernetes?
```

As you can see, the application is working. Now it's time to look at the trace collected from this request. The Istio demo we installed includes Jaeger installation, but it is running in the virtual machine and we need to set up port forwarding to access it from the local host. Fortunately, I have included another `Makefile` target for that:

```
$ make jaeger
kubectl port-forward -n istio-system $(kubectl get pod -n istio-
system -l app=jaeger -o jsonpath='{.items[0].metadata.name}')
16686:16686
Forwarding from 127.0.0.1:16686 -> 16686
Forwarding from [::1]:16686 -> 16686
```

This allows us to access the Jaeger UI via the usual address: `http://localhost:16686/`. Let's go to the **Dependencies | DAG** page first, to see what services were registered by Jaeger during tracing (*Figure 7.3*).

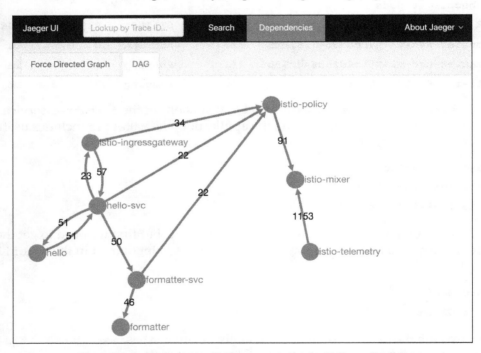

Figure 7.3: Services captured in Jaeger traces for the Hello application

This graph looks a bit strange because our `hello` and `formatter` services appear to be duplicated. If we go back to the `app.yml` deployment file, we will see that we are passing the `app_name` environment variable to our services with values `hello` and `formatter`. Those names are passed to Jaeger tracers as the service names via the `JAEGER_SERVICE_NAME=${app_name}` Java system property. So, we would expect to see a link between the `hello` and `formatter` services on the service graph. Instead, we see those two services hanging off two other nodes, `hello-svc` and `formatter-svc`. These two extra names are the names we gave to the services in the Kubernetes configuration:

```
apiVersion: v1
kind: Service
metadata:
  name: hello-svc
---
apiVersion: v1
kind: Service
metadata:
  name: formatter-svc
```

The spans for them are created automatically by Envoy. The Envoy proxy intercepts both inbound and outbound network calls for each service, which explains why the `hello` service has links in both directions to and from `hello-svc` service. Effectively, the `hello` service is wrapped by the `hello-svc` service. The `formatter` service does not make any outbound calls, so the sidecar only intercepts the inbound call to it, which is indicated by the incoming arrow. Using different names for the actual services and for their Kubernetes counterparts allows us to observe these finer details in the service graph.

What are the other services we see in the graph? They are part of the Istio system. The node `istio-ingressgateway` represents the public API endpoint we are accessing via `curl`. The three nodes on the right, `policy`, `mixer`, and `telemetry`, are the other services of Istio. They are not on the critical path of the main application requests, but are still captured in the same trace. Let's look at that trace in a Gantt chart view. I recommend selecting `hello-svc` in the **Services** dropdown menu to ensure you find the right trace.

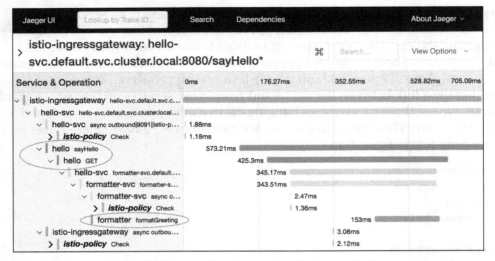

Figure 7.4: A trace with spans produced by the application
(highlighted with red ovals on the left) and by the service mesh

In In the screenshot (*Figure 7.4*), I collapsed the `istio-policy` spans to make room
for the more interesting parts of the trace. We see three spans highlighted with ovals
on the left that are emitted by the white-box instrumentation in Spring Boot. The rest
of the spans are produced by Istio. If we expand one of those, we will see that there
are a lot of additional details captured in the span tags (*Figure 7.5*).

hello-svc.default.svc.cluster.local:8080/sayHello*	Service: **istio-ingressgateway** Duration: **701.13ms** Start Time: **0ms**
∨ Tags	
component	`"proxy"`
node_id	`"router~172.17.0.7~istio-ingressgateway-7f4dd7d699-dvdrd.istio-system-istio-system.svc.cluster.local"`
guid:x-request-id	`"d23285ba-aede-9cc9-a5b3-4e8b285e4abf"`
http.url	`"http://localhost:8080/sayHello/Brian"`
http.method	`"GET"`
downstream_cluster	`"-"`
user_agent	`"curl/7.47.0"`
http.protocol	`"HTTP/1.1"`
request_size	`"0"`
upstream_cluster	`"outbound|8080||hello-svc.default.svc.cluster.local"`
http.status_code	`"200"`
response_size	`"75"`
response_flags	`"-"`
span.kind	`"client"`

> Process: ip - 172.17.0.7

SpanID: f9185a2fed332288

Figure 7.5: Tags in one of the spans produced by Istio

As we can see from the trace, using a service mesh adds quite a bit of complexity to the request-processing pipeline. If we were to run this Hello application without a service mesh and capture a trace, it would contain just three spans: two from the `hello` service and one from the `formatter`. The same trace in the service mesh contains 19 spans. However, if we were to run our simple application in the actual production environment, we would have to deal with many of the same concerns that the service mesh solves for us, so the complexity of the trace is just a reflection of that reality. When tracing via the service mesh, we at least have the visibility into all those additional interactions happening in our architecture.

An acute reader may have noticed that even though I started the chapter with the premise that the service mesh may provide black-box style tracing of our application, we in practice used the application that is internally instrumented for tracing via Spring Boot–OpenTracing integration. What happens if we remove the white-box instrumentation? Fortunately, in our application it is easy to try. All we need to do is remove (or comment out) these Jaeger dependencies from the files `exercise1/hello/pom.xml` and `exercise1/formatter/pom.xml`:

```
<!--
<dependency>
    <groupId>io.jaegertracing</groupId>
    <artifactId>jaeger-client</artifactId>
</dependency>
<dependency>
    <groupId>io.jaegertracing</groupId>
    <artifactId>jaeger-zipkin</artifactId>
</dependency>
-->
```

Let's remove, rebuild, and redeploy the application:

```
$ make delete-app
istioctl delete -f routing.yml
Deleted config: virtual-service/default/formatter-virtual-svc
Deleted config: destination-rule/default/formatter-svc-destination
kubectl delete -f app.yml
service "hello-svc" deleted
deployment.extensions "hello-svc" deleted
service "formatter-svc" deleted
deployment.extensions "formatter-svc-v1" deleted
deployment.extensions "formatter-svc-v2" deleted
```

```
$ make build-app
mvn install
[... skip many logs ...]
docker build -t hello-app:latest .
[... skip many logs ...]
Successfully built 58854ed04def
Successfully tagged hello-app:latest
*** make sure the right docker repository is used
*** on minikube run this first: eval $(minikube docker-env)

$ make deploy-app
istioctl kube-inject -f app.yml | kubectl apply -f -
service/hello-svc created
deployment.extensions/hello-svc created
service/formatter-svc created
deployment.extensions/formatter-svc-v1 created
deployment.extensions/formatter-svc-v2 created
kubectl apply -f gateway.yml
gateway.networking.istio.io/hello-app-gateway unchanged
virtualservice.networking.istio.io/hello-app unchanged
istioctl create -f routing.yml
Created config virtual-service/default/formatter-virtual-svc at
revision 191779
Created config destination-rule/default/formatter-svc-destination at
revision 191781
```

Waits till the pods are running (use the `kubectl get pods` command to check) and send a request:

```
$ curl http://$GATEWAY_URL/sayHello/Brian
Hello, puny human Brian! Morbo asks: how do you like running on
Kubernetes?
```

If we search for traces involving `hello-svc`, we will see that instead of one trace, we have two traces (look for the timestamp on the right, *Figure 7.6*).

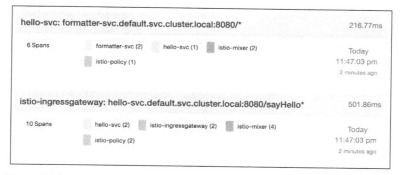

Figure 7.6: Two traces instead of one after we removed white-box instrumentation

If we open the shorter trace (first in the screenshot), we will see that the top two spans represent the egress from the `hello-svc`, and then the ingress to the `formatter-svc`, both captured by the sidecar. The other spans are the administrative activity (calls to the mixer, and so on):

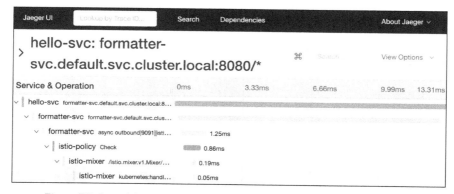

Figure 7.7: One of the two traces after we removed white-box instrumentation

As we can see, without some form of white-box instrumentation, the promise of the service mesh to provide tracing capabilities does not fully hold. It is not difficult to understand why that is. When the `hello` service receives the request forwarded by the sidecar proxy, the request headers contain tracing context. Since the application has no internal instrumentation, this context is not propagated when the service makes an outbound call to the `formatter` service. The sidecar intercepts the outbound call and seeing that it has no tracing context, starts a new trace and injects the needed headers. That's why the trace we opened still showed the `hello-svc` service calling the `formatter-svc` service.

So, how is this supposed to work then? If we read the documentation for systems like Linkerd or Envoy, we will find a fine print saying that in order for tracing to work, the application must propagate a set of known headers from every inbound call to all outbound calls. To try this out, I have added a second controller to the `hello` service, called `HelloController2`, which has the additional logic of copying a set of headers required by Istio from the inbound request to the outbound request:

```java
private final static String[] tracingHeaderKeys = {
        "x-request-id",
        "x-b3-traceid",
        "x-b3-spanid",
        "x-b3-parentspanid",
        "x-b3-sampled",
        "x-b3-flags",
        "x-ot-span-context"
};

private HttpHeaders copyHeaders(HttpHeaders headers) {
    HttpHeaders tracingHeaders = new HttpHeaders();
    for (String key : tracingHeaderKeys) {
        String value = headers.getFirst(key);
        if (value != null) {
            tracingHeaders.add(key, value);
        }
    }
    return tracingHeaders;
}
```

The main handler method invokes this `copyHeaders()` method and passes the result to the `formatGreeting()` method to include in the outbound request:

```java
@GetMapping("/sayHello2/{name}")
public String sayHello(@PathVariable String name,
                       @RequestHeader HttpHeaders headers) {
    System.out.println("Headers: " + headers);

    String response = formatGreeting(name, copyHeaders(headers));
    return response;
}

private String formatGreeting(String name, HttpHeaders tracingHeaders)
{
    URI uri = UriComponentsBuilder
            .fromHttpUrl(formatterUrl)
            .queryParam("name", name)
            .build(Collections.emptyMap());
```

```
    ResponseEntity<String> response = restTemplate.exchange(
        uri, HttpMethod.GET, new HttpEntity<>(tracingHeaders),
        String.class);
    return response.getBody();
}
```

To execute this code path, we only need to send a request to a different URL, `/sayHello2`:

```
$ curl http://$GATEWAY_URL/sayHello2/Brian
Hello, puny human Brian! Morbo asks: how do you like running on
Kubernetes?
```

All looks good; let's try to find the trace in Jaeger, which looks like the screenshot in *Figure 7.8*. Once again, I collapsed the calls to the mixer to remove the distraction. We can clearly see that the proper context transfer is happening and a single trace is starting from the entry into the Istio gateway, and all the way down to the call to the `formatter` service.

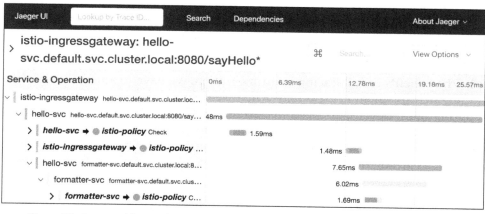

Figure 7.8: A trace without white-box instrumentation but with manual copying of headers

We have come to the most important point of this chapter. A service mesh provides great tracing capabilities outside of the application, but it *does not work without some form of instrumentation*. Should one use full white-box tracing instrumentation or just pass the headers? I recommend using regular tracing instrumentation, for the following reasons:

- The most difficult part of tracing instrumentation is making sure the context is correctly propagated, especially when dealing with asynchronous programming frameworks. There is little difference between propagating the full span or just the headers, as we have to deal with the same difficulties, so neither approach is easier.

- Having full white-box tracing instrumentation in the application allows much more control over data collection. There may be some resource contention that is only visible inside the application and tracing via the sidecar will not reveal anything about it. There may be some business-specific attributes we may want to save to the span that can be very useful during debugging, but the service mesh will never know about them.

- When using an instrumentation like OpenTracing, our application does not need to know which headers it should propagate for the tracing to work, as this knowledge is abstracted by the tracer implementation. This is especially important for general-purpose context propagation, or **baggage**, which we will discuss in *Chapter 10, Distributed Context Propagation*, because some tracing implementations (Jaeger, in particular) use multiple headers to carry the baggage whose names are dependent on the baggage keys. To pass those headers manually, it would not be enough to know the exact header names; the application would have to contain a matching logic to know which headers are part of the trace context.

- When tracing instrumentation is tightly integrated with the application framework used by a service, such as Spring Boot in our examples, the propagation of the context happens automatically with no code changes, so we get a much better guarantee that a particular service will not drop the context because someone forgot to propagate the headers.

Despite the benefits of full tracing instrumentation, we have to admit that it takes more code to implement it, especially when we do not have nice integration, as with Spring Boot. Developers need to learn not only how to pass the context around the application, but also how to start and finish spans, how to annotate them with useful attributes, and how to inject and extract the context when crossing the process boundaries. Learning how to do that adds more cognitive load for the developers.

Using Istio to generate a service graph

We have already seen an example of a service graph earlier in this chapter (*Figure 7.3*). Istio provides another utility service called `servicegraph`, which is able to generate a similar service graph without the help of tracing. To enable access to that service, we again need to set up port forwarding, which we can do with this `Makefile` target:

```
$ make service-graph
kubectl -n istio-system port-forward $(kubectl get pod -n istio-
system -l app=servicegraph -o jsonpath='{.items[0].metadata.name}')
8088:8088
Forwarding from 127.0.0.1:8088 -> 8088
Forwarding from [::1]:8088 -> 8088
```

This allows us to access the service at `http://localhost:8088/`. However, the service does not have a home page in the version of Istio we are using, so we need to access specific URLs. We will take a look at two different graph visualizations provided by Istio: a force-directed graph accessible at `http://localhost:8088/force/forcegraph.html` and a Graphviz-based visualization accessible at `http://localhost:8088/dotviz`. Note that I took the screenshots when running just a single version of the `formatter` service, as otherwise the graph becomes too large and difficult to read, and does not fit a single screenshot.

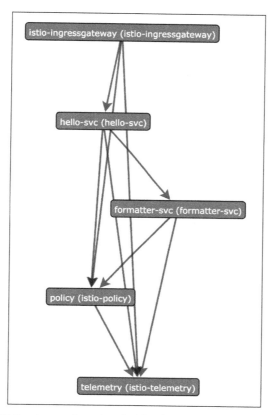

Figure 7.9: Service graph rendered with a force-directed graph algorithm

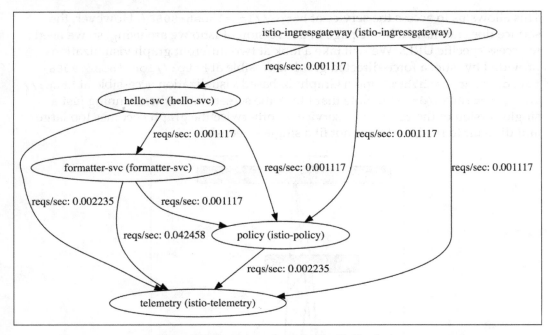

Figure 7.10: Service graph rendered with Graphviz

The graphs produced by Istio resemble the graph generated by Jaeger; however, they do not include the `hello` and `formatter` nodes that were present in the Jaeger graph. This is because the graphs are not generated from the tracing data but from the telemetry collected by the proxy sidecars. Without the tracing information, the sidecars only know about pairwise communications between nodes, but that is enough to construct the graphs we see in the screenshots, and it does not depend on any white-box instrumentation in the services. Another nice thing about Istio service graphs is that they use the data collected in real time, and accept parameters like `filter_empty` and `time_horizon`, which allow you to control whether to show all services or only those actively receiving traffic, and to control the time window.

Distributed context and routing

I want to finish off this chapter with another form of integration of tracing and a service mesh, where we use distributed context propagation of the tracing API to affect the routing of the requests. To run the example, please revert the change to the `pom.xml` files to add back the Jaeger tracer dependencies. Then rebuild and redeploy the application:

```
$ make delete-app
$ make build-app
```

```
$ make deploy-app
$ kubectl get pods
```

As you may remember, I mentioned earlier in this chapter that we deploy two versions of the `formatter` service, v1 and v2, where v2 is passed an extra environment variable, `professor=true`. That version produces a different response, but we have not seen it yet. In order to get it, we need to take a walk down memory lane. In the early days of the internet, there used to be a great web browser called Netscape. One has to be very old, like the Professor, to remember it. What if we pretend to send a request from that browser?

```
$ curl -A Netscape http://$GATEWAY_URL/sayHello/Brian
Good news, Brian! If anyone needs me I'll be in the Angry Dome!
```

There we go; we have a new response from v2 of the `formatter`. The switch `-A` is used to set the `User-Agent` header on the request. Why is this request routed to v2 of the service when others are not? The answer is because we defined a routing rule based on the OpenTracing baggage. First, let's look at the code of the `HelloController`:

```
@GetMapping("/sayHello/{name}")
public String sayHello(@PathVariable String name,
                       @RequestHeader HttpHeaders headers) {
    Span span = tracer.activeSpan();
    if (span != null) {
        span.setBaggageItem("user-agent",
                            headers.getFirst(HttpHeaders.USER_AGENT));
    }

    String response = formatGreeting(name);
    return response;
}
```

We can see here that we are getting the `User-Agent` header from the HTTP request headers and setting it as baggage on the current span with the key `user-agent`. This is the only change in the code. From previous chapters, we already know that the baggage will be automatically propagated to all downstream calls, namely to the `formatter` service. However, the `formatter` service itself does not depend on this baggage. Instead, we defined an Istio routing rule (in the file `routing.yml`) that checks for the string *Netscape* in the header `baggage-user-agent` and forwards the request to v2 of the `formatter-svc`:

```
apiVersion: networking.istio.io/v1alpha3
kind: VirtualService
metadata:
```

```
    name: formatter-virtual-svc
spec:
  hosts:
  - formatter-svc
  http:
  - match:
    - headers:
        baggage-user-agent:
          regex: .*Netscape.*
    route:
    - destination:
        host: formatter-svc
        subset: v2
  - route:
    - destination:
        host: formatter-svc
        subset: v1
```

The name `baggage-user-agent` is formed by the prefix `baggage-` used by Zipkin tracers to pass the baggage values, and the key `user-agent` we defined in the code. Since Jaeger tracers support the Zipkin headers format, we have the integration with Istio working seamlessly.

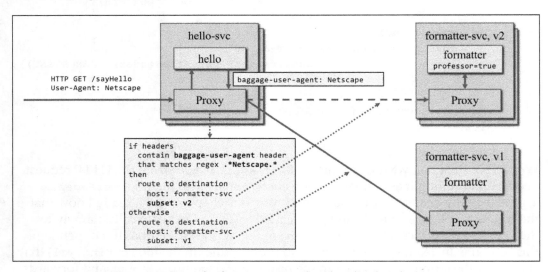

Figure 7.11: Example of routing requests based on distributed context

This is obviously a toy example. Where would one use this functionality in real systems? There may be many applications of this approach, including A/B testing, canary deployments, routing traffic from test accounts differently, and so on. For example, assume we are about to release a new version of some downstream service, and we want to do a canary deployment where only traffic from a specific group of users is routed to that version (for example, only the requests from the company's own employees who are dogfooding the application). The problem is, first we need to run some code in the upper layer to determine whether the user executing the current request is eligible to be routed to the new version, and second, the routing needs to happen somewhere downstream on a per-request basis. The combination of distributed context propagation and service mesh routing works exceptionally well in this case.

Summary

Service meshes are a powerful platform for adding observability features to distributed, microservices-based applications. Without any changes to the application, they produce a rich set of metrics and logs that can be used to monitor and troubleshoot the application. Service meshes can also generate distributed traces, provided that the application is white-box instrumented to propagate the context, either by passing the headers only, or through normal tracing instrumentation.

In this chapter, we have discussed the pros and cons of both approaches and showed examples of the traces that can be obtained with each approach. The sidecar proxies comprise the data plane of the service mesh, and their intimate knowledge of inter-service communications allows for the generation of detailed and up-to-date service graphs. By combining the OpenTracing baggage (distributed context propagation facility) with routing rules in the service mesh, we can perform targeted, request-scoped routing decisions, useful for A/B testing and canary deployments.

So far, we have discussed various ways of extracting tracing data from applications. In the following and last chapter of Part II we will review different sampling strategies that affect which and how much data is captured by the tracing infrastructure.

References

1. Michael Chow, David Meisner, Jason Flinn, Daniel Peek, Thomas F. Wenisch. *The Mystery Machine: End-to-end Performance Analysis of Large-scale Internet.* Proceedings of the 11th USENIX Symposium on Operating Systems Design and Implementation. October 6–8, 2014.

2. Istio: Connect, secure, control, and observe services: `https://istio.io/`.

3. Kubernetes: Production Grade Container Orchestration: `https://kubernetes.io/`.

4. Wikipedia: Enterprise Service Bus: `https://en.wikipedia.org/wiki/Enterprise_service_bus`.

8

All About Sampling

The gathering of monitoring data in production is always a compromise between the costs, in terms of storage and performance overhead, and the expressiveness of the collected data. The more data we collect, the better we hope to be able to diagnose the situation, should something go wrong, yet we don't want to slow down the applications or pay exorbitant bills for storage. Even though most logging frameworks support multiple levels of log severity, a common wisdom is to tune the loggers in production to discard anything logged with the *debug* level or lower. Many organizations even adopt the rule that successful requests should leave no logs at all, and you only log when there is some issue with the request.

Distributed tracing is not immune to this compromise either. Depending on the verbosity of the instrumentation, tracing data can easily exceed the volume of the actual business traffic sustained by an application. Collecting all that data in memory, and sending it to the tracing backend, can have a real impact on the application's latency and throughput. Meanwhile, tracing backends may have their own capacity limitations when processing and storing the data. To deal with these concerns, most tracing systems employ various forms of sampling to capture only a certain portion of the observed traces. For example, without sampling, the Dapper tracer [1] was reported to impose 1.5% throughput and a 16% latency overhead for a web search workload. When using sampling to capture only 0.01% of the traces, the throughput overhead was reduced to 0.06% and the response time slowdown was reduced to 0.20%.

In this chapter, we will review different sampling schemes employed by modern tracing systems; the pros and cons of these schemes, and certain challenges in implementing them. Most of the sampling methods share a common characteristic of trying to make a sampling decision at the level of the whole trace, not its individual spans. This is often referred to as *consistent* or *coherent* sampling. Being able to capture and analyze complete traces, with all the causality between spans preserved, allows much deeper understanding of the request workflow. In contrast, if sampling were performed only on individual spans, it would be impossible to reconstruct the complete call graph of the request flow and the value of the data would be drastically reduced.

Head-based consistent sampling

Head-based consistent sampling, also known as upfront sampling, makes the sampling decision once per trace at the beginning of the trace. The decision is usually made by the tracing libraries running inside the application, because consulting the tracing backend at the point of creating the first span would put the tracing infrastructure onto the critical path of the business requests, which is highly undesirable for performance and reliability reasons.

The decision is recorded as part of the trace metadata and propagated throughout the call graph as part of the context. This sampling scheme is consistent because it ensures that either all spans of a given trace are captured by the tracing system or none of them are. Head-based sampling is employed by the majority of existing industrial-grade tracing systems today.

When the sampling decision must be made at the root of the trace, there is relatively little information available to the tracer on which to base that decision. Nonetheless, there are many algorithms that are used in today's tracing systems to help with making that decision, which we will discuss in the following sections.

Probabilistic sampling

In **probabilistic sampling**, the sampling decision is made based on a coin toss with a certain probability, for example (using a pseudo-language):

```
class ProbabilisticSampler(probability: Double) {
  def isSampled: Boolean = {
    if (Math.random() < probability) {
      return true
    } else {
      return false
    }
  }
}
```

Some tracer implementations make use of the fact that in many tracing systems, the trace ID itself is a randomly generated number and can be used to avoid making a second call to the random number generator, in order to reduce the overhead:

```
class ProbabilisticSampler(probability: Double) {
  val boundary: Double = Long.MaxValue * probability

  def isSampled(traceId: Long): Boolean = {
    if (traceId < boundary) {
      return true
    } else {
      return false
    }
  }
}
```

Probabilistic samplers are by far the most popular in the tracing systems using head-based sampling. For example, all Jaeger tracers and the Spring Cloud Sleuth [2] tracer default to probabilistic samplers. In Jaeger, the default sampling probability is 0.001, that is, tracing one in a thousand requests.

Probabilistic samplers have a nice mathematical property of allowing extrapolation of various measurements based on the spans collected by the tracing backend. For example, assume we collected 100 spans for a certain endpoint X of some service during some time interval. If we know the sampling probability, p, applied to the root span, we can estimate the total number of calls to the endpoint, X, during the time interval to be $100/p$. Such estimates provide very useful data for analyzing patterns across multiple traces, which we will cover in *Chapter 12, Gathering Insights with Data Mining*.

Rate limiting sampling

Another simple implementation of a sampling decision is to employ a **rate limiter**, for example, by using a **leaky bucket algorithm**, which is also known as **reservoir sampling**. The rate limiter ensures that only a fixed number of traces are sampled per given time interval, for example, 10 traces per second or one trace per minute. Rate limiting sampling can be useful in microservices that have very uneven traffic patterns, because probabilistic sampling can only be configured with a single probability value, which could be too small during low-traffic periods and too large during high-traffic periods.

The following code shows a sample implementation of a rate limiter used in Jaeger. Instead of the leaky bucket algorithm terminology, it is implemented as a virtual bank account that has a fixed rate of credits being added to it, up to a maximum balance, and the sampling decision is allowed if we have enough credits to withdraw a certain fixed amount of credits (typically 1.0). Every time a call is made to check the balance, the current credit balance is recalculated based on the elapsed time, and then compared to the withdrawal amount:

```
class RateLimiter(creditsPerSecond: Double, maxBalance: Double) {
  val creditsPerNanosecond = creditsPerSecond / 1e9

  var balance: Double = 0
  var lastTick = System.nanoTime()

  def withdraw(amount: Double): Boolean = {
    val currentTime = System.nanoTime()
    val elapsedTime = currentTime - lastTick
    lastTick = currentTime
    balance += elapsedTime * creditsPerNanosecond
    if (balance > maxBalance) {
      balance = maxBalance
    }
    if (balance >= amount) {
      balance -= amount
      return true
    }
    return false
  }
}
```

Given this `RateLimiter` class, the rate limiting sampler can be implemented by attempting to withdraw the amount of 1.0 units for every call to `isSampled`. Note how this sampler supports rates of sampling less than 1 (for example, one trace in 10 seconds), by setting `maxBalance` to `1.0`:

```
class RateLimitingSampler(tracesPerSecond: Double) {
  val limiter = new RateLimiter(
    creditsPerSecond=tracesPerSecond,
    maxBalance=Math.max(tracesPerSecond, 1.0)
  )

  def isSampled: Boolean = {
    return limiter.withdraw(1.0)
  }
}
```

The rate of sampled traces allowed by the rate limiting sampler usually has
no correlation with the actual traffic going through the application, thus the
extrapolation calculations possible with the probabilistic sampler are not possible
here. For this reason, rate limiting samplers may not be very useful in isolation.

Guaranteed-throughput probabilistic sampling

To partially address the issue of rate limiting for services with spiky traffic,
Jaeger tracers implement a **guaranteed-throughput sampler** that is a combination
of a probabilistic sampler for normal operations and an additional rate limiter for
low-traffic periods. The rate limiter is only consulted when the probabilistic sampler
decides not to sample. This ensures that a given trace point is sampled with at least
a certain minimal rate, hence the name "guaranteed throughput." Here is the basic
algorithm of this sampler:

```
class GuaranteedThroughputSampler(
  probability: Double,
  minTracesPerSecond: Double
) {
  val probabilistic = new ProbabilisticSampler(probability)
  val lowerBound = new RateLimitingSampler(minTracesPerSecond)

  def isSampled: Boolean = {
    val prob: Boolean = probabilistic.isSampled()
    val rate: Boolean = lowerBound.isSampled()
    if (prob) {
      return prob
    }
    return rate
  }
}
```

The reason the lower bound sampler is invoked before checking the result of the probabilistic sampler is to ensure that probabilistic decisions still count toward the rate limits. The real implementation you can find in Jaeger code is a little bit more involved, as it also captures the description of the sampler that made the decision as `sampler.type` and `sampler.param` tags on the root span. Thus, if a trace is sampled because of the probabilistic sampler, the backend can still perform extrapolation calculations.

These guaranteed-throughput samplers are rarely used by themselves, instead forming the basis of **adaptive sampling**, which will be discussed later.

Adaptive sampling

One of the primary reasons we sample traces is to avoid overloading tracing backends with too much data, which they may not be able to handle. It is possible to use simple probabilistic sampling and to tune the probabilities to ensure a steady rate of trace data coming to the tracing backend. However, that assumes the business traffic stays at roughly stable levels, which is rarely the case in practice. For example, most online services handle more traffic during the day than during the night. There are several ways the tracing backends can deal with fluctuating traffic:

- The backend storage may be over-provisioned to handle maximum traffic. The downside is that it leads to wasted capacity during lower-traffic periods.

- The trace ingestion pipeline may be implemented on top of a messaging solution, such as Kafka, which is usually more elastic and easier to scale than a database because it does no processing of the messages, while the database has to index all the incoming data. During the traffic spikes, the excess data that cannot be timely stored in the database is buffered in the message queues. This could lead to a time lag before the tracing data becomes available to the users.

- Another simple option, which is supported in Jaeger by default, is to shed traffic when the database is not able to save all incoming data fast enough. However, this mechanism should only be used as an escape valve during unexpected traffic spikes, not as a way of dealing with normal seasonality. Load shedding happens early in the collection pipeline, in the stateless collectors, which operate on individual spans rather than full traces, and therefore they cannot guarantee that during load shedding they will be able to save or discard the spans consistently for any given trace.

Another common problem with using simple samplers is that they do not distinguish between workloads with different traffic volumes. For example, a Gmail server may have an endpoint `get_mail` that is called a thousand times more often than a `manage_account` endpoint.

If every endpoint were sampled with the same probabilistic sampler, then its probability would have to be small enough to ensure a low overhead and trace volume from the high-traffic get_mail endpoint. It would be too small to get enough traces from the manage_account endpoint, even though that endpoint has enough overhead budget to tolerate higher sampling rates.

Jaeger tracers support a form of sampling strategy called *per-operation sampling*, which uses a separately configured sampler for each operation name that is captured from the root spans, that is, spans that start a new trace. While this may include some inner spans, for example, if the service has some background thread that does some work and starts traces, in practice, this frequently corresponds to the endpoints exposed and traced by the service. Per-operation sampling allows for using different sampling probabilities for endpoints with different traffic volumes. The main challenge is how to determine the appropriate parameters of the samplers across all services and all their endpoints in a large distributed system. Manual configuration of tracers in each service is not a scalable approach in modern cloud-native systems that consist of hundreds, or even thousands, of microservices.

Adaptive sampling techniques try to address these problems by dynamically adjusting sampling parameters throughout the architecture, based on the difference between the actual and the desired rate of trace data generation. They can be implemented in two flavors, depending on whether the observations and adjustments are done locally in the tracers or globally in the tracing backend.

 For simplicity, the discussion in the following sections will be referring to **sampling per service**, but, in practice, the algorithms are implemented at the operation level, that is, **service and endpoint**.

Local adaptive sampling

Local adaptive sampling was described in Google's Dapper paper [1] as a way to automatically customize sampling probabilities across workloads with different traffic. The authors of Dapper proposed an adaptive sampler that still makes probabilistic sampling decisions, but also automatically adjusts the sampling probability over time, with the aim of reaching a certain stable rate of sampled traces. In other words, the tracers are parameterized not by a fixed probability of sampling, but by a desired rate of sampled traces, or the **effective sampling rate**, similar to the rate limiting sampler we discussed earlier. The tracers then automatically adjust their own sampling probability based on the number of traces they end up sampling with the current probability, trying to bring that number close to the target rate. Google did not publish the exact details of the algorithm, but in the next section, we will study something similar, only on the global scale of all service instances.

Global adaptive sampling

Dapper's local adaptive sampling allows us to replace a uniform sampling probability across all services with another uniform parameter for an effective sampling rate, while the actual probability is dynamically adjusted. The target effective rate is still a configuration parameter that needs to be provided to each tracer in each microservice. A single value of this parameter may not be appropriate across the whole architecture:

- Some services may be more important than others and we may want more traces from them
- Some services may only produce small and shallow traces, while others may produce traces with thousands of spans
- Some endpoints in the same service may be very important (for example, StartTrip in the Uber app), while others are not that interesting when traced (for example, a ping with the car location every few seconds)
- Some services may be running only a few instances, while others may run hundreds or thousands of instances, resulting in vastly different volumes of traces

We need to be able to assign different target rates to services and do it dynamically while the service is running. Also, we do not want to manage these parameters manually because it is not scalable given the number of microservices in large architectures.

As we will see in *Chapter 14, Under the Hood of a Distributed Tracing System*, Jaeger client libraries were intentionally designed with a feedback loop from the Jaeger tracing backend that allows the backend to push configuration changes back to the clients. This design allows us to build more intelligent adaptive sampling controlled from the backend. Unlike local adaptive sampling, which has only limited information from a single service instance for making a sampling decision, the backend is able to observe all traces post-collection and calculate adjustments to sampling parameters based on a global view of the traffic patterns.

Goals

There are several different goals we may be trying to achieve with adaptive sampling:

- We may want to ensure that a given service is sampled on average N times per second, across all instances of the service. Since we make a sampling decision once per trace, this is the same as targeting a certain number of **traces per second** (TPS). Note that N can be less than 1 to represent rates of sampling like "one trace per minute."

- Since traces originating from different services may differ in the number of spans by orders of magnitude, another possible objective is to achieve a stable number of *spans per second* flowing to the tracing backend in the sampled traces.

- Different spans can vary significantly in their byte size, depending on how many tags and events are recorded in them. To account for that factor, the target measure can be *bytes per second*, which includes the total byte size of all spans in all traces sampled by a service.

Some of these goals may be more important than the others; it really depends on the distributed system and the verbosity level of tracing instrumentation. Most of them cannot be addressed via local adaptive sampling, since the information is not available at the time of making the sampling decision. The global adaptive sampling algorithm described in the following section can work for all three goals, although, in practice, Jaeger currently only implements the TPS optimization.

Theory

The adaptive sampling used in Jaeger is conceptually similar to the classic **proportional-integral-derivative (PID)** controller used in a variety of applications requiring continuously modulated control, such as cruise control on a vehicle. Imagine that we are driving a car on a highway and want to keep it at a steady speed of 60 mph. We can think of the car as the process that we want to control, by observing its current speed as the measured **process value**, $y(t)$, and affecting it by changing the power output of the vehicle's engine as the **correction signal**, $u(t)$, in order to minimize the **error**, $e(t)$, between the **desired process value**, $r(t)$, of 60 mph and the current speed, $y(t)$. A PID controller (*Figure 8.1*) calculates the correction signal, $u(t)$, as a weighted sum of proportional, integral, and derivative terms (denoted by **P**, **I**, and **D** respectively), which give the controller its name.

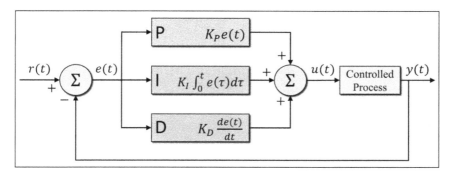

Figure 8.1: A traditional PID controller, whose behavior is defined by the coefficients $K_p, K_I,$ and K_D

Let's apply these terms to the problem of adaptive sampling:

- The process value, $y(t)$, that we want to control is the number of traces sampled for a given service, across all instances of that service during a certain time interval. We can measure it in TPS.

- The desired process value, $r(t)$, is a target TPS that is deemed acceptable given the level of overhead in the instrumented applications and the capacity of the tracing backend.

- The control signal, $u(t)$, is the sampling probability calculated by the algorithm and given back to the clients by the backend.

- The error is standard: $e(t) = r(t) - y(r)$.

As we will see in the following section, the proportional, integral, and derivative terms of the standard PID controller are not well suited for the problem of adaptive sampling directly because of the distributed nature of the implementation.

Architecture

The architecture of Jaeger adaptive sampling is shown in *Figure 8.2*. On the left, we see a number of microservices, each running the Jaeger tracing library that collects tracing data and sends it to the Jaeger collectors (solid lines). The adaptive sampling infrastructure in the collectors calculates the desired sampling probabilities for all services and provides them back to the tracing libraries that periodically poll for that information (dashed lines). We do not show the complete collection pipeline here, as it is not relevant. The adaptive sampling is implemented by four cooperating components that are running inside each Jaeger collector.

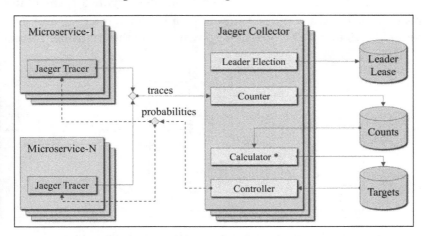

Figure 8.2: Adaptive sampling in Jaeger

The **Counter** listens to all spans received by the collector and keeps track of the number of root spans received from each microservice, and each operation. If the tags in the root span indicate that it was sampled via a probabilistic sampler, it counts as a new sampled trace.

The **Counter** aggregates the counts for a given observation period, τ (usually one minute), and at the end of the period, saves the accumulated counts to the **Counts** table in the database. Since each collector runs a **Counter** component, there are K summaries saved to the database every period, where K is the number of collectors.

The **Calculator** is responsible for calculating the correction signal (sampling probability), $u(t)$, for each service and endpoint pair, depending on the observed number of sampled traces per second, $y(t)$. It first calculates the process value, $y(t)$, by reading all accumulated summaries for this endpoint from the **Counts** table for the last m periods, where m is a configuration parameter (usually 10, corresponding to a lookback interval of 10 minutes). The reason we use a lookback period is to smooth the function by effectively calculating a moving average (similar to the integral term of the PID controller). The **Calculator** then computes the sampling probabilities, $u(t)$, for each service and endpoint, and saves them to the **Targets** table.

To avoid **Calculator** components from different collectors overriding each other's calculations, only one **Calculator** is active at any given time. This is achieved by running a very simple leader election. Each collector contains a **Leader Election** component that periodically tries to save a leader lease tuple, (N,T), to the database, where N is the name or identity of the contender and T is the expiration time of the lease. This is done via a compare-and-set operation on the Cassandra database, with a quorum write. This leader election scheme is not bulletproof, especially in the presence of network delays, when two collectors might think each of them is a leader, but for the purpose of adaptive sampling, it is good enough. The worst that can happen is the mistaken leader will repeat the same probability calculations and overwrite the data.

Finally, the **Controller** component in each collector is responsible for periodically reading the computed probabilities from the **Targets** table, caching them in memory, and sending them back to Jaeger tracers, which periodically poll the collectors for sampling strategies (dashed lines). Once the new probabilities are available to the tracer, it uses them for all new traces.

Calculating sampling probability $u(t)$

When the **Calculator** reads the cumulative counts for m lookback periods, it sums them up and divides by m to obtain the current value of $y(t)$. Then, the desired value of $u(t)$ can be calculated as:

$$u'(t) = u(t-1) \times q \text{, where:}$$

$$q = \frac{r(t)}{y(t)}$$

However, we do not always want to output the exact value $u'(t)$ calculated in the preceding equation. Let's consider a couple of examples. Let's assume that our target rate $r(t) = 10$ TPS, and we observed the current rate as $y(t) = 20$ TPS. That means that the current sampling probability used by the service is too high, and we want to reduce it by half:

$$q = \frac{r(t)}{y(t)} = \frac{10}{20} = \frac{1}{2} \text{. So:}$$

$$u'(t) = u(t-1) \times q = \frac{u(t-1)}{2}$$

This change to the sampling probability is safe to apply ($u(t) \Leftarrow u'(t)$), since it will result in less data sent to the tracing backend. In fact, we want to apply that probability as soon as possible, since we are clearly oversampling this service and may be overloading our tracing backend. Now consider the reverse situation where $r(t) = 20$ and $y(t) = 10$:

$$u'(t) = u(t-1) \times \frac{r(t)}{y(t)} = 2u(t-1)$$

In other words, our target is to sample twice as many traces as we are actually sampling. The intuitive solution would be to double the current sampling probability. However, when we tried this in practice, we observed a lot of volatility in both the levels of sampling probability and the volume of sampled traces, due to the following traffic patterns:

- Some services have periodic spikes in traffic. For example, every 30 minutes some `cron` job wakes up and starts querying the service. During the quiet periods, the tracing backend receives hardly any traces from this service, so it tries to increase the sampling rate by raising the sampling probability, possibly all the way to 100%. Then, once the `cron` job runs, every single request to the service is sampled and it slams the tracing backend with tracing data. This can last for several minutes, since adaptive sampling takes time to react to the traffic and propagate the new sampling strategies back to the clients.

- Another similar pattern occurs with services that may have their traffic drained to another availability zone for a certain period of time. For example, **site reliability engineers** (**SREs**) at Uber have a standing operating procedure to failover the traffic for a certain city during a severe outage, as a way to minimize time to mitigation, while other engineers are investigating the root cause of the outage. During these failover periods, no traces are being received from the service, which again misleads the adaptive sampling into believing it should raise the sampling probability.

To partially address this issue, we do not apply the calculated $u'(t) = u(t-1) \times q$ directly when $q > 1$. Instead, we use a damping function, β, that slows down the rate of increase of the sampling probability (resembling the derivative term in the PID controller). One of damping functions implemented in Jaeger imposes a cap, θ, on the percentage increase of the probability value:

$$\beta\left(\rho_{new}, \rho_{old}, \theta\right) = \begin{array}{ll} \rho_{old} \times (1+\theta), & \dfrac{\rho_{new} - \rho_{old}}{\rho_{olo}} > \theta \\[2ex] \rho_{new}, & otherwise \end{array}$$

Here ρ_{old} and ρ_{new} correspond to the old $u(t-1)$ and new $u'(t)$ probabilities respectively. The following table shows a couple of examples of the impact of this function. In the first scenario, a relatively large probability increase from 0.1 to 0.5 is suppressed, and only allowed to increase to 0.15. In the second scenario, a relatively small probability increase from 0.4 to 0.5 is allowed unchallenged:

	Scenario 1: attempt to increase probability from 0.1 to 0.5	Scenario 2: attempt to increase probability from 0.4 to 0.5
ρ_{old}	0.1	0.4
ρ_{new}	0.5	0.5
θ	0.5(50%)	0.5(50%)
$\dfrac{\rho_{new} - \rho_{old}}{\rho_{old}}$	4.0	0.2
Increase allowed?	$400\% > 50\% \rightarrow no$	$20\% < 50\% \rightarrow yes$
ρ_{final}	0.1*(1+0.5)=0.15	0.5

With the damping function, the final calculation of the control output looks like this:

$$u'(t) = u(t-1)\frac{r(t)}{y(t)}$$

$$u(t) \Leftarrow \begin{cases} u'(t), & u'(t) < u(t-1) \\ \min\big[1, \beta\big(u'(t), u(t-1), \theta\big)\big], & \textit{otherwise} \end{cases}$$

Implications of adaptive sampling

The described adaptive sampling algorithm is controlled by several parameters, such as the observation period, τ, and the lookback interval, m, but, most importantly, the desired sampling rate, $r(t)$, measured in traces per second. In theory, the algorithm works when each service has its own target rate, $r(t)$, but in practice, how do we know what that value should be? The simplest solution is to define a single constant, r, for all services, which guarantees that the tracing backend will be receiving the volume of tracing data it can handle comfortably. This results in all services converging to their own sampling probabilities, so that the volume of traces sampled in each service is roughly the same.

In some cases, this is acceptable. For example, if the capacity of the tracing backend is limited and we would rather have guaranteed representation of all microservices in the architecture than allocate most of the tracing capacity to the high-throughput services.

In other scenarios, we may want to collect more traces from high-throughput services, yet scale the proportions non-linearly. For instance, we can integrate adaptive sampling with the deployment management system that knows how many instances, n, of each service are running. Then we can allocate the tracing budget in *log(n)* proportion. We can also integrate with the metrics system to include other signals in the calculations. Having the adaptive sampling implemented in the tracing backend allows a lot more flexibility in distributing the limited tracing budget.

Extensions

How do we apply the adaptive sampling algorithm to the other two optimization goals: spans per second or bytes per second? In the design described earlier, no collector ever sees the full trace, since they only operate on individual spans, and services in the main application are free to send their tracing data to any collector.

One solution is to implement a partitioning scheme, which we will discuss in the later section on tail-based sampling. However, partitioning requires coordination, which complicates the architecture of the tracing backend. A simpler solution is based on the realization that we do not need the exact counts of spans or bytes per second to compute the desired sampling probabilities: we only need an approximation, since the calculations are already based on aggregate values.

We can run a post-processing job on the data pipeline, which we will discuss in *Chapter 12, Gathering Insights with Data Mining*, and precompute the average size of traces in terms of spans $\overline{S}$ or bytes B. Having these statistics, we can still use the same adaptive sampling design by computing $y(t)$ as:

$$(spans\ per\ second) = (traces\ per\ second) \times S$$

$$or$$

$$(bytes\ per\ second) = (traces\ per\ second) \times B$$

Another possible extension is applying adaptive sampling to calculate the target lower-bound sampling rate that we saw in the guaranteed-throughput sampler. Imagine we deploy a new service that has never been seen before by the tracing backend. The adaptive sampling components in the collectors would have no data to calculate the target sampling probability, $u(t)$, for the new service; instead, they would assign it the default sampling probability, which is by necessity conservatively set to a very low rate.

If the new service is not getting a lot of traffic, it might never get sampled with this probability. The lower-bound rate limiter comes to the rescue and samples at least some small amount of traces, enough to kick-start the recalculations in the adaptive sampler. However, this lower-bound rate is yet another parameter to control our system, and we are back to the question: which value is appropriate for this parameter?

Suppose we set it to one trace every minute. It seems reasonable, so why not? Unfortunately, that does not work too well if we suddenly deploy a thousand instances of the service. The lower-bound rate limiter is local to each instance of the service; each of them is now sampling one trace every minute, or $1000 \div 60 = 16.7$ traces per second. If this happens across hundreds of microservices (and endpoints!), we suddenly have a lot of traces being sampled by the lower-bound rate limiter, instead of the probabilistic sampler that we want. We need to get creative and come up with a scheme of assigning the lower-bound sampling rate that takes into account how many distinct instances of each service and endpoint we are running. One solution is to integrate with a deployment system that can hopefully tell us that number. Another solution is to use the same adaptive sampling algorithm we used to compute probabilities, and apply it to calculate the lower-bound rates appropriate for each service.

Context-sensitive sampling

All sampling algorithms we have discussed so far use very little information about the request executed by the system. There are situations when it is useful to focus the attention on a specific subset of all production traffic and sample it with higher frequency. For example, our monitoring system might alert us that only users using a certain version of the Android app are experiencing problems. It would make sense to increase sampling rates for requests from this app version, in order to collect more complete tracing data and diagnose the root cause.

At the same time, if our sampling happens in the backend services, and not in the mobile app, we do not want to deploy new versions of those services that contain the code evaluating this specific condition for sampling. Ideally, the tracing infrastructure would have a flexible mechanism of describing the context-sensitive selection criteria and pushing them to the tracing libraries in the microservices, to alter the sampling profiles.

Facebook's Canopy [3] is a notable example of a tracing system that supports such infrastructure. It provides a **domain-specific language** (**DSL**) that allows engineers to describe the profile of requests they want to sample at higher rates. The predicates described in this DSL are automatically propagated to the tracing code running in the microservices and executed against the inbound requests for a predefined period of time. Canopy even has the ability to isolate traces sampled via this mechanism into a separate namespace in the trace storage, so that they can be analyzed as a group, independently of the rest of the traces sampled via normal algorithms.

Ad-hoc or debug sampling

Sometimes, we just want to execute a single request against a distributed system and make sure it is sampled. This comes especially handy during development and integration testing. Cloud-native applications often consist of so many microservices that it is nearly impossible to maintain test or staging environments that are fully representative of a production system. Instead, many organizations are implementing infrastructure that supports *testing in production*. An engineer working on a particular microservice can deploy a new version into a staging environment created just for this service, while the rest of the microservices are the normal production instances. The engineer then executes a series of requests against the service, with a special header that instructs the tracing instrumentation that this request should be sampled. The traces collected in this manner are often referred to as *debug* traces.

It is possible to achieve the same result using context-sensitive sampling, by writing a predicate in the DSL that looks for this specific header or some other attribute of the request.

However, not many tracing systems actually support context-sensitive sampling, while most of them support on-demand debug tracing. For example, if an HTTP server is instrumented with Jaeger tracing libraries, a debug request can be initiated by sending a special HTTP header, `jaeger-debug-id`:

```
$ curl -H 'jaeger-debud-id: foo-bar' http://example.com/baz
```

Jaeger will ensure that the trace created for this request will be sampled, and also mark it as a debug trace, which tells the backend to exclude this request from any additional down-sampling. The value `foo-bar` of the header is stored as a tag on the root span, so that the trace can be located in the Jaeger UI via tag search.

Let's try this with the HotROD application. If you do not have it running, please refer back to *Chapter 2, Take Tracing for a HotROD Ride*, for instructions on how to start it and the Jaeger standalone backend. When ready, execute the following command:

```
$ curl -H 'jaeger-debug-id: find-me' 'http://0.0.0.0:8080/dispatch'
Missing required 'customer' parameter
```

The service returns an error, which is expected. Let's pass a parameter that it needs:

```
$ curl -H 'jaeger-debug-id: find-me' \
'http://0.0.0.0:8080/dispatch?customer=123'
{"Driver":"T744909C","ETA":120000000000}%
```

The exact values you receive might be different, but you should get back a JSON output that indicates a successful response. Now let's go to the Jaeger UI. If you have it open with previous results, click on the **Jaeger UI** text in the top-left corner to go to the blank search page. Select the **frontend** service from the **Services** dropdown and enter the query `jaeger-debug-id=find-me` in the **Tags** field (*Figure 8.3*):

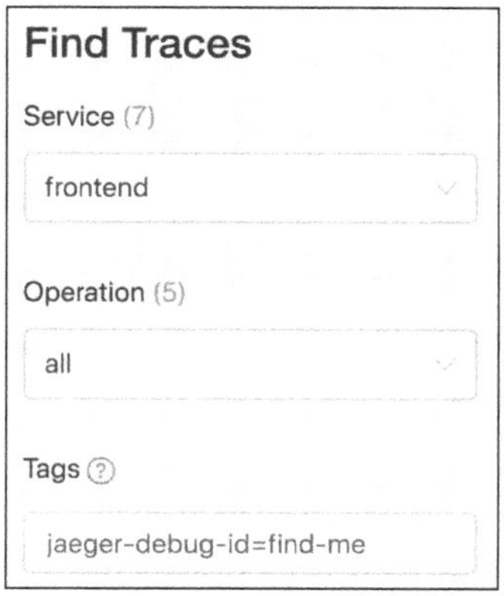

Find Traces

Service (7)

```
frontend
```

Operation (5)

```
all
```

Tags ⓘ

```
jaeger-debug-id=find-me
```

Figure 8.3: Searching for traces by debug id in the Jaeger UI

Now click on the **Find Traces** button at the bottom, and Jaeger should find two traces (*Figure 8.4*):

- One involving only a single span from the frontend service, representing our first request that failed due to a missing argument

- One representing a complete successful request involving six services and 50 or so spans

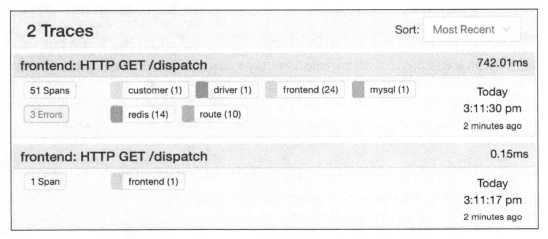

Figure 8.4: Traces found in the Jaeger UI via debug id tag search

Note that the small trace is not marked as having errors, even though it returned to us an error message, and if we inspect it, we will find the HTTP status code `400` (bad request). This may be a bug in the `opentracing-contrib/go-stdlib` we used to instrument the HTTP server. On the other hand, some people may argue that only status codes in the `500-900` range (server faults) should be marked as errors, but not client faults (`400-499`).

If we click into either of these traces and expand their top-level spans, we will find that they both have a tag `jaeger-debug-id` with the value `find-me`. The trace view page has a **View Options** dropdown in the top-right corner. If we select the **Trace JSON** option, we can see that the `flags` field of the root span is set to value `3`, or `00000011` in binary, which is a bitmask where the right-most (least significant) bit indicates that the trace was sampled, and the second right-most bit indicates that it was a debug trace.

```
{
    "traceID": "1a6d42887025072a",
    "spanID": "1a6d42887025072a",
    "flags": 3,
    "operationName": "HTTP GET /dispatch",
```

```
"references": [
],
"startTime": 1527458271189830,
"duration": 106,
"tags": [
  {
    "key": "jaeger-debug-id",
    "type": "string",
    "value": "find-me"
  },
  ...
```

How to deal with oversampling

Any team that is responsible for operating a tracing backend in a large organization will be concerned with making sure that the backend has enough capacity to process and store the trace data, given the current levels of sampling. The end users of tracing typically want the highest sampling rates possible within the constraints of the tracing backend capacity, and with longer retention periods. This inevitably creates a conflict of interests.

In some situations, the tracing team does not even have full control over the sampling rates set by the users. For example, in the Jaeger libraries, the default configuration instantiates a special sampler that constantly consults the tracing backend about which sampling strategies it should use in a given microservice. However, nothing prevents the engineer developing that microservice from turning off the default configuration and instantiating a different sampler, such as a probabilistic sampler with a higher sampling probability. Even if there is no ill intent, it is often useful to run the service with 100% sampling during development, and sometimes people forget to change the setting in the production configuration. The tracing team would want to protect itself from these accidents.

Post-collection down-sampling

One way to protect the tracing backend from overload is with a second round of sampling, after the traces arrive to the collection tier. The approach was described in the Dapper paper, and it is also implemented in Jaeger.

Remember that we want the cumulative sampling to be consistent: if we down-sample one span from a trace, we should discard the whole trace, and vice versa. Fortunately, all spans in a single Jaeger trace share the same trace id, so even though a single collector may not see all spans from a given trace, it is still easy to make a consistent down-sampling decision. We can hash the trace id into a number between 0 and 1 and compare it with the desired down-sampling probability:

```
val downSamplingProbability: Double = 0.1
def downSample(span: Span): Boolean = {
  if (span.isDebug) {
    return false
  }
  val z: Double = hash(span.traceId)
  return z < downSamplingProbability
}
```

This down-sampling technique provides the tracing team with an additional knob they can use to adjust the average global sampling rate and to control how much data is being stored in the trace storage. If a misbehaving service deploys a bad sampling configuration and starts flooding the tracing backend, the tracing team can increase the down-sampling rate to bring the trace volume back within the backend capacity, while contacting the service owners and asking them to fix it. The down-sampling ratio can also be adjusted automatically using an approach similar to adaptive sampling, which we discussed earlier.

It is worth mentioning that using post-collection down-sampling has a few drawbacks. It often confuses engineers who are trying to trace their services, since the number of traces stored in the backend does not match the sampling probabilities defined in the services. It is especially confusing if debug traces are not stored, and for this reason, we explicitly exclude all debug traces from down-sampling in the preceding code example.

Down-sampling also complicates the extrapolation calculations of various statistics based on the tracing data, especially if those calculations are performed offline. We found that if collectors are using non-zero down-sampling, it is best to record the ratio in the traces similarly to how the original sampling probability is recorded in the span tags.

Throttling

Throttling attempts to solve the problem of oversampling at the source, at the moment the sampling decision is made by a tracer on the first span of the trace. Irrespective of how that decision was made, even if it was forced by the user by sending the jaeger-debug-id header, throttling uses another rate limiter to overrule that decision if it deems that the service is starting too many traces (or too many debug traces).

Canopy has been reported to use such throttling in the tracing libraries. At the time of writing, Uber's internal build of Jaeger implements throttling for debug traces, but the functionality is not yet released in the open source version of Jaeger. Selecting the appropriate throttling rate has the same challenges as selecting the lower-bound sampling rate described previously: a single value of the throttling rate may not be suitable for services that serve vastly different traffic volumes.

Most likely, we will be looking to extend the adaptive sampling algorithm to support the calculation of the throttling rate, since in the end, adaptive sampling is just another version of the distributed rate limiting problem.

Tail-based consistent sampling

Clearly, head-based sampling has its benefits and its challenges. It is fairly simple to implement, yet far from simple to manage at scale. There is one other drawback of head-based sampling that we have not discussed yet: its inability to tune the sampling decision to the behavior of the system captured in the traces. Let's assume our metrics system tells us that the 99.9th percentile of the request latency in a service is very high. It means that only one in a thousand requests on average exhibits the anomalous behavior. If we are tracing with head-based sampling and 0.001 probability, we have one in a million chance that we will sample one of these anomalous requests and capture the trace that might explain the anomaly.

Although we could say that one in a million is not that low, given how much traffic goes through modern cloud-native applications, and we probably *will* capture some of those interesting traces, it also means that the remaining 999 traces out of each thousand that we do capture and store in the tracing backend are perhaps *not* that interesting.

It would be nice if we could delay the sampling decision until we see something unusual recorded in the trace, such as an abnormal request latency, or an error, or a call graph branch we have not seen before. Unfortunately, by the time we detect the anomaly, it is too late, since the earlier fragments of the trace that may have caused the abnormal behavior will not be recorded in a tracing system that uses head-based sampling.

Tail-based sampling addresses this problem by making the sampling call at the end of the request execution, when we have the complete trace and can make a more intelligent decision about whether it should be captured for storage or not. What constitutes an *interesting* trace is in fact an active area of academic research. The following are just some examples of potential strategies:

- Sample based on the latency of the top-level request by maintaining a histogram of latency buckets and using rate limiters to ensure equal representation of each bucket among stored traces. That is, we would sample n traces per minute with latency between 0 ms and 2 ms, n traces per minute with latency between 2 ms and 5 ms, and so on.

- Use a similar equal representation technique based on errors captured in the traces, instead of latency. For example, if we observe nine types of errors in the traces, we can sample so that each error will be represented by $1/10^{th}$ of all captured traces, and the remaining $1/10^{th}$ of the population will be traces without errors.

- Given some measure of similarity between traces, we can use clustering techniques to group traces by similarity and sample in the inverse proportion to the size of the cluster that a trace belongs to, to give higher weight to anomalous traces [4].

Another interesting feature of tail-based sampling is that it almost entirely eliminates the problem of oversampling and overload of the tracing backend. Making the sampling decision after collecting the whole trace is equivalent to a pull model, where the tracing backend knows exactly how much data it is requesting and can easily tune it up and down.

The obvious downsides, or at least complications, of tail-based sampling are:

- Trace data collection must be enabled for 100% of traffic. It will introduce a much larger performance overhead compared to head-based sampling where the calls to tracing instrumentation are short-circuited to be effectively no-op when the request is unsampled. To recap, without sampling, the Dapper tracer was reported to impose 1.5% throughput and a 16% latency overhead.

- Until the request execution is completed, and the full trace is assembled and passed through a sampling decision, the collected trace data must be kept somewhere.

It is interesting to note that tail-based sampling changes the *reason* for using sampling. We are no longer trying to reduce the performance overhead on the application. We are still trying to restrict the amount of trace data we store in the tracing backend, but we just said that "all data must be kept somewhere," so how does that work?

The important thing to realize is that we only need to keep all data somewhere while the request execution is in flight. Since most requests in modern applications execute very fast, we only need to hold onto the data for a given trace for mere seconds. After that, we can make a sampling decision, and in most cases, discard that data, since we are still going to be storing the same overall ratio of traces in the tracing backend as we would with head-based sampling. So, because we want to avoid introducing additional performance overhead, keeping the trace data in memory for the duration of the request seems like a reasonable approach.

There are some existing solutions in the market today that successfully employ tail-based sampling. To my knowledge, LightStep, Inc. was the pioneer in this area, with its proprietary LightStep [x]PM technology [5]. In December 2018, SignalFx, Inc. announced that they also rolled out an **application performance monitoring (APM)** solution with tail-based sampling called NoSample™ Architecture [6]. At the same time, a stealth-mode start-up Omnition (`https://omnition.io/`) has been working with the OpenCensus project on building an open source version of OpenCensus collector that supports tail-based sampling [7].

Let's consider how a tail-based sampling architecture could work. In *Figure 8.5*, we see two microservices and two request executions recorded as traces T1 and T2. At the bottom, we see two instances of trace collectors. The objective of the collectors is to temporarily store in-flight traces in memory until all spans for a trace are received and invoke some sampling algorithm to decide if the trace is interesting enough to be captured in the persistent trace storage on the right.

In contrast with the previous architecture diagram, where collectors were shown as a uniform cluster because they were stateless, these new collectors must use a data partitioning scheme based on the trace id, so that all spans for a given trace are sent to the same collector instance.

In the diagram, we show how all spans for traces T1 and T2 are collected in the first and the second collectors respectively. In this example, only the second trace, T2, is considered interesting and sent to the storage, while trace T1 is simply discarded to free up space for newer traces.

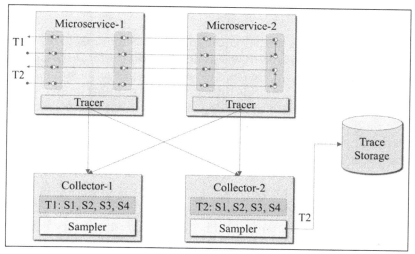

Figure 8.5: A hypothetical architecture for tail-based sampling. Collectors store each trace in memory until it is finished, and spans are partitioned by trace id to ensure that all spans for a given trace end up in a single collector.

What are some of the challenges of implementing this architecture? The data partitioning is certainly an unpleasant addition, as it requires coordination between the collectors to decide which of them owns which range of the partition keys. Usually, this would be achieved by running a separate service, like Apache Zookeeper or an etcd cluster. We would also have to deal with the reshuffling of the partition ring should one of the collectors crash, maybe running each collector with one or more replicas for data resiliency, and so on. Rather than implementing all this new functionality in the tracing system, it would probably be easier to use some existing scalable in-memory storage solution.

Another, perhaps even more interesting, challenge is the cost of sending the tracing data out of the application process to the collectors. In the systems with head-based sampling, this cost is usually negligible due to low sampling rates, but in a tail-based sampling system, we have to send every single span to another server and that is potentially many spans for each business request processed by the service. The cost itself consists of two parts: serializing the trace data into a binary representation for transporting over the wire, and the network transmission. There are a few ways these costs can be reduced:

- Spans data is highly redundant, so a compression scheme may be developed to significantly reduce the size of the data that needs to be shipped out of the application process.

- Instead of sending the data to a remote host, it can be sent to a daemon process running on the host, such as the jaeger-agent process used in many Jaeger deployments. Communication over the loopback interface is less expensive than sending over a real network. However, in this approach we no longer have a single server that receives all spans for a given trace because microservices participating in the trace are most likely running on different hosts. The agents may still need to communicate to a cluster of collectors partitioned by the trace ids and provide some summary about spans stored on the agent. It is difficult to say, without knowing the exact sampling algorithm used to decide which traces are interesting, how much data would need to be sent in that second phase. An educated guess is that we would need to send a significant portion of the span data, which makes this approach less appealing. One benefit it does have is that the daemons may be aware of the partitioning scheme and forward the data directly to the appropriate collector (or storage node), rather than having the same logic in the tracing library.

- Another interesting option would be to use shared memory between the application process and the daemon. This removes the overhead of serializing the traces into a wire format. As with the previous approach, it only makes sense if the collectors only need to know high-level digests about the spans before making the sampling decision.

Finally, before we can make a sampling decision, we need to be sure that the trace is finished, that is, the collector received all spans generated for this trace. This is a harder problem than it seems, because spans can arrive from different hosts in the architecture, even from mobile applications outside of our data center, with unpredictable delays. We will discuss some solutions to this problem in *Chapter 12, Gathering Insights with Data Mining*. The most naive implementation is to simply wait for a certain time interval during which no more spans are received for a trace and then declare the trace finished and ready for sampling.

In summary, implementing tail-based sampling efficiently, with the ability to scale to the trillions of requests per day that are typical for modern internet companies, is an interesting challenge. I am looking forward to an open source solution emerging in this area.

Partial sampling

Let's conclude the overview of the sampling techniques with an approach used in some tracing systems where sampling decision does not guarantee consistent collection of all spans of a trace. It does not mean the sampling decision is made completely randomly at every node of the call graph, but rather that only a portion of the call graph is sampled. Specifically, the sampling decision can be made after detecting an anomaly in the trace, such as unusual latency or an error code. The tracing library is changed slightly to keep all the spans for currently active traces in memory until the entry span is finished. Once the sampling decision is made, we send all those spans to the tracing backend. Even though we will miss the spans from any downstream calls we already made from this service, as they finished the execution without being sampled, at least the inner workings of the current service will be represented in the trace, and we will be able to see which downstream systems were called and possibly caused the error. In addition, we can propagate the fact that we triggered sampling of the current trace backwards in the call graph, to the caller, which would also have all its spans in memory waiting for the completion of the request. By following this procedure, we can sample a subtree of the call graph above the current node, and possibly other future subtrees that the upstream service might execute in response to the error from the service that detected the issue.

Summary

Sampling is used by tracing systems to reduce the performance overhead on the traced applications, and to control the amount of data that needs to be stored in the tracing backends. There are two important sampling techniques: head-based consistent sampling, which makes the sampling decision at the beginning of the request execution, and tail-based sampling, which makes the sampling decision after the execution.

Most existing tracing systems implement head-based sampling that imposes minimum overhead on the applications. Various sampling algorithms can be used to tune the sampling behavior and the impact on the tracing backend. Jaeger implements adaptive sampling that reduces the operational burden for the tracing teams and provides more equitable handling of endpoints with vastly different traffic volumes. A few commercial and open source solutions of tail-based sampling have emerged as well.

This concludes the part of the book dedicated to the data gathering problem in distributed tracing. In *Part III*, we will look into some practical applications and use cases for end-to-end tracing, beyond those that we reviewed in *Chapter 2, Take Tracing for a HotROD Ride*.

References

1. Benjamin H. Sigelman, Luiz A. Barroso, Michael Burrows, Pat Stephenson, Manoj Plakal, Donald Beaver, Saul Jaspan, and Chandan Shanbhag, *Dapper, a large-scale distributed system tracing infrastructure*, Technical Report dapper-2010-1, Google, April 2010.

2. *Spring Cloud Sleuth*, a distributed tracing solution for Spring Cloud: `https://cloud.spring.io/spring-cloud-sleuth/`.

3. Jonathan Kaldor, Jonathan Mace, Michał Bejda, Edison Gao, Wiktor Kuropatwa, Joe O'Neill, Kian Win Ong, Bill Schaller, Pingjia Shan, Brendan Viscomi, Vinod Venkataraman, Kaushik Veeraraghavan, and Yee Jiun Song, *Canopy: An End-to-End Performance Tracing and Analysis System*, Symposium on Operating Systems Principles.

4. Pedro Las-Casas, Jonathan Mace, Dorgival Guedes, and Rodrigo Fonseca, *Weighted Sampling of Execution Traces: Capturing More Needles and Less Hay*. In Proceedings of the 9th ACM Symposium on Cloud Computing, October 2018.

5. Parker Edwards. *LightStep [x]PM Architecture Explained*: `https://lightstep.com/blog/lightstep-xpm-architecture-explained/`.

6. Ami Sharma and Maxime Petazzoni. *Reimagining APM for the Cloud-Native World: Introducing SignalFx Microservices APM™*: `https://www.signalfx.com/blog/announcing-signalfx-microservices-apm/`.

7. OpenCensus Service: `https://github.com/census-instrumentation/opencensus-service`

III
GETTING VALUE FROM TRACING

III

Getting Value from Tracing

9
Turning the Lights On

In the second part of the book, we reviewed various techniques for instrumenting our applications for end-to-end tracing and getting the tracing data out. This next part is all about what we can do with that data, as well as the tracing infrastructure in general.

We have already seen some glimpses of what is possible in *Chapter 2, Take Tracing for a HotROD Ride,* when we ran the HotROD demo application. In this chapter, we will do a more thorough review of the benefits provided by end-to-end tracing, and ways of using the tracing data to help engineers with day-to-day tasks. Some of the ideas presented here are theoretical, meaning that while they are feasible, not all of them are implemented in the existing tracing systems because there is so much to do when you start exploring the possibilities of end-to-end tracing. I hope that you can use some of these ideas as inspiration for what to do with the data generated by your own tracing infrastructure.

Tracing as a knowledge base

One of the most important benefits of tracing is the degree of visibility it gives into the operations of complex distributed systems. Ben Sigelman, one of the creators of the tracing infrastructure at Google, said that when the team deployed tracing there in 2005, "*it was like someone finally turned the lights on: everything from ordinary programming errors to broken caches to bad network hardware to unknown dependencies came into plain view*" [1]. This visibility is important not only when investigating a specific issue or incident, but on a regular basis as the foundation of understanding how the whole application functions, how it is architected, and so on.

Imagine you are a new team member who is not familiar with the system you are hired to work on. How would you learn about the system architecture, deployment modes, or bottlenecks? Documentation is rarely up to date enough to be a reliable source of information. Most engineers would rather build new features than spend time on documenting how the system works. An example from my own experience: I am working on a project of building a new distributed monitoring system for compliance purposes, which started just two months ago. Already the system architecture described in the original **Request for Comments** (**RFC**) document is out of date because better ways were discovered during development and testing. This situation is typical for many teams, especially those that make heavy use of microservices and agile development practices.

If documentation is not reliable, then the only way new team members learn about the system is by asking the existing team members to explain it. This is a slow process that relies on a lot of tribal knowledge, which may also be inaccurate in fast-moving organizations.

Distributed tracing provides a better alternative. By observing the actual interactions between system components that happen in production, it gives us access to automatically maintained, up-to-date information about system architecture, service dependencies, and expected, or sometimes unexpected, interactions. Rather than bugging their more experienced peers, new team members can discover this information on their own, and can learn and understand the system behavior through tooling. The data provided by the tracing infrastructure is very rich, so it allows us to drill down into fine-grained details, such as which endpoints of the downstream services our own endpoint depends on, which data stores and namespaces we are using, which Kafka topics our service is reading and writing, and so on. "Turning the lights on" is indeed a great metaphor.

Service graphs

You have seen examples of the service graphs in previous chapters, some generated by Jaeger, and others generated by the service mesh Istio. There are other open source tools, such as Weaveworks Scope [2] and Kiali [3], that can provide similar service graphs by integrating with other infrastructure components, like service meshes, or simply by sniffing network connections and traffic. These graphs can be extremely useful for quickly grasping the architecture of the system. They are often annotated with additional monitoring signals, such as the throughput of the individual edges (requests per second), latency percentiles, error counts, and other golden signals indicating the health or performance of a service. Various visualization techniques can be used to enhance the presentation, such as representing relative throughput of the edges with line thickness or even animation (for example, Netflix Vizceral [4]), or color-coding healthy and less healthy nodes. When the application is small enough to fit all of its services in a single service graph, the graph can be used as an entry point to the rest of the monitoring stack, as it allows for a quick overview of the application state, with the ability to drill down to the individual components:

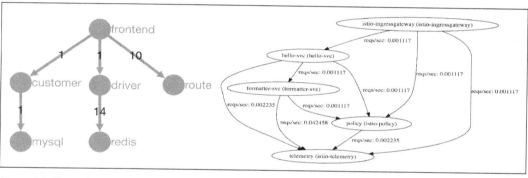

Figure 9.1: Examples of service graphs. Left: architecture of the HotROD application from Chapter 2 discovered by Jaeger. Right: architecture of the Hello application from Chapter 7 discovered by the service mesh Istio.

These service graphs have a number of limitations, however:

- As the applications grow more complex and accumulate a lot more components and microservices, the service graphs of the whole application become too busy and individual nodes become unintelligible, defeating the main benefit of an intuitive overview of the state of the system.

- Microservices often expose multiple endpoints with different traffic patterns and downstream dependencies. Tools that build the graphs at the lower-level network sniffing are often unable to present the information at the endpoint level. Graphs generated by the service mesh can be rendered at the endpoint granularity, but again suffer from becoming too busy to be easily understandable.

- Most graphs are limited to only capturing pair-wise dependencies between services or endpoints. In the preceding diagram, the graph generated by Istio shows that there is a path passing through four services: `hello-svc` | `formatter-svc` | `policy` | `telemetry`. However, there is no way to tell whether this sequence can actually occur in a single distributed transaction. It is possible that the `policy` | `telemetry` calls only happen when the upstream caller is the `hello-svc` service or `istio-ingressgateway`, but not the `formatter-svc` service. When graphs are built by the tools that monitor network activity or non-tracing telemetry from a service mesh, they are fundamentally limited to only showing the edges between the immediate neighbors, and can be quite misleading if one is trying to understand all the dependencies of a given service or needs to decide whether a given downstream service is worthy of an investigation during an outage.

Despite these limitations, pair-wise dependency graphs are the de facto standard among most distributed tracing tools and commercial vendors today.

Deep, path-aware service graphs

To address the limitations of the service graphs composed only of the edges between immediate neighbors, a team at Uber developed a different way of aggregating tracing data and visualizing it as service graphs. First, the interface requires the user to select a service as the focal point of the graph. If the tool is used by a developer who is trying to understand their service's upstream and downstream dependencies, selecting a service is natural. If the tool is used during an incident, then the top-level API service or gateway is usually selected as the starting point. Focusing on one node in the graph allows the tool to filter all unrelated nodes and drastically reduce the size of the overall service graph to a manageable subset.

The tool is able to accurately filter out the irrelevant nodes because it builds the graph from the tracing data by accounting for the actual paths through the architecture observed in the traces. Consider the call graph involving five microservices and their endpoints in *Figure 9.2*, part (**A**). The algorithm collects all unique branches in the tree, starting from the root service **A** and ending at a leaf node. The process is repeated for all traces being aggregated for a certain time window. Then, the final dependency graph for a selected focal service **B** is reconstructed from the accumulated branches by filtering out all paths that do not pass through service **B**, as shown in part (**C**).

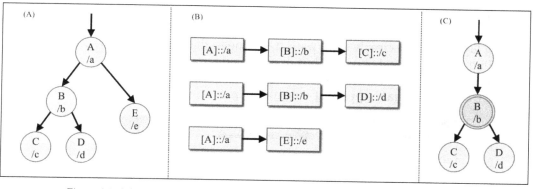

Figure 9.2: (A) sample call graph between services and endpoints. (B) a collection of paths extracted by the algorithm. (C) dependency graph reconstructed from the collected paths after selecting service B as the focal point.

How can we use this technique in practice? *Figure 9.3* shows an example constructed from production data at Uber, with service names obfuscated. Most services shown in the graph have many more immediate neighbors in practice, and if those neighbors were included in the diagram, it would quickly become too busy and unusable. Instead, the diagram is built only from traces that are passing through a selected focal service, in this case, service **shrimp**. By doing that, we can get a much clearer picture of the true dependencies of this service, both upstream and downstream, and not only immediate neighbors.

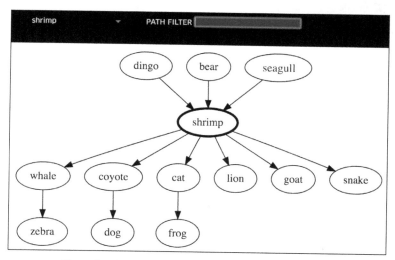

Figure 9.3: Sample path-aware graph with service shrimp selected as the focal point, pictured with a thicker line

The path-based technique of constructing the dependencies graph has another advantage. Consider the **dingo** service in the top layer and the **dog** service in the bottom layer. We can clearly see a path from one to the other in the graph, so it looks like **dingo** depends on **dog**, but does such dependency exist in practice? The underlying path-based data allows us to answer these questions. The screenshots in *Figure 9.4* show what happens if we enter dog or dingo as a path filter:

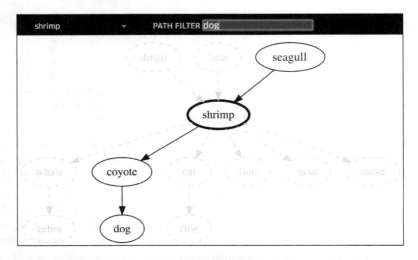

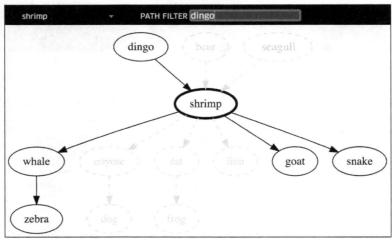

Figure 9.4: Investigating whether the **dingo** service depends on the **dog** service using path-aware filtering, by only showing the paths passing through the **dog** service (left) and through the **dingo** service (right). All paths are passing through the focal service, **shrimp**, shown in the thicker line.

The tool applies the filter by graying out the services in the diagram that are not encountered in any traces passing through the selected service. It makes it obvious that only requests originating from the **seagull** service ever reach the **dog service**, while the requests originating from the **dingo** service the have a very different call graph.

This same tool can be switched to display the dependency graphs at the endpoint level, rather than at a service level as shown in the graph, by creating standalone nodes for every service and endpoint combination. These graphs are typically much larger, such that their visualization again becomes more difficult and usually requires horizontal scrolling. However, they provide a great level of detail when one needs to fully understand the interactions between the services.

 It would be nice if the tool highlighted the matching services, not only the focal service. The path filter is actually just a substring search, so it is possible that it could match more than one service.

Lastly, these graphs can be annotated with performance metrics, such as requests per second going through a particular path or latency percentiles. Performance annotations can quickly highlight problematic areas that require investigation.

Detecting architectural problems

Sometimes, when organizations rush to adopt microservices and break up the existing monoliths, they end up with a "distributed monolith" characterized by a high number of microservices that are tightly interconnected and dependent on each other. It is akin to designing the original monolith without private methods or any form of encapsulation, where every component can call any other component. While this free-for-all approach allows organizations to move quickly in the early phases, eventually the additional complexity of inter-dependencies catches up and slows down the developers' velocity because one can never know whether a small change to one service will have a rippling effect throughout the architecture.

Service graphs, even the basic pair-wise graphs, can illustrate a high degree of connectivity between the services and can be very effective in highlighting these architectural issues of nearly fully connected graphs, and pointing toward the way of fixing them.

For example, we may want to ensure higher affinity between services that belong to the same business domains, such as payments or order fulfilment, while at the same time reducing the connectivity between services in different domains and instead proxying all requests through well-defined API gateways (*Figure 9.5*).

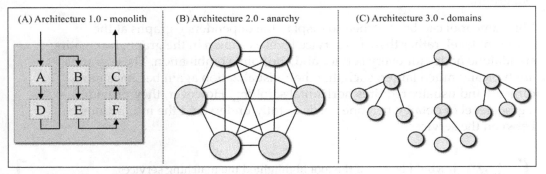

Figure 9.5: (A) Application starts as a monolith. (B) Application evolves into microservices, but without clear boundaries: an almost fully connected "distributed monolith". (C) Application is organized into business domains with clear APIs and boundaries.

Performance analysis

Using tracing data for application performance analysis is the classic use case of distributed tracing. Different aspects of application performance can be investigated via tracing:

- **Availability**: Is the application responding to end user queries? When the application is not responding to end users, or in other words we are in an outage situation, tracing can be used to pinpoint the location in a complex architecture where things go wrong.

- **Correctness**: Does the application provide accurate answers? For example, if you are trying to call a car in the middle of New York City using a ride-sharing mobile app and the system responds with an expected time of arrival of 55 minutes, the correctness of that response is suspicious. Perhaps the system was trying to use a microservice with a highly accurate but slow algorithm, which did not finish in time, and the request failed over to another microservice with a faster but less accurate algorithm. By following the path of a request via a distributed trace, we can analyze how the application arrived at the decision.

- **Speed**: How fast is our application responding to the queries? Understanding the latency profile of a complex distributed application, where dozens of services work together to respond to a single request, is very difficult. Distributed traces collected in production are the prime tool for answering the latency questions.

Note that *detecting* degradation in the preceding performance indicators is a different problem from *diagnosing* it. Detection is often delegated to the metrics systems, which collect highly accurate telemetry without sampling, but heavily aggregate it to minimize the cost of recording. The aggregates are good for monitoring and alerting, but ineffective at explaining the problems. In this section, we will discuss a few techniques for analyzing the application performance with distributed traces.

Critical path analysis

Many tracing tools provide a capability of analyzing a "critical path" in the trace (unfortunately, neither Jaeger nor Zipkin currently implement that functionality). It is a classic technique for understanding how individual components of a parallel execution impact end-to-end latency of the overall distributed transaction. The Mystery Machine paper [5] defined the critical path as follows:

> "*The critical path is defined to be the set of segments for which a differential increase in segment execution time would result in the same differential increase in end-to-end latency.*"

To put it differently, if we can increase the duration of a certain span in the trace without affecting the overall duration of the transaction, then this span is not on the critical path. When analyzing a trace, we are interested in the spans that are on the critical path because by optimizing those, we can reduce the overall end-to-end latency, while optimizing the spans off the critical path is not as useful.

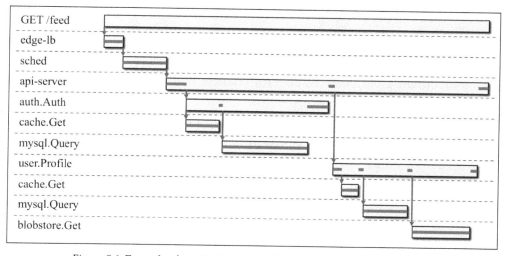

Figure 9.6: Example of a critical path, in red bars striking through the spans, in an imaginary trace for a social media web site.

Figure 9.6 shows how a critical path might look for an imaginary trace for a social media web site. Notice that the critical path is a function not only of the overall trace, but also of the current visualization zoom level. For example, when looking at the complete trace, only small portions of the api-server span are shown on the critical path, since the rest of the time is spent in the downstream calls. However, if we collapse all the details underneath that span, in order to focus on the critical path through the top three services, then the whole api-server span becomes a part of the critical path (*Figure 9.7*).

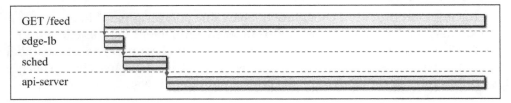

Figure 9.7: Change in the critical path when all following details the "api-server" span are collapsed

How can we use the critical path visualization to improve the end-to-end latency of the request?:

- We can ignore all spans that are off the critical path, as optimizing them will not reduce the latency.

- We can look for the longest span on the critical path. In the preceding example, if we could reduce the duration of any given span by 50%, then doing that for the first mysql.Query span will be the most impactful in reducing the end-to-end latency.

- Finally, we can analyze critical paths across multiple similar traces and focus our attention on the spans that represent the largest average percentage of the critical path, or the spans that are found on the critical path more often than others. Doing that reduces the chances that we spend time optimizing a particular span in a trace that turns out to be an outlier.

Systematic analysis of the critical paths is important for the long-term health of the system. At a recent keynote talk at the Velocity NYC 2018 conference [6], Jaana B. Dogan, an engineer from Google who works on tracing and performance profiling problems, coined a term **critical path driven development (CPDD)**. She observed that availability of every single service in a large architecture is not a goal in itself.

It is more important to see the system from the perspective of the end users, and to ensure that services on the critical path for the end user requests are available and performant. In CPDD, the engineering practices are based on:

- Discovering the critical paths automatically
- Making the critical paths reliable and fast
- Making the critical paths debuggable in production

Tools like distributed tracing play a major role in achieving these practices.

Recognizing trace patterns

One of the simplest ways to benefit from tracing data is to look for certain tracing patterns that are likely indicative of a performance issue. These patterns are surprisingly effective because they are visual, and our brains are very good at quickly analyzing visual information. This section has been inspired by the talk that Bryan Boreham, the director of engineering at Weaveworks, gave at KubeCon EU 2018, where he shared some of the patterns he observed in his experience with distributed tracing [6].

Look for error markers

Let's recall the traces from the HotROD application from *Chapter 2, Take Tracing for a HotROD Ride*. We have seen Jaeger highlighting the spans with a white exclamation point in a red circle if the spans were annotated with an `error` tag. Looking for these markers during an outage can quickly point us to the problematic area of the architecture. In the case of the HotROD trace, out of 13 requests to Redis, the three timed-out requests were responsible for over 40% of the time the application spent to complete the overall operation of loading drivers. Sometimes, the errors are detected later in the execution, that is, a previous request may have returned a bad response, causing the subsequent execution to fail and annotate the span with an error tag, so be on the lookout for those situations. Still, having a visual error marker quickly points us to the area of interest in the trace:

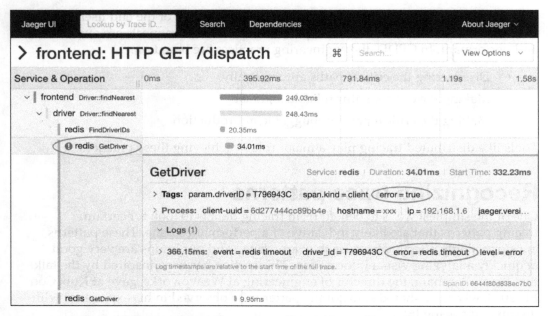

Figure 9.8: Error markers on the spans usually point to a problem in the execution

Look for the longest span on the critical path

As discussed earlier, identifying the critical path through the trace allows us to zero in on the performance bottlenecks. Inspecting and optimizing the longest span on the critical path, such as the **work B** span in *Figure 9.9*, is likely to produce the largest benefit to the overall request latency, rather than trying to optimize the other two work spans.

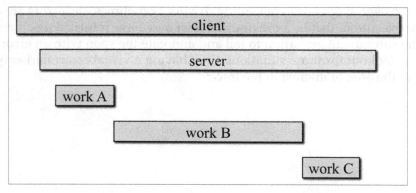

Figure 9.9: Look for the longest span on the critical path as the first candidate for optimization

Look out for missing details

Sometimes, we encounter a trace like the one in *Figure 9.10*. It is feasible that the server was doing some actual work on the CPU between the two spans **work A** and **work B**, but more often than not this pattern indicates missing instrumentation. It is possible the server was waiting on a database query and our database driver is not instrumented for tracing. In cases when we know for sure that the server is doing some internal calculations during that time, adding a properly named span to indicate that makes the trace much more readable for the next person who comes across it.

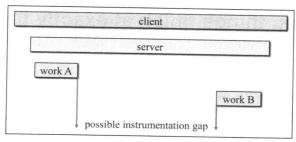

Figure 9.10: A gap between the span in the execution often indicates missing instrumentation

Avoid sequential execution or "staircase"

You have seen an example of this pattern in the HotROD traces in *Chapter 2, Take Tracing for a HotROD Ride*, where the calls to Redis were done sequentially. When this happens, the trace has an easily detectable "staircase" pattern, which is often an indication of suboptimal execution. There are, of course, situations when the algorithm genuinely requires sequential execution of tasks, but more often than not, this pattern is an oversight in the design or simply a masked bug introduced by a layer of abstraction. For example, I have seen many times where using an **object-relational mapping** (**ORM**) library has produced the "staircase" pattern without the developer even realizing that it is happening. The high-level code looks reasonable, for example, a loop over the results of the query, but under the hood, the ORM library might translate each iteration of the loop into a separate SQL query, for example, in order to populate some fields of the object that were not loaded in the initial query.

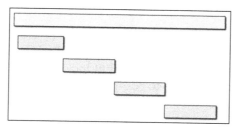

Figure 9.11: Sequential execution, or "staircase", is often suboptimal

The approaches to avoid the "staircase" pattern depend on the specific scenario. In the case of the HotROD example, there was no restriction in the business logic that required us to load driver records from Redis one at a time, so all requests could have been parallelized. Alternatively, many queries can be replaced with bulk queries or joins on the database side, to avoid the individual sub-queries. It is really surprising how often this simple issue occurs in practice, how easy it is to spot with tracing, and how great the resulting performance improvements are, going from seconds or tens of seconds to sub-second latency, for example, on screens like menus or catalogues.

Be wary when things finish at exactly the same time

This last pattern does not always indicate a real issue, but it is nonetheless quite suspicious and warrants further investigation. We have a series of spans that all finish at the same time (perhaps not exactly in the same nanosecond, but relative to the length of the spans the differences are imperceptible). This is unusual for highly concurrent, dynamic systems because things are typically a bit random, starting and finishing at slightly different times.

What could cause a series of spans to finish at *exactly* the same time? One possible explanation is when the system supports timeouts with cancellations. In *Figure 9.12*, the top-level span may have been waiting for the four tasks to finish, but since they did not complete in the allotted timeframe, it canceled them and aborted the whole request. In this scenario, we may want to tune the timeout parameter, or to investigate why the individual work units were taking longer than anticipated.

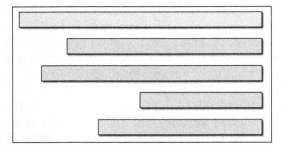

Figure 9.12: Spans finishing at exactly the same time; color us suspicious.

Another example where we can observe this pattern is when there is a resource contention and all the requests are waiting on some lock, such as a long-running database transaction from another request that locked the table. Once the lock is released, our units of work are able to complete quickly. We may want to investigate what it is that is blocking all these spans, by adding additional instrumentation.

You have seen an example of such instrumentation in the HotROD application in *Chapter 2, Take Tracing for a HotROD Ride*, where the database span contained a log statement describing the other transactions waiting on the lock and preventing it from progressing. Breaking the worker spans into smaller chunks may also help. When we have a single span representing a whole unit of work, it does not mean that it was running on a CPU all that time; situations such as being blocked on a mutex are not reflected in the trace without additional instrumentation. By enhancing the instrumentation around the shared resources, we can see more clearly what is preventing the work from progressing.

Exemplars

The techniques we discussed in the previous section typically assume that we are able to obtain a trace that is representative of the problem we are trying to solve. Let's talk about how we can even find those traces among the millions that a tracing infrastructure like Jaeger at Uber collects in just a few hours.

It is a well-known fact in the **Site Reliability Engineering** (**SRE**) discipline that we should never monitor only the average performance indicators, such as mean latency, because doing so obscures many performance outliers. For example, one percent of our users may be experiencing severe latency and an unresponsive application, while our mean latency is perfectly within our desired targets. At internet scale, one percent of users means millions of people affected by poor performance of the application. Most monitoring guidelines recommend monitoring high percentiles of latencies, such as p99 or p99.9. A p99.9 value of one second for latency means that 99.9% of users experience latency less than one second. For the unlucky users in the remaining 0.1%, the requests take longer than one second, and those are the requests we want to investigate by finding the representative traces.

If we know that we are looking for requests taking longer than one second, and we know during which time that abnormal latency was observed, for example, from our metrics dashboard, then we can query the tracing system for representative traces, assuming our sampling rates were high enough to capture them. For example, the search panel in the Jaeger UI allows us to specify the exact time range and the duration of the spans. However, doing so manually is a tedious process and not something we want to be attempting during an outage when every minute counts.

Some of the commercial tracing systems today provide a more user-friendly interface, often referred to as "exemplars". It combines a traditional graph visualization of an observed time series, for example, p99 latency of an endpoint, with examples of spans for the same endpoint, rendered as dots on the same graph (the start timestamp of a span can be used as the x-coordinate, and its duration as the y-coordinate). A time series graph allows us to easily spot unusual spikes in latency, and we can quickly navigate from those regions in the graph to sample traces.

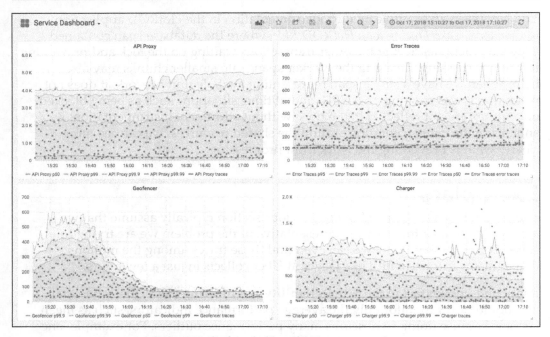

Figure 9.13: Grafana dashboard with trace exemplars
(red dots) overlaid on top of the time series graphs.
Reproduced with permission from Lightstep, Inc.

Combining time series graphs with trace exemplars not only facilitates discovering relevant traces that are representative of a performance degradation, but it is also a great way of educating engineers about the capabilities of tracing systems, by surfacing the information in their on-call workflows and dashboards.

Latency histograms

As the systems grow more complex, even monitoring high percentiles of latency is not enough. It is not uncommon to see requests to the same endpoint of a service exhibit radically different performance profiles, for example, depending on the caller service or other dimensions we may want to associate with the request (for example, a customer account). These performance profiles represent different behaviors in the distributed systems, and we should not be measuring the performance with a single number (even if it's a high-percentile number); we should be looking at the distribution of that number. Latency histograms are a practical approximation of the real performance distribution that we can plot based on the tracing data. Different behaviors of the system often manifest themselves in multi-modal distribution, where instead of the classic bell shape of the normal distribution, we get multiple humps.

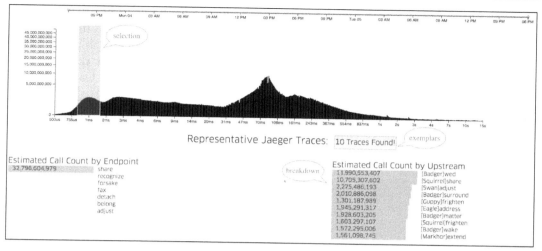

Figure 9.14: Interactive latency histogram built from tracing data

During the Jaeger Salon at KubeCon/CloudNativeCon NA 2017, I demonstrated an internal tool that a team at Uber developed for aggregating production traces and constructing latency histograms for any given service and endpoint, as shown in *Figure 9.14*. The full range of observed latencies is plotted as the *x*-axis, subdivided into many buckets. The *y*-axis is the number of calls to the service/endpoint that had the latency in the given bucket over a certain time window. Since the traces are sampled, the number of calls is extrapolated from the actual number of collected traces and the sampling probability recorded as a tag in the root span:

$$estimated\ call\ count = \frac{observed\ count\ of\ spans\ within\ latency\ bucket}{trace\ sampling\ probability}$$

We can see that the distribution in the histogram is multi-modal, with a couple of humps on the short end (1-3ms), a large hump in the middle (70-100ms), and a long tail going all the way up to 15 seconds. The tool supported the ability to shift time by adjusting the sliders on the timeline at the top. Most importantly, the tool allowed selecting a portion of the distribution and getting a breakdown of the number of calls by the upstream caller, as well as the ability to view sample traces exhibiting the selected latency.

The tool was an early prototype, but it allowed us to visualize and investigate some abnormal behaviors in the system, such as one specific caller often causing slow responses because it was querying for rarely used data that was causing cache misses.

Recently, Lightstep, a commercial vendor that provides a tracing solution called [x]PM, announced [8] a much more advanced and polished version of a histogram presentation, which it calls **Live View**. Unlike the Uber prototype, which was limited in its filtering capabilities, Live View is able to slice and dice the data by a multitude of dimensions, including custom tags that can be added to tracing spans.

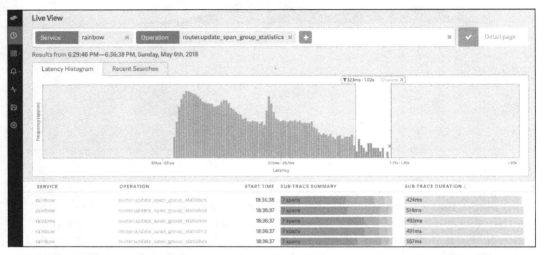

Figure 9.15: Analyzing latency histograms using Live View from Lightstep.
The filter box at the top allows slicing and dicing the data by many dimensions.
Reproduced with permission from Lightstep, Inc.

Investigating performance issues using latency histograms is a step toward a better understanding of the complex behaviors of a distributed system. Preaggregations of traces allow us to make informed decisions about which traces are worth analyzing and ensure that we are not looking at random outliers.

Long-term profiling

Performance optimization is a job that is never done. Applications are constantly evolving, developing new features, and adapting to new business requirements. This adds complexity and introduces new, often unexpected behaviors into the system. Optimizations done previously may no longer apply, or be offset by performance degradation elsewhere, due to new interactions. The discipline of long-term profiling allows us to keep the degradations in check, detect them early, and fix them before they become a real problem.

The simplest step toward long-term profiling is to monitor trends in performance. If we plot the p99.9 latency of an endpoint today and compare it with a plot captured last month, do we see more recent plots being consistently higher? Then we have a degradation. However, we know better by now than to compare two numbers, so instead, we can compare the distributions of latency, via histograms. Do we see today's histogram shifting toward the long tail? Then we have a degradation. We may have also acquired a new mode in the distribution that was not there before.

Monitoring trends via aggregate tracing data has a distinct advantage over traditional measurements because in addition to informing us about degradations, the aggregates also provide insights into the root cause of those changes. Naoman Abbas, an engineer at Pinterest, gave a talk at Velocity NYC 2018 where he presented two analysis techniques that the company applies to understand trends in performance [9].

One of them is an offline analyzer that takes as input a certain description of the trace shape and two timeframes, and runs aggregation over each timeframe to calculate certain cumulative metrics, such as number of traces observed, number of services involved, average overall latency, average self-latency of individual operations, and so on. By comparing the resulting numbers, the engineers can make hypotheses about what changes in the architecture may be responsible for the degradation, then they can test those hypotheses by rerunning the analyzer with more detailed filtering criteria.

The second approach involves real-time extraction of features from fully assembled traces, such as cumulative time spent in the backend spans versus cumulative time spent waiting on the network, or extracting additional dimensions from the traces that can be later used for filtering and analysis, such as the type of client application executing the request (Android or iOS app), or the country where the request originated from. We will discuss this technique in more detail in *Chapter 12, Gathering Insights with Data Mining*.

Summary

In this chapter, I just scratched the surface of all the possibilities of using tracing data for the analysis and understanding of complex distributed systems. With end-to-end tracing finally getting mainstream adoption, I am certain that many more exciting and innovative techniques and applications will be developed by software engineers in the industry and computer scientists in academia. In the following chapters, I will cover more ideas; some based on the tracing data itself, and others made possible by the tracing infrastructure.

References

1. Ben Sigelman. *OpenTracing: Turning the Lights on for Microservices.*
    Cloud Native Computing Foundation Blog: `https://www.cncf.io/`
    `blog/2016/10/20/opentracing-turning-the-lights-on-for-`
    `microservices/`.

2. Weaveworks Scope: `https://github.com/weaveworks/scope`.

3. Kiali: observability for the Istio service mesh: `https://kiali.io`.

4. Vizceral: animated traffic graphs: `https://github.com/Netflix/vizceral`.

5. Michael Chow, David Meisner, Jason Flinn, Daniel Peek, Thomas F. Wenisch.
    *The Mystery Machine: End-to-end Performance Analysis of Large-scale Internet
    Services.* Proceedings of the 11th USENIX Symposium on Operating Systems
    Design and Implementation. October 6–8, 2014.

6. Jaana B. Dogan. *Critical path driven development.* Velocity NYC 2018: `https://`
    `conferences.oreilly.com/velocity/vl-ny/public/schedule/`
    `detail/71060`.

7. Bryan Boreham. *How We Used Jaeger and Prometheus to Deliver Lightning-Fast
    User Queries.* KubeCon EU 2018: `https://youtu.be/qg0ENOdP1Lo?t=1094`.

8. Ben Sigelman. *Performance is a Shape, Not a Number.* Lightstep Blog, May 8,
    2018: `https://lightstep.com/blog/performance-is-a-shape-not-a-`
    `number/`.

9. Naoman Abbas. *Using distributed trace data to solve performance and operational
    challenges.* Velocity NYC 2018: `https://conferences.oreilly.com/`
    `velocity/vl-ny/public/schedule/detail/70035`.

10
Distributed Context Propagation

We discussed in *Chapter 3, Distributed Tracing Fundamentals*, that most tracing systems today use causal metadata propagation, also known as distributed context propagation, as the fundamental substrate for associating tracing events with individual executions. Unlike the trace data collection, the context propagation mechanism is always on for 100% of requests, regardless of the sampling decisions. In *Chapter 4, Instrumentation Basics with OpenTracing*, and *Chapter 5, Instrumentation of Asynchronous Applications*, we have seen that tracing instrumentation APIs, like the OpenTracing APIs, include primitives for implementing context propagation in the applications.

In other chapters, we used OpenTracing baggage, a form of general-purpose context propagation, to implement functionality completely unrelated to tracing: collecting metrics about a specific subset of requests (for example, from a given customer in the HotROD demo in *Chapter 2, Take Tracing for a HotROD Ride*), transparently passing a certain datum through the call graph (the greeting word in *Chapter 4, Instrumentation Basics with OpenTracing*), and even affecting routing decisions done by the service mesh based on some metadata (*Chapter 7, Tracing with Service Mesh*).

As it turns out, there are many other useful applications of context propagation that can be implemented on top of tracing infrastructure. In this chapter, we will look at several examples. However, first I want to address one question you may already have: if end-to-end tracing, as well as other functionality, must be built "on top of" context propagation, shouldn't context propagation be a separate, underlying instrumentation layer, instead of being bundled with tracing APIs? As we will see in the following section, the answer is yes, theoretically it can be separate, but in practice it is more nuanced and there are good reasons for having it bundled with tracing.

> The distributed context propagation mechanism is always enabled for all requests, regardless of the sampling decisions that affect trace data collection.

Brown Tracing Plane

The team at Brown University, led by Prof. Rodrigo Fonseca, has done a lot of research in the space of distributed tracing, including the development of event-based tracing system X-Trace [1], monitoring framework Pivot Tracing [2], which we will discuss in this chapter, and many other projects. They have developed the Tracing Plane [3], a shared set of components that provide core generic metadata propagation (or "baggage", which is where the term came from) on top of which the other projects are built. Recently, the Tracing Plane has been generalized in a more principled way [4] that we are going to review here.

The need for a general-purpose context propagation framework becomes obvious if we consider a large number of existing so-called "cross-cutting" tools that focus on the analysis and management of end-to-end executions in distributed systems, such as using tenant IDs for resource accounting and coordinated scheduling decisions across components; propagating targeting instructions for failure testing and distributed debugging; taint tracking for detecting security policy violations, and many more. I recommend referring to *Chapter 2, Take Tracing for a HotROD Ride*, of Jonathan Mace's PhD thesis at Brown University [5] for an in-depth overview.

Despite their massive potential and usefulness, these tools are challenging to deploy in the existing distributed systems, especially those based on microservices, because they often require modifications to the application source code, similar to tracing instrumentation. The changes can often be logically broken into two parts: the code used to propagate metadata, and the logic of a specific cross-cutting tool.

The context propagation is usually independent of the tool; it only depends on the structure and concurrency model of the application, for example, threads, queues, RPC, and messaging frameworks. The cross-cutting tool logic is usually concerned with the exact semantics of the metadata the tool needs to propagate, but not with the propagation mechanism itself.

Traditionally, the tool instrumentation was closely intertwined with metadata propagation logic, as in the case of tracing instrumentation that we have discussed previously. The tight coupling makes the deployment of the cross-cutting tools more difficult, since the tool authors need to know not only the logic of the tool itself, but also the logic and concurrency model of the application to make sure that the metadata propagation is implemented correctly. The coupling also prevents the reuse of the propagation logic across the tools.

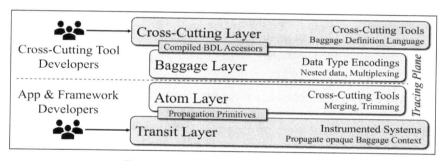

Figure 10.1: Tracing Plane layered design.

The Tracing Plane separates the metadata propagation from the cross-cutting tool instrumentation by providing a layered architecture. At the top of the architecture is the **Cross-Cutting Layer**, which represents the instrumentation of the actual tools, such as end-to-end tracing. Each tool has its own metadata that needs to be propagated, for example, trace and span IDs for tracing. The tools define a schema for their metadata using **Baggage Definition Language** (BDL), which resembles the protocol buffers definition language. A tracing tool like Jaeger may define the baggage schema as follows:

```
bag TracingTool {
    int64 traceID = 0;
    int64 spanID  = 1;
    bool  sampled = 2;
}
```

The Tracing Plane project provides a compiler from BDL to different programming languages. The compiler creates interfaces for accessing and manipulating the data in the baggage, for example:

```
tt := TracingTool.ReadFrom(baggageCtx)
tt.SetSpanID(123)
```

The **Baggage Layer** is the top layer of the Tracing Plane. It provides the cross-cutting layer with access to the metadata in a structured way, performs encodings for data types into cross-platform binary formats, handles nested data types, and allows multiple cross-cutting tools to keep their own metadata in separate namespaces within a single baggage context (multiplexing). The Baggage Layer is optional because the top-level tool is free to access the lower **Atom Layer** directly, but then the tool would have to operate on low-level binary data.

The atom layer is the core context propagation layer. It has no knowledge of the semantics of the metadata stored in the baggage context, which it treats as opaque binary data. The atom layer exposes five operations:

```
Serialize(BaggageContext): Bytes
Deserialize(Bytes): BaggageContext
Branch(BaggageContext): BaggageContext
Merge(BaggageContext, BaggageContext): BaggageContext
Trim(BaggageContext): BaggageContext
```

The first two operations are used for encoding and decoding baggage when execution jumps between processes, for example, as part of an RPC request via HTTP headers. The `Branch` and `Merge` operations are used when execution splits into multiple branches (local forks or outgoing RPC requests) and then joins back. The `Merge` operation has specific semantics of merging baggage items from two contexts, which I will not discuss here (please refer to the paper).

`Trim` is used when there are constraints on the size of the baggage context, for example, when communicating over a protocol that restricts the size of the request metadata (a common occurrence in legacy systems and proprietary protocols).

The operations of the atom layer are used by the **Transit Layer**. This layer itself is not part of the Tracing Plane framework. Instead, it is the actual instrumentation that is written by the application and framework developers to manipulate the baggage context. These developers know the ins and outs of their application or framework; the concurrency semantics of threading and queueing models; details of RPC implementations, and so on. Yet they do not need to know anything about the contents of the baggage context, which allows different cross-cutting tools to be built on top of the instrumentation in the transit layer.

If you have read *Chapter 4, Instrumentation Basics with OpenTracing*, of this book, you will probably see some similarities with OpenTracing:

- The `Inject()` and `Extract()` operations in the `Tracer` interface are similar to Tracing Plane's `Serialize()` and `Deserialize()` operations in the Atom Layer. To be completely agnostic to the transport protocols, the Tracing Plane uses only binary encoding of the baggage, while OpenTracing allows text-based representations.

- Starting a new child span in OpenTracing is somewhat equivalent to the `Branch()` operation because the new span receives its own copy of the baggage that is propagated independently of the parent. OpenTracing does not support reverse propagation (for example, via RPC response headers), and does not define clear semantics of baggage merging when a span is created with more than one parent reference, so there is no equivalent of the `Merge()` operation. The `Trim()` operation is also not defined explicitly in OpenTracing.

- The span API maps to the cross-cutting layer specialized to the domain of end-to-end tracing.

- The OpenTracing instrumentation inside the applications corresponds to the transit layer. It uses the combination of inject and extract methods to encode or decode the context to and from the wire formats, and the **scope** and **scope manager** APIs to propagate the context in-process (please refer to *Chapter 4, Instrumentation Basics with OpenTracing*).

- The `SetBaggateItem()` and `GetBaggageItem()` methods on the span roughly correspond to the rest of the atom layer. Since OpenTracing baggage only supports strings, there is no equivalent of the baggage layer with complex data types and namespaces for different metadata.

A reasonable question at this point would be, why was OpenTracing (as well as other tracing APIs) not implemented with a similar layered architecture as the Tracing Plane? Ironically, even though it was not using this architecture (which was not invented at the time), the very first iteration of what later became OpenTracing was, in fact, called **distributed context propagation (DCP)**. Later, it was renamed to OpenTracing, as the authors realized that the main reason for the project was to make "distributed tracing", first and foremost, more accessible to software developers by reducing the barrier to entry, which is typically the complexity of the white-box instrumentation.

Consider the following OpenTracing instrumentation in Go implemented as HTTP handler middleware:

```go
func MiddlewareFunc(
    tracer opentracing.Tracer,
    h http.HandlerFunc,
) http.HandlerFunc {
    fn := func(w http.ResponseWriter, r *http.Request) {
        parent, _ := tracer.Extract(
            opentracing.HTTPHeaders,
            opentracing.HTTPHeadersCarrier(r.Header),
        )
        span := tracer.StartSpan(
            "HTTP " + r.Method, ext.RPCServerOption(parent),
        )
        defer sp.finish()
        ext.HTTPMethod.Set(span, r.Method)
        ext.HTTPUrl.Set(span, r.URL.String())
        ...
        ctx := opentracing.ContextWithSpan(r.Context(), span)
        h(w, r.WithContext(ctx))
        span.Finish()
    }
    return http.HandlerFunc(fn)
}
```

The call to `tracer.Extract()` would be equivalent to a call to `Deserialize()` in the Tracing Plane. The call to `tracer.StartSpan()` would have to remain if we wanted to keep tracing behavior, but we would also have to add a call to `Branch()` in the Tracing Plane to keep up with the required semantics. In other words, both APIs would need to be actively used in order to extract the context propagation behavior into a shared Tracing Plane implementation.

The tracing practitioners working on the OpenTracing API felt that this would further complicate an already non-trivial tracing instrumentation. On the other hand, focusing on the tracing instrumentation alone, while still providing the option for baggage propagation, was a much easier sell to organizations looking to adopt distributed tracing. As we will see later in this chapter, a lot of cross-cutting tools are still possible to implement, even with the limited version of baggage support available in OpenTracing and other tracing APIs.

Pivot tracing

Pivot Tracing [2] is another fascinating project from Brown University that won the Best Paper Award at **SOSP** 2015 (**Symposium on Operating Systems Principles**). It provides dynamic causal monitoring for distributed systems by allowing users to define, at runtime, arbitrary measurements at one point in the system, and then select, filter, and group these measurements by events in another part of the system for reporting.

We saw a very rudimentary example of this in the HotROD example in *Chapter 2, Take Tracing for a HotROD Ride*, when we measured the time spent on calculating the shortest route in a downstream service and attributed it to the customer ID defined much higher in the call graph. Pivot Tracing takes it to a whole new level by:

- Making the instrumentation dynamic via code injection
- Supporting a complex query language that in turn informs that dynamic instrumentation

The paper discussed the evaluation of this query:

```
FROM bytesRead IN DataNodeMetrics.incrBytesRead
JOIN client IN FIRST(ClientProtocols) ON client ⇒ bytesRead
GROUP BY client.procName
SELECT client.procName, SUM(bytesRead.delta)
```

This query is applied to HDFS data nodes that are processing requests from different clients running HBase, Map-Reduce, and direct HDFS clients. The query involves the data from two trace points: one high in the stack, called `ClientProtocols`, which captures the type and process name of the client, and the other running on the data nodes at the bottom of the stack, called `DataNodeMetrics`, which collects various statistics, including the number of bytes read from disk for a given request (`incrBytesRead`).

The query groups all requests by the `client.procName` and calculates the total amount of disk usage per client. It looks pretty similar to the HotROD example, but in HotROD, we had to not only hardcode the calculation of the time spent, but also manually attribute it to two parameters in the metadata: session ID and customer name. If we wanted to do the aggregation by a different parameter, for example, by the `User-Agent` header from the browser, we would have to change the code of the `route` service. In Pivot Tracing, we only need to change the query!

Another novel mechanism in Pivot Tracing is the ability to do causal "happened-before" joins as represented by the symbol ⇒ in the query. Both `DataNodeMetrics` and `ClientProtocols` are just events produced by the trace points, and a production system will be generating thousands of these events per second.

The happened-before join allows the joining of only those events that are causally related, in this case client requests causing disk reads. In Pivot Tracing implementation, the happened-before joins were restricted to events occurring in the same distributed transaction, but in theory, they could be extended to a wider definition of causality, such as events from one execution influencing another execution.

The paper demonstrates how Pivot Tracing was used to diagnose a performance issue in HDFS and discover a bug in the implementation. Due to the dynamic nature of Pivot Tracing queries, the authors were able to iteratively issue more and more specific queries to the system, grouping the results, and throughput metrics by various dimensions, until they were able to find the root cause of the issue and demonstrate the software bug. I recommend reading the paper for a detailed walkthrough of that investigation.

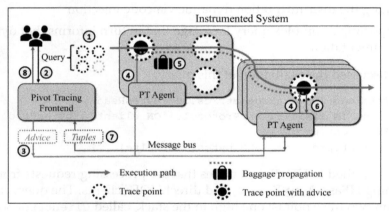

Figure 10.2: Overview of Pivot Tracing.

Let's discuss how Pivot Tracing is able to achieve all that. The implementation was targeted at systems implemented in Java, which allows dynamic instrumentation of the applications via byte code manipulation and the injection of trace points. Trace points emit events that contain certain attributes, such as values of the in-scope variables. Pivot Tracing can also work with the existing (permanent) trace points in the code. The preceding diagram illustrates how it evaluates the queries:

1. The events of the trace points define a vocabulary for the queries, for example, events `ClientProtocols` and `DataNodeMetrics.incrBytesRead`, and their attributes, `procName` and `delta`, used in the preceding query.

2. The operator constructs a query that they want to evaluate in the system using the supported vocabulary.

3. The Pivot Tracing frontend analyzes the query and compiles it to an intermediate representation called "advice" that is distributed to Pivot Tracing agents embedded in the applications.

4. The agent maps the instructions in advice to code that it installs dynamically at relevant trace points.

5. When the execution passes through trace points, they execute the code from advice. Certain instructions in advice tell the trace points to pack certain attributes of the observed events into the metadata context and propagate it with the execution via baggage, for example, in the query the `procName` attribute is packed by the first invocation of the `ClientProtocols` trace point and later accessed (unpacked) by the `incrBytesRead` trace point to produce a data tuple.

6. Other instructions in advice may tell the trace points to emit data tuples.

7. Data tuples are aggregated locally and streamed over the message bus to the Pivot Tracing backend.

8. The frontend performs final aggregations and produces reports.

It is interesting to note that in general, implementing a happened-before join could be very expensive, requiring all tuples to be aggregated globally in the cluster prior to evaluating the join. Pivot Tracing greatly simplifies this process by relying on baggage to capture and propagate relevant group-by attributes (at the cost of increased request size), so that the actual join is performed implicitly, when the attributes are extracted from baggage and included in the emitted tuples.

Pivot Tracing does not implement its own baggage propagation. Instead, it relies on the Tracing Plane functionality that we discussed earlier. However, from the description of the algorithm, it is easy to see that its requirements on the baggage mechanism are pretty minimal and can be easily satisfied by the OpenTracing implementation, for example, by encoding a single baggage item with the key `pivot-tracing` and a JSON string as the value. There are some edge cases that the Tracing Plane handles via the merging of baggage contexts, such as parallel executions that both increment the same counter, but in many systems these merges are not required (as long as we can represent the execution via the span model).

Since Pivot Tracing is able to install instrumentation dynamically, it can co-exist with an OpenTracing instrumentation and make use of the OpenTracing baggage for its query evaluation.

Chaos engineering

To address the massive impact of system downtime on business revenues, many organizations are adopting Chaos Engineering in order to gain confidence that their systems are fault-tolerant, that is, built to anticipate and mitigate a variety of software and hardware failures. Many organizations are implementing internal "failure as a service" systems, such as **Failure Injection Testing (FIT)** [6], **Simian Army** [7] at Netflix, **uDestroy** at Uber, and even commercial offerings like `https://gremlin.com`.

These systems advocate treating Chaos Engineering as a scientific discipline:

1. *Form a hypothesis*: What do you think could go wrong in the system?
2. *Plan an experiment*: How can you recreate the failure without impacting users?
3. *Minimize the blast radius*: Try the smallest experiment first to learn something.
4. *Run the experiment*: Monitor the results and the system behavior carefully.
5. *Analyze*: If the system did not work as expected, congratulations, you found a bug. If everything worked as planned, increase the blast radius and repeat.

Unfortunately, having the infrastructure for fault injection is only half the battle. The more difficult part is coming up with adequate **failure scenarios**: combinations of faults across a distributed system. We can view this as a general **search problem**: funding a set of fault injection scenarios (preferably a minimal set) that exercise all failure modes that exist in the application. The number of distinct scenarios is exponential in the number of potential faults, and therefore is intractable for exhaustive search.

The most common approaches for creating failure scenarios are random search and programmers-guided search. Random search has the advantage of simplicity and generality, but it is unlikely to discover deep or cascading failures involving a combination of rare conditions, and it often wastes a lot of resources by testing scenarios that are redundant or could be proven to not affect the end user. Leveraging the intuition of domain experts is difficult to scale to large architectures. In organizations like Uber, with over 3,000 individual microservices, there are hardly any engineers, even the most senior ones, who can keep the full complexity of the system in their head, and anticipate non-trivial failures.

A recent study at Netflix [8] demonstrated the use of **Lineage-driven Fault Injection (LDFI)** as a technique for guiding the search through possible fault-injection scenarios. One of the most critical user interactions with the Netflix site is the "app boot" workflow: the loading of the main page with metadata and the initial list of videos for the user. It is a very complex request that touches dozens of internal microservices and has hundreds of potential failure points. Brute force exploration of that search space would require approximately 2^{100} experiments. By using the LDFI technique, the full space of failure scenarios was covered with just 200 experiments, and the team discovered "11 new critical failures that could prevent users from streaming content, several of which involved 'deep' failure scenarios involving a combination of service fault events."

The full description of the LDFI technique is beyond the scope of this book. However, the existing end-to-end tracing infrastructure at Netflix played a critical role in enabling it. The LDFI service was continuously monitoring distributed traces collected in production and using them to build long-lived models of *dependencies* within individual executions and *redundancy* across them.

The models were used to construct *lineage* graphs used by LDFI to reason backwards (from effects to causes) about the impact that some combination of faults could have on a successful outcome. Those combinations that could be proven to have the potential to cause user-visible failure were then tested using the FIT infrastructure [7]. The requests matching the criteria for the failure scenarios were decorated with metadata describing the faults under test, such as adding latency to specific service calls or failing those calls completely. These fault instructions encoded in the metadata were passed through the call graph using, you guessed it, distributed context propagation.

The use of collected end-to-end traces to guide the exploration of the failure search space is very interesting. However, the use of metadata propagation for delivering fault instructions to the services is of particular interest in the context of this chapter. Many "failure as a service" systems support execution scripts that can target specific services, service instances, hosts, and so on, for fault injection. However, many non-trivial fault scenarios cannot be expressed in these terms because they need the faults to be scoped to specific *transactions*, not just specific *components* in the system.

The time sequence diagram in *Figure 10.3* illustrates a replication bug in Kafka that was reproduced by the LDFI technique. Three Kafka replicas are configured to handle a single partition, but when they send their membership message (**M**) to the **Zookeeper**, a temporary network partition causes the messages from **Replicas B** and **C** to be lost, and **Replica A** becomes the leader, while believing that it is the sole surviving replica. The client's request (**C**) also acknowledges via message (**L**) that **Replica A** is the leader. When the client writes (**W**) the data to **Replica A**, the write is acknowledged (**A**) as successful. Immediately after that, the **Replica A** crashes, thus violating the message durability guarantee.

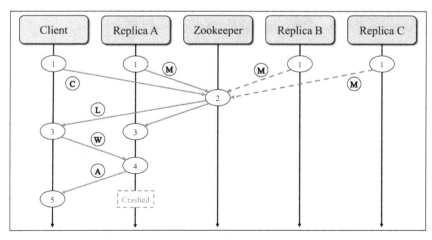

Figure 10.3: Time sequence diagram illustrating a previously discovered Kafka replication bug reproduced via LDFI.

It is easy to see that even with fault instructions propagated via metadata, this particular bug is very hard to reproduce because a number of faults must be carefully orchestrated in time to simulate the failure scenario and there are at least four different RPC chains involved. However, using metadata propagation is still a very valuable technique for delivering targeted fault instructions to the system components in the context of specific requests.

Traffic labeling

At a high level, adding metadata to request context and propagating it through the call graph is a way of partitioning the overall traffic to the application along a number of dimensions. As an example, if we label each external request with the type of company product it represents (for Google it could be Gmail, Docs, YouTube, and so on, and for Uber it could be Ridesharing, Uber Eats, Uber Bikes, and so on) and propagate it in the metadata, then we can get a pretty accurate picture of how much traffic served by a data center is attributed to each product line. Strictly speaking, the Pivot Tracing and LDFI techniques I discussed earlier can also be considered as partitioning of the traffic, but the values they pass through metadata are very complex and high cardinality. In this section, I will talk about traffic labeling that uses low-cardinality dimensions.

Testing in production

Testing in production is a common practice today because given the complexity of the internet-scale distributed systems, it is often impossible to provide the same level of coverage of different edge cases and the variety of user behaviors that we might observe in production by simulating them in the staging environments. Some testing requests may only read the data, while others make changes to the system state, for example, a simulated rider taking a simulated Uber ride.

Some services in the system may identify the requests as test traffic by looking at the data involved, for example, a simulated Uber rider account is likely to have a special marker in the database. However, many services may not have that knowledge. For example, a generic storage layer, while having access to the test account marker, would not know to look for it in the data. Therefore, it is useful to label the traffic generated by test accounts from the root of the call graph by propagating a label like tenancy, indicating whether the traffic is synthetic or real production. There are multiple ways that the system components may use such a label:

- Let's assume you own some downstream service and you provision it to handle a certain level of traffic. You will probably setup the monitoring of the traffic volume coming to your service and define alerts when that volume exceeds a certain threshold (even if you use auto-scaling you may want to do that for cost reasons).

Now imagine that some upstream service a couple of levels above you in the stack is doing a capacity or resiliency test by generating a lot of synthetic test traffic. Without using something like `tenancy` metadata to recognize that traffic, your service will not be able to tell if the increase in traffic is due to real production growth or just synthetic tests. Your alerts might start firing for no reason! On the other hand, if you know that the synthetic traffic will be labeled accordingly, you can define your alerts to only fire on the growth of real production traffic and ignore the synthetic spikes. In *Chapter 11, Integration with Metrics and Logs*, we will look at concrete ways this can be achieved very easily.

- Some components may be configured to recognize the traffic with test tenancy and automatically switch to **read-only** mode or to direct the writes to a different database.

- Some components may not want to serve synthetic traffic from production clusters at all (that is, they are not quite ready for testing in production). The test tenancy metadata can be used by the routing layers to redirect the requests to a staging cluster.

Debugging in production

If we embrace the philosophy of testing in production, in part because we cannot construct staging environments that reproduce production, then we should also talk about debugging in production, and especially debugging microservices. No matter how powerful end-to-end tracing is, it is still limited to the information collected by the preprogrammed trace points. Sometimes we need to inspect the full state of the application, step through code, and change some variables, to understand the issue or find a bug. This is where the traditional debuggers shine. However, in a *microservices-based* application, the state is spread out across many processes, and each process has many states for all of the concurrent requests it is processing at any given time. If we want to debug the behavior of a particular request, we may need to attach debuggers to instances of different services, possibly in different languages, and we also need to figure out which instance of a given service is going to receive our request.

One of the very interesting projects that helps to solve this problem is the **Squash debugger** [9], developed by Solo.io, Inc. Squash consists of three components:

1. The Squash user interface is just a plugin to popular IDEs, like Visual Studio Code or IntelliJ. You can set breakpoints in your microservices as if you're developing locally, and the Squash plugin will coordinate with the Squash server to install those breakpoints in the services running in the production cluster.

2. The Squash server holds information about the breakpoints and orchestrates Squash clients.

3. The Squash client is a daemon process that runs alongside the applications, contains the binaries for the debuggers, and allows the attaching of the debuggers to the running microservice process.

Squash integrates with **service mesh Istio** by providing a filter for the Envoy proxy that can initiate a debugging session for requests that contain certain markers, for example, a special header. To isolate the instance from other production requests, Squash can clone the full state of the process into another instance and attach a debugger to that private instance, without affecting the rest of the production traffic. I recommend watching some of the talks about Squash for more information.

How is this related to traffic labeling and context propagation? We do not want to start hitting the breakpoints on random production requests, possibly affecting real users. At the same time, we may need to hit breakpoints in multiple microservices processing our hand-crafted request. This coordination becomes much easier with metadata propagation. We can define the breakpoints to be only enabled when an HTTP request has a particular baggage item encoded in the request headers and issue the top-level request to the system with that baggage item set, for example, using Jaeger baggage syntax:

```
$ curl -H 'jaeger-baggage: squash=yes' http://host:port/api/do-it
```

If the services are instrumented with OpenTracing and Jaeger, this baggage item will be propagated through the call graph automatically and trigger the breakpoints. To allow multiple developers to debug in production, the baggage item may be set to some token or username, to ensure that each developer only gets their breakpoints triggered by their hand-crafted request.

Developing in production

If we do not have a staging environment approximating production, then developing microservices that interact with other services is also a challenge. Even if we do have a staging cluster, the process of deploying the code there is usually not very snappy (building a container, uploading it to the registry, registering a new service version, and so on). A much faster way is if we can run the service instance locally and proxy the production traffic. For the downstream services, it is easier: we can just set up the tunnels. But what if our service needs upstream services from production to get a sensible request? What if we want to use the production mobile app to execute a high-level user workflow and have our local instance serve a portion of that execution? Fortunately, there are solutions for this problem as well. For example, **Telepresence** [10] integrates with Kubernetes and can replace a production service with a proxy that forwards all requests to another service instance that we may be running on a laptop, from our favorite IDE, with our favorite debugger attached.

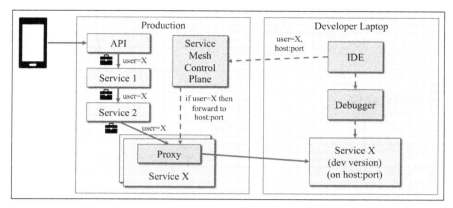

Figure 10.4: Developing in production by proxying to a development version of service X.

The diagram in *Figure 10.4* illustrates this approach. The developer starts a local instance of the service they want to debug (**Service X**), possibly from an IDE and with a debugger attached. The **IDE** plugin communicates with a control server in production, which could be a **Service Mesh Control Plane** (for example, Istio) or a dedicated debugging server that the routing proxy recognizes.

The **IDE** sends instructions about which requests should be intercepted, for example, only those that have the user=X label propagated via metadata. The user then makes a regular production request, even from a mobile app. The API server authenticates the user and stores user=X in the baggage, which is then used by the routing proxy (or by a library embedded in the application) to intercept those specific requests and forward them to the service instance on the developer's laptop.

Similar to the Squash example, the key to this approach is knowing which traffic should be redirected to the local instance, and which traffic should remain in production. Using traffic labeling via distributed context propagation provides an elegant solution to this problem.

Summary

In this chapter, we discussed how the metadata propagation mechanism can be separated from the tracing instrumentation that depends on it, for example, using the approach from the Tracing Plane, and why this is not always done in practice. We reviewed a number of cross-cutting techniques and tools for solving the problems of monitoring, debugging, and testing distributed systems that are not dependent on tracing directly, but depend on distributed context propagation. Having tracing instrumentation in the distributed systems makes these additional tools much easier to implement.

We briefly touched upon using traffic labeling to affect application metrics and alerts. In the next chapter, we will cover that in more detail, as well as other integrations between tracing, metrics, and logging systems.

References

1. X-Trace: `http://brownsys.github.io/tracing-framework/xtrace/`.

2. Pivot Tracing: `http://pivottracing.io/`.

3. Brown Tracing Plane: `http://brownsys.github.io/tracing-framework/tracingplane/`.

4. Jonathan Mace, Rodrigo Fonseca. *Universal Context Propagation for Distributed System Instrumentation*. Proceedings of the 13th ACM European Conference on Computer Systems (EuroSys '18).

5. Jonathan Mace. *A Universal Architecture for Cross-Cutting Tools in Distributed Systems*. Ph.D. Thesis, Brown University, May 2018.

6. Kolton Andrus, Naresh Gopalani, Ben Schmaus. *FIT: Failure Injection Testing*. The Netflix Tech Blog: `https://medium.com/netflix-techblog/fit-failure-injection-testing-35d8e2a9bb2`.

7. Yury Izrailevsky, Ariel Tseitlin. *The Netflix Simian Army*. The Netflix Tech Blog: `https://medium.com/netflix-techblog/the-netflix-simian-army-16e57fbab116`.

8. Peter Alvaro, Kolton Andrus, Chris Sanden, Casey Rosenthal, Ali Basiri, Lorin Hochstein. *Automating Failure Testing at Internet Scale*. ACM Symposium on Cloud Computing 2016 (SoCC'16).

9. Squash: Debugger for microservices: `https://github.com/solo-io/squash`.

10. Telepresence: Fast, local development for Kubernetes and OpenShift microservices: `https://www.telepresence.io/`.

11
Integration with Metrics and Logs

In the previous chapter, we reviewed several techniques that rely on distributed context propagation, which often comes built in with the tracing libraries. The notion of a request context that travels along the requests in a distributed transaction is becoming increasingly important for monitoring distributed systems, not just by means of distributed tracing, but even with the more traditional monitoring tools such as metrics (or stats) and logs. By enriching metrics and logs with the metadata from request context, we can observe behavioral patterns in the applications that otherwise would be hard to notice just by looking at the aggregates. This is quickly becoming a new norm in the observability industry and is one of the reasons that projects such as OpenCensus come out with combined APIs for metrics, logs, and tracing, all of which are tightly linked with distributed context propagation.

In this chapter, we will look at many integration points between these monitoring tools, using a version of our favorite, the Hello application. We will see how metrics and logs can be enriched with request metadata, how tracing instrumentation can be used to replace explicit metrics instrumentation, and how logs and traces can be bidirectionally integrated with each other.

Three pillars of observability

If you have followed the application monitoring and performance management space in the past few years, whether at conferences or in the news and tech blogs, you have probably heard the term "three pillars of observability" used to refer to metrics, logs, and distributed tracing. While some people have strong, very-amusing-to-read (strong language warning!), and partially justified objections [1], [2] to this term, we can look at these three areas as different approaches to recording events occurring in the applications. In the end, all of these signals are collected by instrumentation in the code, triggered by some events we deem worthy of recording.

Ideally, when we troubleshoot a performance problem, we would like to know as much as possible about what the application was doing at the time, by recording all possible events. The main challenge we face is the cost of collecting and reporting all that telemetry. The three "pillars" primarily differ in their approach to data collection and the associated costs.

Metrics are often the cheapest to collect, with the smallest impact on the application performance, because metrics typically deal with simple numeric measurements that are heavily aggregated to reduce the data volume; for example, to measure the throughput of a REST service, we just need an atomic counter and to report just a single int64 number once a second. Very few applications would be adversely impacted by the cost of reporting such a measurement. As a result, metrics are often used as highly accurate "monitoring signals" to keep track of the application health and performance, while at the same time, they are highly ineffective at explaining performance problems, due to the very same aggregation and lack of context.

Metrics as a monitoring tool are generally useful for monitoring individual entities, such as a process, a host, or an RPC endpoint. Since metrics can be easily aggregated, they can be used to monitor higher-level entities by combining individual time series, for example, observing throughput or latency of a NoSQL database cluster by aggregating stats from individual nodes via averages, min or max, and percentiles. It is a common practice to partition a single logical metric, for example, an endpoint error count, into multiple time series by adding extra dimensions, such as the host name, availability zone, or data center name, and so on.

Older metrics protocols, such as Graphite StatsD, supported time series partitioning by encoding the dimensions into the metric name as positional arguments, for example, the host name `host123` in the second position: `servers.host123.disk.bytes_free`. The Graphite query language allows aggregation via wildcards:

```
averageSeries(servers.*.disk.bytes_free)
```

Newer protocols supported by metrics systems, such as CNCF Prometheus [3] or Uber's M3 [4], take a more structured approach and capture these dimensions as named labels:

```
disk_bytes_free{server="host123", zone="us-east-1"}
```

Capturing metrics with extra dimensions provides more investigative power to the operators, who can narrow down the time series aggregates to specific infrastructure components. Unfortunately, since most metrics APIs are not context-aware, the dimensions typically represent static metadata available at the process level, such as host name, build version, and so on.

Logging frameworks perform no aggregation and report the events as-is, ideally in the so-called "structured format" that is machine friendly and can be automatically parsed, indexed, and processed by the centralized logging infrastructure. You will see an example of this log format in this chapter.

Most logging frameworks record events as a stream of records that may be tagged with the name of the execution thread (for example, this is a standard practice in Java), which helps slightly with inferring causal relationships between the events; however, that practice becomes less useful with the proliferation of frameworks for asynchronous programming. In general, event correlation is a problem not solved particularly well by logs as a toolset. The verbosity of the logs can be another challenge for high-throughput services; to combat it most logging frameworks support leveled logging where messages are explicitly classified by the developer as debug, info, warning, error, and so on. Is it a common practice to disable any debug-level logs in production and to keep even higher levels to an absolute minimum, especially for successful requests.

Sampling is sometimes used to reduce the logging volume and performance overhead, typically in the form of rate limiting rather than any more context-sensitive techniques. Since sampling takes effect at the log streams of individual nodes or processes, it makes logs correlation across multiple services even harder. On the plus side, it allows the teams owning a particular service to make cost and benefit decisions about how much log data is worth keeping for their service; for example, a load balancer might produce a bare minimum number of logs, while a payment handling service might log a lot more information, even when both services participate in the same distributed transaction.

Distributed tracing instrumentation, in many aspects, is very similar to logging, only even more structured. The main difference is that tracing explicitly captures causal relationships between the events, which makes it immensely more powerful at troubleshooting the behavior of distributed and highly concurrent systems compared to logging. Tracing is also fully aware of the distributed request context, which allows us to apply more intelligent sampling techniques that reduce the data volume and overhead, while consistently preserving the events collected at different components of a distributed system during a specific execution. Furthermore, because tracing libraries themselves are often responsible for distributed context propagation, they can lend this context awareness to the other two "pillars," as we will see in this chapter.

Prerequisites

Since we are talking about integrating tracing with logs and metrics, we will run the backends for all three of these monitoring tools:

- Jaeger for traces
- Prometheus for metrics
- The ELK stack (Elasticsearch, Logstash, Kibana) for logs

This section provides instructions on setting up the environment to run the Hello application.

Project source code

The code can be found in the Chapter11 directory of the book's source code repository on GitHub. Please refer to *Chapter 4, Instrumentation Basics with OpenTracing*, for instructions on how to download it, then switch to the Chapter11 directory, from which all example code can be run.

The source code of the application is organized in the following structure:

```
Mastering-Distributed-Tracing/
  Chapter11/
    exercise1/
      client/
      formatter/
      hello/
      lib/
    elasticsearch/
    kibana/
    logstash/
    prometheus/
    docker-compose.yml      pom.xml
```

The application is composed of two microservices, `hello` and `formatter`, and a `client` app, all defined in the `exercise1` submodule. We will review their roles in the following section. The microservices are using some shared components and classes defined in the `lib` module.

The other top-level directories specify configurations for the monitoring tools. The `docker-compose.yml` file is used to spin up all of them as a group, including the two microservices from the Hello application. The Hello clients are run separately, outside of Docker containers.

Java development environment

Similar to the examples in *Chapter 4, Instrumentation Basics with OpenTracing*, we will need JDK 8 or higher. The Maven wrappers are checked in and will download Maven as needed. The Maven project in `pom.xml` is set up as a multi-module project, so make sure to run `install` to install the dependencies in Maven's local repository:

```
$ ./mvnw install
[... skip a lot of Maven logs ...]
[INFO] Reactor Summary:
[INFO]
[INFO] chapter11 0.0.1-SNAPSHOT ................. SUCCESS [  0.492 s]
[INFO] lib ..................................... SUCCESS [  1.825 s]
[INFO] exercise1 ............................... SUCCESS [  0.020 s]
[INFO] hello-1 ................................. SUCCESS [  2.251 s]
[INFO] formatter-1 ............................. SUCCESS [  0.337 s]
[INFO] client-1 0.0.1-SNAPSHOT ................. SUCCESS [  0.421 s]
[INFO] ------------------------------------------------------------
[INFO] BUILD SUCCESS
[INFO] ------------------------------------------------------------
```

Running the servers in Docker

Once the Java artifacts are built, all the server components, including the Hello application microservices and the monitoring backends, can be run via `docker-compose`:

```
$ docker-compose up -d
Creating network "chapter-11_default" with the default driver
Creating chapter-11_jaeger_1        ... done
Creating chapter-11_elasticsearch_1 ... done
```

```
Creating chapter-11_hello-1_1        ... done
Creating chapter-11_formatter-1_1    ... done
Creating chapter-11_prom_1           ... done
Creating chapter-11_logstash_1       ... done
Creating chapter-11_kibana_1         ... done
```

We pass the `-d` flag to run everything in the background. To check that everything was started correctly, use the `ps` command:

```
$ docker-compose ps
            Name                        Command              State
------------------------------------------------------------------------
-
chapter-11_elasticsearch_1   /usr/local/bin/docker-entr ...    Up
chapter-11_formatter-1_1     /bin/sh -c java      -DJAEG ...    Up
chapter-11_hello-1_1         /bin/sh -c java      -DJAEG ...    Up
chapter-11_jaeger_1          /go/bin/standalone-linux - ...    Up
chapter-11_kibana_1          /bin/bash /usr/local/bin/k ...    Up
chapter-11_logstash_1        /usr/local/bin/docker-entr ...    Up
chapter-11_prom_1            /bin/prometheus --config.f ...    Up
```

Sometimes Elasticsearch takes a long time to complete its startup process, even though the preceding `ps` command will report it as running. The easiest way to check that it's running is to `grep` for Kibana logs:

```
$ docker-compose logs | grep kibana_1 | tail -3
kibana_1          | {"type":"log","@timestamp":"2018-11-
25T19:10:37Z","tags":["warning","elasticsearch","admin"],"pid":1,"mes
sage":"Unable to revive connection: http://elasticsearch:9200/"}
kibana_1          | {"type":"log","@timestamp":"2018-11-
25T19:10:37Z","tags":["warning","elasticsearch","admin"],"pid":1,"mes
sage":"No living connections"}
kibana_1          | {"type":"log","@timestamp":"2018-11-
25T19:10:42Z","tags":["status","plugin:elasticsearch@6.2.3","info"],"pid"
:1,"state":"green","message":"Status changed from red to green -
Ready","prevState":"red","prevMsg":"Unable to connect to
Elasticsearch at http://elasticsearch:9200."}
```

We can see that the top two logs indicate Elasticsearch not being ready, while the last log reports the status as green.

Declaring index pattern in Kibana

Before we can use Kibana to explore collected logs, we need to define an index pattern for `logstash`. The `Makefile` includes a target to streamline this one-time setup step:

```
$ make index-pattern
curl -XPOST 'http://localhost:5601/api/saved_objects/index-pattern' \
 -H 'Content-Type: application/json' \
 -H 'kbn-version: 6.2.3' \
 -d '{"attributes":{"title":"logstash-
*","timeFieldName":"@timestamp"}}'


{"id":"5ab0adc0-f0e7-11e8-b54c-f5a1b6bdc876","type":"index-
pattern","updated_at":"…","version":1,"attributes":{"title":"logstash
-*","timeFieldName":"@timestamp"}}
```

From this point, if we execute some requests against the Hello application, for example:

```
$ curl http://localhost:8080/sayHello/Jennifer
Hello, Jennifer!
```

then we can find the logs in Kibana by accessing it at `http://localhost:5601/` and selecting the **Discover** menu item in the sidebar:

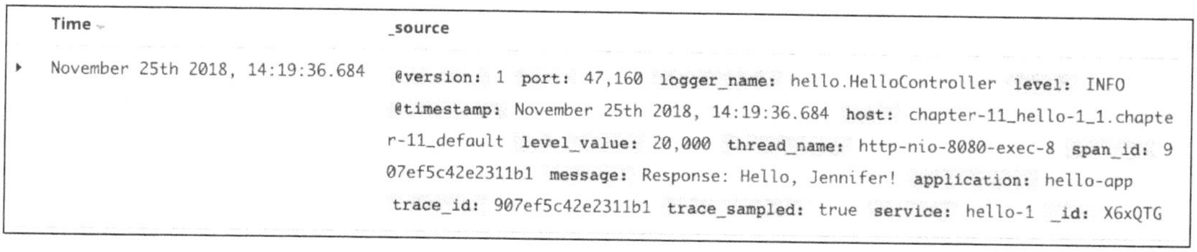

Time ⌄	_source
▸ November 25th 2018, 14:19:36.684	@version: 1 port: 47,160 logger_name: hello.HelloController level: INFO @timestamp: November 25th 2018, 14:19:36.684 host: chapter-11_hello-1_1.chapter-11_default level_value: 20,000 thread_name: http-nio-8080-exec-8 span_id: 9 07ef5c42e2311b1 message: Response: Hello, Jennifer! application: hello-app trace_id: 907ef5c42e2311b1 trace_sampled: true service: hello-1 _id: X6xQTG

Figure 11.1: Example of a log message from the Hello application, as displayed in Kibana

Running the clients

There is only one client application, but it takes certain parameters (via Java system properties) that control its behavior. The included `Makefile` contains two targets, `client1` and `client2`, to run the client in two different modes, from two different Terminal windows, for example:

```
$ make client1

./mvnw spring-boot:run -pl com.packt.distributed-tracing-chapter-
11:client-1 -Dlogstash.host=localhost -Dclient.version=v1 -
Dfailure.location=hello-1 -Dfailure.rate=0.2

[... skip initial logs ...]

[main] INFO  client.ClientApp.logStarted - Started ClientApp in 6.515
seconds (JVM running for 15.957)

[main] INFO  client.Runner.runQuery - executing
http://localhost:8080/sayHello/Bender

[main] INFO  client.Runner.runQuery - executing
http://localhost:8080/sayHello/Bender

[main] ERROR client.Runner.runQuery - error from server

[main] INFO  client.Runner.runQuery - executing
http://localhost:8080/sayHello/Bender

[main] ERROR client.Runner.runQuery - error from server
```

As you can see, the clients repeatedly execute the same HTTP request against the Hello application, and some of those requests are successful, while others fail. We will discuss later the meaning of the parameters accepted by the clients.

The Hello application

The Hello application we will use in this section is very similar to the one we used with the service mesh in *Chapter 7, Tracing with Service Mesh*. It consists of only two services: `hello` and `formatter`. The following diagram describes the overall architecture of this exercise:

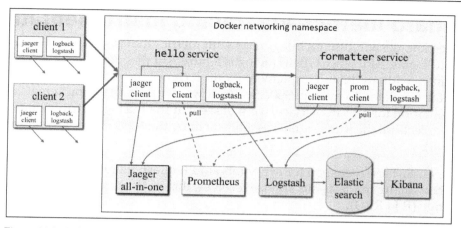

Figure 11.2: Architecture of the Hello application and its monitoring components and backends

All components of the Hello application are configured with a **jaeger client**, a **prom client**, and the **logback** logging framework with a `LogstashTcpSocketAppender` plugin that sends the logs directly to **Logstash**, which saves them to **Elasticsearch**. **Kibana** is the web UI used to query logs from storage. The Prometheus client accumulates the metrics in memory, until the **Prometheus** server pulls them via an HTTP endpoint. Since the Prometheus server runs inside the networking namespace created by `docker-compose`, it is not configured to scrape metrics from the two clients that run on the host network.

As before, we can also access the Hello application via `curl`:

```
$ curl http://localhost:8080/sayHello/Jennifer
Hello, Jennifer!
```

Integration with metrics

There are two types of integrations we are going to review: emitting metrics via tracing instrumentation and partitioning metrics by the request metadata attributes.

Standard metrics via tracing instrumentation

In this section, we will discuss integration with metrics that is somewhat unique to the OpenTracing API. Since OpenTracing is a pure API that describes distributed transactions, without default implementations, it can be implemented to generate data that is unrelated to tracing. Specifically, if we think about a typical metrics instrumentation for an RPC service, we will see that the tracing instrumentation already collects all the same signals as advocated by the **RED (Rate, Error, Duration)** method [5]:

- We start a server span for every inbound request, therefore we can count how many requests our service receives, that is, its throughput or request rate (R in RED).

- If the request encounters an error, the tracing instrumentation sets the `error=true` tag on the span, which allows us to count errors (E in RED).

- When we start and finish the server span, we signal the trace points to capture the start and end timestamps of the request, which allows us to calculate the duration (latency) of the request (D in RED).

In other words, tracing instrumentation is already a superset of the dedicated instrumentation for core metrics that people often use to describe their microservices. To see it in action, make sure that you started the servers and the clients as described in the *Prerequisites* section, then open the Prometheus web UI at `http://localhost:9090/`. In the **Expression** box enter the following query:

```
sum(rate(span_count{span_kind="server"}[1m]))
by (service,operation,error)
```

This query looks for a metric named `span_count`, with a `span_kind="server"`, label since the other kinds of spans in the trace do not map well to the service's RED signals.

Since it would be meaningless to aggregate all the requests across both services and all their endpoints, we group the results by service name, operation name (that is, the endpoint), and the error flag (true or false). Since each microservice is only exposing a single endpoint, grouping by service and operation is equivalent to grouping by either one alone, but when we include both in the query, the legend under the graph is more descriptive, as can be seen in *Figure 11.3*. We can also plot the 95th percentile of request latency with the following query (using the `span_bucket` metric):

```
histogram_quantile(0.95,
sum(rate(span_bucket{span_kind="server"}[1m]))
by (service,operation,error,le))
```

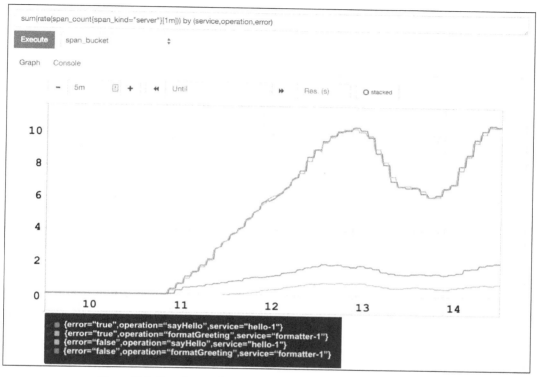

Figure 11.3: Four time series representing the successful (top two lines)
and failed (bottom two lines) request rates from the Hello application

Of course, many of us are already accustomed to seeing these kinds of dashboards. The difference here is that the microservices in the Hello application do not have any special instrumentation to emit these metrics, even though it is very possible that the underlying RPC frameworks (in our case, Spring Boot) do have the ability to generate similar metrics. Instead, the application is using tracing auto-instrumentation for Spring, which you have already seen in previous chapters:

```
<dependency>
    <groupId>io.opentracing.contrib</groupId>
    <artifactId>opentracing-spring-cloud-starter</artifactId>
</dependency>
```

The instrumentation provides us with the description of a transaction and various measurements. In order to convert that description into Prometheus metrics, we can use another library (imported in our `lib` module):

```
<dependency>
    <groupId>io.opentracing.contrib</groupId>
    <artifactId>opentracing-metrics-prometheus</artifactId>
    <version>0.2.0</version>
</dependency>
```

This library implements the OpenTracing API as a decorator around another `Tracer` implementation and uses the callbacks from the trace points to calculate span metrics. Our services first instantiate the normal Jaeger tracer, then wrap it in the metrics decorator, as can be seen in the `TracingConfig` class from the `lib` module:

```
@Bean
public io.opentracing.Tracer tracer(CollectorRegistry collector) {
    Configuration configuration = Configuration.fromEnv(app.name);
    Tracer jaegerTracer = configuration.getTracerBuilder()
            .withSampler(new ConstSampler(true))
            .withScopeManager(new MDCScopeManager())
            .build();

    PrometheusMetricsReporter reporter = PrometheusMetricsReporter
            .newMetricsReporter()
            .withCollectorRegistry(collector)
            .withConstLabel("service", app.name)
            .withBaggageLabel("callpath", "")
            .build();
    return io.opentracing.contrib.metrics.Metrics.decorate(
            jaegerTracer, reporter);
}
```

Note the additional metrics labels configured via `withConstLabel` and `withBaggageLabel`. The former adds the service name ("hello-1" or "formatter-1") to all metrics emitted by this decorator. We will discuss where the baggage label becomes useful in the following section.

You may ask, if we can get similar RED metrics for a service using traditional metrics libraries, why bother doing it via tracing instrumentation? One of the main benefits is the standardization of the metrics names that we can get from different services, potentially built on top of different application frameworks; for example, if we enable metrics directly from the Spring Boot framework, they are very likely to be named very differently from the metrics emitted from another application built on top of another framework, such as, Dropwizard.

However, metrics emitted by the decorator we used in this exercise are going to be the same across all frameworks. As a bonus, the service and operation names used as labels in the metrics will have an exact match to the service and operation names collected in the actual traces. By correlating the time series with traces in this way, we can enable bi-directional navigation between traces and time series in the monitoring UIs, and we can annotate spans in a given trace with accurate statistical measures, for example, automatically calculating which percentile of latency distribution a given span represents.

The decorator approach is not the only way to get metrics emitted by the tracing instrumentation. Although we did not discuss it in *Chapter 2, Take Tracing for a HotROD Ride*, the Jaeger tracer in Go has an optional module that can emit metrics using an observer pattern, rather than a decorator pattern. If we run the HotROD demo application with the `--metrics=prometheus` flag and execute a few car orders from the UI, we can pull the metrics generated for the HTTP request by the RPC metrics plugin:

```
$ curl -s http://localhost:8083/metrics | grep frontend_http_requests
# HELP hotrod_frontend_http_requests hotrod_frontend_http_requests
# TYPE hotrod_frontend_http_requests counter
hotrod_frontend_http_requests{endpoint="HTTP-GET-
/",status_code="2xx"} 1

hotrod_frontend_http_requests{endpoint="HTTP-GET-
/",status_code="3xx"} 0

hotrod_frontend_http_requests{endpoint="HTTP-GET-
/",status_code="4xx"} 1

hotrod_frontend_http_requests{endpoint="HTTP-GET-
/",status_code="5xx"} 0

hotrod_frontend_http_requests{endpoint="HTTP-GET-
/dispatch",status_code="2xx"} 3

hotrod_frontend_http_requests{endpoint="HTTP-GET-
/dispatch",status_code="3xx"} 0

hotrod_frontend_http_requests{endpoint="HTTP-GET-
/dispatch",status_code="4xx"} 0

hotrod_frontend_http_requests{endpoint="HTTP-GET-
/dispatch",status_code="5xx"} 0
```

You saw in *Chapter 7, Tracing with Service Mesh,* that using a service mesh is another way of getting standardized metrics out of our microservices, which has a similar benefit of the consistent labeling of metrics and traces. However, in situations where deploying a service mesh is not an option, emitting metrics from tracing instrumentation can be a viable alternative.

Adding context to metrics

Perhaps a much more useful integration between metrics and tracing instrumentation is providing context awareness to the metrics. If we let the clients run for a few minutes, we can get the following graph of the request rates:

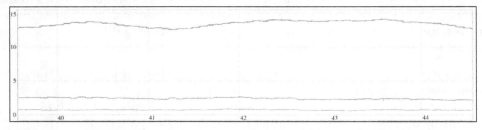

Figure 11.4: Four time series representing the successful (top two lines) and failed (bottom two lines) request rates from the Hello application. The y-axis is the count of spans in a certain group and the x-axis is the time (minute of the hour).

The top two lines represent the successful requests at each of the services:

```
span_count{error="false",operation="sayHello",service="hello-1"}
span_count{error="false",operation="formatGreeting",service="forma
tter-1"}
```

The bottom two lines represent errors (the rate of errors from the `hello` service is higher):

```
span_count{error="true",operation="sayHello",service="hello-1"}
span_count{error="true",operation="formatGreeting",service="formatt
er-1"}
```

From the chart in *Figure 11.4*, we know that a certain percentage of requests are failing, but we do not know why, and the metrics provide little context to understand the why. In particular, we know that our services are being accessed by two clients that have different configurations, so it is possible that the clients cause different behaviors in the application. It would be nice to see that in the chart. However, to do that we need to label our metrics with metadata that represents the client version, which is not known to the two microservices from the HTTP requests. This is where our old friend baggage comes into play. In the `lib` module, we have a helper service `CallPath`, with a single method, `append()`:

```
public void append() {
    io.opentracing.Span span = tracer.activeSpan();
    String currentPath = span.getBaggageItem("callpath");
    if (currentPath == null) {
        currentPath = app.name;
    } else {
        currentPath += "->" + app.name;
    }
    span.setBaggageItem("callpath", currentPath);
}
```

This method reads the baggage item called `callpath` and modifies it by appending the current service name. The controllers in both microservices call this method from their HTTP handlers, for example, in the `formatter` service:

```
@GetMapping("/formatGreeting")
public String formatGreeting(@RequestParam String name) {
    logger.info("Name: {}", name);

    callPath.append();
    ...

    String response = "Hello, " + name + "!";
    logger.info("Response: {}", response);
    return response;
}
```

The clients also call this method, which puts the client name, for example, `client-v1`, as the first segment of the call path. Note that we have to start the root span in the clients to have a place to store the baggage item, as otherwise the span will only be created by the `RestTemplate` when making the outbound call.

```
public void run(String... args) {
    while (true) {
        Span span = tracer.buildSpan("client").start();
        try (Scope scope = tracer.scopeManager().activate(span,
false))
        {
            callPath.append();
            ...
            runQuery(restTemplate);
        }
        span.finish();
        sleep();
    }
}
```

Finally, this `callpath` baggage item is being added to the metrics label by the decorator we discussed in the previous section because we configure the reporter with the `withBaggageLabel()` option:

```
PrometheusMetricsReporter reporter = PrometheusMetricsReporter
        .newMetricsReporter()
        .withCollectorRegistry(collector)
        .withConstLabel("service", app.name)
        .withBaggageLabel("callpath", "")
        .build();
```

To see this in action, all we need to do is to add the `callpath` to the group-by clause of the Prometheus query:

```
sum(rate(span_count{span_kind="server"}[1m]) > 0)
by (service,operation,callpath,error)
```

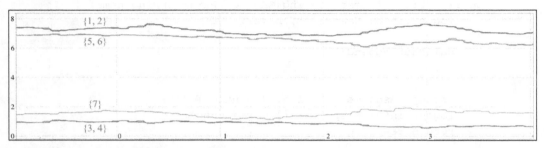

Figure 11.5: Additional time series shown when we add the "callpath" label to the group-by clause. The x-axis is the count of spans in a certain group and the y-axis is the time (minute of the hour).

Unfortunately, without the interactivity and mouse-over popups available in the real dashboard, it is hard to see what is going on here, so let's look at the raw data that is available in Prometheus in the **Console** tab, next to the **Graph** tab (formatted as a table for better readability, where the `service`, `operation`, `error`, and `callpath` labels are pulled into columns):

#	Callpath	Service (that emits metric)	Operation	Error	Value
1	client-v2->hello-1	hello-1	sayHello	false	7.045
2	client-v2->hello-1->formatter-1	formatter-1	formatGreeting	false	7.058
3	client-v2->hello-1	hello-1	sayHello	true	0.691
4	client-v2->hello-1->formatter-1	formatter-1	formatGreeting	true	0.673
5	client-v1->hello-1	hello-1	sayHello	false	6.299
6	client-v1->hello-1->formatter-1	formatter-1	formatGreeting	false	6.294
7	client-v1->hello-1	hello-1	sayHello	true	1.620

We can now see interesting patterns emerging. Let's focus only on rows **3**, **4**, and **7**, which represent failing requests according to the label `error=true`, and ignore successful requests in rows **1-2** and **5-6**. From the `callpath` label, we can see that the requests in rows **3** and **4** originate from `client-v2`, and in row **7** from `client-v1`.

Requests from `client-v1` never reach the `formatter` service and have a higher rate of failure (1.62 failures per second) than requests from `client-v2` (about 0.7 failures per second, rows **3-4**).

Requests from `client-v2` all appear to fail in the `formatter` service because the failure rates in rows **3-4** are almost the same. This fact may not be apparent, but we know from the architecture of the application that if the `formatter` service fails, then the `hello` service will fail as well. Therefore, if the `hello` service was failing independently of the `formatter` service, it would not have made the call down the chain and its failure rate would have been higher. In summary:

- Requests from `client-v1` fail almost twice as often as from `client-v2`
- Requests from `client-v1` fail in the `hello` service, while request from `client-v2` fail in the `formatter` service

Now that we have deduced that the error patterns are caused by the version of the client, let's confirm the hypothesis by looking at the code. The failures in the Hello application are simulated with the help of the `ChaosMankey` class in the `lib` module. During initialization, it reads two parameters from Java system properties:

```
public ChaosMonkey() {
  this.failureLocation = System.getProperty("failure.location", "");
  this.failureRate = Double.parseDouble(System.getProperty
    ("failure.rate", "0"));
}
```

The field `failureLocation` contains the name of the microservice where we want to simulate the failure. The field `failureRate` contains the desired probability of this failure occurring. Before making an HTTP request, the clients are calling the `maybeInjectFault()` method on `ChaosMonkey` that probabilistically stores the desired failure location in the `fail` baggage item:

```
public void maybeInjectFault() {
    if (Math.random() < this.failureRate) {
        io.opentracing.Span span = tracer.activeSpan();
        span.setBaggageItem("fail", this.failureLocation);
    }
}
```

The microservices `hello` and `dispatcher` make a call to another method of ChaosMonkey, `maybeFail()`, before responding to the incoming HTTP requests, for example:

```
@GetMapping("/formatGreeting")
public String formatGreeting(@RequestParam String name) {
    ...

    chaosMonkey.maybeFail();

    String response = "Hello, " + name + "!";
    logger.info("Response: {}", response);
    return response;
}
```

The `maybeFail()` method compares the current service name with the value of the `fail` baggage item, and if there's a match, throws an exception:

```
public void maybeFail() {
    io.opentracing.Span span = tracer.activeSpan();
    String fail = span.getBaggageItem("fail");
    if (app.name.equals(fail)) {
        logger.warn("simulating failure");
        throw new RuntimeException(
            "simulated failure in " + app.name);
    }
}
```

Finally, the `Makefile` defines the configuration of the two versions of the client that control the failure injection mechanism and explain the metrics pattern we observed in Prometheus:

```
CLIENT_V1 := $(CLIENT_SVC) \
    -Dclient.version=v1 \
    -Dfailure.location=hello-1 \
    -Dfailure.rate=0.2
CLIENT_V2 := $(CLIENT_SVC) \
    -Dclient.version=v2 \
    -Dfailure.location=formatter-1 \
    -Dfailure.rate=0.1
```

We see that `client-v1` is instructed to induce failures in the `hello` service for 20% of the requests, which explains why we never saw the error call path reaching to the `formatter` service. `client-v2` is instructed to induce failures in the `formatter` service for only 10% of the requests, which explains the difference in the error rates we observed.

Context-aware metrics APIs

The technique for adding context-based labels to the metrics works well when the metrics are emitted by the tracing instrumentation. However, applications can often generate many other custom metrics, such as the size of an internal cache, the current queue depth, and so on. Even RPC-related metrics may sometimes be difficult to emit via tracing instrumentation; for example, to measure the byte size of the request payload, the instrumentation needs access to the request object, which is outside of the scope of the OpenTracing API and therefore cannot be captured by the decorator tracer implementation we used in the previous sections.

In these situations, the instrumentation falls back onto traditional metrics APIs, for example, by directly calling the client library of the metrics system (for example, the Prometheus client) or by using an abstraction layer, such as Micrometer in Java (`https://micrometer.io`). Most traditional metrics APIs are created without the support for distributed context, making it harder to annotate the metrics with additional request-scoped metadata, like the `callpath` label in our earlier example.

In the languages where the request context is passed around through thread-local variables or similar mechanisms, it is still possible to enhance the traditional metrics APIs to extract the extra labels from the context without altering the API. In other languages, including Go, the metrics APIs need to be enhanced to accept the context as one of the arguments to the functions that take the measurements; for example, the popular microservices framework Go kit [6] defines the `Counter interface` like this:

```
type Counter interface {
    With(labelValues ...string) Counter
    Add(delta float64)
}
```

The `Add()` function gathers the actual measurements, but it does not accept the `Context` object. We can work around that by creating a helper that would extract the context-scoped label values from the context, for example:

```
type Helper struct {
    Labels []string
}

func (h Helper) Add(ctx context.Context, c Counter, delta float64)
{
    values := make([]string, len(h.Labels))
    for i, label := range h.Labels {
        values[i] = labelValueFromContext(ctx, label)
    }
    c.With(values).Add(delta)
}
```

This could be a viable approach, but it has the downside that the application developer must remember to invoke this helper instead of calling the `Add()` function with context directly on the `Counter` object. Fortunately, newer frameworks, such as OpenCensus, are being developed as fully context-aware, so that "forgetting" to use the right function is not an option:

```
// Record records one or multiple measurements with the same context
// at once. If there are any tags in the context, measurements will be
// tagged with them.
func Record(ctx context.Context, ms ...Measurement) {}
```

Integration with logs

Similar to metrics, logs often suffer from the lack of request-scoped context and their investigative power can be improved by capturing some of that context in the fields of structured log records.

Structured logging

Before we go further, let us briefly talk about structured logging. Traditionally, the logging frameworks generate the log lines as plain strings, an example of which you can see in the output of the Hello application clients:

```
25-11-2018 18:26:37.354 [main] ERROR client.Runner.runQuery - error
from server

25-11-2018 18:26:37.468 [main] INFO  client.Runner.runQuery -
executing http://localhost:8080/sayHello/Bender

25-11-2018 18:26:37.531 [main] ERROR client.Runner.runQuery - error
from server

25-11-2018 18:26:37.643 [main] INFO  client.Runner.runQuery -
executing http://localhost:8080/sayHello/Bender
```

While these strings do have a certain structure that can be parsed by the log aggregation pipeline, the actual messages are unstructured, making them more expensive to index in the log storage. For example, if we wanted to find all logs with a specific URL, we would need to express the question as a substring or regex query, as opposed to a much simpler `url="..."` query.

When we use structured logging, we express the same information as a proper structure, for example, using the JSON format:

```
{
    "@timestamp": "2018-11-25T22:26:37.468Z",
    "thread": "main",
    "level": "INFO",
    "logger": "client.Runner.runQuery",
    "message": "executing HTTP request",
    "url": "http://localhost:8080/sayHello/Bender"
}
```

When expressed this way, the logs can be indexed much more efficiently and provide various aggregation and visualization capabilities, such as those available in Kibana.

In this chapter's exercise, we will use the standard **SLF4J** API, which does not support the log messages as structured data. However, we do configure the structured formatter for the logs when we send them to Logstash. It can be found in `resources/logstash-spring.xml` files in every module, for example, in client:

```
<appender name="logstash"
   class="net.logstash.logback.appender.LogstashTcpSocketAppender">
      <destination>${logstash.host}:5000</destination>
      <encoder class="net.logstash.logback.encoder.LogstashEncoder">
         <customFields>
            {"application":"hello-app", "service":"client-1"}
         </customFields>
      </encoder>
</appender>
```

In addition to the fields defined in the configuration, attributes stored in the **Mapped Diagnostic Context** (**MDC**) are also automatically added as fields to the log messages.

Correlating logs with trace context

Before distributed tracing was becoming mainstream, developers often used custom methods of propagating some unique request ID and including it in the logs, in order to make the logs a bit more useful and allow filtering them down to a single request.

Once we have tracing instrumentation in place, we already have the context propagation problem solved, and the trace ID is just as good as correlation ID to bring together the logs for a given request. We can do even better and include the span ID, which allows us to associate the logs with specific spans in the trace, making them even more contextual and useful.

The Hello application in this chapter includes this form of integration. As you may recall from *Chapter 4, Instrumentation Basics with OpenTracing*, the OpenTracing API for Java defines the concept of scope managers that are responsible for keeping track of the currently active span.

The OpenTracing API library provides a default scope manager implementation that is usually used by the tracers, but since it was designed to be pluggable, it can be extended via the Decorator pattern (although not yet via the Observer pattern). The `lib` module includes one such extension, `MDCScopeManager`, implemented as a subclass of the standard `ThreadLocalScopeManager`. It overrides the `activate()` method and returns `ScopeWrapper`, a decorator that wraps the scope returned from the superclass. The constructor of the wrapper contains the main business logic:

```
ScopeWrapper(Scope scope) {
    this.scope = scope;
    this.previousTraceId = lookup("trace_id");
    this.previousSpanId = lookup("span_id");
    this.previousSampled = lookup("trace_sampled");4

    JaegerSpanContext ctx = (JaegerSpanContext)
scope.span().context();
    String traceId = Long.toHexString(ctx.getTraceId());
    String spanId = Long.toHexString(ctx.getSpanId());
    String sampled = String.valueOf(ctx.isSampled());

    replace("trace_id", traceId);
    replace("span_id", spanId);
    replace("trace_sampled", sampled);
}
```

As you can see, it casts the current span context to the Jaeger implementation and retrieves the trace ID, span ID, and the sampling flag, which are then stored in the MDC using the `replace()` method. The `lookup()` method is used to retrieve previous values of these attributes, which are restored once the scope is deactivated:

```
@Override
public void close() {
    this.scope.close();
    replace("trace_id", previousTraceId);
```

```
    replace("span_id", previousSpanId);
    replace("trace_sampled", previousSampled);
}

private static String lookup(String key) {
    return MDC.get(key);
}

private static void replace(String key, String value) {
    if (value == null) {
        MDC.remove(key);
    } else {
        MDC.put(key, value);
    }
}
}
```

When we instantiate the Jaeger tracer in the `TracingConfig`, we pass it the custom scope manager:

```
Configuration configuration = Configuration.fromEnv(app.name);
Tracer jaegerTracer = configuration.getTracerBuilder() //
        .withSampler(new ConstSampler(true)) //
        .withScopeManager(new MDCScopeManager()) //
        .build();
```

Let's see how all this integration works in Kibana. We have already seen the logs found in Kibana in the Prerequisites section. To the left of the log display, there is a vertical section listing all field names that Elasticsearch has discovered in the log stream produced by our services, including fields such as **application**, **service**, **trace_id**, and so on. When you mouse-over those fields, the **add** button appears, which allows you to add the fields to the **Selected Fields** section at the top of the sidebar. Let's select at least three fields: **service**, **level**, and **message**, in this order. We do not have to add the timestamp, as Kibana will automatically display it:

Figure 11.6: Selecting fields in Kibana to display the logs

Once the fields are selected, we will see a display of the logs that is much easier to read:

	Time ▾	service	level	message
▸	November 25th 2018, 20:05:52.052	hello-1	INFO	Response: Hello, Bender!
▸	November 25th 2018, 20:05:52.047	formatter-1	INFO	Name: Bender
▸	November 25th 2018, 20:05:52.037	hello-1	INFO	Name: Bender
▸	November 25th 2018, 20:05:52.021	hello-1	INFO	Response: Hello, Bender!
▸	November 25th 2018, 20:05:52.019	formatter-1	INFO	Response: Hello, Bender!
▸	November 25th 2018, 20:05:52.017	hello-1	INFO	Name: Bender
▸	November 25th 2018, 20:05:52.017	hello-1	INFO	Calling http://formatter-1:8082/formatGreeting?name=Bender
▸	November 25th 2018, 20:05:51.926	hello-1	INFO	Response: Hello, Bender!
▸	November 25th 2018, 20:05:51.923	formatter-1	INFO	Response: Hello, Bender!
▸	November 25th 2018, 20:05:51.915	hello-1	INFO	Calling http://formatter-1:8082/formatGreeting?name=Bender

Figure 11.7: Logs displayed by Kibana after selecting only a subset of the fields

As we could have expected, the logs are not very usable, since the logs from different concurrent requests are all mixed up. How would we use that to investigate a problem, such as the error rates that we were seeing with the metrics? If we scroll the results, we will see, at some point, the logs with the message "simulating failure". Let's focus on those by adding a filter in the query textbox at the top of the UI:

```
message:"simulating failure"
```

Hit the search button and we might get results like in *Figure 11.8*.

	Time	service	level	message
▸	November 25th 2018, 20:44:02.733	hello-1	WARN	simulating failure
▸	November 25th 2018, 20:44:02.231	hello-1	WARN	simulating failure
▸	November 25th 2018, 20:44:01.921	hello-1	WARN	simulating failure
▸	November 25th 2018, 20:44:01.271	hello-1	WARN	simulating failure
▸	November 25th 2018, 20:44:00.989	formatter-1	WARN	simulating failure
▸	November 25th 2018, 20:44:00.187	formatter-1	WARN	simulating failure
▸	November 25th 2018, 20:43:59.603	formatter-1	WARN	simulating failure
▸	November 25th 2018, 20:43:58.991	hello-1	WARN	simulating failure

Figure 11.8: Logs filtered to contain a specific message

Now expand one of the records using the triangle on the left (for example, from the `formatter` service). We can see, as an example, that the log message was added by the `lib.ChaosMonkey` class, as expected. Near the bottom of the list of fields, we find `trace_id`, `span_id`, and `trace_sampled` fields added by our `MDCScopeManager`:

t	application	hello-app
t	host	chapter-11_formatter-1_1.chapter-11_default
t	level	WARN
#	level_value	30,000
t	logger_name	lib.ChaosMonkey
t	message	simulating failure
#	port	48,534
t	service	formatter-1
?	span_id	b3413aade04979e4
t	thread_name	http-nio-8082-exec-8
?	trace_id	610d71be913ffe7f
?	trace_sampled	true

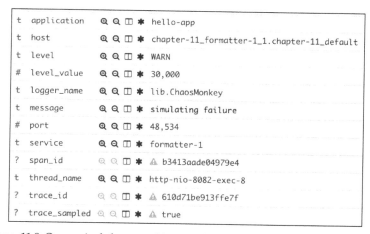

Figure 11.9: Once a single log record is expanded, it shows a list of fields and values

We can now search for all logs for that specific request by replacing the query for the message text with a search by trace ID:

```
trace_id:610d71be913ffe7f
```

Since we happened to pick the simulated failure in the `formatter` service, we already know from our previous investigation with metrics that this request came from `client-v2`. However, this is not reflected in the log fields because the clients share the same `logback-spring.xml` configuration file that is not parameterized for the client version (let's leave it as an exercise):

Time ⌄	service	level	message
▸ November 25th 2018, 20:44:01.041	client-1	ERROR	error from server
▸ November 25th 2018, 20:44:00.989	formatter-1	WARN	simulating failure
▸ November 25th 2018, 20:44:00.988	formatter-1	INFO	Name: Bender
▸ November 25th 2018, 20:44:00.975	hello-1	INFO	Calling http://formatter-1:8082/formatGreeting?name=Bender
▸ November 25th 2018, 20:44:00.972	hello-1	INFO	Name: Bender
▸ November 25th 2018, 20:44:00.953	client-1	INFO	executing http://localhost:8080/sayHello/Bender

Figure 11.10: A list of log records for a single request

This final search result represents the full execution of a request, starting at the client and ending with the client logging the error message "error from server." Granted, this is not particularly exciting in this simple application, but it would be much more useful when we deal with a real production system that involves dozens of microservices executing a single request.

Context-aware logging APIs

Similar to the metrics example, we were able to rely on the fact that both the tracing context and the MDC in log frameworks use thread-local variables to store the context. Even though we were able to sync up the MDC attributes with the current span, the same approach would not work if we wanted to log the `callpath` baggage value. This is because the custom scope manager we used only updates the MDC when the span is activated, while the `CallPath` class can update the baggage at any time. The design of the OpenTracing baggage API is partially to blame for that, as it allows mutable state of the context, rather than requiring a copy-on-write context.

In the languages where thread-locals are not available, we are back to the same overall problem of having access to the context when using the off-the-shelf logging APIs not designed with context propagation in mind. Ideally, we would like to see logging APIs in Go that require the context as the first argument to all the logging methods, so that implementations of that API could pull the necessary metadata out of the context into the log fields. This is currently an active area of design, with the OpenCensus project looking to introduce context-aware logging APIs.

Capturing logs in the tracing system

Since our `docker-compose.yml` file included Jaeger's `all-in-one`, we can use it to look up the request we previously found in Kibana, by entering the trace ID in the textbox at the top of the Jaeger UI (which is available at the usual address, `http://localhost:16686/`):

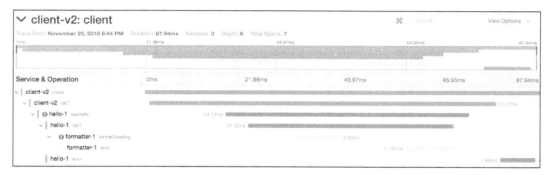

Figure 11.11: Trace of the request we previously found in Kibana

One extra benefit of OpenTracing–Spring Boot integration is that all log records generated by the application using the logging API are automatically attached to the currently active span (in the version of integration we used, it is only available for the Logback logging framework and can be turned on and off via the application properties). If we expand the root "client" span in the trace, we will see four logs; two generated by the Jaeger client when the baggage is updated in the span, and the bottom two appended by the OpenTracing–Spring Boot integration, in a similar structured format (*Figure 11.12*).

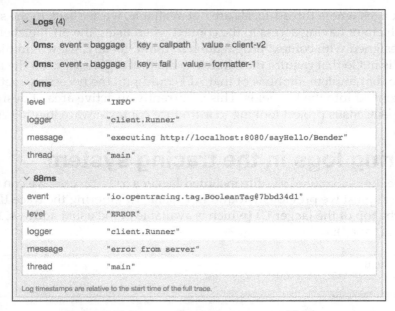

Figure 11.12: Four span logs in the root span of the trace

If you are interested, the code for this integration is in the `SpanLogsAppender` class found in the `io.opentracing.contrib.spring.cloud.log` package in the GitHub repository `https://github.com/opentracing-contrib/java-spring-cloud/`.

Having all the log statements displayed in the right place in the trace view can be extremely informative and a much better experience in troubleshooting than looking at the same logs in Kibana, even if filtered by the trace ID. It does not mean that all logs must always be sent to the tracing backend: as long as the log records capture the span ID, they can be lazily pulled from the logging backend by the tracing UI.

This brings us to the last topic of this chapter.

Do we need separate logging and tracing backends?

To summarize, correlating logs with trace context provides the following benefits:

- We can use the log storage to search for logs for a single request, via trace ID.
- We can use the rich infrastructure that already exists in many organizations for processing and aggregating logs to gain operational insights in aggregate, and then drill down to individual traces, since all logs are tagged with a trace ID.

- We can build integration between tracing UIs and the logging storage to pull the logs by trace and span ID into trace visualizations, and display them in the right contextual place in the trace.

- In some cases, as in the example of OpenTracing–Spring Boot integration, the log messages can be redirected to be stored as span logs in the tracing backend.

All these integrations beg a question: should the logging and tracing backends be separate in the first place? After all, traces are just a more specialized and structured form of log events. When we discussed Pivot Tracing in *Chapter 10, Distributed Context Propagation*, we saw the following query:

```
FROM bytesRead IN DataNodeMetrics.incrBytesRead
JOIN client IN FIRST(ClientProtocols) ON client ⇒ bytesRead
GROUP BY client.procName
SELECT client.procName, SUM(bytesRead.delta)
```

Nothing in this query is tied to tracing instrumentation; it is just an expression over the set of events and measurements generated from the application, with a causal join (⇒). It would be great if we could express these queries against events emitted by all kinds of instrumentation, for example, a bytesRead.delta measurement might come from a field in a structured log message (ignoring for the moment the causal propagation performed by Pivot Tracing).

Another example is the service from honeycomb.io that is built around the idea of collecting raw, rich, structured events, and providing querying, aggregation, and charting capabilities on top of that. As long as the events capture some causality (which can be automatically provided, as you have seen in this chapter), the data can be used to build both time series and traces. At some point of system scale, the events need to be sampled, so the Honeycomb offering does not completely remove the need for metrics if we want highly accurate measurements for monitoring, but as far as troubleshooting and debugging complex systems goes, it makes little distinction between logging and tracing events.

Of course, there are scenarios where tracing ideas seem not really applicable to some events, for example, for the application's bootstrap logs, which are not tied to any distributed transaction. However, even in that example, someone had to press the button somewhere to kick off the deployment, or another instance of this service died somewhere else causing this instance to start, so there is still a notion of some distributed orchestration workflow that could be modeled as a trace to understand its causality. In any case, if we treat all logs as equal events, some of which may or may not have the context-based causality links, then the only difference between them is in how we analyze those events.

These are not particularly prescriptive answers, but this is a topic that people are starting to seriously think and talk about, so we can hope for better answers to come out soon.

Summary

Metrics, logs, and traces are often called the "three pillars of observability", a term that does not do justice to each tool individually, or in combination, and makes many software organizations inclined to check all three boxes, sometimes by using three different vendors, without getting any better observability for their systems.

In this chapter, we discussed how metrics and logs lack the investigative and debugging power when applied to distributed systems because in their standard forms, they are not aware of the distributed request context and cannot provide a narrative for a single execution. I showed how combining these tools with context propagation and tracing enhances their ability to explain system behavior.

I used a simple Hello application to demonstrate these integrations in practice and we applied techniques that we first discussed in *Chapter 10, Distributed Context Propagation*, such as using the OpenTracing baggage (a form of context propagation) to pass around fault injection instructions, and using the cumulative call path string to partition our metrics.

The chapter touched upon the general lack of, and the need for, context-aware APIs for metrics and logging in the industry. While using context propagation provided by tracing is a workable solution, developing context-aware monitoring APIs would be much easier if there were general-purpose, tool-agnostic context propagation APIs, similar to the Tracing Plane we reviewed in *Chapter 10, Distributed Context Propagation*.

In the next chapter, we will return our attention exclusively to end-to-end tracing and discuss some data mining techniques that can be used to gain application insights from the large corpus of traces.

References

1. Charity Majors. There are no three pillars of observability. On Twitter: `https://twitter.com/mipsytipsy/status/1003862212685938688`.

2. Ben Sigelman. *Three Pillars, Zero Answers: We Need to Rethink Observability.* KubeCon + CloudNativeCon North America 2018: `https://bit.ly/2DDpWgt`.

3. Prometheus: Monitoring system and time series database: `https://prometheus.io/`.

4. M3: open source metrics platform built on M3DB, a distributed timeseries database: `https://m3db.io/`.

5. Tom Wilkie. *The RED Method: key metrics for microservices architecture*: `https://www.weave.works/blog/the-red-method-key-metrics-for-microservices-architecture/`.

6. Go kit: A toolkit for microservices: `https://gokit.io/`.

12

Gathering Insights with Data Mining

Let us finish Part III of the book with a discussion of perhaps the most exciting and promising area for future exploration for the practitioners of end-to-end tracing. Distributed tracing data provides a treasure trove of information about our distributed systems. I have already shown that even inspecting a single trace can be an exceptionally insightful exercise that often helps engineering teams understand performance issues and identify the root causes. However, even with low probability of sampling, software systems operating at internet-scale can record millions or even billions of traces per day. Even if every engineer in the company looks at a few traces each day, it is going to add up to a tiny fraction of all the data collected by the end-to-end tracing backend. It is a shame to let the rest of this data go to waste, when we can build data mining tools to process all of it; create useful aggregations; discover patterns, anomalies, and correlations; and extract insights that otherwise will not be apparent by looking at individual traces.

A very important reason to work with aggregations is to avoid being misled by one-off traces that could be outliers; for example, if we find a trace where the latency of some span is very high, is it worth investigating and debugging? What if its latency was 15 seconds, but the overall 99.9 percentile of latency for this service is still under a second? We could waste hours of engineering time chasing after a random outlier that may have no impact on the system **service level objectives (SLOs)**. Starting the investigation from the aggregates, like the latency histograms we discussed in *Chapter 9, Turning the Lights On,* and narrowing it to a few traces that are known representatives of a certain class, is a much better workflow.

We discussed some examples of aggregate data in *Chapter 9, Turning the Lights On,* such as deep dependency graphs, latency histograms, trace feature extractions, and so on. Bulk analysis of tracing data is a relatively new field, so we can expect many more examples to surface in blog posts and conference talks in the future. Very often, the process of finding a root cause of a pathological behavior in the system is an iterative process that involves defining a hypothesis, collecting data to prove or disprove it, and moving on to another hypothesis. In this process, the prefabricated aggregations can be useful as a starting point, but generally, the data analysis framework needs to be more flexible to allow the exploration of patterns and hypotheses that may be very unique to a given situation or a person doing the analysis.

In this chapter, rather than focusing on any specific aggregations or reports produced with data mining, we will discuss the principles of building a flexible data analysis platform itself. We will build a simple aggregation using the Apache Flink streaming framework that will cover several architectural aspects needed for any trace analysis system. We will also discuss some approaches that the other companies with mature tracing infrastructure have taken.

Feature extraction

The number of possible aggregations and data mining approaches is probably only limited by engineers' ingenuity. One very common and relatively easy-to-implement approach is "feature extraction." It refers to a process that takes a full trace and calculates one or more values, called **features**, that are otherwise not possible to compute from a single span. Feature extraction represents a significant reduction in the complexity of the data because instead of dealing with a large **directed acyclic graph (DAG)** of spans, we reduce it to a single sparse record per trace, with columns representing different features. Here are some examples of the trace features:

- Total latency of the trace
- Trace start time
- Number of spans
- Number of network calls

- Root service (entry point) and its endpoint name
- Type of client (Android app or iOS app)
- Breakdown of latency: CDN, backend, network, storage, and so on
- Various metadata: Country of origin of the client call, data center handling the request, and so on

Since features are computed per trace and in near real time, they can also be viewed as time series, and used to monitor trends, feed into alerts, and so on. Facebook's distributed tracing system Canopy [1] stores extracted features in an analytical database that allows even deeper exploratory analysis by filtering and aggregating the data across many feature dimensions.

Components of a data mining pipeline

There are probably many ways of building near real-time data mining for traces. In Canopy, the feature extraction functionality is built directly into the tracing backend, whereas in Jaeger, it can be done via post-processing add-ons, as we will do in this chapter's code exercise. Major components that are required are shown in *Figure 12.1*:

- **Tracing backend**, or tracing infrastructure in general, collects tracing data from the microservices of the distributed application
- **Trace completion trigger** makes a judgement call that all spans of the trace have been received and it is ready for processing
- **Feature extractor** performs the actual calculations on each trace
- An optional **Aggregator** combines features from individual traces into an even smaller dataset
- **Storage** records the results of the calculations or aggregations

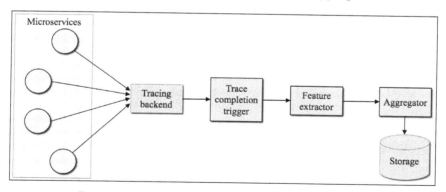

Figure 12.1: High-level architecture of a data mining pipeline

In the following sections, I will go into detail about the responsibilities of each component.

Tracing backend

The data pipeline needs the source of tracing data to process, and the tracing backend acts as that source. A distinct characteristic of the tracing backend in this scenario is that it receives tracing spans from many services in a distributed application asynchronously, often out of order, and sometimes not at all due to network failures. A backend like Jaeger simply puts all spans it receives into storage, one by one, and does not attempt to reason about which spans belong to which trace. It can only reassemble the full trace at query time.

Trace completion trigger

This random nature of spans collection presents a problem for data mining because it is difficult to know that all spans for a given trace have been received and stored by the tracing backend. Some spans may be coming all the way from mobile devices via public networks, and it is not unusual for the mobile devices to batch those spans and send the batches periodically, rather than immediately upon span completion. Trace completion trigger is responsible for observing all the spans received by the tracing backend and making a judgement call that a trace is ready for processing in the data mining pipeline. It is a judgement call, rather than a determination, because it is nearly impossible to guarantee that all spans have indeed arrived. Tracing systems employ various heuristics to help them make that decision.

Probably the most commonly used and the simplest approach is to wait for a predetermined time interval after receiving the first span for a previously unseen trace. As an example, we might have domain knowledge that most of the requests to our application are serviced within a few seconds. We can pick an interval that will fit nearly all requests, such as 30 seconds or one minute, and declare the trace complete after that time elapses. Despite its simplicity, this approach has a few obvious downsides:

- Networks, especially mobile networks, vary significantly in quality, so there may be a small population of end users who routinely experience latency well above the p99 percentile. If we choose the wait window that is too short, we will be incorrectly deciding that the traces for their requests are complete (false positives).

- If we select the time window that is too large, to reduce the false positives, then the latency of the data mining pipeline increases accordingly. As an example, if the pipeline is doing aggregations useful for root cause analysis of outages, and our time window is 10 minutes, then the on-call engineers would have to wait for 10 minutes after receiving an alert before they could use the data from the pipeline.

- It is very common for very large distributed systems to have workflows that operate on vastly different time scales. For example, while many RPC-based workflows are very quick (a few seconds in the worst case), some operational workflows, like deploying a new version of a service across many nodes, may take minutes or even hours. A single time window threshold is not suitable in these cases.

There are other heuristics that can improve the accuracy of the time-window-based trace completion trigger. Some of them need to be implemented in the tracing libraries that receive callbacks from the trace points. As an example, keeping track of how many children spans were created for a given parent span (inside the same process) allows for some basic sanity checks in the trigger whether all those children spans have been received. The trace completion trigger can use a larger time window for slower workflows, yet detect that a trace for a short workflow is complete based on these sanity checks of the DAG.

The trace completion trigger can also be given some statistics about previously observed behaviors of the system, collected through another round of data mining over historical data. The statistics can show approximate distribution of latencies for each endpoint of each service, which can help the trigger to build estimates of when each in-flight trace should complete. Perhaps the trace completion trigger can even be built using machine learning.

In summary, implementing a trace completion trigger is not a trivial task if we want to do anything beyond a simple time window wait. Almost any implementation is not going to be completely accurate and have the absolute minimum decision latency, so the aggregations performed in the later stages of the analysis pipeline need to be aware of that.

Feature extractor

The feature extractor receives a complete trace and runs the business logic to calculate useful features from it. The features can vary from simple numerical values, such as the total span count, to more complex structures. As an example, if we want to build a path-aware service graph that we discussed in *Chapter 9, Turning the Lights On*, then for each trace we may want to produce a collection of (path, count) pairs. The code exercise we will do in this chapter will be generating the former type of features: count of spans by services found in the trace graph.

The feature extractor is where most of the custom logic resides, and it should be extensible to allow adding more calculations. The common part across those individual extractors is the data model representing the trace as a DAG. Canopy authors described a specially designed higher-level trace model that is constructed from the raw tracing data and makes it easier to write aggregations and business logic.

The model ideally should also provide some API to allow writing graph queries against the trace DAG. In some cases, the users may only want to extract features from a subset of all traces passing through the system, so the graph queries can also be used as a filtering mechanism.

Depending on how the trace completion trigger is implemented, it is possible that the trigger may fire more than once if some stray spans arrive to the backend later than the first trigger fired. The feature extractor may need to deal with these situations.

Aggregator

The aggregator is an optional component. Since we reduce the rich span graph to a small set of features, it is often not expensive to store the computed set of features as a single record per each trace, especially if the underlying storage directly supports aggregate queries. The aggregator in this case is a no-op; it simply passes each record to the storage.

In other cases, storing each record may be too expensive or unnecessary. Consider the pair-wise service graphs we saw in the Jaeger UI. The underlying data structure for that graph is a collection of DependencyLink records records; for example, in Go:

```
type DependencyLink struct {
    Parent    string  // parent service name (caller)
    Child     string  // child service name (callee)
    CallCount uint64  // # of calls made via this link
}
```

Many of these link records can be generated for each trace. It is not important to keep each of them in the storage, since the final service graph is an aggregation of many traces over a period of time. This is typically the job of the aggregator component. For the service graph use case, it would group all DependencyLink records from many traces by the (parent, child) pairs and aggregate them by adding up the callCount values. The output is a collection of DependencyLink records where each (parent, child) pair occurs only once. The aggregator is called for a set of features extracted from a trace (after the trace completion trigger), accumulates the data in memory, and flushes it to permanent storage after a certain time window, for example, every 15 minutes or whichever interval is appropriate.

Feature extraction exercise

In this code example, we will build an Apache Flink job called SpanCountJob for basic feature extraction from traces. Apache Flink is a big data, real-time streaming framework that is well suited to processing traces as they are being collected by the tracing backend. Other streaming frameworks, like Apache Spark or Apache Storm, can be used in a similar way. All these frameworks work well with the messaging queue infrastructure; we will be using Apache Kafka for that.

Since version 1.8, the Jaeger backend supports Kafka as an intermediate transport for spans received by the collectors. The **jaeger-ingester** component reads the spans from a Kafka stream and writes them to the storage backend, in our case **Elasticsearch**. *Figure 12.2* shows the overall architecture of the exercise. By using this deployment mode of Jaeger, we are getting traces fed into **Elasticsearch** so that they can be viewed individually using the Jaeger UI, and they are also processed by **Apache Flink** for feature extraction. The feature records are stored in the same **Elasticsearch** and we can use the **Kibana UI** to look at them and to build graphs.

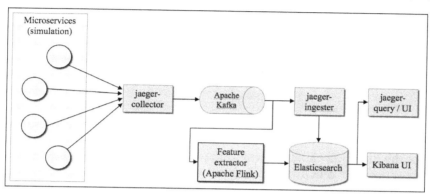

Figure 12.2: Architecture of the feature extraction example

We will need a steady source of tracing data. Any application that continuously produces traces will do, for example, the Hello application from *Chapter 11, Integration with Metrics and Logs,* with repeatedly running clients, or even HotROD from *Chapter 2, Take Tracing for a HotROD Ride,* with a `curl` command running in a loop. Instead, we will use a microservices simulator (`https://github.com/yurishkuro/microsim`) that can simulate sufficiently complex architectures that can be easily changed to produce a different shape of the traces.

The feature extraction job will count the number of spans per service in each trace it receives and write a trace summary record to Elasticsearch. *Figure 12.3* shows how one of these records might look in Kibana. It includes the `traceId` field, a timestamp, and a group of columns nested under `spanCounts` in the format `{serviceName}::{endpointName}: {number of spans}`.

Time	_source
▸ December 19th 2018, 19:23:54.832	traceId: 0000000000000000717D5C3696A64E6B @timestamp: December 19th 2018, 19:23:54.832 spanCounts.ui::HTTP GET: 1 spanCounts.redis::/GetDriver: 10 spanCounts.driver::/FindNearest: 1 spanCounts.route::/GetShortestRoute: 10 spanCounts.customer::HTTP GET: 1 spanCounts.redis::/FindDriverIDs: 1 spanCounts.frontend::HTTP GET: 12 spanCounts.driver::HTTP GET: 11

Figure 12.3: Trace summary record shown in Kibana

While this feature extractor is very simple, it serves as an illustration of the data mining pipeline and includes all of the components we discussed previously, except for the aggregator, which is not needed in this example.

Prerequisites

As you can see in *Figure 12.2*, there are quite a few components that we need to run in order to bring up the exercise architecture. Fortunately, most of the components can be run in Docker containers. The only two components that we will need to run directly are the microservices simulator (in Go) and the Apache Flink feature extraction job (Java).

This section provides instructions on setting up the environment and running the exercise.

Project source code

The code of the Flink job can be found in the Chapter12/ directory of the book's source code repository on GitHub. Please refer to *Chapter 4, Instrumentation Basics with OpenTracing*, for instructions on how to download it, then switch to the Chapter12 directory, from where all example code can be run.

The source code of the application is organized in the following structure:

```
Mastering-Distributed-Tracing/
   Chapter12/
     Makefile
     docker-compose.yml
     elasticsearch.yml
     es-create-mapping.json
     hotrod-original.json
     hotrod-reduced.json
     kibana.yml
     pom.xml
     src/
```

There is only one Java artifact built by this project, therefore all the source code is located in the top src/ directory. The docker-compose.yml file is used to spin up other components: Jaeger backend, Apache Kafka, Elasticsearch, and Kibana. elasticsearch.yml and kibana.yml are the configuration files for Elasticsearch and Kibana respectively. The hotrod*.json files are the profiles for the microservices simulator.

Running the servers in Docker

All the required components of the exercise except for the Apache Flink job can be run via `docker-compose`:

```
$ docker-compose up -d
Creating network "chapter-12_default" with the default driver
Creating chapter-12_elasticsearch_1      ... done
Creating chapter-12_jaeger-ingester_1    ... done
Creating chapter-12_zookeeper_1          ... done
Creating chapter-12_jaeger-collector_1   ... done
Creating chapter-12_kafka_1              ... done
Creating chapter-12_jaeger_1            ... done
Creating chapter-12_kibana_1            ... done
```

We pass the `-d` flag to run everything in the background. To check that everything was started correctly, use the `ps` command:

```
$ docker-compose ps
     Name                        Command               State
-----------------------------------------------------------------------
chapter-12_elasticsearch_1    /usr/local/bin/docker-entr ...   Up
chapter-12_jaeger-collector_1  /go/bin/collector-linux          Up
chapter-12_jaeger-ingester_1   /go/bin/ingester-linux           Up
chapter-12_jaeger_1           /go/bin/query-linux              Up
chapter-12_kafka_1           /etc/confluent/docker/run        Up
chapter-12_kibana_1          /bin/bash /usr/local/bin/k ...   Up
chapter-12_zookeeper_1        /etc/confluent/docker/run        Up
```

Sometimes, Elasticsearch and Kafka take a long time to complete their startup process, even though the `ps` command will report them as running. The easiest way to check is to `grep` the logs:

```
$ docker-compose logs | grep kibana_1 | tail -3
kibana_1        | {"type":"log","@timestamp":"2018-11-
25T19:10:37Z","tags":["warning","elasticsearch","admin"],"pid":1,"mes
sage":"Unable to revive connection: http://elasticsearch:9200/"}
kibana_1        | {"type":"log","@timestamp":"2018-11-
25T19:10:37Z","tags":["warning","elasticsearch","admin"],"pid":1,"mes
sage":"No living connections"}
```

```
kibana_1          | {"type":"log","@timestamp":"2018-11-
25T19:10:42Z","tags":["status","plugin:elasticsearch@6.2.3","info"],"
pid":1,"state":"green","message":"Status changed from red to green -
Ready","prevState":"red","prevMsg":"Unable to connect to
Elasticsearch at http://elasticsearch:9200."}
```

We can see that the top two logs indicate Elasticsearch not being ready, while the last log reports the status as green. We can also check the Kibana UI at `http://localhost:5601/`.

To check if Kafka is running, it is easier to search for `jaeger-collector`, which will keep restarting until it can connect to the Kafka broker:

```
$ docker-compose logs | grep collector_1 | tail -2
jaeger-collector_1  | {"level":"info","ts":1545266289.6151638,
"caller":"collector/main.go:151","msg":"Starting jaeger-collector
HTTP server","http-port":14268}

jaeger-collector_1  | {"level":"info","ts":1545266289.615701,"
caller":"healthcheck/handler.go:133","msg":"Health Check state
change","status":"ready"}
```

The health check status `ready` indicates that the collector is ready to write to Kafka.

Defining index mapping in Elasticsearch

Once we start running the feature extraction job, it will be writing data to the `trace-summaries` index in Elasticsearch. The records will contain a field called `@timestamp` holding the start time of the trace encoded as the number of milliseconds since Unix epoch. In order for Elasticsearch and Kibana to recognize this field as a timestamp, we need to define the index mapping first:

```
$ make es-create-mapping
curl \
        --header "Content-Type: application/json" \
        -X PUT \
        -d @es-create-mapping.json \
        http://127.0.0.1:9200/trace-summaries
{"acknowledged":true,"shards_acknowledged":true,"index":"trace-
summaries"}
```

Java development environment

Similar to the examples in *Chapter 4, Instrumentation Basics with OpenTracing,* we will need JDK 8 or higher. The Maven wrappers are checked in and will download Maven as needed. The included `Makefile` provides a helper target `run-span-count-job` that spins up a local instance of the Flink environment (mini-cluster) and runs the job:

```
$ make run-span-count-job

./mvnw package exec:java -Dexec.mainClass=tracefeatures.SpanCountJob

[INFO] Scanning for projects...

 [... skip a lot of Maven logs ...]

INFO - Starting Flink Mini Cluster

 [... skip a lot of Flink logs ...]

INFO - Kafka version : 2.0.1

INFO - Kafka commitId : fa14705e51bd2ce5

INFO - Cluster ID: S2HliBxUS9WLh-6DrYLnNg

INFO - [Consumer clientId=consumer-8, groupId=tracefeatures]
Resetting offset for partition jaeger-spans-0 to offset 0.

INFO - Created Elasticsearch RestHighLevelClient connected to
[http://127.0.0.1:9200]
```

The last two lines (your order may be different) indicate that the job has connected to the Kafka broker and to Elasticsearch. We can leave the job running from this point and create some traces to give it data to process.

Microservices simulator

Any application instrumented with Jaeger can be used to feed the data to the Flink job. To demonstrate how this job can be used to monitor trends, we want an application that can generate continuous load and can change the shape of the traces so that we can see the differences in the trace summaries. We will be using a microservices simulator `microsim`, version 0.2.0, from `https://github.com/yurishkuro/microsim/`. The source code for this chapter includes two JSON files describing the simulation profiles that model the HotROD demo application from Jaeger. Let's run the simulator to generate a single trace. We can run it either as a Docker image (recommended), or from source.

Running as a Docker image

The `Makefile` includes a number of targets that start with `microsim-`, for example:

```
$ make microsim-help
docker run yurishkuro/microsim:0.2.0 -h
Usage of /microsim:
  -O    if present, print the config with defaults and exit
  -c string
        name of the simulation config or path to a JSON config file
(default "hotrod")
 [ . . . ]
```

To run the actual simulation, let's use the `microsim-run-once` target:

```
$ make microsim-run-once
docker run -v /Users/.../Chapter12:/ch12:ro --net host \
    yurishkuro/microsim:0.2.0 \
    -c /ch12/hotrod-original.json \
    -w 1 -r 1
{"Services": [long JSON skipped]
 [ . . . ]
2018/12/19 20:31:16 services started
2018/12/19 20:31:19 started 1 test executors
2018/12/19 20:31:19 running 1 repeat(s)
2018/12/19 20:31:19 waiting for test executors to exit
```

In the `docker run` command, we are asking to run the program on the host network, so that it can locate the `jaeger-collector` via `localhost` name, which is the default setting in `microsim`. We also mount the chapter's source code directory to `/ch12` inside the container, so that we can access the simulation profile configuration files.

Running from source

The simulator is implemented in Go. It has been tested with Go version 1.11, and should work with later versions as well. Please refer to the documentation for Go installation instructions (`https://golang.org/doc/install`).

Download the source code:

```
$ mkdir -p $GOPATH/src/github.com/yurishkuro
$ cd $GOPATH/src/github.com/yurishkuro
$ git clone https://github.com/yurishkuro/microsim.git microsim
$ cd microsim
$ git checkout v0.2.0
```

The `microsim` project uses `dep` as the dependency manager that needs to be installed. Please see the instructions at `https://github.com/golang/dep#installation`. On macOS, it can be installed via `brew`:

```
$ brew install dep
$ brew upgrade dep
```

Once `dep` is installed, download the project dependencies:

```
$ dep ensure
```

Now you should be able to build the simulator:

```
$ go install .
```

This will build the `microsim` binary and install it in under `$GOPATH/bin`. If you have that directory added to your `$PATH`, you should be able to run the binary from anywhere:

```
$ microsim -h
Usage of microsim:
  -O   if present, print the config with defaults and exit
  -c string
       name of the simulation config or path to a JSON config file
[ . . . ]
```

Now try to run the simulator to generate a single trace:

```
$ microsim -c hotrod-original.json -w 1 -r 1
{"Services": [ . . . long JSON skipped . . . ]
 [ . . . ]
2018/12/19 20:31:16 services started
2018/12/19 20:31:19 started 1 test executors
2018/12/19 20:31:19 running 1 repeat(s)
2018/12/19 20:31:19 waiting for test executors to exit
 [ . . . ]
```

Verify

If we now look at the terminal where the Flink job is running, we should see that it generated a single trace summary, indicated by a log line like this:

```
3> tracefeatures.TraceSummary@639c06fa
```

Define an index pattern in Kibana

The last preparation step is to define an index pattern in Kibana to allow us to query for trace summaries and to plot trends:

```
$ make kibana-create-index-pattern
curl -XPOST 'http://localhost:5601/api/saved_objects/index-pattern' \
    -H 'Content-Type: application/json' \
    -H 'kbn-version: 6.2.3' \
    -d '{"attributes":{"title":"trace-summaries",
        "timeFieldName":"@timestamp"}}'
{"id":"...", "type":"index-pattern", "updated_at":"...", "version":1,
"attributes":{"title":"trace-
summaries","timeFieldName":"@timestamp"}}
```

You can also do it manually in the Kibana UI. Go to `http://localhost:5601/` and click on the **Discover** item in the side menu. It will ask to create an index pattern, and will show three indices found in Elasticsearch: two created by Jaeger when it stores the raw spans, and the `trace-summaries` index created by the Flink job (*Figure 12.4*):

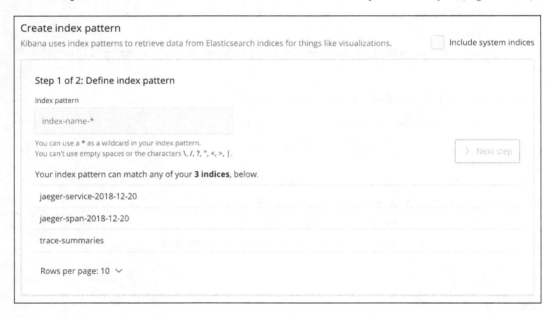

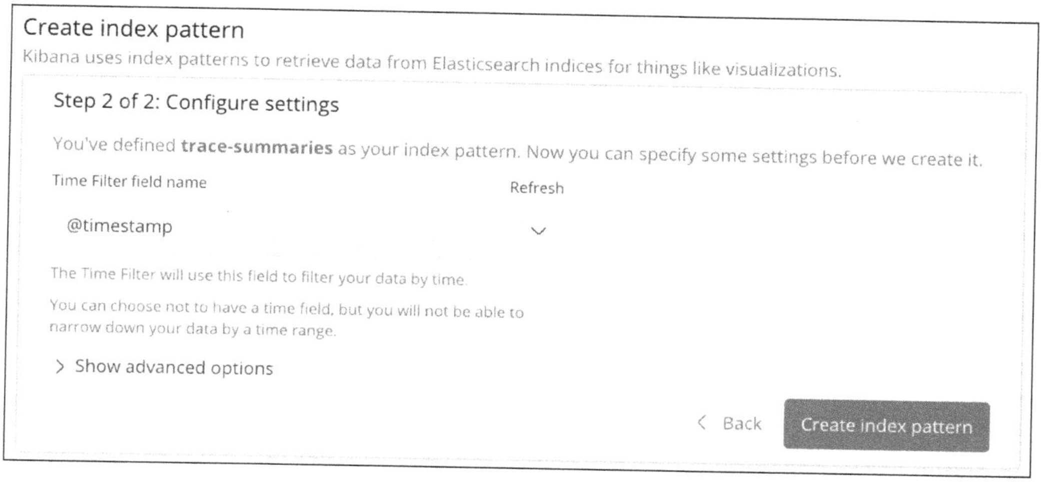

Create index pattern
Kibana uses index patterns to retrieve data from Elasticsearch indices for things like visualizations.

Step 2 of 2: Configure settings

You've defined **trace-summaries** as your index pattern. Now you can specify some settings before we create it.

Time Filter field name   Refresh

  @timestamp   ⌄

The Time Filter will use this field to filter your data by time.

You can choose not to have a time field, but you will not be able to
narrow down your data by a time range.

  〉 Show advanced options

                                                  ‹ Back   Create index pattern

Figure 12.4: Creating an index pattern in Kibana

Type `trace-summaries` into the **Index pattern** textbox and click **Next step**. On the next screen, open the dropdown menu for **Time Filter field name** and select the **@timestamp** field. Then click on the **Create index pattern** button. Kibana will create an index and display a table of all the fields it discovered in the single trace summary records we saved, including the span count fields, like `spanCounts.frontend::/dispatch` or `spanCounts.frontend::HTTP GET`.

Once the index pattern is created, you can look at the trace summary records on the **Discover** tab; you should see an entry similar to the one shown in *Figure 12.3*.

The Span Count job

Let's look at how the `SpanCountJob` is implemented. The Jaeger collector writes spans to Kafka in Protobuf format, so we need a way to parse them. The `package io.jaegertracing.api_v2` is auto-generated by the Protobuf compiler from the IDL file found in the Jaeger codebase (`model/proto/model.proto` in Jaeger v1.8). Protobuf-generated classes are not particularly convenient to work with in Flink, so in the `model` package we define a simplified model of the trace that only contains the span data that we need for the purpose of the span count calculations:

```
public class Span implements Serializable {
    public String traceId;
    public String spanId;
    public String serviceName;
    public String operationName;
    public long startTimeMicros;
    public Map<String, String> tags;
}
```

The class `model.ProtoUnmarshaler` is used to convert the spans from the Protobuf model to the simplified `Span` type. These `spans` are then aggregated into a `Trace` type:

```
public class Trace {
    public String traceId;
    public Collection<Span> spans;
}
```

As we discussed previously, this requires waiting for all spans of the given trace to arrive to the tracing backend from all the participating microservices. So, the first part of the job implements the trace completion trigger using a simple time window strategy of waiting for five seconds (in the local simulation we usually don't need to wait longer than that). Then the job performs feature extraction and generates a trace summary:

```
public class TraceSummary implements Serializable {
    public String traceId;
    public long startTimeMillis;
    public Map<String, Integer> spanCounts;
    public String testName;
}
```

The trace summary is converted to a JSON and stored in Elasticsearch by the `ESSink` class.

Let's look into the code of the `SpanCountJob` itself. It starts by defining the data source as a Kafka consumer:

```
Properties properties = new Properties();
properties.setProperty("bootstrap.servers", "localhost:9092");
properties.setProperty("group.id", "tracefeatures");

FlinkKafkaConsumer<Span> consumer = new FlinkKafkaConsumer<>(
        "jaeger-spans",
        new ProtoUnmarshaler(), properties);


// replay Kafka stream from beginning, useful for testing
consumer.setStartFromEarliest();
```

Here we are providing the address of the Kafka broker via properties to `FlinkKafkaConsumer`, a standard component of the Flink distribution. We tell it to read from the Kafka topic `jaeger-spans`, and pass `ProtoUnmarshaler`, which converts the data from Protobuf to the `model.Span` type. For testing purposes, we also instruct it to start consuming data from the beginning of the topic on every run. In a production setting, you will want to remove that instruction.

The main body of the job consists of these five statements:

```
DataStream<Span> spans = env.addSource(consumer).name("spans");
DataStream<Trace> traces = aggregateSpansToTraces(spans);
DataStream<TraceSummary> spanCounts = countSpansByService(traces);

spanCounts.print();
spanCounts.addSink(ESSink.build());
```

The function `aggregateSpansToTraces()` plays the role of the trace completion trigger, and `countSpansByService()` is the feature extraction logic. Let's look at them individually.

Trace completion trigger

```
private static Time traceSessionWindow = Time.seconds(5);

private static DataStream<Trace> aggregateSpansToTraces(
        DataStream<Span> spans
) {
    return spans
        .keyBy((KeySelector<Span, String>) span -> span.traceId)
        .window(
            ProcessingTimeSessionWindows
              .withGap(traceSessionWindow)
        )
        .apply(new WindowFunction<Span, Trace, String, TimeWindow>() {
            @Override
            public void apply(
                String traceId, TimeWindow window,
                Iterable<Span> spans, Collector<Trace> out
            ) throws Exception {
                List<Span> spanList = new ArrayList<>();
                spans.forEach(spanList::add);

                Trace trace = new Trace();
                trace.traceId = traceId;
                trace.spans = spanList;
                out.collect(trace);
            }
        });
}
```

It looks a bit busy, but in fact the main magic is in the first two stream operators. `keyBy()` tells Flink to group all incoming records by a designated key; in our case by trace ID. The output of this operator is a stream of span groups where every group has spans with the same trace ID. The `window()` operator forces the span accumulation in each group to continue for a certain period of time. Flink has different notions of time (**processing time**, **event time**, and **ingestion time**), each having different implications for the job's behavior.

Here we are using processing time, which means that all time-based functions, such as windowing operators, use the current system clock on the machine executing the respective operation as the timestamp of the record. The alternative is to use event time, defined as the time that each individual event occurred on its producing device. Since spans have a start and end time, there is already ambiguity of which timestamp can be used as the event time. More importantly, the machines and devices that produce the original spans can have various clock skews between them, especially among mobile devices. We generally do not want our stream processing to be dependent on those timestamps, so we're using the processing time.

We could have also used the ingestion time, which means each record is assigned a timestamp equal to the current system clock of the machine executing the source operator (that is, where records enter the Flink job). In our example, we are running a job with a single windowing operator on a single-node cluster, thus using the ingestion time would be equivalent to the processing time.

One operational downside of using the processing time for trace completion trigger is when the job experiences a lag, maybe if it was down for a couple of hours for whatever reason. When it starts again and resumes the processing of a Kafka topic, there will be a large volume of spans in Kafka that it needs to process. Those spans would have arrived to Kafka at a normal rate, but when the job is catching up, it might read them much faster, and as a result their processing time is going to be much closer to each other than during the normal operations. The job may need to keep a lot more data in memory because all record timestamps would congregate at the beginning of the time window, yet the job would have to wait for a full window interval while processing a much higher data volume from the backlog.

The second aspect of the windowing strategy we use is "session windows." Unlike the other type of windows supported in Flink, session windows are not fixed in length. Instead, they are sensitive to the activity, that is, the arrival of new items with the same key. The session window closes after it receives no new events during the specified time interval, in the selected notion of time. In our case, since we are using processing time, it would be five seconds after no new spans arrive for a given trace, according to the system clock. This approach alleviates some of the problems of the fixed size windows we discussed earlier in this chapter.

Once the window closes, the aggregation `WindowFunction` is invoked. In this function, we receive a stream of spans (with the same trace ID because of the earlier `keyBy` operator), and we convert them to a `Trace` object. Thus, the output of our trace completion trigger is a stream of `Trace` objects, ready to be processed and aggregated. If we wanted to deploy different types of feature extraction jobs, this first part would be common among them.

There is an implicit cost to this first stage of the job that may not be obvious due to the somewhat misleading simplicity of the code. The windowing operators do not perform any incremental aggregations; instead, they store all the `model.Span` objects in memory until the window closes. In a real production setting, Flink can partition the work across many processing nodes, so that the nodes do not run out of memory. To avoid data loss if a node fails, Flink supports checkpointing that allows it to save all intermediate in-memory states to persistent storage. This is where things may get expensive, especially if we design the data pipeline in such a way that every new feature extraction requires a separate Flink job: each of those jobs will be implementing the trace completion triggers with steep memory and checkpointing requirements.

An alternative approach could be to throw away most of the span data before doing the window aggregation, only keeping trace and span IDs. That would require a lot less memory and a much smaller data volume at checkpointing.

After the window closes, the trace ID (and optionally a set of span IDs) can be emitted from the single job to another Kafka topic, indicating that a given trace is complete and ready for processing. A multitude of other Flink jobs with the actual feature extraction logic can consume that secondary topic

Feature extractor

The second function, `countSpansByService()`, contains the actual feature extraction logic.

```
private static DataStream<TraceSummary> countSpansByService(
    DataStream<Trace> traces
) {
    return traces.map(SpanCountJob::traceToSummary);
}
```

The function itself is very simple, since it delegates to another function to convert a `Trace` to a `TraceSummary`:

```
private static TraceSummary traceToSummary(Trace trace) throws
Exception {
    Map<String, Integer> counts = new HashMap<>();
    long startTime = 0;
    String testName = null;
    for (Span span : trace.spans) {
```

```
                String opKey = span.serviceName + "::" +
        span.operationName;
                Integer count = counts.get(opKey);
                if (count == null) {
                    count = 1;
                } else {
                    count += 1;
                }
                counts.put(opKey, count);
                if (startTime == 0 || startTime > span.startTimeMicros) {
                    startTime = span.startTimeMicros;
                }
                String v = span.tags.get("test_name");
                if (v != null) {
                    testName = v;
                }
            }
        TraceSummary summary = new TraceSummary();
        summary.traceId = trace.traceId;
        summary.spanCounts = counts;
        summary.startTimeMillis = startTime / 1000; // to milliseconds
        summary.testName = testName;
        return summary;
    }
```

Here we see that feature extraction can be rather simple. Counting spans does not require building a DAG of spans; we only need to iterate through all spans and build a map of service or operation to counts. We also compute the smallest timestamp across all spans and designate it as the trace timestamp, which allows us to visualize the span counts by service as time series.

Observing trends

Now that we have our job running and we understand what it is doing, let's run some experiments. The two JSON files with profiles for the microservices simulator model the architecture of the HotROD demo application we covered in *Chapter 2, Take Tracing for a HotROD Ride*. The second profile file, hotrod-reduced.json, is nearly identical to hotrod-original.json, except that the simulator is instructed to make only five calls to the route service instead of the usual 10 calls. This difference would affect the SpanCountJob. To do the experiment, let the simulator run with the original profile for a few minutes:

```
$ make microsim-run-original
docker run -v /Users/.../Chapter12:/ch12:ro --net host \
    yurishkuro/microsim:0.2.0 \
    -c /ch12/hotrod-original.json \
    -w 1 -s 500ms -d 5m
```

```
[ . . . ]
2018/12/23 20:34:07 services started
2018/12/23 20:34:10 started 1 test executors
2018/12/23 20:34:10 running for 5m0s
```

If you built the `microsim` binary locally, you can run:

```
$ microsim -c hotrod-original.json -w 1 -s 500ms -d 5m
```

Here, we tell the simulator to run a single worker (`-w 1`) for five minutes (`-d 5m`) and to sleep for half a second (`-s 500ms`) after each request executed against the architecture. If you look at the terminal where the Flink job is running, you should be seeing the job printing lines about the trace summaries it generates:

```
3> tracefeatures.TraceSummary@4a606618

3> tracefeatures.TraceSummary@5e8133b

4> tracefeatures.TraceSummary@1fb010c3

1> tracefeatures.TraceSummary@147c488

3> tracefeatures.TraceSummary@41e0234e

2> tracefeatures.TraceSummary@5bfbadd2

3> tracefeatures.TraceSummary@4d7bb0a4
```

If we go to the **Discover** screen in Kibana, click on the time range in the top-right corner and select **Quick | Last 15 minutes**, we should see the examples of the trace summaries stored in the index (*Figure 12.5*).

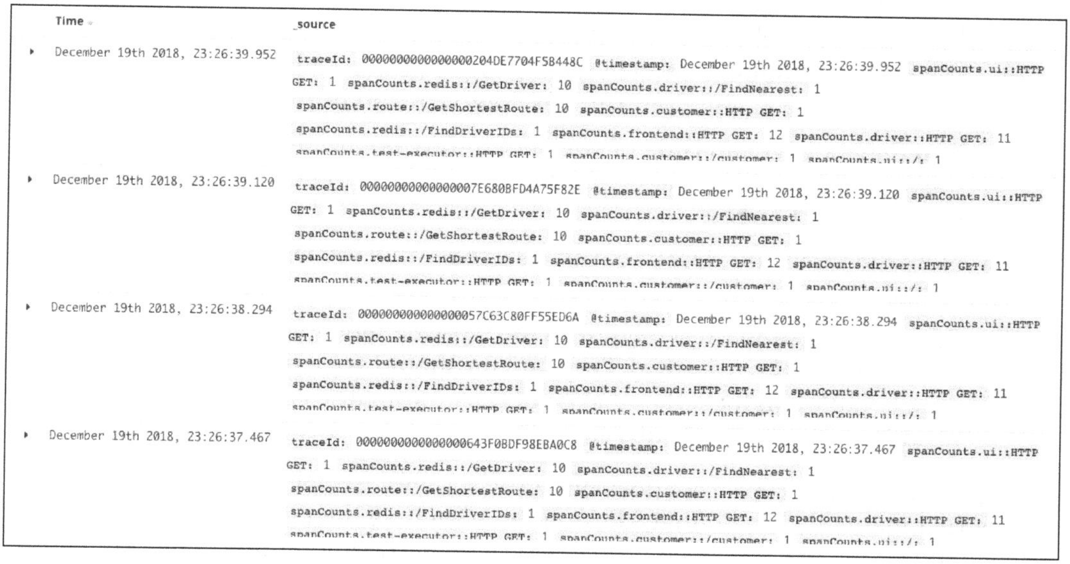

Figure 12.5: Trace summary samples in Kibana

After the first run of the simulator is finished, do a second run with the `reduced` profile:

```
$ make microsim-run-reduced
docker run -v /Users/.../chapter-12:/ch12:ro --net host \
        yurishkuro/microsim:0.2.0 \
        -c /ch12/hotrod-reduced.json \
        -w 1 -s 500ms -d 5m
[ . . . ]
2018/12/23 20:34:07 services started
2018/12/23 20:34:10 started 1 test executors
2018/12/23 20:34:10 running for 5m0s
```

Or using the locally built binary:

```
$ microsim -c hotrod-reduced.json -w 1 -s 500ms -d 5m
```

After this second run, we can plot the trend of changes in the average span count for the `route` service. To save some time, I have included a file called `kibana-dashboard.json` that contains a pre-made dashboard configuration. To import it into a blank Kibana, follow this process:

1. Make sure that you created the `trace-summaries` index pattern as described in *Prerequisites* by running `make kibana-create-index-pattern`.

2. Open a fresh copy of Kibana at `http://localhost:5601/`.

3. Go to **Management**, then **Saved Objects**. You should see three tabs: **Dashboards, Searches**, and **Visualizations**, all with zero count.

4. Click on the **Import** button in the top-right corner. Choose the `kibana-dashboard.json` file. Confirm: **Yes, overwrite all objects**.

5. You may now get an **Index Patterns Conflict** popup that offers to associate the objects being imported with the `trace-summaries` index pattern. Press **Confirm all changes**.

6. Now the three tabs, **Dashboards, Searches**, and **Visualizations**, should refresh and each should show the count of one.

7. Select the **Dashboard** screen from the left-side menu and pick the newly imported dashboard called **Trends**. You should see a dashboard with two panels: a plot on the left and a list of trace summaries on the right. You may need to adjust the time interval in the top-right corner to see the data.

If the preceding import process does not work for you, do not despair; it is easy to reconstruct manually. To do that, click on the **Visualize** item in the side bar menu. You should see an empty screen with **Create a visualization** button. Click on it and on the next screen, select the **Line** chart type from the **Basic Charts**.

Kibana will ask if you want to create a visualization from a new search or a saved search. Under the new search select the **trace-summaries** index. Kibana will open an empty chart view and a side panel on the left where you can specify parameters. Make sure you are on the **Data** tab in that panel, and in the **Metrics/Y-Axis** section specify:

- **Aggregation**: Average
- **Field**: spanCounts.route::/GetShortestRoute

Then in the next section, **Buckets**, select **X-Axis** from the table as the bucket type, and for **Aggregation** select **Date Histogram**. **Field** and **Interval** should automatically populate with **@timestamp** and **Auto** (*Figure 12.6*). Hit the run button (blue square with white triangle at the top of the sidebar) and you should see a plot similar to the one shown in *Figure 12.7*. If you do not see any data points, make sure your time range selector in the top-right corner corresponds to the time when you ran the simulations.

Figure 12.6: Specifying line chart parameters in Kibana

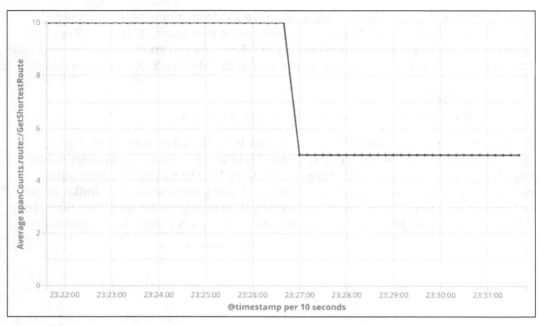

Figure 12.7: Plot of a trend of average span count per trace for service "route", endpoint "/GetShourtestRoute"

Of course, the chart itself is not especially exciting and very much expected: we changed the simulation profile to call the route service five times per trace instead of 10 times, and that is exactly what we see in the chart. However, if we use this technique in production, it can provide powerful regression detection capabilities. I picked a very simple-to-implement feature for this exercise; there are many more interesting features that can be extracted from traces.

If we continuously capture those features as time series, we can run anomaly detection algorithms on them and create alerts that can pinpoint non-trivial problems in a distributed architecture. More importantly, trace summaries can be enriched with various *metadata* and even *attributes* from the traces, such as customer accounts, user names, and so on. As an example, the microsim program records the name of the test configuration as a tag on the root span, for example test_name = "/ch12/ hotrod-original.json" (*Figure 12.8*):

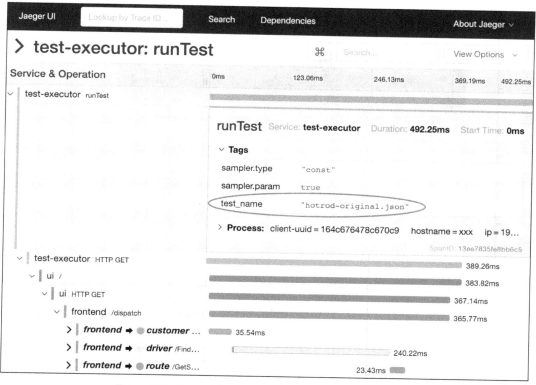

Figure 12.8: Name of the test included as a tag on the root span

The feature extractor, part of the `SpanCountJob` class, already extracts this tag into a `testName` field of `TraceSummary`.

Let's do another experiment: run `microsim` with both configurations simultaneously. For example, execute these `make` commands (or the binaries directly) in separate terminal windows:

```
$ make microsim-run-original
$ make microsim-run-reduced
```

After the simulations finish, refresh the chart we used previously (you may have to adjust the time frame). The average span count is now oscillating around the value of 7.5, which is an average of 10 and 5 from the two streams of traces processed at roughly similar rates, with some randomness introduced by imperfect alignment with the time buckets (*Figure 12.9*).

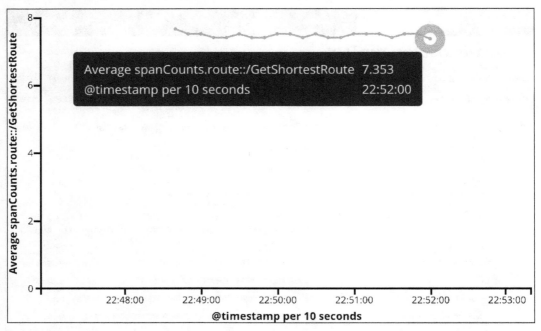

Figure 12.9: Average count of GetShortestRoute spans per trace when running both simulations in parallel

Since we expect the normal average value to be 10, this time series indicates some issue in the system. However, it does not point to the root cause, that is, that there is another simulation running with a different shape of the call graph. Fortunately, because our trace summaries include the testName feature, we can use it to group the trace summaries and visualize them as two different time series, one per simulation.

To do that in Kibana, navigate to the **Visualize** page from the left-sidebar menu. If you loaded the dashboard from the provided JSON file, select the **GetShortestRoute** chart from the list. If you created it manually, you should already have the edit options for the graph on the screen. Under **Buckets/X-Axis**:

- Click **Add sub-buckets**
- Select **Split Series** as the bucket type
- For **Sub Aggregation**, select **Term** at the end of the dropdown list
- For **Field**, select **testName**

Apply the changes by clicking on the blue square with the white triangle. Kibana should show two perfectly horizontal lines at levels 10 and 5, for the original and reduced simulation configurations respectively (*Figure 12.10*). The root cause for the drop of the average GetShortestRoute span count is now obvious.

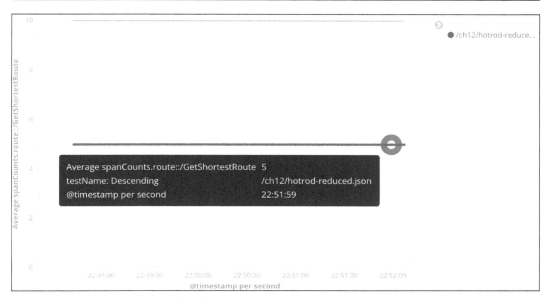

Figure 12.10: Average count of GetShortestRoute spans per trace partitioned by the testName attribute

This last example is very similar to the capabilities touted by many companies in the monitoring space, which allow for partitioning of monitoring time series by multiple dimensions, from various metadata sources. Here we do the same, but with the time series built from trace features, some of which (the `testName` attribute) are used as group-by dimensions. Thus, by storing the trace summaries in the raw form in a storage capable of answering analytical queries, we open up many exploration possibilities for hypotheses formulated by engineers.

Another benefit of feature extraction that we implemented here is that it is easy to navigate from the anomalies that show up in the trends to sample traces. We can select the time range around the anomaly in the first exercise (*Figure 12.7*), that is, when we started getting five calls to the route service instead of 10, by dragging the mouse horizontally on the chart (a technique known as **brush select**).

If you use the dashboard, the representative trace summaries will show in the right panel, otherwise switch to the **Discover** tab to find them. Copy one of the trace IDs and use it to find the trace in the Jaeger UI, for example, `http://localhost:16686/` `trace/942cfb8e139a847` (you will need to remove the leading zeroes from the `traceId` included in the trace summary).

As you can see in *Figure 12.11*, the trace only has five calls from the `frontend` service to the `route` service, instead of the usual 10. If we had a more integrated UI, instead of off-the-shelf Kibana, we could make this navigation from the chart to the trace view completely seamless. With Elasticsearch as the backing store, the query used to generate the chart is an aggregation query that computes an average per time bucket, and I am not sure if there is a way to instruct Elasticsearch to return sample document IDs (in our case, trace IDs) as exemplars for the aggregation buckets.

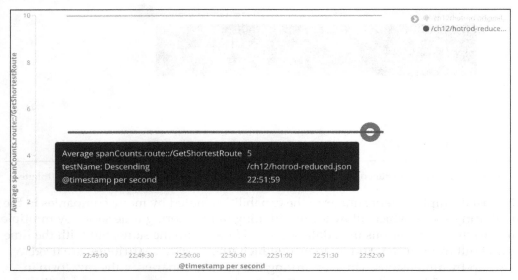

Figure 12.11: Sample trace in Jaeger UI showing an anomalous number of calls (five) to the "route" service

Beware of extrapolations

There is one potential problem with making conclusions based on the preceding techniques we discussed. It is very common for high-scale systems to use distributed tracing with low probability of sampling. The Dapper paper mentioned that Google sampled traces with probability of 0.1%, and from recent conversations with Google developers, it may be sampling even less: 0.01% of traces.

When we build feature extraction and aggregations, we make statements about certain statistical properties of a full distribution of requests in the production system, but we base them on a very small percentage of those transactions. It is a well-known rule in statistics that the smaller the sample size, the larger the margin of error.

How do we know that the data we derive via data mining is not complete garbage, statistically speaking? Unfortunately, there is no simple formula here because the statistical significance of the results depends not only on the sample size, but also on the question we are trying to answer with the data, that is, the hypothesis. We may not need highly accurate data to investigate the hypothesis, but we should know the margin of error and decide if it is acceptable. My recommendation is to seek help from your data scientists for the specific use cases.

Fortunately, most companies do not operate at the scale of Google or Facebook and might afford a much higher rate of trace sampling. They may also tolerate the performance overhead of the tail-based sampling approach that we discussed in *Chapter 8, All About Sampling*. Tail-based sampling opens up new possibilities for data mining because it needs to keep full traces in the memory of the collectors before sampling them. It is possible to build an infrastructure into those collectors to run feature extractors in line with the collection, on the full population of requests, guaranteeing very accurate results.

Historical analysis

So far, we have only talked about real-time analysis of tracing data. Occasionally, it may be useful to run the same analysis over historical trace data, assuming it is within your data store's retention periods. As an example, if we come up with a new type of aggregation, the streaming job we discussed earlier will only start generating it for new data, so we would have no basis for comparison.

Fortunately, the big data frameworks are very flexible and provide a lot of ways to source the data for analysis, including reading it from databases, or HDFS, or other types of warm and cold storage. In particular, Flink's documentation says it is fully compatible with Hadoop MapReduce APIs and can use Hadoop input formats as a data source. So, we can potentially use the same job we implemented here and just give it a different data source in order to process historical datasets .

While these integrations are possible, as of the time of writing, there are not very many open source implementations of trace analysis algorithms. The Jaeger team at Uber is actively working on building such tools, as well as teams from other open source projects, like Expedia's Haystack.

Ad hoc analysis

In October 2018, the members of the tracing team from Facebook gave a presentation at the Distributed Tracing – NYC meetup [2], where they talked about a new direction that they are taking with their tracing system, Canopy. While not based on open source technologies like Apache Flink, the feature extraction framework in Canopy was conceptually similar to the approach we presented in this chapter.

The API for building new feature extractions was open to all Facebook engineers, but it often had a steep learning curve and required fairly deep familiarity with the overall tracing infrastructure and its data models. More importantly, new feature extractors had to be deployed in production as part of Canopy itself, which meant the Canopy team still had to be deeply involved in reviewing the code and deploying the new analysis algorithms. Finally, feature extraction was primarily designed to work on live data, not on historical data. All of this was creating enough procedural friction to make feature extraction and data mining not very accessible or attractive to rank-and-file engineers at Facebook as a platform for performance investigations.

The team realized that they needed to democratize the tooling and remove themselves from the critical path of developing new data analysis algorithms. They observed that there are three classes of data analysis:

- **Experimentation with small data sets**: When someone has an idea for a new feature, it is not easy to get the exact calculation or algorithm right on the first try. Running iterative experiments on large data sets is also time consuming. Ideally, the engineers should have a playground where they can try out various algorithms on small production data sets, to prove that they are getting some useful signal from a new feature.

- **Experimentation with historical data sets**: Once an engineer is happy with the small-scale experiments, they may want to run them on a larger historical population of traces to verify that the new algorithm or feature still gives a strong and useful signal, that is, it was not just an anomaly of a small sample. Ideally, the historical experiment can be run with the same code developed in the first step.

- **Permanent deployment as a streaming job**: If after running the experiment on a large historical dataset the engineers still observe that they are getting a useful signal from the new feature extraction, they may want to deploy it in production to run continuously as a real-time streaming job, to calculate the feature for all future traces, start observing trends, defining alerts, and so on. Once again, ideally, they should be able to do it using the same code as for the first two steps.

The Facebook team decided that supporting Python and Jupyter Notebooks was the best way to gain wider adoption among engineers and data scientists. The previous version of Canopy used a custom **domain-specific language** (**DSL**) for describing the feature extraction rules. For example, this was a program to calculate how long rendering of the page in the browser took:

```
BrowserThread = ExecUnits() | Filter(name='client')
Begin = BrowserThread() | Points() | First()
End = BrowserThread() | Points() | Filter(marker='display_done')
How_long = End | Timestamp() | Subtract(Begin) | Timestamp()
   | Record('duration)
```

 Note: A trace in Canopy's event-based data model consists of "execution units" that contain "points."

The DSL was difficult to learn, and the resulting code was difficult to maintain by the engineering teams, often requiring the involvement of the tracing team. In contrast, Python is a well-known language, and it is very popular among data scientists. Feature extraction code expressed in Python is much easier to understand and maintain. The speakers did not show the Python function equivalent to the preceding program; however, it might look like this:

```
def browser_time_to_display(trace):
    browser_thread = trace.execution_units[attr.name == 'client']
    begin = browser_thread.points[0]
    end = browser_thread.points[attr.marker == 'display_done']
    return end.timestamp - begin.timestamp
```

Here is an example of a program the Facebook team did provide, which counts the number of expensive (over 10 seconds) database calls in a trace:

```
def count_expensive_db_calls(trace):
    count = 0
    for execution_unit in trace.execution_units:
        if execution_unit.db_duration_ms > 10000:
            count += 1
    return count
```

An engineer can use this program to investigate a single trace or a small set of traces, for example, by running it in a Jupyter Notebook. Then the same program can be run in a batch mode against a large volume of historical data, to validate the hypothesis about a performance issue. Facebook has an internal infrastructure similar to AWS Lambda or serverless compute that makes running a Python program against large data sets very easy.

Finally, if the engineer decides that this particular feature is worthy of continuous monitoring and alerting, the same code can be deployed as a streaming job.

The Facebook tracing team said that they learned some important lessons by developing this data analysis platform:

- Engineers at Facebook have really interesting ideas and tools that they want to apply to the tracing data.

- However, traces themselves can be hard to understand and manipulate, especially as more and more of the architecture is instrumented and the traces become really large, including tens of thousands of data points.

- Traces cover a very wide variety of workflows and heterogenous applications, from mobile apps and browsers, to storage and messaging backends. Building a single "do-it-all" tool is often impossible, or at least not productive. Such a tool might be so complex that it would take a power user to be able to understand it.

- By allowing simple programmatic access to the traces, including through such convenient exploratory and visualization frameworks as Jupyter Notebook, the infrastructure team removes itself from the critical path of data analysis and enables the rest of the engineers to use their domain knowledge and ingenuity to build very specific data analysis tools that solve the right problems.

Summary

Even though distributed tracing is still a bit of a novelty in the software engineering industry, the open source world is making great strides in making free tracing infrastructure available to anyone, from data gathering via projects like OpenTracing, OpenCensus, and W3C Trace Context, to storing and processing the data via many open source tracing backends like Jaeger, Zipkin, SkyWalking, and Haystack. As the tracing infrastructures become commodities, data mining and data analysis are going to be the areas of the main focus of research and development.

In this chapter, we covered some basic techniques for building data analysis tools on top of the tracing data, including looking at some of the challenges, such as trace completion triggers, which do not yet have perfect solutions.

We ran through an exercise of building a feature extraction framework and a sample span count job that can be used as a foundation for a full-featured platform.

Finally, we reviewed a very promising approach from the Facebook tracing team of enabling "write once, run thrice" ad hoc analysis and giving the rest of the engineers a platform to build domain-specific tools for trace data exploration.

In the next chapter, we will focus on solving some organization challenges of deploying tracing infrastructure in large organizations that operate complex distributed systems.

References

1. Jonathan Kaldor, Jonathan Mace, Michał Bejda, Edison Gao, Wiktor Kuropatwa, Joe O'Neill, Kian Win Ong, Bill Schaller, Pingjia Shan, Brendan Viscomi, Vinod Venkataraman, Kaushik Veeraraghavan, Yee Jiun Song. *Canopy: An End-to-End Performance Tracing and Analysis System*, Symposium on Operating Systems Principles, October 2017.

2. Edison Gao and Michael Bevilacqua-Linn. *Tracing and Trace Processing at Facebook*, Presented at Distributed Tracing NYC meetup, October 23, 2018: `https://www.meetup.com/Distributed-Tracing-NYC/events/255445325/`.

VI
DEPLOYING AND OPERATING TRACING INFRASTRUCTURE

13

Implementing Tracing in Large Organizations

"These and other clichés will be available to you all for one more day of training with me."

— *Col. O'Neill, Stargate SG-1*

We have arrived at the last part of this book. Hopefully, by now you are convinced that end-to-end tracing is an invaluable and must-have tool in your arsenal for monitoring and managing the performance of complex distributed systems. *Parts II and III* of this book are primarily addressed to the users of distributed tracing, covering topics from how to instrument applications, to how to use tracing data to gain insights into system behavior and perform root cause analysis.

In a large organization, someone needs to be in charge of actually deploying and maintaining tracing infrastructure, so that the users can reap the benefits. Often, this is the job of a dedicated tracing team, or a larger observability team, or an even larger (in scope, not necessarily in size) infrastructure team. No matter how it is named or structured, this team is responsible for operating the tracing infrastructure, which we will discuss in the next chapter, and for making sure that infrastructure gathers comprehensive and accurate data from the business applications.

Even though we discussed many technical aspects of data gathering in *Part II*, there are many non-technical organizational challenges that need to be solved, especially in large engineering organizations. In this chapter, we will discuss these challenges and some approaches to addressing them. Just like in business, there is no one-size-fits-all technique that guarantees success, and each organization may be sufficiently unique to require improvisation and custom solutions. The recommendations in this chapter are based on the lessons learned from my discussions with colleagues from other companies, as well as my own experience with rolling out distributed tracing at Uber. Treat them as good practices and recipes, rather than a manual.

Why is it hard to deploy tracing instrumentation?

Before we talk about solving the organizational challenges of deploying tracing, let's talk about what those challenges are. What is so different about end-to-end tracing? It seems all we need to do is add some instrumentation, just like we do for gathering metrics or logs. We spent several chapters in *Part II* on the technical aspects of adding instrumentation, including solutions to make it easier through auto-instrumentation, so what have we missed?

Consider a small tech company that has about a dozen software engineers. If this company embraces the idea of microservices-based architecture, it can build a system that contains from 10 to 20 microservices. Most engineers would know what each service does, if not necessarily the details of how they all interact. If they decide to add distributed tracing instrumentation to the system, it is generally not a large task, and it can be accomplished by one or two people in a short period of time.

Contrast this with a large organization that has hundreds or even thousands of engineers. Melvin Conway observed in his 1967 paper [1] that "*organizations which design systems...are constrained to produce designs which are copies of the communication structures of these organizations*"(an adage also known as **Conway's law**). Following this reasoning, the design of a system based on microservices would naturally mirror the hierarchical structure of the organization, where each team develops and operates a small number of microservices and has little knowledge of how the microservices in the other parts of the organization are implemented.

Unless the system has been built from the start on top of a strongly unified application development infrastructure, for example, a single application and dependency injection framework, or a single RPC framework, then deploying tracing instrumentation across the whole system inevitably requires massive amounts of domain knowledge around the design of each group of microservices developed by individual teams. It is intractable for a small, centralized tracing team to research all the different ways the microservices are built by different teams, least of all to go and add tracing instrumentation to them. If just a couple of motivated people can do this work in a small company, in a large organization this work must be decentralized.

This brings us to the main challenge that is unique to distributed tracing instrumentation compared to the other monitoring techniques: the *motivation* or the *lack of incentives*. If the organization follows the DevOps principles, then engineers who develop the applications are also on-call for those systems in production. When you are on call, you are very much interested in getting good observability for your application, at minimum for monitoring its health. Therefore, you have an incentive to add instrumentation such as metrics to your own application or microservice. However, observability via distributed tracing is inherently a global property of the whole system. It requires the participation of numerous microservices, and, according to Conway's law, numerous organizational units or teams. If one team decides to add tracing instrumentation to all their services, it does not significantly move the needle on increasing the overall system's observability through tracing, unless other teams also do that.

This psychological problem is one of the biggest road blocks for wide-scale adoption of distributed tracing. If some of the technical challenges can be solved through purely technical solutions, then this problem requires social engineering and cultural changes in the organization. In the remaining sections, we will discuss both types of solutions.

Reduce the barrier to adoption

Given the incentives mismatch problem we just discussed, one of the best ways of getting tracing instrumentation into all applications is to ensure that it requires no work whatsoever by the adopting teams, that is, it comes for free, by default. Of course, this is easier said than done. There may be situations when tracing cannot be added without requiring some code changes in the application. For example when I joined Uber, the engineering organization had just started adopting Go as the programming language for the backend services. The practice of threading the `context.Context` object through the code was not widespread, and the type itself was not even a part of the Go standard library (it was defined in `golang.org/x/net/context` and only moved to the standard `context` package in Go version 1.7). As a result, the context propagation was non-existent in many applications, making distributed tracing impossible without code changes.

A similar situation existed in many Node.js applications where context propagation had to be implemented by passing an application-specific object through the code.

These problems may still exist today, but they have become less pronounced, as many Go applications today are written in the recommended style with context propagation, and Node.js runtime supports features like continuation-local storage, which allows for implicit context propagation.

In the following sections, we will review some of the other techniques that reduce the barrier to adoption for distributed tracing.

Standard frameworks

Feature velocity is one of the most valuable properties of software development to the business supported by that software. Sometimes, the desire to increase feature velocity leads to situations where engineers are encouraged to use whichever tools get them to production the fastest:

- You just came from a Ruby on Rails shop? Go implement the next service in Ruby.
- Spent the last five years working with Node.js? Build the next backend service in Node.js.
- Familiar with the Spring framework in Java? Go for it. What, not Spring, but Dropwizard? Go for it.

This approach can lead to a highly fractured ecosystem of the software run by the company. Even for a small team of a dozen engineers, it seems unsustainable, as everyone needs to be familiar with every other technology or framework to make code changes in different services. Yet the situation is not uncommon, if not to such an extreme degree as shown.

At some point during the organization's growth, the velocity starts to slow down due to the overhead of context switching. The system becomes less reliable as the infrastructure teams are not able to provide common infrastructure services and components, such as the metrics library, for every combination of programming language and application frameworks used.

It seems obvious that by standardizing on a small set of technologies, the teams can become more efficient, easily transfer skillsets between teams, and so on. It is especially important for deploying tracing instrumentation, since every framework in use by the engineers may require special instrumentation. The application developers may not have enough understanding of tracing to do it correctly (tell them to read this book—wink), therefore that task often falls onto the central tracing team. It is difficult to scale the efforts of the tracing team if it needs to instrument dozens and dozens of frameworks.

Once the organization converges onto a small set of programming languages and frameworks, making the tracing instrumentation come for free becomes easier. The selection of the frameworks to standardize on should include considerations of how well they are instrumented for observability, which includes distributed tracing. Just like security, the observability cannot be an afterthought. These days, there is no excuse for the frameworks used to build microservices to be designed without observability features or at least extension points that allow improved observability through middleware and plugins.

In-house adapter libraries

In the past, many companies built internal frameworks (application or RPC), such as Finagle at Twitter. If you are in one of those situations, then it makes deploying tracing instrumentation even easier by enabling it automatically as part of the initialization of the respective framework, since you have full control over it. These days, there are many choices available in open source, so building an internal version from ground up is uncommon. However, this does not mean that your infrastructure team has no leverage.

Along with the standardization efforts, the infrastructure team can build an internal adapter of the framework. For example, consider the Spring framework in Java. It is very flexible and there are probably numerous ways an application can be constructed on top of it, and wired with additional dependencies for numerous infrastructure concerns, for example, which metrics or logging library to use, how to find the service discovery system, or where to find the configuration and secrets in production. This diversity is actually detrimental to the overall organization; it's the same problem as we discussed in the previous section, only on the scale of a single framework.

The infrastructure team can provide a library that bundles some of these configuration components together to allow the application developers to focus on the business logic instead of the infrastructure wiring. Instead of depending on the open source Spring framework, they can depend on the internal adapter that brings Spring as a transitive dependency and forces a standard way to initialize and configure the application. These adapter libraries are a convenient place to enable the tracing instrumentation as well, transparently to the application developer.

This principle also applies to the tracing libraries. As we discussed in *Chapter 6, Tracing Standards and Ecosystem*, there are efforts to standardize various data formats involved in distributed tracing, but those efforts are still in progress. As a result, when deploying tracing instrumentation across many applications in an organization, the infrastructure developers need to make a number of choices:

- If they are using OpenTracing, which tracer implementation they want to use
- Which wire format for the context propagation the tracer will be using

- How the tracer should export trace point data, for example, encoding, transport, and so on
- How the sampling should be configured

As an example, Jaeger clients support over 20 configuration parameters. The uniformity of this configuration is important because if two applications configure tracers to use different wire formats for context propagation, then the traces will be broken, as the tracers will not be able to understand each other. The solution: encapsulate all these decisions into an internal adapter library and let the application developers import the adapter instead of the concrete tracing library. By doing so, we consolidate the control of the tracing configuration in the hands of the tracing or the infrastructure team.

Tracing enabled by default

If you have standard libraries and internal adapters, make sure tracing is enabled in them by default. Requiring application developers to enable it explicitly is an unnecessary friction that only creates a barrier to adoption. Tracing libraries may be configurable to disable the instrumentation in rare cases where it is warranted, for example, for performance reasons, but a normal microservice should never need to disable tracing. If you are using any scaffolding tools for creating new application templates, make sure that tracing is initialized and enabled by default.

Monorepos

One of the benefits of microservices-based architecture is the autonomy provided to the teams supporting different microservices. This autonomy sometimes translates into each service having its own source code repository. In contrast, in a **monorepo (monolithic repository)** the code for all services is co-located in the same source code repository. Monorepos are employed by many tech companies, including Google, Facebook, Uber, Microsoft, and Twitter [2]. The discussion of the pros and cons of monorepos is beyond the scope of this chapter, and there are some challenges with scaling to large repositories. However, if you do work in a monorepo, it is very beneficial to the infrastructure teams, and can be very helpful in rolling out end-to-end tracing.

Google was one of the early adopters of distributed tracing on a large scale. Two factors played an important role in the success of the tracing rollout: a single standard RPC framework and a monorepo. Although this is probably a simplification, the Dapper team only needed to add tracing instrumentation to the RPC framework that was widely adopted across the company, and all applications received that change automatically due to the monorepo.

Monorepos greatly facilitate upgrades to the infrastructure libraries. Due to the global nature of distributed tracing, some features of the tracing libraries cannot be utilized until they are deployed across many microservices involved in distributed transactions. Upgrading a tracing library in hundreds of independent repositories is significantly more difficult than upgrading it once in a monorepo, especially when the new version of the library introduces breaking API changes. The upgrade of the monorepo can usually be done by the tracing team, but that approach does not scale to the multirepo situation.

Monorepos do not fully address the upgrades of the applications in production. They make it easy to ensure that the code of each application is using the latest versions of the tracing libraries, but someone still needs to build and deploy that code. It is possible that some of the applications are in maintenance mode and are not being upgraded in production for many months. Mature organizations typically have policies that address that issue, such as a requirement that every application must be redeployed every so often, or even by doing automatic deployments.

Integration with existing infrastructure

Sometimes it is possible to deploy distributed tracing by relying on the existing infrastructure and solutions already built into the applications. A good example is how Lyft used Envoy in a service mesh to provide tracing capabilities to most of the applications without any additional code changes or library integrations. The applications at Lyft had already been built with some mechanisms to propagate HTTP headers end-to-end, and we saw in *Chapter 7, Tracing with Service Mesh*, that it can be sufficient to make the service mesh do the rest and generate the spans representing the RPC requests. Some other companies piggyback on the existing request ID propagation and logging mechanisms to extract the tracing information.

The goal here is to be able to collect some form of tracing data with minimal involvement of the application developers. The ideas of distributed tracing and context propagation are not new; many legacy applications may already have some form of instrumentation that can be turned into proper tracing data with a bit of ingenuity. It is better to have incomplete data than no data at all. Often it is much easier to implement some central data conversion tools that can adapt differently formatted data into the format understood by your tracing backend than to try to replace the existing instrumentation with something new.

Where to start

In the previous sections, we discussed techniques that can help with making the tracing rollout a "zero touch" process, that is, without requiring any additional manual work by all the application teams.

Sadly, very often a completely hands-off approach is not feasible, otherwise we would have seen a much higher rate of tracing adoption in the industry. Therefore, since we need to spread the work across the organization, we need to address some organizational questions:

- Where do we start?
- Is it all-or-nothing or can we do an incremental rollout?
- How do we get buy-in from the management and application developers?

Once again, I do not presume to have a rule book that guarantees success. I have, however, observed some common patterns from discussions with industry practitioners. The most common advice people give is this: start with the workflows that are most important to your business. For example, for a ridesharing app it is more important that the workflow for taking a ride is working than the workflow for bookmarking a location. Ideally, both should be in great shape, but outages do happen, and the financial and reputational impact of an outage in the ride-taking workflow is orders of magnitude larger than the other one. Tracing is a powerful tool for troubleshooting applications during an outage, so it makes sense to prioritize the rollout of instrumentation by ranking the workflows according to their importance to the business.

[Start with the workflows that are most important to your business.]

The all-or-nothing approach is simply not feasible if we are already in the position where manual work is required because in a large organization, full rollout may take months. Once we know the most valuable workflows, we can start working towards instrumenting the endpoints that serve those workflows. This is the time for the tracing team to get their hands dirty and really dive into some of the application code to understand the landscape better. Typically, some API service is the entry point to any workflow, so we can start there. Incidentally, in a well-designed API service, an instrumentation implemented for one endpoint should work equally well for all other endpoints, so the impact of the tracing team's work is actually larger than just the main workflow.

People often do not realize that even for workflows served by dozens of microservices, the call graph is rarely very deep. In a system that mostly uses RPCs to communicate between microservices, rather than queues and messaging, the call graph can be a shallow tree with just a few levels, while the branching factor accounts for the large number of nodes. It means that if we instrument the top level (the API service) and then only the services in the second level, that incomplete instrumentation can already greatly improve the observability of the system and allow us to narrow down the causes of outages to a small subset of services.

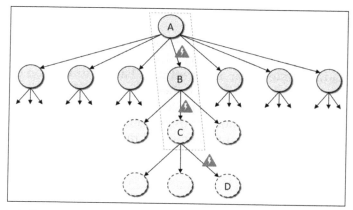

Figure 13.1: A shallow call graph with only the top-two levels instrumented for tracing still allows us to significantly narrow down the scope of the outage investigation (box with dashed line). Circles with solid borders represent instrumented services, while a dashed border represents services without tracing instrumentation. Triangles with lightning indicate errors or performance problems.

As shown in *Figure 13.1*, we can observe the errors or performance problems in the requests passing through services **A** and **B**, and given adequate instrumentation in service **B**, we might also be able to detect that the errors are coming from service **C**, not the other dependencies of **B**. Given the lack of instrumentation in **C**, we know nothing about its dependencies in the fourth level of the tree, but we still get a pretty accurate picture of where to look for the root cause, compared to a state when the system had no tracing instrumentation.

This incremental tracing rollout can quickly bring return on investment by shortening the time it takes to investigate outages. The tracing team can focus its attention on building tools for trace data analysis and let the peer pressure influence application developers in the lower stacks of the workflow to implement tracing in their services.

As an example, let's assume that service **D** is the one often causing the outages. If you are a first responder responsible for the overall workflow and you see the trace graph in *Figure 13.1*, your natural reaction would be to page the on-call person for service **C**, since you can trace the error there, but you cannot see any further. The on-call person for service **C** cannot actually fix the problem, so after some investigation, they realize that service **D** is responsible and they page the on-call for **D**. Eventually the developers of service **C** may realize that if they just instrument their service for tracing, then the first responder could page the on-call for D directly, without waking them up.

The *who is to blame?* question can be a sufficient motivator for teams and their managers to do the work to enable tracing instrumentation, or it may not be, in which case some other approaches are needed, such as changing the culture.

Building the culture

It is great to see that the culture of building applications that include observability features is gaining traction in the industry. Back in the days when I was working on derivatives trading systems for an investment bank, our version of application health monitoring was a trader calling on the phone (a landline, mind you) and complaining that they couldn't book or price their trades. Today, systems that automatically expose metrics to monitor their health are commonplace, while systems that support distributed tracing are still rare. Similarly, many engineers are familiar with tools like Prometheus and Grafana, and less familiar with distributed tracing tools. There are some things we can do to change this culture.

Explaining the value

It is hard to sell someone on a product that they do not need. This is not the case with end-to-end tracing, which has a clear value proposition, but people just don't know about it. At Uber, we have given a number of internal talks showing how to use the tracing tools and what problems they are addressing. We have also included lessons on tracing, as well as the overall observability, in the boot camp that newly hired engineers are required to take. This helps with raising awareness of good observability practices and tooling.

Integrating with developer workflows

Engineers spend more time using the tools that are in front of them than those that need to be found somewhere else. If we can integrate the tracing tools into engineers' daily routines, it creates a virtuous feedback loop where they start suggesting new features or even building their own analysis tools based on the tracing data.

We saw in *Chapter 10, Distributed Context Propagation,* how Squash debugger uses tracing instrumentation to deliver breakpoint information to the microservices encountered by a specific request. While this technique itself does not expose the user to the tracing tools directly, the fact that it depends on the context propagation of the tracing infrastructure can serve as a motivation to developers to instrument their services.

When backend engineers work on new features, they often need to send realistic requests to their microservice, sometimes indirectly through a higher-level service, or even a mobile app. The interaction between microservices may be fairly complicated and easy to break during development. Tracing can be very useful in surfacing the exact execution of the request in these cases. We discussed in *Chapter 8, All About Sampling,* that the Jaeger tracers understand a special HTTP header, `jaeger-debug-id`, which can be used to force sampling of a given request and to find that request in the Jaeger UI by a correlation ID. This allows us to integrate the use of tracing tools into the development workflows.

The integration with on-call and alerting tools is perhaps the most impactful technique. There are two types of alerting that can be used to include tracing information:

- The most common case is alerting from metrics, that is, time series. For example, we can set up a threshold alert that fires if the 99th percentile of some endpoint latency exceeds some value. The system generating the alert can query the tracing backend for representative samples of that condition and include links to the sample traces in the alert text as it is dispatched via a communication channel like email or PagerDuty. An engineer receiving this alert can jump right into the tracing tool, which gives them rich context about the outage.

- In other cases, you may develop a black-box testing system that does not look at the metrics from the services, but instead acts as a real user and executes some synthetic test requests against the backend. This system can generate alerts based on repeated failures of some tests. Since it fully controls the execution of the requests, it can be aware of the trace IDs corresponding to those requests (it can even start a trace itself). The link to the specific trace is included in the alert text, similar to the previous example, but it is much more precise, as it points to the trace of the exact request that caused an error.

Finally, I want to mention a talk given by Ted Young from Lightstep at KubeCon 2018 in Seattle [3]. The talk was titled *Trace Driven Development* and proposed a thought-provoking idea of writing unit tests expressed as expectations over the trace data collected from the execution of a request. For example, given an account in a banking application, the test checks that the account cannot allow withdrawals of amounts larger than the current balance:

```
model = NewModel()

model("Accounts cannot withdraw more than their balance")
  .When(
    LessThan(
      Span.Name("fetch-balance").Tag("amount"),
      Span.Name("withdrawal").Tag("amount")))
  .Expect( Span.Name("rollback") )
  .NotExpect( Span.Name("commit") )
  .Expect(
    Span.Name("/:account/withdrawl/")
      .HttpStatusCode(500))

Check(model, testData)
```

As we can see, the expectations of the test are expressed as queries over some trace model (the syntax is a pseudo-language at this point). The talk proposed that the same exact code can be used not only as a unit test, but also as an integration test against a staging environment, and even as a continuous test in production that also acts as a monitoring tool for the correctness of the operations. Ted concluded the talk with an observation that currently our development and monitoring practices are often divorced and that if monitoring is not useful during development, then the quality of the monitoring code suffers, since there is no feedback loop. The proposed approach puts the monitoring (tracing) code directly into the development process.

Tracing Quality Metrics

To finish this chapter, let's talk about a reporting system we implemented internally at Uber, called **Tracing Quality Metrics**. It is part of a larger reporting system that provides various metrics about the quality of engineering artifacts, with rollups from individual microservices to teams, to divisions, and up to all of engineering. The objective of this system is to help with keeping up and raising the overall quality of engineering across the company by tracking measurable indicators, such as code coverage; availability of integration, capacity, and chaos testing; efficiency; compliance; microservices metadata, such as who is on-call, and many others. The tracing quality of a service is one of the metrics tracked by that system, as shown in *Figure 13.2*.

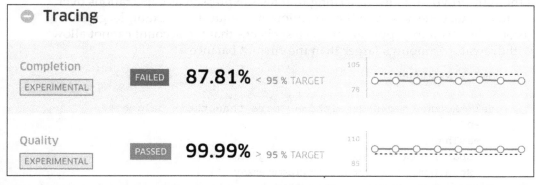

Figure 13.2: Summary of trace quality metrics for a microservice, with current (left) and historical (right) levels

We developed the tracing quality report when we realized that having just a "yes or no" indicator for tracing instrumentation was not enough to adequately track adoption of distributed tracing by the applications. Even though a given service may have some tracing instrumentation in it and collect some tracing data, the instrumentation may be done incorrectly, or it may be incomplete, such as passing the tracing context to some downstream calls but not all of them.

We have implemented a streaming job that performs analysis of all collected traces and looks for common mistakes and omissions, which we call **quality metrics**. For each quality metric, the job calculates how many traces satisfied the criteria, and how many did not. The ratio of failures to the total number of traces gives a simple score between 0 and 1 (or as a percentage). *Figure 13.3* shows an example of a breakdown of individual metrics for a single service `api-gateway`. The **Metric** column lists the metrics and links to the documentation explaining what the metric means, what conditions may cause it to fail, and ways to fix it. The columns **Num Passes** and **Num Failures** link to sample traces in the respective category, so that the service owner can investigate what happened.

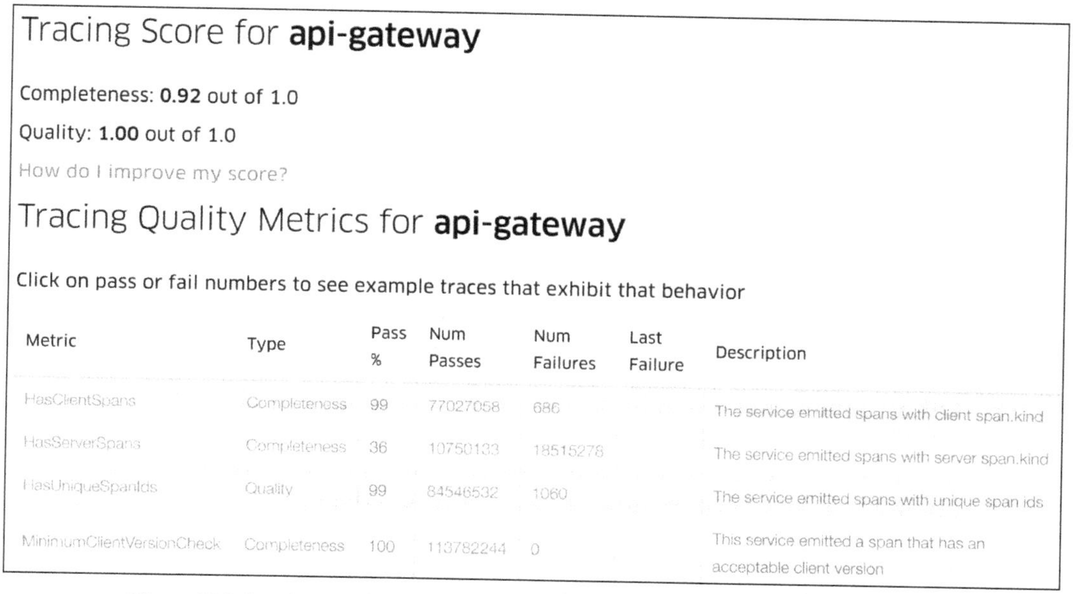

Tracing Score for **api-gateway**

Completeness: **0.92** out of 1.0

Quality: **1.00** out of 1.0

How do I improve my score?

Tracing Quality Metrics for **api-gateway**

Click on pass or fail numbers to see example traces that exhibit that behavior

Metric	Type	Pass %	Num Passes	Num Failures	Last Failure	Description
HasClientSpans	Completeness	99	77027058	686		The service emitted spans with client span.kind
HasServerSpans	Completeness	36	10750133	18515278		The service emitted spans with server span.kind
HasUniqueSpanIds	Quality	99	84546532	1060		The service emitted spans with unique span ids
MinimumClientVersionCheck	Completeness	100	113782244	0		This service emitted a span that has an acceptable client version

---

Figure 13.3: Breakdown of Tracing Quality Metrics for a single service, "api-gateway"

The metrics are categorized into three groups:

- **Completeness**: Having a low score in this category means the traces are likely to be broken, for example, one part of the trace is reported with one trace ID, and another part of the trace with a different trace ID, preventing full reassembly in the backend. Some examples of completeness metrics include:
    - `HasServerSpans`: Let's say we have a trace where service A calls service B. Service A has good instrumentation and emits a client-side span, indicating via the `peer.service` tag that it's calling service B. Service B, on the other hand, does not emit any server-side span for this trace. We count this trace ID as a failure in service B.

- ° `HasClientSpans`: Similar to `HasServerSpans`, with the roles of services A and B reversed.

- ° `MinimumClientVersionCheck`: This metric checks the version of the Jaeger tracer library used to emit each span and compares it with a minimal acceptable version. Strictly speaking, running an old client does not necessarily lead to broken traces, but we have included it in the completeness score because there may be some features missing from the old tracer libraries that can cause various problems for trace collection.

- **Quality**: Criteria in this category measure usefulness of the data collected in the trace, for example:

  - ° `MeaningfulEndpointName`: This metric ensures that the spans are given meaningful names that can be used for grouping. For example, a server handling a REST endpoint such as `/user/{user}/profile` may report server-side spans with the operation names `GET` and `POST`. While this does not break the trace, it makes it harder to analyze, since all endpoints will be grouped under the `GET` and `POST` names.

  - ° `UniqueClientSpanID`: This metric verifies that a service does not issue multiple spans with the same span ID. We have seen this issue occasionally, usually because of invalid instrumentation.

- **Other**: Some criteria that indicate a problem that may not be easily attributable to a service or actionable by the service developers. They may also indicate some issues that we have not yet elevated to the quality category because no automated process depends on them.

The breakdown screen calculates the average for the completeness and quality categories, which are also reported to the overall quality tracking system. The reporting system allows us to analyze which microservices, teams, or even groups within the company have low tracing quality scores and work with them and their management on improving the coverage. There may be many reasons why a given organization has low cumulative tracing scores: they may be using non-standard frameworks that do not have tracing instrumentation and need some help, or they may be using different technologies, for example, some specific forms of queueing and messaging that are not well supported by the mainstream instrumentation. It may also be simply a matter of prioritization and the teams need a presentation explaining the value and benefits of tracing.

The tracing quality report has been our main go-to tool for driving and tracking the adoption of tracing instrumentation at Uber.

Troubleshooting guide

When we just started a push for wide adoption of tracing at Uber, there were a lot of questions coming to the tracing team in emails, tickets, and online chat: *Why doesn't this work? I am not seeing spans; how do I investigate?* and so on. We have aggregated many of those questions and distilled them into a step-by-step guide for troubleshooting tracing instrumentation given the specifics of Uber's development and production environments. This guide drastically reduced the number of support tickets and questions, freeing the team up to focus on better integration with existing popular frameworks and enabling application developers to solve their problems without waiting for the feedback from the tracing team.

Don't be on the critical path

The practitioners of distributed tracing and performance optimization should know all about not being on the critical path. This applies to the organizational aspects as well. A tracing team cannot scale its effort in a large organization if it needs to go and make changes in hundreds of microservices. Tracing Quality Metrics was specifically designed to be a self-service tool that service owners may consult, make changes to the instrumentation, and check if that improves the metrics, all without involving the tracing team. The same principle applies to all other advice in this chapter: the tracing team should be doing surgical strikes to improve instrumentation in widely used frameworks, providing excellent documentation and troubleshooting guides, and focusing on the tracing platform. Ultimately, application developers are the domain experts for their own applications, the internal structure of those applications, and the internal threading model. The objective of the tracing team is to make the initial integration as frictionless as possible and allow the application developers to improve the instrumentation with the specifics of their application.

Summary

Deploying tracing instrumentation and infrastructure in large organizations is a challenging task, given the variety of technologies and frameworks usually present in mature companies, whether through acquisitions or through *build fast, use whichever tools you want* policies. Even with good practices around standardization and consolidated infrastructure, the sheer number of different business problems that engineers need to solve dictates a wide variety of tools, from various databases to numerous machine learning frameworks. The industry has not reached the point where all these tools are designed with support for distributed tracing and we can just plug a tracer, and start collecting consistent tracing data across the whole ecosystem. If you find yourself in such an organization, it can take many months or even years to gain high levels of adoption.

In this chapter, we discussed various techniques that facilitate that task by attacking it from different angles, through technical as well as organizational and cultural solutions. I have previously given two talks on similar topics: *Distributed Tracing at Uber Scale* [4] and *Would You Like Some Tracing with Your Monitoring?* [5], and the topic clearly seemed to resonate with the audience, indicating that this is indeed a significant pain point. I am hoping these thoughts will help people navigate their way in this area. If you have other ideas or stories about adoption, I would be interested to hear them–send me a direct message on Twitter: @yurishkuro.

In the next and last chapter, we will address more technical aspects of operating tracing infrastructure, such as deploying and running the tracing backend, dealing with traffic spikes and sampling abuses, multi-tenancy, and multiple data centers.

References

1. Conway, Melvin E.(April 1968), *How do Committees Invent?*, Datamation, 14 (5): 28–31: http://www.melconway.com/Home/Committees_Paper.html.

2. Monorepo. Wikipedia: https://en.wikipedia.org/wiki/Monorepo.

3. Ted Young. *Trace Driven Development: Unifying Testing and Observability.* KubeCon – CloudNativeCon North America 2018: Seattle: https://kccna18.sched.com/event/GrRF.

4. Yuri Shkuro. *Distributed Tracing at Uber Scale.* Monitorama PDX 2017: https://vimeo.com/221070602.

5. Yuri Shkuro. *Would You Like Some Tracing with Your Monitoring?* KubeCon – CloudNativeCon North America 2017, Austin: https://youtu.be/1NDq86kbvbU.

14
Under the Hood of a Distributed Tracing System

This last chapter is aimed at engineers or DevOps people tasked with deploying and operating a distributed tracing backend in their organization. Since my own experience is mostly related to Jaeger, I will be using it as an example. I will try to avoid focusing on very specific details of Jaeger configurations, since they may change after the book is published while the project continues evolving. Instead, I will use them to illustrate the general principles and the decisions you need to make when deploying a tracing platform. Many of the topics that we will discuss apply equally well to any other tracing backend, and even to using hosted solutions like AWS X-Ray and Google Stackdriver, or offerings from commercial vendors.

Why host your own?

As the creator and a maintainer of an open source tracing system, I would obviously have a conflict of interest if I were to advocate for everyone to run their own tracing backend. By no means would this be the right answer for all organizations. There are many reasons when it makes more sense to use a hosted solution; the complexity of operating yet another distributed system is one of the major reasons to look for commercial or freemium vendors that will take care of receiving, storing, and processing the traces for you. However, there are also benefits to operating a tracing backend by yourself, some of which I want to briefly mention here.

Customizations and integrations

Commercial offerings are often, by necessity, designed as general-purpose solutions, aimed at satisfying the needs of many different customers. Yet every organization is unique in its history and its needs, and sometimes an organization may need features that may not make sense to others, and therefore may not have a sufficient business case for the vendor to implement.

When you use an open source product, it is often easier to customize to your needs and integrate with your existing systems. As an example, suppose you are looking at a Gantt chart view of a distributed trace and you want to have access to various other infrastructure services associated with a given microservice, for example, trigger a rollback of a recent deployment, page the on-call person, open a Grafana dashboard with metrics, find out how many compute resources it is using, and so on. There is not a lot of standardization in the industry for solving all of these use cases with a small number of infra systems, and a vendor solution is unlikely to provide support for every possible combination, especially if it requires running some code as part of the tracing backend to interface with those other systems.

The other side of integrations is being able to include tracing views with other web applications you may be running internally. As an example, the Jaeger frontend views can be embedded into other applications, as was recently demonstrated [1] by the Kiali project, an observability tool for service mesh Istio.

Bandwidth cost

As you get serious about tracing your distributed architecture, you may start producing so much tracing data that the cost of bandwidth for sending all this data to a hosted solution may become a problem, especially if your company's infrastructure operates in multiple **data centers** (**DCs**). The cost of network traffic inside a DC is always orders of magnitude lower than sending it to the cloud. Having said that, this particular consideration may only matter to very large, internet-scale companies.

Own the data

This, perhaps, is the main reason to host your own tracing platform. As I have tried to show in *Chapter 9, Turning the Lights On*, and *Chapter 12, Gathering Insights with Data Mining*, tracing data is an incredibly rich source of insights you can extract about the behavior of complex systems. This industry is very new and there are not many general-purpose data mining solutions for tracing out there yet.

If you want to build additional processing and data mining that is specific to the unique properties of your architecture or business, you need access to the raw tracing data. While some hosted solutions provide a way to retrieve the tracing data, it is not very cost effective (the bandwidth costs are doubled), and it is much easier to do while the data is being collected from your applications. We saw in *Chapter 12, Gathering Insights with Data Mining*, how easy it was to add data mining jobs on top of the already-existing data collection pipeline used by Jaeger.

Bet on emerging standards

Whether you decide to deploy an open source tracing platform like Jaeger or Zipkin, use a commercial vendor, or even build your own, there are a few critical choices you need to make to future-proof your efforts. Instrumenting a code base is expensive and time-consuming, so you only want to do it once. Vendor-neutral standards like OpenTracing give you the flexibility of changing your mind later about which tracing backend you want to use. However, the OpenTracing API does not dictate how the trace context is represented on the wire, leaving this decision to the implementations, and ultimately to you, since many implementations are configurable. As an example, the Jaeger clients can use Jaeger's native trace context format [2], or the B3 headers popularized by the Zipkin project [3].

Similarly, the OpenCensus libraries also support B3 headers, as well as the emerging W3C Trace Context format [4]. In some way, choosing the propagation format is even more important than choosing the instrumentation API. As we discussed in *Chapter 13, Implementing Tracing in Large Organizations*, there are techniques, such as in-house adapter libraries, that can minimize the exposure of application developers to the details of the tracing instrumentation.

By upgrading the adapter libraries, which are under your control, you might think that you can change the propagation format already used in production. Yet in practice, even if you have a monorepo and you can force all microservices to pick up a new version of the tracing library, it may still take a long time, in the order of months, until all microservices in production are re-deployed with the new version.

If applications use a different trace context propagation format, it effectively means you have traces broken all over the place. The only way to achieve a switch of the propagation format in production from X to Y is to do a phased rollout:

1. Configure tracing libraries to be able to read both the X and Y format from the inbound requests, but only send format X in the outbound requests.

2. Once all services are upgraded to understand format Y from the inbound requests, upgrade the libraries again to start sending format Y in the outbound requests.

3. Once all services are upgraded for the second time, you can make the third change to the libraries configuration and instruct them to not parse the format X.

If each of these steps takes several months to rollout, we can see that we are potentially looking at a very long migration period. It is possible to shorten it slightly by combining the first two steps and including both formats X and Y in the outbound requests, at the expense of increasing the volume of network traffic across all of your applications.

In conclusion, it is best to avoid these pains if you can. As we discussed in *Chapter 6, Tracing Standards and Ecosystem*, the W3C Trace Context format is emerging as the standard for trace context propagation, which will be supported by most commercial vendors, cloud providers, and open source projects. It also provides you with interoperability in case your applications are relying on other cloud services.

Architecture and deployment modes

Many tracing backends, including the Jaeger backend that we will use as an example, are themselves implemented as microservices-based distributed systems that consist of multiple horizontally-scalable components. Some of those components are optional, which allows different deployment configurations depending on the needs of your architecture.

Basic architecture: agent + collector + query service

Figure 14.1 shows the basic architecture of Jaeger that we were running at Uber in 2017. It includes the main components that are common to many tracing backends.

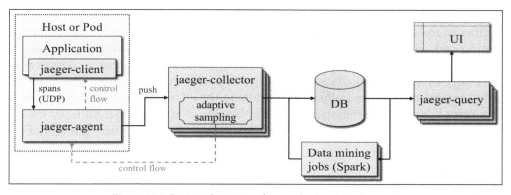

Figure 14.1: Basic architecture of Jaeger backend deployment

Client

The client library, or the tracing library, or the tracer, is the code that runs inside the business application. For example, the application that is instrumented with OpenTracing would be making calls to the OpenTracing API, and the Jaeger client library that implements that API would be using those calls to extract tracing data from the application. The client library is responsible for exporting the data to the tracing backend. The most common implementation is to stash the tracing data into an internal memory buffer, to move it off the critical path of the request, and then send it in batches to the tracing backend asynchronously, for example, from a separate background thread.

Most Jaeger tracers support multiple formats for data exports, as well as multiple protocols, for example, the spans can be converted to a Thrift message and sent to a UDP port on the localhost (to be received by the agent), or as a JSON message to an HTTP port on the collector. Which configuration to choose depends on the specifics of your deployment environment. Sending data to the agent has the benefit of requiring minimal configuration of the client, since the agent is typically configured to be available on the localhost. Using the UDP port means that the messages are sent as fire-and-forget and could be discarded if the host is overloaded or the agent is not keeping up with reading them off the UDP port.

Submitting spans via HTTP protocol directly to the collector requires that the clients are given the address of the collector, which tends to complicate the configuration and deployment of the business applications. It may also require running or configuring a third-party load balancer to avoid creating hot spots in the cluster of collectors. However, in some cases this is the only possible configuration; for example, if your application is deployed to the AWS Lambda platform, you don't have the option of running the agent as a sidecar next to the application.

The diagram in *Figure 14.1* shows that there is a feedback loop from the collectors to the clients called the **control flow**. It is a pull-based mechanism for updating certain configuration settings in the tracers and most importantly, the sampling strategies when they are controlled by the adaptive sampling component in the collectors, which we discussed in *Chapter 8, All About Sampling*. The same channel can be used to pass other parameters to the clients, such as throttling limits that control how many debug traces the application is allowed to initiate, or the baggage restrictions that control which baggage keys the application is allowed to use.

Agent

The Jaeger agent implements the sidecar design pattern, which we discussed in *Chapter 7, Tracing with Service Mesh,* by encapsulating the logic of submitting data to the collectors, including service discovery and load balancing, so that it does not need to be repeated in the client libraries in each programming language. It is a pretty simple and mostly pass-through component of the Jaeger backend. There are two primary modes of deploying the agents:

- As a host-level agent that runs either on bare metal [5] or as a Kubernetes `DaemonSet` or something similar

- As a sidecar running next to the business application, for example, inside the same Kubernetes pod [6]

At Uber, we have a dedicated infrastructure for deploying host-level agents across the fleet, so for us, running Jaeger agents directly on the hosts is the best approach. The sidecar approach works best if you need to support multi-tenancy, discussed later in this chapter.

Similar to Jaeger clients, the agents also employ a memory buffer for the tracing data they receive from the clients. The buffer is treated as a queue that supports load shedding by discarding the oldest items when there is no more space in the buffer to add new spans.

Collector

The Jaeger collectors are stateless, horizontally scalable services that perform a number of functions:

- They receive span data in either Jaeger or Zipkin formats, in a variety of encodings (JSON, Thrift, or Protobuf), over a variety of network protocols (HTTP, TChannel, or gRPC).

- They convert and normalize span data to a single internal data model.
- They send the normalized spans to a pluggable persistent storage.
- They contain the adaptive sampling logic that observes all inbound span traffic and generates sampling strategies (discussed in *Chapter 8, All About Sampling*).

The collectors also employ a configurable internal memory queue used to tolerate the traffic spikes better. When the queue is full, the collectors can shed the load by dropping data. They are also capable of consistent down-sampling of the traffic. These features are described later in this chapter.

Query service and UI

Query service is another stateless component that implements a query API for searching and retrieving traces from the storage. The same binary also serves the static HTML assets that are used by the Jaeger UI.

Data mining jobs

The data mining jobs perform post-processing and aggregation of the trace data, such as building the service dependency graphs (for example, Spark jobs [7] in the Jaeger project) or computing tracing quality scores, discussed in *Chapter 9, Turning the Lights On*, and *Chapter 13, Implementing Tracing in Large Organizations*, respectively. Typically, these jobs store the data in the same database, so that it can be retrieved and visualized by the Jaeger UI.

Streaming architecture

As more and more services were being instrumented with distributed tracing at Uber, we realized that the simple push architecture we originally deployed had certain drawbacks. In particular, it was struggling to keep up with the traffic spikes, especially during routine DC failovers that Uber SREs perform to test capacity and disaster recovery.

We were using Apache Cassandra as the storage backend for traces, which was under-provisioned to handle all of the traffic during failovers. Since collectors are designed to write to the storage directly and have only a limited amount of memory for the internal buffer for smoothing short bursts of traffic, during failovers the internal buffers would fill up quickly and the collectors were forced to start dropping data.

Normally, the tracing data is already sampled, so dropping more of it should not be an issue; however, since the spans from a single trace can arrive to any one of the stateless collectors, some of the collectors may end up dropping them while others store the remaining spans, resulting in incomplete and broken traces.

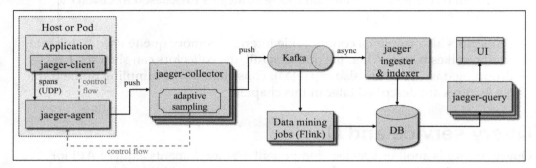

Figure 14.2: Streaming architecture of the Jaeger backend deployment

To address this problem, we turned to a streaming architecture, based on Apache Kafka (*Figure 14.2*). Kafka is heavily used at Uber, processing several trillion messages daily. Kafka installations have a lot of capacity, much more than our Cassandra cluster used for traces, so as a sink for tracing data, Kafka is much more elastic than Cassandra during traffic spikes. It is also more efficient, since the messages stored in Kafka are just raw bytes, while in Cassandra the spans are stored in a specific domain model.

We implemented a new storage type supported by the Jaeger collectors to allow them to write spans to Kafka. We added two new components, **ingester** and **indexer**, whose jobs were to read the spans from a Kafka stream, and to store and index them in the storage. The separation into two components was beneficial with Cassandra as the trace storage backend because Jaeger does not use Cassandra's built-in indices and instead directly builds lookup tables, which requires more writes to the storage. Since indexing spans for querying is a lower-priority task, we were able to decrease the latency of ingestion by moving the indexing to a separate component working at its own pace.

The result of this architectural change was that we were able to eliminate indiscriminate data loss during traffic spikes, at the expense of increased latency for the availability of traces in the persistent storage.

The second significant benefit was that the stream of spans available in Kafka allowed us to build more efficient, streaming-based data mining jobs. As part of this work, we switched from the Apache Spark to the Apache Flink framework, because Flink provides a true streaming platform for data mining and it was easier for us to deploy on Uber's infrastructure, but in the end, both frameworks are probably equally capable of handling the task of processing tracing data.

Multi-tenancy

Multi-tenancy refers to the ability of a single system to serve the needs of different customers, or tenants, while providing isolation of their data. This requirement is very typical for hosted commercial solutions, but many organizations have similar requirements internally, for example, for regulatory reasons. Each organization may have a different notion of what constitutes a tenant and what exact requirements for multi-tenancy are imposed on the tracing backend. Let's consider some of them separately and discuss what implications they have on the tracing backend, and how we can implement them.

Cost accounting

Tracing infrastructure incurs certain operational costs for processing and storing the traces. Many organizations have internal policies where systems are charged back for the resources they consume from other systems. If you instrument your service to generate 10 spans for each RPC request, while a neighbor service only produces two spans per RPC, then it's reasonable to charge your service more for the resources of the tracing backend. At the same time, when you or your neighbor developer look at the traces, you can see the same data, across both services. The data access is not restricted per tenant.

This scenario is easy to implement with Jaeger and most tracing backends. The tracing spans are already tagged with the name of the service that emitted them, which can be used for cost accounting. If we need a coarser notion of the tenant, such as at the level of a division or business domain rather than an individual microservice, then it can be captured in the span tags.

As an example, Jaeger tracers support the configuration parameter that defines "tracer-level tags", or the tags that are automatically applied to every span emitted by the service without the need for the instrumentation to set those tags directly (*Figure 14.3*). The values of these tags can be configured via the environment variable JAEGER_TAGS, which accepts a comma-separated list of key=value pairs, for example:

```
JAEGER_TAGS="tenant=billing,service-instance=text-executor-0"
```

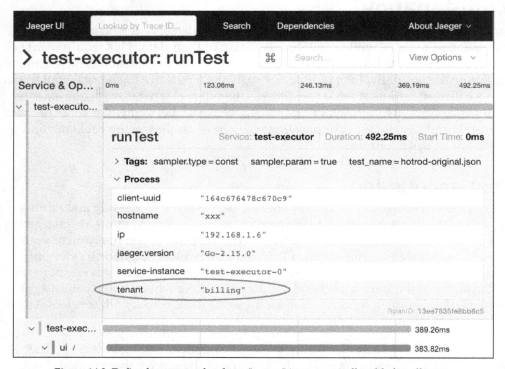

Figure 14.3: Defined as a tracer-level tag, "tenant" is automatically added to all spans

Since all users of the tracing backend in this scenario are still able to see each other's data, this is not a real multi-tenancy. Accordingly, it does not require any special deployment aside from defining the tenant in the applications' environment variables.

Complete isolation

Similar to hosted solutions or **Software as a Service (SaaS)**, each tenant may want to have complete isolation of their data from all other tenants. This is not possible today with Jaeger without deploying isolated installations of the Jaeger backend for each tenant.

The main reason why this use case is more difficult to support is because it requires the storage implementation to be tenant-aware. Multi-tenant storage can take different forms, with no guarantee that any particular solution will satisfy all use cases. As an example, if we use Cassandra for storage, there are at least three different options to support multi-tenancy: isolated clusters, a shared cluster with different keyspaces, and a shared cluster with a single keyspace where tenancy is an attribute of the span data. All these options have their strengths and weaknesses.

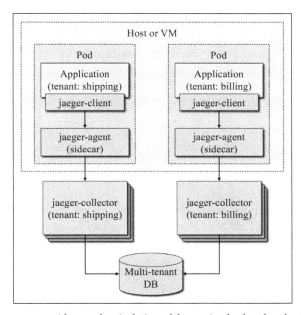

Figure 14.4: Multi-tenant setup with complete isolation of the tracing backend and a tenancy-aware storage

Aside from multi-tenant storage, there are other implications of providing complete isolation, especially for the internal deployments. If you use a vendor-hosted tracing backend to collect the spans, your own software stack is already (hopefully) isolated, even if you run on a cloud platform. Therefore, the configuration for reporting tracing data is going to be identical in all microservices. However, if you are deploying a tracing infrastructure internally and you need isolation by tenant, it may require running multiple per-tenant stacks of the tracing backend components. As an example, the two internal tenants may be sharing the compute resources, for example, a Kubernetes cluster. If the Jaeger agent runs as a `DaemonSet`, then the spans from different tenants might be mixed up if their applications happen to be scheduled on the same host. It is best to run the Jaeger agent as a sidecar, so that it can forward the data to the appropriate tracing backend (*Figure 14.4*).

Granular access controls

At the high end of the complexity scale is the scenario where a corporation needs granular control to the data access, for example, a single request may span three different business domains within an organization. Some users may be authorized to see the trace data across all three domains, while others only within their own domain.

This scenario goes somewhat against the premise of distributed tracing as a tool that provides end-to-end visibility into the execution of distributed requests. If you can only see a portion of the trace, you are not getting end-to-end visibility.

However, the situation might become more common once more cloud services start implementing distributed tracing and correlating the internal traces with the external requests. As an example, Google and Amazon are unlikely to expose all the intricate details of the internal execution in Spanner or DynamoDB to their customers.

How can a single tracing backend satisfy these data access requirements and still be useful? One option is that the data aggregations that are performed by the backend can still operate on the full set of data, and access to the aggregation results is controlled, similar to the access to the raw traces. This might be quite difficult to guarantee, as there are various known techniques where the aggregate data might reveal information that was otherwise not accessible from the raw data with granular access control. A discussion of this topic is outside the scope of this book.

To implement granular access controls at the level of raw trace data, the data (spans) needs to be tagged with tenancy attributes, and the tracing backend and its data querying components must always be aware of the tenancy information. To my knowledge, no existing tracing system goes to this extreme today.

Security

Multi-tenancy goes hand in hand with security, both for data access controls by the users and for securing the data transmission channels from the application to the tracing backends. Jaeger and other tracing backends have mixed support for these two types of security. Many components support **transport-level security (TLS)** between the internal parts of the backend, such as communications between Jaeger agents and collectors using gRPC with TLS-enabled, or communication with the storage backends that can also be configured with TLS certificates.

On the other hand, the Jaeger query service provides no built-in authentication or authorization for users. The motivation for this gap is to leave this function to external components that can be deployed alongside the Jaeger query service, such as Apache httpd [8] or Keycloak [9] proxies.

These networking tools are dedicated to developing solutions for securing other components and integrating with additional services, such as single sign-on and other authentication mechanisms. By leaving the security aspects to them, the tracing backend developers can focus on tracing-related functionality and not reinvent the wheel. The only downside is that the granular access controls described in the previous sections are not possible, since they do require domain knowledge about the traces.

Running in multiple DCs

Many large corporations run their systems from multiple DCs, whether to ensure business continuity in the face of DC failures or to improve user-experienced latency by routing user requests to the closest DC. One of the popular approaches to thinking about multi-DC deployments is by looking at **zones** and **regions**. A zone, or availability zone, is a DC that is independent of any other DCs, such that a failure or disaster in zone X should not cause a failure in zone Y. A region is a group of zones that are independent, but geographically close to each other, with high bandwidth network links between them to reduce the latency. For example, Amazon cloud locations are composed of AWS regions, such as `us-east-1` in N. Virginia or `us-west-1` in N. California, and each region has many availability zones, such as `us-east-1a`, `us-east-1b`, and so on.

Making a cross-zone request can impose an order of magnitude penalty on the latency and cross-region request up to two orders of magnitude. Given this limitation, the recommended design pattern for distributed systems hosted in those DCs is to ensure that most of the traffic between microservices occurs within a single zone, to minimize the overall latency of the requests. This is good news for distributed tracing, since we can expect most of the traces to be collected from microservices operating within the same zone. However, there may be cases where the requests do need to jump across zones or even regions. This could happen due to an outage in one of the dependent microservices and your routing infrastructure, for example, a service mesh, may route the request to another zone, with the assumption that it's better to take longer to serve the request than to fail completely.

This could also happen for legitimate reasons due to the design of the application, for example, a global company like Uber may store user profiles, favorite locations, trip history, and so on, in DCs close to the user's home location, for example, in one or more zones of the EU region for a user who lives in Paris. When that user travels to New York, the mobile app requests are going to be routed to zones in the U.S. regions, since that's where the fulfillment (ride-matching) services are likely operating. The services from the U.S. region will need to access user data located in the EU region. Granted, the data may be replicated on-demand and cached, but at least one request would be a cross-region request, and that's the request we probably want to trace, since it will exhibit unusual latency. Therefore, our tracing infrastructure may need to deal with these requests spanning multiple DCs.

There is, of course, a simple solution of running all of the tracing backend components in just one region, with some replication for resiliency. However, as we discussed earlier in this chapter, this may be prohibitive due to the network bandwidth costs. It is also highly inefficient, since the majority of the requests in a well-designed system will be local to a single zone. An efficient solution would be to only incur a cross-zone bandwidth cost for traces that are themselves cross-zone and handle all other traces locally.

Capturing origin zone

One of the possible solutions to this problem is to capture the name of the zone where the trace begins and propagate it as part of the trace context throughout the call graph, always capturing the value in the generated spans. Let's call this value `origin_zone`. The collectors receiving the spans can inspect the `origin_zone` field and use static mapping to know whether the spans can be processed locally, that is, saved to storage or sent to a local Kafka topic, or need to be forwarded to collectors in another zone.

Assume that the request originated in zone X and some part of it was executed in zone Y. Using the preceding algorithm, the trace will only be processed in zone X. If we are running data mining and aggregation jobs in every zone, we probably want the same trace to be processed by both X and Y zones. This is difficult to achieve with stateless routing via collectors because by the time we find out that part of the trace was executing in zone Y, we may have already processed spans that were created in zone X.

The solution here is to rely on post-processing, for example, by using the trace completion trigger we discussed in *Chapter 12, Gathering Insights with Data Mining*. The routing algorithm will ensure that all spans from this trace will arrive to zone X, but every span nonetheless can capture the zone where it was actually emitted. Once the trace completion trigger declares the trace as finished, we can inspect all spans in that trace, and if any of them have the emitting zone other than X, we can send that trace for replication to that other zone (or zones). If requests spanning two zones are rare, requests spanning even more zones are exponentially rarer, so we are not talking about huge replication costs, yet we allow the data mining and aggregation jobs local to each zone to have a more complete picture.

One downside of the `origin_zone` approach is a small increase in the size of the request, since we need to propagate the extra value throughout the call graph. Another downside is that it requires having the foresight to implement tracing libraries with the behavior of capturing and propagating the zone in the first place. I have to admit, when I was just starting to design Jaeger, I was very new to distributed tracing, and this particular trick did not occur to me.

Neither was it used in the other tracing systems I studied, for example, OpenZipkin. Even using the baggage mechanism, which was built into the Jaeger clients from the beginning, would not help.

It could be used to propagate the `origin_zone` as part of the trace context, but it would be only available in the application at runtime, since baggage items are not stored in the spans.

To enable this approach in the already deployed tracing infrastructure requires an upgrade of tracing libraries in many applications, which is something that can take a long time. Note that we are only talking about capturing and propagating the original zone; recording in which zone a given span was emitted is much easier, as we can do that by enriching the span in the agents or collectors, since they know in which zone they are running.

Cross-zone federation

Another problem related to multi-zone deployment is getting a cross-zone view of the system. For example, if our service has a certain SLO for p99 latency and the service is deployed over a dozen zones, we don't want to go to a dozen different URLs to check that number. This is an example from metrics, but we can replace the latency SLO with any other feature that is only available from traces.

Another example is if we want to query for traces across all zones. Answering these questions becomes much easier if you have only a single location for all of your tracing data, but as we already discussed, that approach may not scale well. The alternative is to build a federation layer that can fan out the requests to multiple tracing backends and aggregate the results. Jaeger does not have such a component today, but we will most likely build it in the future.

Monitoring and troubleshooting

As with any other distributed system, the tracing backend itself must be observable. Jaeger exposes numerous metrics for all of its components, from the client libraries to the backend components. Typical metrics include stats for the number of spans created, received, processed, sampled and non-sampled, and so on. As an example, the following are some of the metrics emitted by the Jaeger client in the `frontend` service of the HotROD application (from *Chapter 2, Take Tracing for a HotRod Ride*):

```
hotrod_frontend_jaeger_started_spans{sampled="n"} 0
hotrod_frontend_jaeger_started_spans{sampled="y"} 24
hotrod_frontend_jaeger_finished_spans 24
hotrod_frontend_jaeger_traces{sampled="n",state="joined"} 0
hotrod_frontend_jaeger_traces{sampled="n",state="started"} 0
hotrod_frontend_jaeger_traces{sampled="y",state="joined"} 0
hotrod_frontend_jaeger_traces{sampled="y",state="started"} 1
```

As we can see, it reports the number of started and finished spans, partitioned by the sampled flag, and the number of traces started or joined. Here is another group of metrics:

```
hotrod_frontend_jaeger_reporter_queue_length 0
hotrod_frontend_jaeger_reporter_spans{result="dropped"} 0
hotrod_frontend_jaeger_reporter_spans{result="err"} 0
hotrod_frontend_jaeger_reporter_spans{result="ok"} 24
hotrod_frontend_jaeger_sampler_queries{result="err"} 0
hotrod_frontend_jaeger_sampler_queries{result="ok"} 0
hotrod_frontend_jaeger_sampler_updates{result="err"} 0
hotrod_frontend_jaeger_sampler_updates{result="ok"} 0
hotrod_frontend_jaeger_span_context_decoding_errors 0
hotrod_frontend_jaeger_throttled_debug_spans 0
hotrod_frontend_jaeger_throttler_updates{result="err"} 0
hotrod_frontend_jaeger_throttler_updates{result="ok"} 0
```

Here we see statistics about the reporter, a sub-component of the tracer that is responsible for exporting the spans to the agent or collector. It reports the current length of its internal queue, how many spans it sent out (successfully or not), and how many spans it dropped because the internal buffer was full. Other Jaeger backend components are similarly chatty about their internal state. For example, this group of metrics from the agent describes how many batches and spans in those batches it forwarded to the collectors:

```
jaeger_agent_tchannel_reporter_batch_size{format="jaeger"} 1
jaeger_agent_tchannel_reporter_batches_failures{format="jaeger"} 0
jaeger_agent_tchannel_reporter_batches_submitted{format="jaeger"} 42
jaeger_agent_tchannel_reporter_spans_failures{format="jaeger"} 0
jaeger_agent_tchannel_reporter_spans_submitted{format="jaeger"} 139
```

Here is another, significantly truncated set that describes the behavior of the UDP server that receives spans as packets from the clients; the packet size; how many were processed or dropped because the internal queue was full; the current queue size; and how many packets could not be parsed:

```
thrift_udp_server_packet_size{model="jaeger",protocol="compact"} 375
thrift_udp_server_packets_dropped{model="jaeger",protocol="compact"} 0
thrift_udp_server_packets_processed{model="jaeger",protocol="compact"} 42
thrift_udp_server_queue_size{model="jaeger",protocol="compact"} 0
thrift_udp_server_read_errors{model="jaeger",protocol="compact"} 0
```

These metrics can be very helpful in troubleshooting deployment problems, such as if you make a mistake in setting up the networking configuration between the components in Kubernetes. They can also be used as the sources of production alerts, for example, you would want to make sure that the `packets_dropped` counter remains at zero during normal operations.

The Jaeger query service is also instrumented with OpenTracing and can be configured to send traces back to Jaeger. That instrumentation can be especially useful if the query service experiences latency, because all database access paths are generously decorated with spans.

Resiliency

I want to finish this chapter with a brief discussion of the importance of designing a tracing backend that is resilient to potential, often unintentional, abuse. I am not talking about an under-provisioned cluster, as there is little that can be done there. While operating Jaeger at Uber, we have experienced a number of tracing service degradations or even outages due to a few common mistakes.

Over-sampling

During development, I often recommend engineers to configure the Jaeger tracer with 100% sampling. Sometimes, inadvertently, the same configuration is pushed to production, and if the service is one of those serving high traffic, the tracing backend gets flooded with tracing data. It does not necessarily kill the backend because, as I mentioned previously, all Jaeger components are built with in-memory buffers for temporary storage of spans and handling short traffic spikes, and when those buffers are full, the components begin shedding their load by discarding some of the data. Unfortunately, the resulting degradation in the quality of the data is nearly equivalent to the backend being down completely, since most of the Jaeger components are stateless and are forced to discard data without any consistency (unlike the sampling that ensures full traces are sampled and collected).

There are several remediation strategies that we employed at Uber:

- The Jaeger collectors have a configuration that can enable additional down-sampling in the collectors. We can increase the percentage of spans preemptively dropped by the collectors before they reach the memory buffer. This is based on the hash of the trace IDs and thus guarantees that the spans in the same trace will be consistently down-sampled, even if they are handled by different stateless collectors. This degrades the service for all users but preserves the quality of the data that is still being collected. It gives us time to work with the team to rollback the change to the bad config.

- We recommend all our engineers to use adapter libraries instead of open source Jaeger clients. The adapter libraries disable the ability to manually configure sampling strategy in production, so that a service will always use the strategy provided to it by the Jaeger collectors.

Debug traces

Debug traces are created when the application explicitly sets a `sampling.priority=1` tag on a span. There are certain command-line tools at Uber that are used mostly for debugging purposes, such as a utility to send Thrift requests, similar to `curl`.

The utility was automatically forcing the debug flag on all traces it originated, because it was useful for developers to not have to remember to pass an additional flag. Unfortunately, on many occasions, developers would create some ad hoc scripts, maybe for one-off data migrations, that used such utilities repeatedly with high frequency. Unlike the regular over-sampling that can be somewhat mitigated by the down-sampling in the collectors, the debug traces were intentionally excluded from the scope of the down-sampling.

To address this problem, we implemented additional throttling in the Jaeger clients that rate limits the application when it is trying to create a debug trace. Since the debug flag was designed mostly for manually issued requests, the throttling is initialized with a generous rate limit that is unlikely to be exhausted by executing the utility manually, but can be quickly used if the utility is run repeatedly in a loop. Deploying a new version of a tracer library across many applications takes a long time; however, in our case, we had a few sets of known offenders (utilities) that we were able to quickly upgrade.

Traffic spikes due to DC failover

I explained this use case earlier in this chapter. Normally, an increase in traffic would not be a problem because our adaptive sampling would quickly reduce the sampling probabilities across the board. Unfortunately, we have a certain percentage of high-value traffic used for automated root cause analysis that comes with the debug flag and is not subject to throttling or adaptive sampling. We do not have a good solution to this problem other than increasing the capacity of the tracing cluster (mostly storage) to withstand these spikes. The Kafka-based streaming ingestion helps us to not lose any data, but it creates delays in the availability of traces, which negatively impacts the automated root cause analysis system.

Perpetual traces

This is just a peculiar story from production that I want to mention, not a persistent issue. There was a bug in the instrumentation of certain systems at Uber in the early days of rolling out Jaeger. The system was implementing a gossip protocol where all nodes in the cluster periodically informed other nodes of some data changes. The bug was causing the nodes to always reuse the span from the previous round of gossip, meaning that new spans were perpetually generated with the same trace ID, and the trace kept growing in the storage, creating all kinds of issues and out-of-memory errors. Fortunately, the behavior was easy to spot, and we were able to locate the offending service and fix its instrumentation.

Very long traces

Here I am talking about traces that had over 100 million spans in them. One explicit negative side effect of these traces is that in the Cassandra storage implementation, the trace ID is used as a partition key, so all these spans reside on the same Cassandra node and form a very large partition that is known to cause degradation in Cassandra performance. We are still yet to identify the root cause of this behavior, but the remediation strategy we are implementing is to introduce an artificial upper limit on the number of spans the ingester is allowed to save per trace ID.

Summary

In this chapter, we discussed many aspects of operating the tracing backend, from architecture and deployment choices to monitoring, troubleshooting, and resiliency measures. I intentionally kept the discussion at a slightly abstract level because I feel the concrete details about configuring and deploying Jaeger are probably going to become quickly outdated and therefore are better left for Jaeger documentation. Instead, I tried to only use Jaeger as an illustration of general principles that will be useful to anyone deploying and operating a tracing infrastructure, whether it is Jaeger or any other competing solution.

References

1. Alberto Gutierrez Juanes. *Jaeger integration with Kiali*. Kiali project blog: `https://medium.com/kialiproject/jaeger-integration-in-kiali-13bfc8b69a9d`.

2. Jaeger native trace context format: `https://www.jaegertracing.io/docs/1.8/client-libraries/#propagation-format`.

3. Zipkin's B3 context format: `https://github.com/openzipkin/b3-propagation`.

4. W3C Trace Context headers: `https://github.com/w3c/trace-context`.

5. Juraci Paixão Kröhling. *Running Jaeger Agent on bare metal*. Jaeger project blog: `https://medium.com/jaegertracing/deployment-strategies-for-the-jaeger-agent-1d6f91796d09`.

6. Juraci Paixão Kröhling. *Deployment strategies for the Jaeger Agent*. Jaeger project blog: `https://medium.com/jaegertracing/running-jaeger-agent-on-bare-metal-d1fc47d31fab`.

7. Jaeger Spark jobs for service dependency graphs: `https://github.com/jaegertracing/spark-dependencies`.

8. Lars Milland. *Secure architecture for Jaeger with Apache httpd reverse proxy on OpenShift*: `https://medium.com/@larsmilland01/secure-architecture-for-jaeger-with-apache-httpd-reverse-proxy-on-openshift-f31983fad400`.

9. Juraci Paixão Kröhling. *Protecting Jaeger UI with an OAuth sidecar Proxy*. Jaeger project blog: `https://medium.com/jaegertracing/protecting-jaeger-ui-with-an-oauth-sidecar-proxy-34205cca4bb1`.

Afterword

Congratulations, you have reached the end of the book! Sometimes, when I finish a book, I think, *finally, it's over!* Other times, I think, *wait, it's over? I wish there was more!* So, which "R" are *you* filled with: relief, or regret?

We covered a lot of ground in this book. I am confident that you have a much better understanding of distributed tracing, which is a fairly complex and often challenging field. I am also confident that you still have many questions. I still have many questions myself as well! Tracing is still a very new field, and with many more people getting into it, I expect to see a lot of innovation.

My team at Uber has pretty grandiose plans for the future of tracing. Uber's architecture is growing more and more complex every day, counting thousands of microservices and spanning many data centers. It is becoming obvious that managing this infrastructure in an automated fashion requires new techniques, and the capabilities of distributed tracing place it at the center of those techniques. For example, Google engineers wrote the famous SRE book [1], where they advocate for an SLA-driven approach to reliability. Unfortunately, it sounds much simpler than it is in practice.

One of the main API gateways at Uber has over 1,000 different endpoints. How do we even start assigning each of them SLOs such as latency or availability? An SLO is easier to define when you have a concrete product and can estimate an impact of SLO violation on the business. However, an API endpoint is not a product; many of them often work in complex combinations for different products. If we can agree on the SLO of a product or a workflow, how do we translate that to the SLOs of the many API endpoints? Even worse, how do we translate that to SLOs for thousands of microservices sitting below the API? This is where distributed tracing comes in. It allows us to automatically analyze the dependencies between microservices and the shapes of the call graphs for different business workflows, and this can be used to inform the SLOs at multiple levels of the call hierarchy. How exactly? I don't know yet; stay tuned.

Take another example: automatic rollbacks of service deployments. The idea is simple: start rolling out a new version of a service to canary instances, and if things start going wrong, then rollback. Yet how do we know that things have started going wrong? A service has its own health signals, so we can watch for those, but that's often not enough. Our service may be serving requests normally, but the responses may in some way negatively affect another service one or more layers above. How do we detect that? Monitoring the health of all services does not help, because many of them are not even related to the workflows our service is part of. Tracing, once again, can give us the big picture needed to automatically understand the impact our service rollout is having on the rest of the architecture, and figure out if it needs to be rolled back.

There are more examples like this. Many organizations, including Uber, are forging ahead with microservices-based architectures, but they have only scratched the surface of the capabilities that distributed tracing opens up for managing those architectures. The future is quite exciting.

At the same time, the distributed tracing field has many other, less advanced, challenges it still needs to overcome. I have a wish list of things that I would really like to see happen in the industry sooner:

- Standardization of context propagation format is critical for the interoperability of applications instrumented with different tracing libraries. The W3C Distributed Tracing Working Group made good progress on defining the standard for Trace Context, but right now, it only covers HTTP transport, and does not include a standard header for passing baggage or transmitting context over non-HTTP protocols such as AMQP (Advanced Message Queuing Protocol).

- Standard instrumentation API and the corresponding body of reusable instrumentation. Both the OpenTracing and OpenCensus projects had as one of their primary goals the acceleration of distributed tracing adoption, but in practice, the existence of two competing, yet conceptually nearly identical, APIs achieved exactly the opposite, as the rest of the industry is unsure which standard to back and integrate into their solutions. The two projects are in active discussions about converging to a single standard.

- Standardization of trace format is useful for interoperability, but critical for the development of universal tools that can work with tracing data. There is actually plenty of prior art in this area, for example, the Eclipse Trace Compass [2] tool supports a number of different trace formats (although they are not specifically *distributed* trace formats), such as the Common Trace Format [3] used by many kernel tracing tools for Linux, or the Trace Event format used by Trace Viewer [4], the JavaScript frontend for Chrome, about:tracing, and Android's systrace.

- Universal visualization tools. Currently, each tracing system implements its own frontend, even though very often they have near identical functionality. A standard trace format would allow building reusable components for visualization, such as the plexus module in Jaeger, which is used as the basis for the trace comparison feature released in Jaeger v. 1.8.

- Reusable data mining tools. I firmly believe data mining is the future of distributed tracing, but at the moment, there are hardly any data mining tools available in the open source, in part due to a lack of a standard trace format.

- Better integration with observability tooling. The notion of "three pillars of observability" does a disservice to the industry by promoting the idea that these three technologies are independent and that by combining these three distinct solutions, we get better observability for the systems. As we discussed in *Chapter 11, Integration with Metrics and Logs*, adding awareness of the request context to metrics and logs significantly increases their investigative power. But I would like to go further and have a truly integrated experience where the context of my investigation, for example, the high-level workflow I am troubleshooting, the time range, the specific call path, and so on, is carried over across different views, whether I am looking at a latency histogram or a health signal time series, or logged events.

In closing, I want to issue a call to action: join us! Jaeger is an open source project and we welcome contributions. If you have an idea, open a ticket in the main Jaeger repository [6]. If you already implemented it and achieved interesting results, write a blog post and tweet about it @jaegertracing or mention it on our online chat [7]; we are always looking for interesting case studies (and can help you to promote them). In turn, I am committed to continuing to release the advanced features we are building for distributed tracing at Uber as open source tools.

Happy tracing!

References

1. Niall Richard Murphy, Betsy Beyer, Chris Jones, Jennifer Petoff. *Site Reliability Engineering: How Google Runs Production Systems.* O'Reilly Media, 2016.

2. Eclipse Trace Compass. An open source application to solve performance and reliability issues by reading and analyzing traces and logs of a system: https://www.eclipse.org/tracecompass/.

3. Common Trace Format. A flexible, high-performance binary trace format: https://diamon.org/ctf/.

4. Trace-Viewer. The JavaScript frontend for Chrome about:tracing and Android systrace: https://github.com/catapult-project/catapult/tree/master/tracing.

5. plexus. A React component for rendering directed graphs: https://github.com/jaegertracing/jaeger-ui/tree/master/packages/plexus.

6. Jaeger backend GitHub repository: https://github.com/jaegertracing/jaeger.

7. Jaeger project online chat: https://gitter.im/jaegertracing/Lobby.

Other Books You May Enjoy

If you enjoyed this book, you may be interested in these other books by Packt:

Distributed Computing with Go

V.N. Nikhil Anurag

ISBN: 978-1-78712-538-4

- Gain proficiency with concurrency and parallelism in Go
- Learn how to test your application using Go's standard library
- Learn industry best practices with technologies such as REST, OpenAPI, Docker, and so on
- Design and build a distributed search engine
- Learn strategies on how to design a system for web scale

Mastering Go

Mihalis Tsoukalos

ISBN: 978-1-78862-654-5

- Understand the design choices of Golang syntax
- Know enough Go internals to be able to optimize Golang code
- Appreciate concurrency models available in Golang
- Understand the interplay of systems and networking code
- Write server-level code that plays well in all environments
- Understand the context and appropriate use of Go data types and data structures

Leave a review - let other readers know what you think

Please share your thoughts on this book with others by leaving a review on the site that you bought it from. If you purchased the book from Amazon, please leave us an honest review on this book's Amazon page. This is vital so that other potential readers can see and use your unbiased opinion to make purchasing decisions, we can understand what our customers think about our products, and our authors can see your feedback on the title that they have worked with Packt to create. It will only take a few minutes of your time, but is valuable to other potential customers, our authors, and Packt. Thank you!

Index

wget
  reference 86
World Wide Web Consortium (W3C) 197

X

X-Ray 197

Z

Zipkin 196
zones 393

CPSIA information can be obtained
at www.ICGtesting.com
Printed in the USA
FFHW010844060419
51541678-56987FF